BALI *Art, Ritual, Performance*

BALI *Art, Ritual, Performance*

Edited by Natasha Reichle

Essays by Francine Brinkgreve, Garrett Kam,
Natasha Reichle, and David J. Stuart-Fox

Entries by Francine Brinkgreve, Natasha Reichle,
and David J. Stuart-Fox

ASIAN ART MUSEUM
CHONG-MOON LEE CENTER
FOR ASIAN ART AND CULTURE

Copyright © 2010 by the Asian Art Museum of San Francisco

ISBN: 978-0-939117-55-0 (cloth) / 978-0-939117-56-7 (paper)

The Asian Art Museum–Chong-Moon Lee Center for Asian Art and Culture is a public institution whose mission is to lead a diverse global audience in discovering the unique material, aesthetic, and intellectual achievements of Asian art and culture.

Photography of objects in the exhibition, by catalogue number: Ben Grishaaver: 9, 10, 28, 29, 39, 43, 63, 96, 97, 98, 99, 100. Gustra: 5, 22. Kaz Tsuruta: 15, 23, 27, 38, 41, 44, 46, 55, 56, 61, 62, 64, 70, 88, 108, 116, 117. Additional photography was provided by the lending institutions.

All rights reserved. No part of this book may be reproduced in any form, electronic or mechanical, without permission in writing from the publisher, except by a reviewer, who may quote brief passages in a review.

1 3 5 7 9 8 6 4 2
FIRST PRINTING

CONTENTS

A Note about Spelling   6
Director's Preface   *Jay Xu*   7

Essays
Bali: Art, Ritual, Performance   *Natasha Reichle*   9
Ritual Arts and Implements of Balinese Priests   *David J. Stuart-Fox*   35
Palm Leaf and Silkscreen: Balinese *Lamak* in Transition   *Francine Brinkgreve*   61
Offerings in Bali: Ritual Requests, Redemption, and Rewards   *Garrett Kam*   87
W. O. J. Nieuwenkamp and His Royal Lion Offering-Box   *Francine Brinkgreve*   117

Catalogue of the Exhibition   133

Glossary   366
Bibliography   368
Index   373

A NOTE ABOUT SPELLING

In general Balinese names are used throughout both the essays and entries of this catalogue. There are many variations in the spelling of Balinese terms. For instance, one commonly sees *batara, bhatara,* and *betara* as a word for deity. In this case, we have chosen the former. We have tried to be uniform in our choices, and we apologize for inconsistencies. The names of the major Hindu epics, the Ramayana and Mahabharata, maintain their Sanskrit spelling. Quotations from other sources may contain Sanskrit spellings, or Dutch spellings of Indonesian or Balinese words. Dutch spellings were widely used before a unified system of spelling was introduced in 1972.

When Sanskrit names for deities were adopted in Bali, certain changes in spelling and pronunciation occurred. The letter V is most often replaced by a W, but occasionally by a B. The sound SH is replaced by the S sound. In Balinese and Indonesian a C is pronounced CH. So in Bali the Indic deity Vishnu is known as Wisnu, a *vajra* is a *bajra,* Shiva is Siwa, *chakra* is spelled *cakra*.

Sanskrit names for all major deities and characters from the Hindu epics mentioned in the catalogue are supplied in the glossary. Although Sanskrit equivalents for these names are given, it is important to remember that the characters of these deities have localized personalities when they manifest themselves at different temples in Bali.

One of the two major lending institutions, the National Museum of Ethnology, Leiden, is occasionally referred to in the catalogue by its Dutch name, the Rijksmuseum voor Volkenkunde, Leiden; the abbreviation RMV refers to objects coming from its collections. In the notes of the catalogue, objects from the Tropenmuseum, Amsterdam, sometimes have the abbreviation TM before the inventory number.

JAY XU
DIRECTOR'S PREFACE

More than eighty years ago, the anthropologist Margaret Mead recorded her impressions of the island of Bali:

> Upon the hundreds of stone altars of Bali, there lay not merely a fruit and a flower, placed as visible offering to the many gods, but hundreds of finely wrought and elaborately conceived offerings made of palm leaf and flowers, twisted, folded, stitched, embroidered, brocaded into myriad traditional forms and fancies. There were flowers made of sugar and combined into representations of the rainbow, and swords and spears cut from the snow-white fat of sacrificial pigs. The whole world was patterned, from the hillsides elaborately terraced to give the maximum rice yield, to the air which was shot through with music, the temple gates festooned with temporary palm-leaf arras over their permanent carved façade, to the crowds of people who, as they lounged, watching an opera or clustered around two fighting cocks, composed themselves into a frieze....Their lives were packed in intricate and formal delights.

Mead's observations of Bali in the 1930s may seem tinged with romanticism today, but the richness and vibrancy of the cultural traditions of the island are as evident now as they were then. Bali continues to inspire artists, performers, scholars, and movie stars, all drawn to a unique culture where art is an integral part of daily life.

Bali: Art, Ritual, Performance—the first major exhibition of arts of Bali presented in the United States—explores the dynamism of Balinese cultural life. This catalogue, the exhibition, and the accompanying public programs emphasize Balinese objects of ritual importance, with explanations of the ceremonies that sanctify them, and the performances that enliven them.

The exhibition would not have been possible without the generous cooperation of two Dutch museums, the Rijksmuseum voor Volkenkunde, Leiden (National Museum of Ethnology, Leiden) and the Tropenmuseum, Amsterdam, which together lent the majority of the objects to this exhibition. It has been a pleasure working with the staff of these institutions and forging closer ties with European museums possessing outstanding collections of Asian art. In particular, Francine Brinkgreve and David Stuart-Fox of the Rijksmseum voor Volkenkunde were true colleagues in the production of this exhibition and catalogue. The Rijksmuseum, Amsterdam; the Nusantara Museum, Delft; W. E. Bouwmann; and a private collector in the Netherlands also lent important objects.

Thanks are also due to lenders in the United States, including the American Museum of Natural History, the Library of Congress, the Fowler Museum of Cultural History, Mary Catherine Bateson, Lily Belcher, Anne and Timothy Kahn, and other private lenders.

Jay Xu is director of the Asian Art Museum–Chong-Moon Lee Center for Asian Art and Culture in San Francisco, one of the largest museums in the Western world devoted exclusively to Asian Art; its collection of more than 17,000 artworks spans 6,000 years of history. The museum is a public institution whose mission is to lead a diverse global audience in discovering the unique material, aesthetic, and intellectual achievements of Asian art and culture.

Presentation at the Asian Art Museum was made possible by grants from the National Endowment for the Humanities; United Airlines; Margaret and Al Njoo; the Koret Foundation; the Henry Luce Foundation; the Creative Work Fund, a program of the Walter and Elise Haas Fund supported by the William and Flora Hewlett Foundation and the James Irvine Foundation; the Walter and Elise Haas Fund; the Phyllis C. Wattis Foundation; the Mary Van Voorhees Fund of the San Francisco Foundation; and Pacific Gas & Electric; with additional support from the Richard and Rhoda Goldman Fund.

The Indonesian community in the Bay Area, and scholars and consultants in Bali and elsewhere have been invaluable friends and advisers. Particular thanks to Endang Sri Hardiati, Garrett Kam, Jero Ni Made Renten, Bruce Carpenter, Thomas Murray, Consuelo McHugh, Merrill Randol Sherwin, Martha Hertelendy, and Alexandra and Dennis Lenehan. We appreciate the suggestions and helpful advice of I Made Moja, Lisa Tana, Kompiang Metri-Davies, I Made Surya, Judy Slattum, Wayne Vitale, Thomas Cooper, Adrianna Williams, Hildred Geertz, and Adrian Vickers. So many others contributed in ways big and small that is impossible to name them all.

Many members of the staff of the Asian Art Museum were instrumental in preparing this exhibition. Foremost among them is Natasha Reichle, associate curator of Southeast Asian art, who brilliantly curated the exhibition and wrote and oversaw the content of this catalogue. Because of the importance of performance and ritual to the culture of Bali, public programming and video play an essential part in contextualizing the role of the objects on view. Director of education Deborah Clearwaters was an early collaborator in the conception of this exhibition and worked tirelessly with her team in the Education department, especially Allison Wyckoff and Lorraine Tuchfeld.

Each department of the museum contributed to the preparation of the exhibition: Sharon Steckline, Robin Groesbeck, Nahry Tak, Lauren Waycott, and Aino Tolme in Museum Services; Mark Fenn and the entire Conservation staff; Susie Kantor in the Curatorial department; and many others. Dino Piacentini and Kristin Paine worked long hours writing grants for this project. Kaz Tsuruta photographed many objects, and Aino Tolme managed photo permissions. Exhibition designer Stephen Penkowsky is consistently brilliant, and the Preparation team led by Brent Powell executes his plans with skill and good humor.

The catalogue's production was capably overseen by Thomas Christensen, who also did the design and typesetting. Kristina Youso, James Donnelly, and Theresa Duran edited, proofread, and indexed the text. Their contributions are deeply appreciated.

The arts of Bali have long inspired visitors from around the world—the Mexican artist Miguel Covarrubias and the American novelist Vicki Baum, represented here, are only two of many. Through this catalogue and exhibition we hope that a new generation will find inspiration, as Margaret Mead did, in the "intricate and formal delights" of Bali.

NATASHA REICHLE
BALI: ART, RITUAL, PERFORMANCE

DESA, KALA, PATRA

In Balinese there is a phrase, *desa, kala, patra*, which roughly translated means *place, time, situation*. On one level it refers to the localization of customary practices, which can differ from north to south, east to west, village to village. But in a larger sense it suggests the need for contextualization, the necessity of trying to understand how meanings of events or objects are unique to specific circumstances and can differ by location and over time. When thinking about Balinese art and this exhibition I kept returning to this phrase, realizing how each object chosen was made by a specific person, in certain place, over a defined period, for a particular patron, to serve a unique purpose. But in the relatively short period of time since the production of these works, knowledge of much of this context has been lost. Shown now, in a museum setting, the objects remain separated from the forces that originally gave them meaning.[1] This is especially true of objects whose active agency is often conceived only in the midst of ritual or performance. For the Balinese, a statue is not a deity in its own right, merely a receptacle for the visitation of the divine.[2] It is through ritual acts—invitations to the gods, ornamentation of temples, presentations of offerings, and incantations of mantras—that vessels become sacred objects.

Balinese ritual practices are highly sensory experiences; during a temple ceremony one can smell incense and flowers, hear the shimmering notes of at least one gamelan orchestra, feel and taste the sprinkle of holy water. Hildred Geertz writes that in a museum each work is "virtually stripped of its original context,"[3] and it is true that no museum can recreate the cultural milieu that produced these objects. Despite this, all is not lost. The fact that ritual remains an integral part of day-to-day life in Bali means that many of the objects displayed in this exhibition are still used today in much the same manner as they may have been one hundred years ago. Although practices vary by place and time, one can still see temple ceremonies or performances today that match descriptions recorded by ethnologists in the 1930s. I hope that in the essays and entries for this catalogue, and in the photographs and videos accompanying the exhibition, layers of meaning can be illuminated and some semblance of the significance of these fascinating objects can be understood.

The stories of how these artworks came into museums and private collections add other aspects of meaning to them. The vast majority of pieces in the exhibition come from the collections of the Tropenmuseum, Amsterdam, and the Rijksmuseum voor Volkenkunde,

Photos in this essay are by Natasha Rechle unless otherwise noted.

1 They have also gained new meanings: souvenir, colonial booty, ethnographic object, artwork, etc.

2 Many statues will never serve as "seats for the gods," but instead function as images that decorate a temple and transform it into a site where the gods feel welcomed and honored. It is primarily smaller statues, stored for much of the year within the temple shrines, or images made of ephemeral materials, that serve as temporary abodes for the deities on ceremonial occasions.

3 Hildred Geertz, *The Life of a Balinese Temple: Artistry, Imagination, and History in a Peasant Village* (Honolulu: University of Hawaii Press, 2004), 7.

Leiden, two Dutch museums with among the finest collections of Indonesian material outside of Asia. Other Dutch lenders include the Rijksmuseum, Amsterdam, and Nusantara Museum, Delft. The Netherlands were a colonial presence in Indonesia for more than three hundred years, so it is no surprise that these institutions have such rich holdings.[4] The history of colonial collections has been the focus of research for several Dutch and Indonesian scholars and institutions, especially the Rijksmuseum voor Volkenkunde, Leiden, which has been working with the Museum Nasional, Indonesia, on exhibitions and publications exploring their shared cultural heritage.[5]

Delving into this colonial history reveals the myriad paths that objects have taken from Bali to the Netherlands. Some objects were collected as loot after military expeditions; others were commissioned by government officials for world fairs; gifts were given as part of diplomatic exchanges; objects were bought from artists; other items were taken as souvenirs by Dutch colonial administrators. Many more pieces do not have a traceable provenance. The objects in the exhibition coming from American institutions—the American Museum of Natural History, the Fowler Museum of Cultural History, and the Library of Congress—tend to have been collected or made by Western tourists and scholars who traveled to Bali in the 1930s.

The phrase *desa, kala, patra* also made me think of this exhibition and catalogue as a product of early-twenty-first-century scholarship and as a museum enterprise, limited in scope by money, conservation issues, expertise, and personal taste. Attempting to do justice to representing the arts of such a culturally diverse and intriguing place as Bali is daunting. Thomas Reuter writes that "a piece of social research can never provide more than a partial and temporary interpretation of another culture as experienced from the unique position of a particular historical subject."[6] The joy of working with the arts and artists of Bali is that even a partial glimpse is full and rewarding.

CULTURAL LIVES

A tiny island in the Indonesian archipelago, surrounded by powerful neighbors, Bali reverberates in the public imagination to an extent far greater than its size might indicate. Indeed, it is one of the most well-known places in Southeast Asia—long celebrated as an exotic locale and a honeymoon paradise—although many know very little about why it gained this reputation.[7] Although the island is a mere ninety-five miles from east to west, sixty-nine miles from north to south, it is home to tens of thousands of temples, which come alive in annual festivals to honor the gods and ancestral deities. It is the diversity of this island, the wealth of ceremony and spectacle, that has made Bali such a favored subject

---

4 The Dutch East India Company (Vereenigde Oost-Indische Compagnie), known as the V.O.C., established its first permanent trading post in West Java in 1603. The Netherlands claimed colonial control of the region in 1800. They remained colonial powers until Indonesia's independence, with a brief British interregnum in 1811–1816 during the Napoleonic Wars. The Dutch did not gain full colonial control of Bali until 1908.

5 Endang Hardiati and Pieter ter Keurs, ed., *Indonesia: The Discovery of the Past* (Amsterdam: KIT Publishers, 2006); Pieter ter Keurs, ed., *Colonial Collections Revisited* (CNWS Publications, 2007).

6 Thomas Reuter, "Indonesia in Transition: Concluding Reflections on Engaged Research and the Critique of Local Knowledge," in *Inequality, Crisis and Social Change in Indonesia: The Muted Worlds of Bali* (London; New York: RoutledgeCurzon, 2003), 211.

7 For a history of the West's envisioning of Bali, see Adrian Vickers, *Bali, A Paradise Created* (Berkeley, CA: Periplus Editions, 1989).

of study. Hundreds of scholars have come to Bali to examine its cultural life, its music and dance traditions, its woodcarving, painting, and textiles.

Yet defining the "cultural life" of Bali is difficult and problematic. As Degung Santikarma writes:

> Bali is not harmonious, homogenous, and static. It is—and has long been—the home of many competing strands of thought and many different ways of being Balinese. It is an ever-changing mosaic, shifting its design to meet new ideas imported from outside, whether they be the Chinese-derived *barong* figure or the old Chinese *pis bolong* coins used in offerings, or the Harley Davidsons and heavy metal that make up today's youth culture. And Bali does not stop at the island's borders, but encompasses Balinese living in the Diaspora of Jakarta, Australia, Europe or America, or the transmigration areas of Sumba, Sumatra, and Sulawesi. Bali also encompasses—whether the Balinese like it or not—a semi-permanent population of thousands of Western expatriates as well as Indonesian migrants, many of them married to Balinese or converted to Balinese Hinduism, who may even participate in events that Balinese call cultural, such as religious ceremonies, the traditional arts, or the speaking of the Balinese language.[8]

8 Degung Santikarma, "The Power of 'Balinese Culture,'" in *Bali: Living in Two Worlds: A Critical Self-Portrait,* ed. Urs Ramseyer and I Gusti Panji Trisna (Basel: Museum der Kulturen, Basel; Schwabe, 2001), 32.

9 The divide between these islands marks the Wallace Line, a division between the ecozones of Asia to the west and Australasia to the east. The strait here is so deep that most animal species could not pass between islands; thus very different fauna are found on either side of the divide.

The exhibition this catalogue documents can explore only some elements of the cultural lives of Balinese. One focus is the intersections of art, ritual, and performance. These divisions are, of course, a Western construct; the categories overlap and intermingle in Balinese life. A mask, when properly carved and sanctified by a priest, becomes a receptacle for a deity. When worn during a ritual dance, it becomes an apotropaic force. Palace doors mark the division between the world of the outsiders and the private domain of the court. Palace architecture mimics temple architecture (the king was sometimes referred to as a "visible god"), and doors placed in a stepped gateway metaphorically recall the sacred mountain home of the gods. A handful of simple palm leaves, woven together, properly blessed, and placed upon a shrine, becomes an offering to the gods and a plea for the fertility of the harvest.

GEOGRAPHY AND FERTILITY

About eight degrees south of the equator, Bali lies in the middle of the vast Indonesian archipelago. To the west, separated by a narrow and shallow strait, is the island of Java. A short but deep strait lies between Bali and its neighbor to the east, Lombok.[9] Bali is a small island of a little over two thousand square miles, shaped in a rough diamond. It is densely populated, especially in the fertile sloping terraces of the southern part of the island. It is hard not to lapse

Fig. 1. Map of Bali.

10 Peter Bellwood, "The Origins and Dispersals of Agricultural Communities in Southeast Asia," in *Southeast Asia from Prehistory to History* (London; New York: RoutledgeCurzon, 2004), 25.

11 I Made Suastika, "Traces of Human Life Style from the Palaeolithic Era to the Beginnings of the First Century AD," in *Burials, Texts and Rituals,* ed. Brigitta Hauser-Schäublin and I Wayan Ardika, vol. 1, Göttinger Beiträge zur Ethnologie (Göttingen: Universitätsverlag Göttingen, 2008), 169.

into what James Boon calls "brochurese" when talking about the setting of Bali, especially the patchwork of verdant rice fields that descend from the mountains to the sea. Other regions are more arid, particularly the west, north, northeast, and the far southern Bukit peninsula.

Although the Indonesian archipelago has been occupied since Paleolithic times, the majority of current inhabitants are descendants of an Austronesian-speaking people who moved south from Southern China and Taiwan in a number of stages beginning around 3000 BCE.[10] Burial sites in north Bali dating from around the beginning of the first millennium contain pottery, jewelry, and bronze and iron implements of an early metal age culture spread by these immigrants.[11] Bronze artifacts found throughout Indonesia, probably dating from the early centuries CE, demonstrate connections with bronzes from the Northern Vietnamese Dongson culture. The almost two-meter-high drum called the "Moon of Pejeng" is the most remarkable example of early bronze casting found in Bali. It is uncertain whether it was manufactured in Bali, but other smaller artifacts indicate bronze production on the island. (For more on early bronzes see cat. no. 1.)

Trade routes from the eastern "Spice Islands" (Maluku or Moluccas) to China and India passed by the northern coast of Bali. The mention of sandalwood and spices in Indian and Roman sources indicates these goods were already actively traded at the beginning of the first millennium CE.[12] Although Bali did not have any significant spices or natural resources to export, there is evidence that traders stopped at ports along the north coast. The sites of Sembiran and Pacung have produced large numbers of rouletted sherds of pottery originating from Arikamedu in present-day Tamil Nadu, South India.[13] Archaeologists estimate the dates of these sherds to be in the first two centuries CE.[14] Analysis of a human tooth found at one of the sites indicates the possible presence of Indian traders in Bali in these early centuries of the Common Era.[15]

The topography and natural resources of Bali have marked its culture in profound ways. A chain of volcanoes crosses the island from Gunung Merbuk in the west to the most sacred and tallest mountain, Gunung Agung, in the east. These mountains have formed the island. Repeated volcanic eruptions have laid down layer after layer of rich soil. Rivers flowing from their slopes have rent deep ravines. These gorges run primarily from the north to the south, dividing the land into a series of long, sloping ridges. Because of this essential characteristic of the landscape, and because of the importance of its volcanoes, the Balinese do not orient themselves toward the cardinal directions, but rather in relation to the mountains around them. The terms *kaja* indicates up the ridge toward the mountains, and *kelod*, down toward the sea.[16]

Myths relate that the sacred mountain Gunung Agung was brought to Bali from India via Java. It is called a broken-off part of Mount Meru, the central axis of the Hindu universe and the home of the god Siwa. Bali's most sacred temple, Pura Besakih, lies on the slopes of Mount Agung. Deities are affiliated with other major geographical landmarks. The mountain lakes are linked with goddesses, who have temples dedicated to them along their shores. Networks of temples also appear throughout the complex systems of irrigation. Much of the ritual life of the Balinese revolves around ceremonies involving water and the fertility of the island. Dewi Sri, the goddess of rice, Dewi Pertiwi, the earth goddess, Dewi Melanting, goddess of seeds and prosperity, and Wisnu, the god associated with water, play the largest roles in these rites.

The centrality of rice to Balinese village culture is impossible to overestimate.[17] Rice has, for thousands of years, been the staple of the Balinese diet and an important component of most ritual offerings. Every morning after the first rice of the day is prepared, small offerings are presented to the unseen spirits before any members of the family partake. Raw grains of rice, cooked and colored rice, rice "cookies," rice porridge, and rice-paste figures are all used in offerings. The importance of rice agriculture in Balinese society can also be

12 I Wayan Ardika, "Archaeological Traces of the Early Harbour Town," in *Burials, Texts and Rituals,* ed. Brigitta Hauser-Schäublin and I Wayan Ardika, vol. 1, Göttinger Beiträge zur Ethnologie (Göttingen: Universitätsverlag Göttingen, 2008), 154.

13 I Wayan Ardika, "Archaeological Traces of the Early Harbour Town," 151.

14 I Wayan Ardika and Peter Bellwood, "Sembiran: The Beginnings of Indian Contact with Bali," *Antiquity* 65, no. 247 (1991): 229.

15 J. Stephen Lansing et al., "Reply," *Antiquity* 80, no. 307 (2006): http://antiquity.ac.uk/projgall/lansing/index.html#response.

16 Besides *kaja* and *kelod,* the directions of the sunrise, *kangin,* and sunset, *kauh,* as well as intercardinal directions, are important in many aspects of Balinese life. See the essays by David Start-Fox, Garrett Kam, and Francine Brinkgreve (on *lamak*) in this volume.

17 Some regions of the island (especially the west and north) are today too dry to cultivate rice, although it seems that that was not necessarily the case prior to the twentieth century. Brigitta Hauser-Schäublin, "Sembiran and Julah — Sketches of History," in *Burials, Texts and Rituals,* ed. Brigitta Hauser-Schäublin and I Wayan Ardika, vol. 1, Göttinger Beiträge zur Ethnologie (Göttingen: Universitätsverlag Göttingen, 2008), 9–10, 12.

Fig. 2. Nini, "rice mother" (or grandmother), sheaves of rice made as a temporary residence for the rice goddess.

18 Arlette Ottino, *The Universe Within: A Balinese Village through Its Ritual Practices* (Paris: Karthala, 2000), 84–85; Thomas Reuter, *Custodians of the Sacred Mountains: The Ritual Domains of Highland Bali* (Canberra: The Australian National University, 1996), 372.

19 R. Goris, *Bali: atlas kebudajaan; Cults and customs; Cultuurgeschiedenis in beeld* ('s-Gravenhage: W. van Hoeve, 1955), 38; Roy Hamilton, *The Art of Rice: Spirit and Sustenance in Asia* (Los Angeles: UCLA Fowler Museum of Cultural History, 2003), 260.

20 The introduction of new strains of rice in the late 1960s led to new harvesting practices. The shorter rice is cut with sickles and threshed in the fields.

seen in the many agricultural rituals and shrines dedicated to the pre-Indic rice goddess, Dewi Sri, to whom there are more shrines dedicated than any other deity in Bali. Rice paddies everywhere are marked with simple shrines dedicated to the goddess, and shrines to the goddess can also be found next to rice granaries and in village temples. Before, during, and after the rice-growing cycle, ceremonies are performed by farmers and their families to protect the fields and ensure fertility.

Images of goddesses are made of both ephemeral substances like plant matter and more permanent material like wood and metal. Before the harvest, a number of unthreshed stems are collected into a bundle called a *nini* (rice mother), which serves as a temporary residence for the rice goddess.[18] The *nini* are placed near the main irrigation inlet to the rice fields. Lontar palm leaves are also used to make figures that are associated with fertility and the rice goddess (cat. nos. 6, 7, 8). These finely plaited figures, called *cili*, are placed on small shrines in the rice fields or in homes or businesses.[19] Dewi Sri and her consort Rambut Sedana, together referred to as Sri Sedana, are often represented by statues made of wood and old Chinese coins. Harvest festivals celebrate the couple and the fertility they bring. These statues are vivified by ritual—they come alive during ceremonies when the deities are invoked and come down to temporarily "inhabit" the statues.

The importance of rice in Balinese society can also be seen in the care taken to produce the implements of its harvest. Special ritual finger knives and rice paddles (decorated with the faces of deities) were traditionally used for the harvest of rice.[20] The small knives were designed to fit into the palm of the farmer's hand, to allow her to harvest a single stalk. Local lore explains that these easily hidden tools were used so that the rice goddess would not be frightened. After the rice was cut, it was gathered into sheathes to be stored. A rice paddle was used to even the ends of the sheaves before storage in the rice barn. The shapes of these gathered sheaves of rice, tied at the middle with a spreading crown of grain at the top, are said to be the inspiration for *cili* figures.[21]

While rice remains the staple of the Balinese diet, there have been remarkable changes to Bali's agricultural practices, especially in the second half of the twentieth century. The use of new strains of faster-growing rice, commercial fertilizers, and pesticides has changed the methods and routines of agricultural production for many farmers.[22] Farming has also been affected by the exponential growth of tourism, resulting in steep increases in the value of land, in some cases, and land dispossession in the face of tourist complexes in others. In commercially developed areas, efforts to build tourist amenities with a "rice field view" has cut off that view for the full-time residents and turned backbreaking field labor into a backdrop for tourist amusement. Although the impact of tourism is often couched in terms of cultural change, the environmental impact of millions of tourists is just as evident.

BELIEFS

One thousand years ago, one could see evidence of Hindu religious practices throughout much of Southeast Asia. Today, however, Bali is the only place in this vast region where these once widespread Indic traditions remain strong.[23] As it is practiced today, the religion of the Balinese combines worship of deities associated with nature, ancestral deities, and gods from the Hindu pantheon. When writing about "the Balinese," the authors of this catalogue largely speak of the Hindu Balinese, ignoring the small but important segments of Muslim and Christian communities.[24] The unique practices of immigrant communities, or Balinese of Chinese ancestry, or of mountain communities with rituals divergent from, and not recognized by, the Hindu majority, are also beyond the scope of this book.[25]

There is no word in Balinese for religion, and the concept of religion as being separate from traditions or culture is a foreign one. Before the second half of the twentieth century, practices that are today deemed religious were conceived of by most Balinese as village customs.[26] The Sanskrit term *agama* was adopted to encompass the many rites and rituals of Balinese "religious" life. The majority religion has been called many names: *Agama Tirta*, *Agama Hindu Bali*, *Agama Hindu*, among others.[27] Each of these names reflects different concerns. *Agama Tirta*, or the religion of holy water, brings the significance of water in Balinese ritual life to the forefront. The role of holy water is vital in all ceremonies. The importance of water in ritual finds vivid parallel in the complex networks of irrigation that have sustained the island for over a thousand years.

While deities connected to nature and agriculture are among the most important in Balinese life, deified ancestors are also of great significance. It is believed that, after the proper rites, the soul of the deceased is released from earthly bonds and becomes an ancestral spirit, who may be reincarnated back into the family in a further generation. During the ten-day-long ceremony of Galungan, occurring every 210 days, Balinese pay homage to their deified ancestors, who come down from their mountain abodes to visit their descendants at ancestral shrines in family compounds. The *pura puseh* (navel temple) of a village is for the worship of the ancestors of the village founders. Members of the same

21 See Francine Brinkgreve's essay in this volume for more on the use of figures of this type in altar hangings (*lamak*).

22 J. Stephen Lansing, *Priests and Programmers: Technologies of Power in the Engineered Landscape of Bali* (Princeton, NJ: Princeton University Press, 1991).

23 This is excepting South Asian immigrant communities in Southeast Asia.

24 Fredrik Barth, *Balinese Worlds* (Chicago: University of Chicago Press, 1993).

25 Reuter, *Custodians of the Sacred Mountains;* Thomas Reuter, *The House of Our Ancestors: Precedence and Dualism in Highland Balinese Society* (Leiden: KITLV, 2002).

26 Michel Picard, "The Discourse of Kebalian," in *Staying Local in the Global Village,* ed. Raechelle Rubinstein and Linda Connor (Honolulu: University of Hawaii Press, 1999), 49.

27 Michel Picard, "What's in a Name? Agama Hindu Bali in the Making," in *Hinduism in Modern Indonesia: A Minority Religion between Local, National, and Global Interests,* ed. Martin Ramstedt (London; New York: RoutledgeCurzon, 2004), 56–75.

Left: Fig. 3. Turtle-shaped stone sarcophagi, Museum Gedung Arca Purbakala, Bedulu.

Right: Fig. 4. Cremation tower for royal cremation ceremony in Ubud, July 2008.

28 There are many other names for temples for particular descent groups. For more on the complex hierarchy of temples in Bali, see David Stuart-Fox, *Pura Besakih: Temple, Religion and Society in Bali* (Leiden: KITLV, 2002), 53–65.

29 I Made Sutaba, "Preliminary Notes on Ancestor Statues in Bali," *Bulletin of the Indo-Pacific Prehistory Association* 16 (1997): 229–232.

30 Turtles play important roles in Hindu mythology that spread at a later date to Bali. Their meaning in these early megalithic sculptures in unknown.

genealogical line worship their common ancestors at clan temples (*pura dadia*) or regional ancestral origin temples (*pura kawitan*).[28]

Some of the earliest megalithic objects in Bali include statues, sarcophagi, and terraced platforms. These ancient stone remains likely date from the beginning of the first millennium CE and are all thought to be linked to ancestor worship.[29] Dozens of stone sarcophagi have been found, the most remarkable of which take the form of turtles with human faces.[30] Care for the dead as expressed in ancient burial customs continues today in the quite different form of elaborate funerary ceremonies.

The Balinese commemorate all major events in the life cycle of an individual, but none quite as spectacularly as death. The act of cremation releases the ties that bind a spirit to this world, allowing the soul to journey to the next world. There are many ceremonies that accompany these last rites, including the creation of towers and animal-shaped sarcophagi. On an auspicious date, the body of the deceased is placed within a highly decorated pagoda-like cremation tower. The cremation tower is used to transport the corpse to the cremation grounds. There, the body is transferred into an animal-shaped effigy for cremation. The form of the sarcophagus varies; the higher castes often use a bull-shaped effigy, while other status groups use effigies in the form of different real or mythical animals. Special offerings

and holy water are placed with the body inside the effigy, prayers are said, and then the effigy and the cremation tower are burned. The relative time and expense put into these elaborate public displays proclaim the eminence of the deceased and the status of their descendants, thus serving an important political function.

Many of the objects used in Bali's famous funerary rituals, such as the towers that carry bodies to the cremation grounds, the animal-shaped sarcophagi in which bodies are cremated, or the flower effigies (*puspa-sarira*) prepared for the second cremation, are made of ephemeral materials and are burned during ceremonies. Evidence suggests that in earlier times, more permanent materials were used to venerate the dead. Early wood, stone, and bronze statues of paired couples, such as cat. nos. 15, 17, and 18, seem to indicate that, from the tenth to the fifteenth centuries, objects composed of durable materials were made to commemorate the ancestors.

Stone statues of single and paired figures are still found in some of the older Balinese temples and are thought to represent royal couples. Some are clearly identified as such by inscription. Crowned and richly ornamented bronze figures such as those in the Asian Art Museum's collection (cat. no. 15; dated to 1400–1600 CE) relate to the tradition of making paired figures in stone, but how they may have

Left: Fig. 5. Sarcophagus in the shape of a composite animal, Pura Dalem, Padangtegal, July 2008.

Right: Fig. 6. Ancestor statue, Pura Tegeh Koripan, Penulisan, Bangli.

been used or worshipped is unknown. In the past four hundred years, the tradition of making these commemorative images out of stone and metal has died out.

Museum collections indicate that in the early decades of the 1900s, large numbers of wooden paired male and female images were collected by Western visitors, but their functions are not clearly documented. Scholarly knowledge about wooden statues is limited, but such figures may relate to ancestor worship as well. The difficulty of dating these objects, and the presumption that older statuary would have decayed in the humid climate, has led most scholars to date these images to the 1800s and early 1900s, but it is possible that some are much older. The identity of these paired figures is also still uncertain: do they represent a continuation of the ancestor statues made in bronze, or do they represent other deities, or even characters from literature?

One of the most striking differences between religious practices in Bali and those in Java (and India) is the role of statuary and temples. Temples in Bali have been described as open-air theaters. They are largely abandoned except for days of ritual importance. Temples are not considered the home of the deities; rather, they are a place where, on special occasions, the people can welcome the gods when they visit. Large stone statues of deities do not play as significant a role in Balinese Hinduism as they do in Indian Hinduism. More important to the Balinese are smaller images that are stored away for much of the year and taken out on special anniversaries. The images and the temples come alive on these important days, when the deities descend and inhabit the sacred vessels.

Another feature of Balinese Hinduism is the use of carved, hollow, wooden animals or decorated palanquins that act as vehicles for the deities during ritual processions. (See Francine Brinkgreve's essay on the lion offering-box, p. 117.) Several striking examples of these vehicles are in this exhibition, ranging from an exquisite lion-shaped ivory box to an elaborate two-meter-long palanquin with gold finials. On ceremonial occasions, an image of a deity may be taken out of its enclosed shrine and paraded through the village, to another temple, or to the ocean. Sometimes small images of the deities are placed on the carved animal's back; at other times the symbol of the deity is carried within the animal itself. The many vehicles for the gods point to the importance of rituals involving the procession of deities—often from the temple to the sea for purification ceremonies.

The Balinese believe in a host of unseen forces (*niskala*): some known throughout the island, such as the major Hindu deities Siwa, Wisnu, and Durga; others specific to a certain locale. Even the well-known deity Durga, the consort of Siwa, takes different forms and meanings in different villages. Stephen Lansing writes:

One of the distinguishing features of Bali-Hindu ... is that the gods are supposed to "blow like the wind" through Bali and alight from time to time at various temples. It is only when resident at a temple that they have a personality. Durga, for example, may be called Durga at temple X, and have a well-defined personality, but at temple Y three miles to the north she will have a different name and perfectly distinct personality when she comes to "visit."[31]

Fig. 7. Balinese priest holding a bell (*Martha Hertelendy photo*).

The thousands of temples on the island provide sites to welcome the gods on ceremonial occasions. These temples range in scale from simple family shrines in every family compound to large regional temples to the highest temple of Pura Besakih. Depending on the region, most villages have two or three temples: frequently a *pura puseh,* temple of origin, *pura desa,* temple of the village, and *pura dalem,* temple of death. Numerous other temples are associated with specific locales or natural sites, with water and irrigation, and with kin groups or professions. Complex networks of relationships exist between temples and among the deities that visit them.

Most individuals "belong" to numerous temples. When villagers belong to a temple they are said "to carry it on their heads" (*sane nyungsung pura*), a phrase that evokes the act of bearing the deities aloft during processions.[32] The saying also points to the active role of the worshiper in his or her interaction with the divine. An individual's work for a temple involves many acts that make a deity's visit more hospitable. This includes the decoration of the temple grounds and the preparation and presentation of offerings. Balinese life is full of ceremonies and rituals, which are often marked by the presentation of offerings to the unseen deities. Besides rituals for the gods (*dewa yadnya*), rituals for the demons (*buta yadnya*), and rituals for the ancestors (*pitra yadnya*), there are also rituals concerned with the human life cycle (*manusa yadnya*) and consecration ceremonies for priests (*rsi yadnya*).

Various types of priests and ritual practitioners fulfill the needs of the community. The high priests of the Brahman caste (*pedanda*) are generally considered the most holy and are responsible for officiating at important ceremonies. They know ancient prayers and are able to prepare the holy water that is needed for any Balinese ritual. The *pedanda*'s wife helps with these rituals and assumes her husband's duties upon his death. Priests who have undergone a lower level of consecration rituals are called *pemangku. Pemangku* officiate

31 J. Stephen Lansing, *Evil in the Morning of the World: Phenomenological Approaches to a Balinese Community.* (Ann Arbor: Center for South and Southeast Asian Studies, University of Michigan, 1974), 2.

32 Geertz, *The Life of a Balinese Temple,* 13–14.

BALI: ART, RITUAL, PERFORMANCE 19

at more routine events. They are affiliated with specific temples and have more intimate contact with temple members than do high priests. Some *pemangku* are renowned as healers, and are trained to use sacred diagrams to cure the afflicted. (See the essay by David Stuart-Fox on page 35.)

Balinese religious practices remain highly localized. Much of the worship at temples is not directed toward easily recognizable Hindu deities, but toward local indigenous deities, ancestral deities, and gods associated with wealth and agricultural prosperity. As described by Hildred Geertz, the primary gods of the Pura Desa Batuan in Gianyar are Ida Betara Ratu Puseh, the god of the realm of Batuan; Ida Betara Ratu Desa, the deified original ancestor of the region; Ratu Sanghyang Aji Saraswati, a deity associated with the Hindu goddess Saraswati but who manifests in ancient copper inscriptions of the temple; and Ida Sanghyang Rambut Sedana, deities associated with fertility and well-being.[33] Often temples are interconnected through complicated networks of alliance. The temples in the northern Balinese village of Pacung, for example, include shrines not only for deities associated with local sites but also for deities associated with temples of regional importance (Gunung Agung, Lake Batur, etc.).[34]

As Margaret Wiener writes: "In precolonial Bali there was no clearly demarcated domain of action that could be termed 'religion' since all power was understood to derive from relationships to invisible forces."[35] Balinese engage with a variety of unseen forces, both deities and demons. Westerners are often taken aback by the preponderance of images of wrathful deities or beings in Balinese art. The Balinese conceive of the cosmos as forever shifting between good and evil, and feel the need to acknowledge and propitiate both sides.[36] Certain places and objects are considered *tenget*, a word that has been defined as "sacred" but also conveys the sense of metaphysically charged, or inhabited, by unseen powers. A *tenget* site or object enables the interaction of humans and spiritual beings, both benevolent and malevolent. The conception of specific locations as spiritually charged, and worship of these highly localized deities, point to the continuation of pre-Hindu religious traditions and practices.

When the Indonesian Ministry of Religion was founded in 1946, the Balinese religion was not included among the nationally recognized religions.[37] To qualify for inclusion a religion had to be monotheistic, possess a holy book and prophet, be international in scope, and have members of more than one ethnic group. In an effort to have their cultural practices included among the official Indonesian religions, Balinese reformists tried to reframe the disparate beliefs and practices of the island under a rubric that could

---

33 Geertz, *The Life of a Balinese Temple*, 45–46.

34 I Wayan Patera, "Sanggah Dawa in the Life of Pacung Community," in *Burials, Texts and Rituals,* ed. Brigitta Hauser-Schäublin and I Wayan Ardika, vol. 1, Göttinger Beiträge zur Ethnologie (Göttingen: Universitätsverlag Göttingen, 2008), 122.

35 Margaret Wiener, *Visible and Invisible Realms: Power, Magic, and Colonial Conquest in Bali* (Chicago: University of Chicago Press, 1995), 73–74.

36 Hildred Geertz suggests that the impetus for Balinese ritual comes from anxiety of "impending or continuing physical suffering due to godly anger, demonic greed, ancestral anger, or the anger of other human beings." She believes "all Balinese rituals are at base propitiations of potentially destructive spiritual beings; these propitiatons are followed by rituals of gratitude to the beings and forces that have accepted propitiation and are willing to desist from hurting their people and to actively protect them." Geertz, *The Life of a Balinese Temple*, 73.

37 Michel Picard describes the negotiations of the language regarding religion in the construction of the Indonesian constitution in Picard, "What's in a Name? Agama Hindu Bali in the Making," 1–34.

be recognized by the national government.[38] Some Balinese who did not belong to the highest castes also sought changes in the religion, which they saw as highly hierarchical. Publications of Balinese intelligentsia of the time indicate that the desire for recognition stemmed not merely from a desire for their religion to be recognized alongside other world religions, but also a desire to avoid proselytization from Islamic and Christian believers.[39] The reframing of religion involved stressing connections with modern Hindu movements in India and deemphasizing the diverse localized practices of the island. On some levels this process of "Hinduization" was as much about politics as about religion.[40]

Agama Hindu Bali was acknowledged as a section of the Indonesian Ministry of Religion in 1958. The name acknowledges Hinduism, but specifies it in terms of a local variant. Discussions and disagreements continued among Balinese as to whether this new concept of a Balinese religion should encompass and strengthen indigenous traditions, which combined Indic religions, ancestor worship, and animism, or if the official Balinese religion should codify practices and become aligned with Indian Hinduism as defined by groups like the religious agency, Parisada Hindu Dharma.[41] The name Agama Hindu was adopted by the Indonesian government in 1965 and demonstrates a further step away from localization and toward alignment with Hinduism in other parts of the world, particularly India. This movement, while not necessarily changing the ritual life of the Balinese, has certainly influenced the ways Balinese conceive of their religion and discuss it.[42] This debate has resulted in many Balinese conceptualizing their belief systems as a religion, and viewing them in a larger political context.

HISTORIES: COURT AND CULTURE

Bali is situated along trade routes connecting the Spice Islands, China, and India. These ancient routes not only brought goods; they also spread ideas. During the first millennium, many regions in Southeast Asia adopted and adapted aspects of Indic civilization, especially language, religion, and court culture. Initial contacts with traders from India most likely occurred in the centuries before the first millennium CE, but we do not see evidence of the adoption of Indic religions in Bali until around the eighth or ninth century CE. Clay stupas and impressed seals, as well as stone statuary and rock-cut architecture, provide evidence of the introduction of both Buddhist and Hindu religions. Inscriptions indicate the spread of complex Indic ideas about caste, calendrical systems, and kingship.[43]

From the late ninth century, inscriptions on stone and copper plates describe the first recorded kingdoms of Bali and chronicle a growing network of connections between

38 This involved stressing concepts like the existence of one almighty but imperceptible god, Sanghyang Tunggal or Sanghyang Widhi Waça. It also emphasized the importance of the Vedas and the Hindu epics, the Ramayana and Mahabharata.

39 Picard, "What's in a Name? Agama Hindu Bali in the Making," 63.

40 Picard, "What's in a Name? Agama Hindu Bali in the Making," 57.

41 Of course the Hinduism of India is as diverse as anywhere else. As Frits Staal writes, "In Bali, as in Sri Lanka, Burma, Thailand, the other countries of Southeast Asia, and indeed in Nepal and on the Indian subcontinent itself, it is often impossible to make a sharp distinction between Hindu, Buddhist, and 'animist.' ... What we actually find in Bali is a kind of totality in which features that can be differently labeled when one looks at their historical origins have merged ..." Frits Staal, "The Sound of Religion," *Numen* 33, no. 2 (December 1986): 206.

42 Geertz, *The Life of a Balinese Temple*, 37–40.

43 The idea of caste was adopted from India with the division of people into four hereditary categories, Brahmana, Ksatria, Wesia, and Sudra. These divisions were at one time associated with certain occupations: priest, ruler, merchant, and commoner. The first three categories are known in Bali as the *anak jero,* or inside people. Commoners were called *anak jaba,* or outsiders. For more on caste, see Leo Howe, *The Changing World of Bali: Religion, Society and Tourism* (London; New York: Routledge, 2005), 12–15.

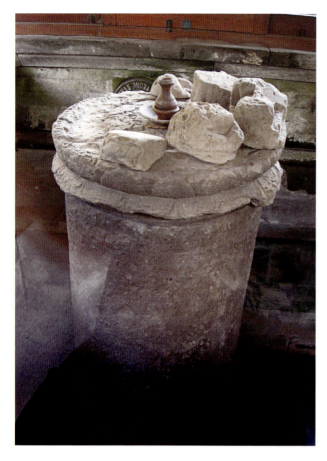

Fig. 8. Blanjong inscription, 913 CE, Pura Blanjong, near Sanur.

44 J. Stephen Lansing, *The Three Worlds of Bali* (New York, NY: Praeger, 1983), 29–31.

45 I Wayan Ardika, "Blanjong: An Ancient Port Site in Southern Bali, Indonesia," in *Form, Macht, Differenz: Motive und Felder ethnologischen Forschens,* ed. Elfriede Hermann, Karin Klenke, and Michael Dickhardt (Göttingen: Universitätsverlag Göttingen, 2009), 252.

46 The inscription is written in early Nagari letters that used the Ancient Balinese language and the Old Balinese letters that used Sanskrit language.

47 Ardika, "Blanjong: An Ancient Port Site in Southern Bali, Indonesia," 254.

48 August Johan Bernet Kempers, *Monumental Bali: Introduction to Balinese Archaeology and Guide to the Monuments* (Berkeley; Singapore: Periplus Editions, 1991), 99.

court, village, and temple or monastery. Many of these early inscriptions are royal edicts pronouncing regulations, obligations, and taxes imposed on local communities. The inscriptions are written in Sanskrit and Old Balinese. Sanskrit was used in proclamations praising rulers. The inscriptions in Old Balinese discuss a wider variety of subjects, including relations between rulers, villages, and members of different religious establishments, both Hindu and Buddhist. Craftsmen, artists, musicians, and performers are mentioned in many of these inscriptions, giving an indication of the rich cultural life in Bali at the beginning of the second millennium, and also offering a window onto interactions between court and village. "Royal troupes" are described, as well as village performers, and groups that moved between village and court. The frequent mention of the artists and performers in these early inscriptions led anthropologist Stephen Lansing to hypothesize that the performing arts served as a tool for the spread of Indic ideas.[44]

The first mention of a Balinese ruler can be found in the Blanjong inscription dated 913 CE.[45] This 1.77-meter-high pillar was found in the southern coastal village of Sanur and is still on display near the Pura Blanjong temple. The partially decipherable inscription is in two languages, Old Balinese and Sanskrit, and is written in two scripts.[46] It praises a ruler by the name of Adipatih (King) Kesari Warmmadewa, who has achieved victory over his enemies at Gurun and Suwal, two places of uncertain location. Scholars suggest that King Kesari was the first of a dynastic line, as several other later rulers have names containing Warmmadewa.[47] One of the scripts used in the inscription, early Nagari, is also used in early Buddhist inscriptions, leading scholars to believe King Kesari may have been Buddhist.[48]

By the beginning of the second millennium CE, Bali seems to have been divided into numerous small "kingdoms." The geography of the island, marked by ridges and long ravines, provided natural territorial divisions. Our historical picture of this time is limited, mostly pieced together from inscriptional and archaeological evidence. Bali's relationship with Java, the much larger island to the west, was marked by periods of both engagement and hostility.

In the mid-tenth century (c. 960 CE), Udayana, a Balinese king of the Warmmadewa dynasty, married an east Javanese princess, Gunapriya Dharmapatni.[49] A number of early inscriptions in Old Balinese mention both of their names. But later inscriptions

Fig. 9. Gunung Kawi, eleventh-century royal monuments, near Tampaksiring (*Dennis Lenehan photo*).

are in the Old Javanese language, suggesting increasing Javanese influence on the island.[50] Their court seems to have been based in central Bali near Pejeng, where there are considerable archaeological remains. King Udayana's last dated inscription is from 1011. A dated stone statue of a pair of figures from that same year has been associated with the royal couple. The statue is now kept at the Pura Tegeh Koripan, along with many other stone statues of royally attired standing figures.

A son of this Balinese-Javanese union, named Airlangga, moved to Java and eventually ruled there in the early eleventh century; two other sons stayed and ruled in Bali. The spectacular site of Gunung Kawi, with its rock-cut temple facades carved into the hillside, may have been made in commemoration of one of these kings, Anak Wungsu.[51] There is little information about contacts with Java in the next few centuries. But it is evident that a shared literary culture developed, with prose and poetry in Old Javanese (Kawi) being written and read on both islands. For both regions, models for kingship appear to have been drawn from this rich literary tradition, including Javanese adaptations of the Hindu epics, the Ramayana and Mahabharata, as well as tales of Javanese princes and kings (Malat tales).

In 1284 the east Javanese Singasari court sent armies into Bali. The Majapahit dynasty court chronicle, the Nagarakrtagama, mentions this incursion as well as a second military

49 The name Warmmadewa derives from the Sanskrit Varma or Varman and was often used in the renal names of rulers of South and Southeast Asia.

50 Lansing, *The Three Worlds of Bali*, 32.

51 Bernet Kempers, *Monumental Bali*, 151–157.

BALI: ART, RITUAL, PERFORMANCE 23

expedition from east Java to Bali in 1343.[52] This latter event plays a seminal role in indigenous Balinese histories, which describe the appointment of a Javanese vassal ruler, as well as the distribution of Balinese land to Javanese nobles.[53] Many Balinese trace their lineages back to these "Majapahit invaders" from Java, considering this "conquest" to be the source of Bali's high culture and civilization.[54] One important Balinese historical work upon which these lineages are based is called the Babad Dalem, a text probably written in the eighteenth century.[55] Other Balinese of the Brahman caste trace their ancestry to the Javanese who fled to Bali after the fall of the Majapahit dynasty and the conversion of the Javanese courts to Islam.

There are various scholarly opinions concerning this story of Majapahit origins for the Balinese people: some scholars have dismissed the idea that Javanese nobility even settled on Bali after the Majapahit incursion; others have tried to find correspondences to these claims in European accounts.[56] Little evidence points to Java's direct control over Bali during this period, although inscriptions indicate a ruler of Majapahit's most eastern province may have had nominal control over parts of the island.[57] Nonetheless, similarities between the islands were often noted. In the Nagarakrtagama, the court chronicler of the Majapahit king Rajasanagara stated: "Among the outer islands Bali conforms with all the customs of Java."[58] European visitors also commented on the similarities between the customs of the two islands. Among other things, the temple architecture of Bali bears resemblances to East Javanese temple complexes. But other Balinese monuments, statues, and inscriptions demonstrate that the cultural ties between Java and Bali go back centuries before the Majapahit dynasty.

By the mid-fifteenth century, a kingdom called Gelgel was established in the southern part of the island. Early Dutch explorers were awed by the grandeur of the court at Gelgel, which was the last Balinese kingdom to have centralized control of much of the island. An account written by Aernoudt Lintgenszoon in 1597 describes the king (possibly Dalem Seganing): "He is also a curious man who has people of all nations and foreign lands in his court, and yet he daily tries to obtain more, and thus he offers friendship to all because if they can speak the language, they can counsel him. And he is well disposed to foreign nations."[59]

In his discussion of the geography of Bali, anthropologist and social scientist Clifford Geertz called the island a "snug little amphitheater." Geertz's use of the term "amphitheater" is elaborated in his arguments that Bali (in the nineteenth century) was a theater state, propped up by organized spectacle. Many of Geertz's theories have been contested, but the

52 Mpu Prapanca, *Desawarnana (Nagarakrtagama)*, trans. Stuart Robson (Leiden: KITLV, 1995), vv. 41: 1, 49: 4.

53 Helen Creese's work discusses the reasons why Majapahit origins were so important to the formations of Balinese identity in the eighteenth century. Helen Creese, *In Search of Majapahit: The Transformation of Balinese Identities* (Clayton, Vic.: Monash University, Monash Asia Institute, 1997). The idea of the unified "golden age" of the Majapahit dynasty was also important to the burgeoning nationalist movements of the early twentieth century. S. Supomo, "The Image of Majapahit in Later Javanese and Indonesian Writing," in *Perceptions of the Past in Southeast Asia,* ed. A. Reid and David Marr (Singapore: Heinemann Educational Books [Asia], 1979), 171–185.

54 An exception is the Bali Aga people, who live mostly in the highlands of Bali.

55 Helen Creese discusses some of the difficulties of interpreting historical events as described in these genealogical texts. Helen Creese, "Balinese Babad as Historical Sources; A Reinterpretation of the Fall of Gelgel," *Bijdragen tot de Taal-, Land- en Volkenkunde* 147, no. 2/3 (1991): 236–260.

56 Henk Schulte Nordholt, *The Spell of Power: A History of Balinese Politics, 1650–1940* (Leiden: KITLV Press, 1996), 23; Hans Hagerdal, "Bali in the Sixteenth and Seventeenth Centuries; Suggestions for a chronology of the Gelgel period," *Bijdragen tot de Taal-, Land- en Volkenkunde* 151, no. 1 (1995): 101–124.

idea of Bali as a site of spectacle and performance continues to resound today, although the audiences, patrons, and performances have changed over the years. The metaphor of an amphitheater suggests looking inward, and Bali's orientation towards its central mountains is often emphasized in discussions of its geography. But this metaphor belies the cosmopolitan nature of Bali, which was noted by its earliest European visitors.

Although Bali is often spoken of in contrast to its neighbor Java, the two islands have many commonalities, and can be seen as sharing a long-lasting cultural heritage. Western scholars have often framed histories of Bali as contrasting with those of Muslim Java; however, Balinese histories from the eighteenth and nineteenth century are deeply tied to the idea of Majapahit Java as the origin of Balinese identity. In Adrian Vickers's article on conceptions of Hinduism and Islam in Indonesia, he notes that differences in religion were not of paramount importance in Balinese narratives.[60] Both Javanese kingdoms and Balinese kingdoms looked to the Majapahit as an important and shared point of origin. Narrative traditions played large roles in cementing this shared cultural heritage. Stories of the Javanese prince Panji were important on both islands, and depictions of characters from these stories can be seen in performance (*gambuh* dance dramas), paintings (see cat. no. 70), and sculpture (cat. nos. 20 and 21).

The sixteenth and seventeenth centuries saw a growth of Balinese power in the region, with periods of Balinese sovereignty in the far eastern parts of Java and in the west on the neighboring island of Lombok. This period is thought of as a golden age in Balinese history. By the end of the seventeenth century, though, Gelgel's power had waned, and Bali was fragmented into a number of principalities often competing for dominance. European perceptions about Bali as a hostile place—a fierce island with constantly battling rulers—were formed during this period. Bali was known in the West as a land of warring princes, a center of the slave trade, and an island staunchly resistant to Dutch incursion.

For years the island's main exports had been rice, cotton cloth, and livestock, but after 1650 a burgeoning slave trade developed.[61] According to one estimate over 150,000 slaves were sold in Bali between 1650 and 1830, often in exchange for opium. Large numbers of Balinese were shipped to Batavia (now Jakarta), the center of the Dutch colonial government, where they worked as household servants or agricultural laborers. Others were forced into military service or sent to work at other colonial outposts as far away as Cape Town and Mauritius. Constant warfare between the fragmented kingdoms provided rulers with captives who were sold into slavery.

By the 1800s, the many small warring principalities in Bali had stabilized into

57 Creese, *In Search of Majapahit,* 6.

58 Mpu Prapanca, *Desawarnana: (Nagara-krtagama),* trans. S. O. Robson (Leiden: KITLV Press, 1995), 79:3.

59 Adrian Vickers, *Travelling to Bali: Four Hundred Years of Journeys* (Kuala Lumpur; New York: Oxford University Press, 1994), 39–40; Howe, *The Changing World of Bali,* 1–17.

60 Adrian Vickers, "Hinduism and Islam in Indonesia: Bali and the Pasisir World," *Indonesia* 44 (1987): 31.

61 Alfons van der Kraan, "Bali: Slavery and Slave Trade," in *Slavery, Bondage, and Dependency in Southeast Asia,* ed. Anthony Reid (New York: St. Martin's Press, 1983), 315–340.

62 Helen Creese, Darma Putra, and Henk Schulte Nordholt, ed., *Seabad puputan Badung: perspektif Belanda dan Bali,* 1st ed. (Jakarta: Pustaka Larasan, 2006).

63 Margaret Wiener argues that suicide is the wrong term to describe this action, which was not an act of despair but "calm, fearless steadfastness" and a "will to surrender ... completely to the invisible world." Wiener, *Visible and Invisible Realms,* 325–328.

64 Although they had firearms, they did not use them.

65 Wiener, *Visible and Invisible Realms,* 314–330.

nine separate kingdoms: Klungkung, Buleleng, Karangasem, Mengwi, Badung, Bangli, Tabanan, Gianyar, and Jembrana. With the exception of Mengwi, which fell in 1891 to neighboring kingdoms, these remain the regencies of Bali today. Although the Dutch had long been a strong colonial presence in other parts of Indonesia, they had taken less interest in Bali, which could not provide them with the vast plantations that were cultivated in Java, Sumatra, and the Maluku islands. So it was not until the mid-nineteenth century that the Netherlands sought to consolidate their empire in Indonesia (and ensure that no other colonial power gained a foothold) by gaining control of Bali. Using the pretext of punishment for the plundering of shipwrecks along Bali's coral reefs, the Dutch made a number of campaigns against the northern kingdoms. It took over three decades before Buleleng, Jembrana, and Karangasem finally came under complete colonial control in 1882. In 1906, the Dutch turned toward the south and again launched a series of campaigns.[62] After landing at the coastal village of Sanur they marched toward Kesiman, only to find the palace in flames and the local ruler dead, killed by his priest in anticipation of the Dutch attack.

The armies then advanced upon the palace of Denpasar in Badung. As the Dutch troops approached, the members of the court filed out, willfully marching into the gunfire of the Dutch troops in a mass action called a *puputan* (ending/finishing).[63] Dressed in white, the color associated with purification (the color a body is wrapped in before cremation), the Balinese advanced in waves, bearing lances and ceremonial daggers (*kris*).[64] Women threw pieces of gold at the Dutch soldiers, and then stood pointing at their hearts, waiting to be killed. Palaces were burned and the slain bodies of the royal families stripped of their jewelry. That afternoon the Dutch army marched on to Pamecutan, to the palace of the co-reigning ruler of Badung, where they met the same reception. The raja of the neighboring kingdom of Tabanan surrendered, and then killed himself in prison along with his son. Two years later the Dutch marched upon the last independent kingdom in south Bali, Klungkung, and again encountered a final *puputan*, marking the end of indigenous rule on the island.[65]

The Dutch artist W.O.J. Nieuwenkamp witnessed the *puputan* of Badung and described it in a letter to his family a few days after the events:

> I have not yet made up my mind whether or not to write letters to the Handelsblad [newspaper] about the war. I am quite certain that anything I write will differ radically from the (news given in) the officially embellished telegrams; and such a letter would make me a lot of enemies. I am very curious

to know what the newspapers will have to say about the taking of Den Pasar, the capital, or will they turn it into an heroic feat. Nonetheless, there was absolutely no question of battle. Our troops stood with canons in front of the entrance to the palace; some hundred or so Balinese came outside, men and women and children. The men knifed the women and children to death, then allowed themselves to be shot dead by the soldiers. Absolute hordes of Balinese kept on coming, and in the same way 1800 died. (I wonder what the official numbers will turn out to be?) The ruler himself came out in a palanquin in all his splendour, and allowed himself to be killed. In the entire campaign, we lost only four men, a clear proof that there was not real battle [...] In a couple of days I shall be going to Den Pasar, it is still in a dreadful mess; they are still busy burying the dead.[66]

66 Francine Brinkgreve, "Balinese Rulers and Colonial Rule: The Creation of Collections, and Politics," in *Indonesia: The Discovery of the Past,* ed. Endang Hardiati and Pieter ter Keurs (Amsterdam: KIT Publishers, 2006), 130.

Word of the *puputans* did reach the Netherlands and the armies' actions were denounced, but the government moved quickly to promote an arcadian view of the island, where the villagers, now free from the yoke of despotic rajas, could be free to follow age-old rituals and create beautiful art.

COURTLY ARTS

Before the Dutch annexation of Bali, the rulers of each small kingdom controlled territory and the services of the people who lived within it. Villagers cultivated land, served in armies, and provided labor for spectacular ritual displays of the ruler's status. Local rulers advanced their prestige by promoting the idea of the king as divine ruler. The connections between court and temple were complex and deeply intertwined. Each palace contained its own temple, and larger "state temples" were the site of worship of deceased and now deified rulers. There are many parallels in temple and palace architecture; both are composed of a series of courtyards, containing pavilions and other buildings. These courtyards are often laid out with the entrance closer to the sea (*kelod*) and its farthest courtyard, containing the royal living quarters or altars for the deities, closest to the mountains (in the *kaja* direction).

Gates and doorways are extremely important in Balinese architecture. In temples, they mark the threshold between the secular and sacred spaces; in a palace compound, they divide the public realm from the private quarters of the court. Often these portals are the most ornate part of a palace or temple compound, and the materials, size, and details of their composition indicate the status of the ruler or the wealth of the village. As liminal spaces, they are charged with power—places where offerings must always be left.

Fig. 10. Temple gate, Pura Kehen, Bangli (*Dennis Lenehan photo*).

67 In fact, kings and priests were sometimes called *susuunan,* a word that means borne on the head. Wiener, *Visible and Invisible Realms,* 154.

Little remains of the palace architecture of the southern Balinese kingdoms of Klungkung and Badung. The royal compounds were burnt to the ground during the early twentieth-century Dutch invasions. The Dutch artist W. O. J. Nieuwenkamp salvaged objects from the destruction, many of which are on view in the exhibition. (See Francine Brinkgreve's essay.) One of the most spectacular of these objects is a pair of four-meter-tall palace doors. The doors come from the palace of Denpasar, in the Balinese kingdom of Badung. After the sack of Badung, Nieuwenkamp recovered the doors, which were going to be used as a bridge by Dutch soldiers. These beautifully carved objects are rare remnants of royal architecture and give us a glimpse of what the palace portal once looked like.

Other indications of royal life can be seen in furnishings, paintings, jewelry, textiles, and regalia. Evidence of the patronage of painting at the court, as well as the Balinese court's adaptation of Hindu myths, can be seen in painted objects made for royalty. A gilt palanquin from the Museum Nusantara, Delft, collected in the nineteenth century, displays painted scenes from the Hindu epic, the Mahabharata. This nobleperson's vehicle calls to mind the palanquins used to carry images of the gods. The similarity was no doubt intentional, and in ritual occasions, such as royal funerals, members of the family are still borne aloft in ceremonial processions.[67] During a Dutch auction of loot from the palace, Nieuwenkamp purchased two large headboards from the palace of Tabanan. One depicts scenes from the Indian epic, the Ramayana, while the other shows a story of the Hindu god of love's disastrous attempts to rouse the god Siwa from his meditation. A canopy for such a bed is painted with another narrative scene, in this case a story of the mythical bird Garuda, one of the most beloved figures in Indonesian mythology. Because of the destruction, fire, and looting that accompanied the Dutch conquest of southern Bali between 1906 and 1908, these are rare surviving examples of pre-1900 court furnishings.

Other types of royal regalia and accoutrements include *kris* (ceremonial daggers), jewelry, implements for chewing betel (a mild stimulant once popular in much of South and Southeast Asia), boxes for the storage of ancient texts, and sumptuous textiles, shimmering with gold thread. The elegance of these items all serve to enhance or express royal prestige. The *kris*, which has great significance throughout the Indonesian archipelago, was among a ruler's most important possessions—a powerful heirloom that could possess supernatural agency. Ornate boxes for the presentation of betel were required in any court, and the offering of betel to a guest was obligatory. The components of betel—betel leaf, areca nut, and lime—are also an important part of any offering to the gods.

The courts were not only major patrons of painters, carvers, smiths, and weavers; they were also important in the development and patronage of Balinese literary and performing arts. Each palace had at least one gamelan orchestra, whose instruments were ornately carved and often decorated with gold leaf. The courts supported other types of performing arts, often bringing the most skilled artisans from the villages to the palace. Kings paid for spectacular costumes, with gold headdresses and fine textiles. Stories from early travelers to Bali emphasize how important the performing arts were in the construction of the prestige of the ruler. When a Thai trader visited a court in north Bali in 1846, he was entertained over two nights with shadow puppet performances and a dance drama. After performances, the ruler extensively questioned the trader about similar traditions in Thailand.[68]

Fig. 11. Princess from the Ubud royal family carried in procession during a cremation ceremony, July 2008.

The conquest of Bali led to a shift of patronage from the courts to the villages. The Dutch wrested power from the kings, whom they perceived as despotic rulers, and set up a new administrative system. Eventually, in the face of rising nationalist sentiments, the traditional rulers were restored in an attempt to maintain peace and order. While much of their former political power had been lost, they still maintained considerable wealth. There had always been interaction between court and village artists, of course, with the most talented artists receiving patronage from the courts. As the courts declined, however, patronage of the arts shifted more and more to the villages, especially to the community associations known as *banjar*. Artists now concentrated their efforts on art for the village temples, for the community, and eventually for a new group of patrons—tourists.

Masked dance performances were especially significant in village cultural life. Today, most villages possess at least one performance mask. The most famous masked dance in Bali involves the wrathful deity Rangda and a playful, lion-like creature known as Barong; the two are said to fight to keep balance and harmony in the world. The masks

68 The trader, Chinkak, refers to the king of Klungkung, but it is believed the ruler might actually have been the king of Buleleng. Charnvit Kaset-siri, "The Statement of Chinkak on Bali," *Indonesia* 7 (1969): 83.

Fig. 12. *Barong bangkal,* boar *barong,* Banjar Mukti, Singapadu.

in this drama are considered sacred divinities in their own right and are stored in temple shrines. In different regions of Bali, Barong takes the form of other animals, including a tiger, boar, and elephant, among others. A wide variety of other masks were used in dance drama performances, many drawing their repertoire from the Hindu epics, or from quasihistorical stories originating in East Java.

PARADISE COLLECTED: WESTERNERS IN BALI, WHAT THEY SAW AND WHAT THEY TOOK

In the aftermath of the final conquest of the island, the image of Bali in the West was recreated and marketed as a tropical Eden, replete with temples, musicians, and barebreasted ladies.[69] While early visitors romanticized the island, describing it as a paradise in which a rich artistic culture flourished in an idyllic landscape, they also saw the island as a kind of "living museum" that preserved a once widespread ancient culture.[70] All this belied the fact that the early decades of the twentieth century were a time of extreme difficulty for the Balinese people, with poverty, natural disasters, and epidemics. The reality of this hardship was kept out of tourist photos and the carefully crafted propaganda promoting the island.[71]

The Dutch justified their overthrow of the Balinese rajas by claiming that they were

69 Vickers, *Bali, A Paradise Created;* Michel Picard, *Bali: Cultural Tourism and Touristic Culture* (Singapore: Archipelago, 1996).

70 This idea had first been articulated a century earlier by Thomas Stamford Raffles, who was the lieutenant governor of Java during the British interregnum (1811–1816).

despotic rulers of foreign (Majapahit Java) origin.[72] Aims of the early colonial government were to preserve the culture of Bali and to restore a more egalitarian society to the people. Ironically, it was the very rulers who were deposed who were the major patrons of the arts. Also, in drawing attention to the inequities of life under the former rulers, the Dutch inadvertently pointed to the parallel inequities of colonialism. Eventually the rulers of Bali were restored, but with drastically reduced authority.

> Emasculating the despots served to justify the *puputan* atrocities and legitimized large-scale political reform; keeping them in place as puppet rulers concealed political domination. Enforcing traditional Balinese ritual, arts and religion made it look as if no change had taken place, thus validating the policy of cultural preservation. Eulogising the rice terraces masked poverty, and glorifying Bali as exotic and beautiful facilitated tourism.[73]

The promotion of Bali as a chic bohemian destination was extremely successful. The list of early Western visitors includes luminaries of the arts, entertainment, and high society worlds: Charlie Chaplin, Al Hirschfeld, Noël Coward, Doris Duke, Barbara Hutton, Leopold Stowkowski, and H. G. Wells, among many others. A comment section of a hotel register in the 1930s included this tongue-in-cheek commentary from Noël Coward (speaking of his fellow traveler Charlie Chaplin):

> As I said this morning to Charlie
> There is far too much music in Bali
> And although as a place it's entrancing
> There is also a thought too much dancing
> It appears that each Balinese native
> From the womb to the tomb is creative
> And although the results are quite clever
> There is too much artistic endeavor[74]

Some of these Western travelers just came for short visits; others stayed, studied, and wrote substantial ethnologies about the island. The most influential of these included the artist Walter Spies, the dancer Beryl de Zoete, the composer and ethnomusicologist Colin McPhee, the dancer Katharane Mershon, the Mexican artist Miguel Covarrubias, and the anthropologists Margaret Mead and Gregory Bateson. In many ways these visitors wanted to see Bali as a timeless exotic locale where age-old traditions continued; in doing so they implicitly supported the Dutch government's efforts to "preserve the culture" of the island.[75]

---

71 There were Dutch critics of the colonial endeavor to promote the island. Tessel Pollman writes, "Critical Dutch comment upon the actual misery and poverty of the people in the east and the north, the new rigidity to which the Hindu caste-system in Bali has developed under colonial rule, the high taxes which the Dutch-Indies Government imposes on poor people, the stunting wealth of the Rajas who are the highest native civil servants as well, the appalling housing of the poor, the syphilis and the tuberculosis, the exploitation of the women, the labor of children from the age of four, the opium-addiction which increases as the Government opens more and more profitable opium-dens, the compulsory labor for Government projects, the unspeakable dirt, the concentration of the culture in the southern areas where life becomes richer and the disappearance of culture from the villages where life becomes poorer, the obligatory character of Balinese culture in public life, and the restrictions of freedom of speech and unions." Tessel Pollman, "Margaret Mead's Balinese: The Fitting Symbols of the American Dream," *Indonesia* 49 (October 1989): 12.

72 Howe, *The Changing World of Bali*, 20–21.

73 Howe, *The Changing World of Bali*, 26.

74 Frank Clune, *To the Isles of Spice with Frank Clune: A Vagabond Voyage by Air from Botany Bay to Darwin, Bathurst Island, Timor, Java, Celebes and French Indo-China* (New York: E. P. Dutton, 1942), 317.

75 Pollman, "Margaret Mead's Balinese: The Fitting Symbols of the American Dream."

The exploration of Balinese interactions with Western visitors in the early twentieth century is only touched upon in this exhibition and is a topic that is rich for further exploration. Here we look at the early interactions of some influential Westerners with Bali using four individuals as case studies: C. M. Pleyte, a Dutch curator; Miguel Covarrubias, a Mexican artist; Vicki Baum, an Austrian writer; and Margaret Mead, an American anthropologist. By examining the objects collected by these individuals, or the images of Bali created by them, the exhibition will consider how increasing contact with Westerners in the early 1900s influenced the West's perception of the island and ultimately impacted art production in Bali. Until the twentieth century, most "art" objects in Bali functioned in ritual contexts, where they might be intertwined with spectacle and performance or could be considered to be imbued with power. With the development of tourism, these traditions continued, but some objects and performances also began to be detached from ritual contexts—evolving in new and fascinating directions.

Although tourists in the 1930s feared that the unique culture of Bali was doomed to disappear in the face of Westernization, it clearly has not. The Mexican artist and ethnographer Miguel Covarrubias bemoaned the fact that the Balinese were "only too willing to adopt any new idea," without acknowledging that the island's unique culture was formed over centuries of such interactions with the outside world. Bali is changing, faced with the pressures of globalization and modern popular culture, but it was never a static entity to begin with. More than a thousand years ago the Balinese adapted and innovated as they incorporated Indic ideas into what must have been an already complex network of indigenous beliefs. Likewise, today, the Balinese have taught and learned from generations of artists from other countries, and Balinese art and performance continue to have an impact on international artists of all kinds. With the growth of tourism in Bali, a new art market—one which catered to Western tastes and generated artworks and performances divorced from their original, spiritual contexts—did, in fact, appear. Rather than replacing traditional Balinese arts and culture, however, this new tourist market coexists with ritual-based Balinese cultural production.

The majority of objects in this exhibition were made before World War II, which brought a halt to the flow of tourists to Bali and began a period of turmoil and hardship. The Japanese occupied the island in 1942. Three days after their surrender in 1945, Indonesian nationalists declared independence, and revolutionary factions fought the Dutch until 1949. Another period of intense bloodshed occurred in the mid-1960s, after the overthrow of President Sukarno and the subsequent massacre of tens of thousands of Balinese in so-called "Communist witch hunts" throughout the island.[76]

Tourism returned in the late 1960s and 1970s, and the numbers of foreigners visiting the island increased stratospherically. In the years before World War II, up to 2000 foreigners had visited the island annually; by 2002, approximately 1.5 million foreign tourists and an equal number of domestic tourists were visiting Bali every year. In the past decade, global political and economic events have influenced the flow of tourism, especially the bombings of 2002. The art produced in the second half of the twentieth century continued to meet the ritual needs of the community, but also developed to meet the burgeoning needs of the tourist markets and the international art markets. This material is beyond the scope of the present exhibition, but is certainly in need of further examination.

There are so many worthy subjects of study in the consideration of Balinese art that any selection of essays can do justice only to a few. Those in this catalogue fill some gaps in material not presented in the exhibition, explain in greater depth some objects that are on display, and discuss Balinese ritual offerings, some of which will be constructed as part of the exhibition.

David Stuart-Fox's essay examines the roles of different types of priests in Bali, and their use of objects in acts of ritual and healing. Specifically, he discusses the *kajang*, a decorated cremation shroud used in cremation rituals (cat. no. 43), and *rerajahan*, magic drawings (cat. no. 39) illustrated with figures and sacred syllables. In his exploration of these drawings, Stuart-Fox suggests intriguing connections between their symbolism and Tantric traditions elsewhere.

One of Francine Brinkgreve's essays is formed around an exquisite object, an animal-shaped ivory offering box from southern Bali. Her essay traces the history of this object, shedding light on both colonial collecting practices and on the possible ritual uses of the box. Garrett Kam and Francine Brinkgreve (in her other essay) both address the ephemeral arts of Bali, exploring ritual decorations and offerings. Their essays complement both objects in the exhibition (palm leaf fertility figures and *lamak* cloth hangings) and the offerings that will be constructed by ritual specialists in the museum during the course of the exhibition. Both men and women participate in the manufacture of offerings, but the daily responsibility of making a family's temple offerings has most often been in the hands of women. These artists have not had the

[76] For a study of this period in history, see Geoffrey Robinson, *The Dark Side of Paradise: Political Violence in Bali* (Ithaca: Cornell University Press, 1995).

Left: Fig. 13. Men preparing a *penjor* at Pura Kehen, Bangli.

Right: Fig. 14. Women making rice-paste offerings, Pejeng Kauh.

recognition that painters and sculptors of the island have received, in part because of the temporary nature of the works, and in part because of the artwork's integration into daily life.

Offerings can be found everywhere in the Balinese landscape—in every family compound, at every bridge or crossroads, on the dashboards of cars, in front of every shop and restaurant. Although the materials used to make them are often fundamentally simple—leaves, flowers, foodstuffs—there is a complex symbolism in the arrangement of colors and shapes. After the offerings are presented to the gods, demons, or ancestral deities, they are destroyed, eaten by animals, or left to decompose. For major celebrations, ritual specialists make even more elaborate offerings, requiring weeks to construct. While it is impossible to permanently preserve these ephemeral arts, Kam's and Brinkgreve's essays greatly enrich our understanding of these traditions, explaining their significance and examining their changing forms in contemporary times.

DAVID J. STUART-FOX
RITUAL ARTS AND IMPLEMENTS OF BALINESE PRIESTS

BALINESE HINDUISM

Present-day Hinduism in Bali is the rich and unique result of intellectual and creative contact of the Balinese people with Indian religions over a period of two thousand years. By the beginning of the Common Era, traders from India had reached the north coast of Bali, a link in the developing trade routes through the waters of Nusantara (an appropriate term for what is now modern Indonesia). However, despite the existence of ancient objects of Indian origin and even the presence of Indian genes in the population, until well into the twentieth century direct contact with India was of lesser significance than the mediation of Indic religions and culture by way of neighboring Java.[1] The presence of the two great Indic religions, Hinduism and Buddhism, is indicated in the earliest known inscription of 896, written in the Old Balinese language and an Indic Pallava-derived script. The earliest polities in Bali, although making use of Indic concepts of kingship and statecraft, were probably organized largely along principles of Austronesian kinship and domain structure. It was on this Austronesian base—and Bali in the late metal age (first–eighth centuries) was a relatively advanced society—that the Indic religions were to flourish.

Although there is evidence of contact between Bali and Central Java in the eighth–early tenth centuries, the era of the great monuments of Borobudur and Prambanan, it was after the center of Javanese power moved to East Java early in the tenth century that the political and religious histories of Bali became entwined with those of Java, even to family ties between their rulers. Old Javanese became the language of both government and religion. However, although strongly influenced by Java, Bali remained essentially independent until the Singasari (thirteenth century) and Majapahit (late thirteenth–fifteenth centuries) periods when Bali was subjugated militarily. Throughout these centuries Hinduism and Buddhism maintained an important presence at the court and in surrounding villages.

Balinese religious history, apart from information gleaned from inscriptions, is a story of a small number of highly influential Brahman priests, usually bearing the title Rsi (Resi) or Mpu (Empu), all of whom are said to have come to Bali from Java. The legendary Rsi Markandeya is said to have introduced Hinduism to Bali from Java, sometime in the middle of the first millennium. Mpu Kuturan is said to have arrived early in the tenth century, and made important reforms in the fields of both doctrine and temple organization; a number

[1] Since the 1950s a small number of Balinese scholars have studied in India, and one or two Indians in Bali. Classic Hindu texts previously unknown in Bali, like the Vedas and Upanishads, have been translated into Indonesian. Later, the Sai Baba and Hare Krishna movements gained adherents in Bali. See Leo Howe, *Hinduism and Hierarchy in Bali* (Oxford: Currey, 2001).

Left: Fig. 1. A *pemangku* temple priest presents worshipers' offerings during the yearly festival at Pura Dalem Puri, Besakih (Karangasem). *Photo David Stuart-Fox.*

Right: Fig. 2. Official *pemangku* priests of Pura Besakih officiate at the yearly *usaba ngeed* ritual. Besakih (Karangasem). *Photo David Stuart-Fox.*

2 These two priests are among the Balinese Sapta Rsi, the "seven holy men" from whom, according to traditional genealogies, many of the major Balinese kin groups are descended.

3 See Andrea Acri, *Saivism in Ancient Indonesia: The Sanskrit-Old Javanese 'Tutur' Literature from Bali* (unpublished *tesi di laurea*, Rome, 2005) for an introductory survey, with particular reference to Java.

of religious texts are associated with this name, which however is also that of a high court functionary. His brother Mpu Bharadah, court priest of Airlangga, one of Java's most famous kings, is the distant ancestor of the Ksatria and Brahmana (Brahman) kin groups of Bali.[2] Mpu Nirartha was court priest of King Baturenggong (sixteenth century), during whose reign the kingdom of Gelgel reached the apogee of its power and glory; he was a major literary figure, founder of important temples, and the ancestor of the *brahmana siwa* kin groups. His nephew, Mpu Asthapaka, the last to arrive, is the ancestor of the *brahmana buda* kin group. The two kinds of Brahman priest, the *pedanda siwa* and *pedanda buda*, belong to these respective kin groups.

Unfortunately, though, the stories of the great priests help little in understanding the development of Hindu doctrines and practices in Bali. The same can be said for Buddhism as well, for within Balinese Hinduism there are Buddhist elements, particularly in the ritual texts of the *pedanda buda*, one of the two categories of Brahman high priest. Epic texts, some in prose but many in poetry, are primarily derived from the great Indian Hindu myths and epics, particularly the Mahabharata and Ramayana. In the Indonesian context, these originate from the Old Javanese period, and can be fairly accurately dated. Doctrinal texts, what the Balinese call *tutur*, are rarely dated; some indeed are from the Old Javanese period but others were written in Bali in Old Javanese language idioms, known as Kawi. Few scholars have delved into this highly esoteric field, and no one has attempted a survey of the concepts and development of doctrines in Balinese Hinduism.[3] There seems to be, however, some general agreement. For example, although terms and ideas from other Hindu traditions may appear, the main Balinese tradition is the Saiva-siddhanta, a predominantly South Indian school, with a dualistic philosophical system in which ritual and mantra play important roles. This is particularly the case with regard to the rituals of the Brahman high priests. A second point of agreement is the extensive influence of Tantric ideas and practices.

It is said that Hinduism in Bali is a religion of orthopraxis rather than orthodoxy, where the correct enactment of ritual plays a more important role than the correct understanding of ideas. Bali is indeed particularly famous for its rituals, which are highly elaborate and very colorful, and which take place virtually on a daily basis. In fact, evidence suggests that during the last century Balinese rituals have become even more elaborate, so much so that leading religious figures are calling for a reevaluation of this tradition, to simplify rituals and further the understanding of the concepts that underlie them.

As in all religions, in Bali also there is a wide difference in the depth of understanding among Hindu adherents. The average villager or urban dweller performs the rituals that he or she has to perform, or plays his or her role in the enactment of communal rituals, helping with preparations, making offerings, carrying the gods, or performing a ritual dance. Traditionally, it was believed that not everyone was suitable for receiving deeper knowledge. This tradition of *aywa wera*, literally "do not disseminate," kept knowledge within priestly, particularly Brahman, families. This tradition has only within the last fifty years or so begun to lose its power, but many esoteric traditions and interpretations still remain essentially secret.

BALINESE PRIESTS

In Balinese Hinduism there are many kinds of priests, in the broad sense of any ritual expert who acts as intermediary between human and nonhuman realms, or what the Balinese call the *sekala* (visible) and *niskala* (invisible) realms. Many types of priests exist, each with its own name, title, and consecration ritual, but these can more or less be grouped into two major categories: the *sulinggih* or high priest with *madiksa* as rite of consecration, and the *pemangku*, with *mawinten* as rite of consecration. In terms of numbers the *pemangku* is far more numerous, but in terms of influence and ritual status the *sulinggih*, particularly the Brahman high priest, is more important. There is no gender discrimination in entry to Balinese priesthoods; all are open to both male and female, generally as a married couple. The priestess adds the term *istri* (meaning "female") after the priestly title.

To become a *pemangku* is open to everyone, male or female, from any of the four castes (*warna*). A "temple" *pemangku* has in his (or her) charge the rituals of a village, kin group, or some other kind of temple to which he has rights and duties (figs. 1–3). Such a position may be inherited, or chosen by the worship-group or by divine selection (trance). A "private" *pemangku* becomes so of his own volition, often in connection with a particular vocation such as shadow-play puppeteer (*dalang*) or healer (*balian*). In fact, the consecration ritual

Left: Fig. 3. The nine official *pemangku* of Pura Besakih perform their collective *ajang* ritual. Pura Banua, Besakih (Karangasem). *Photo David Stuart-Fox.*

Right: Fig. 4. A *pemangku* sprinkles holy water over the heads of worshipers at a temple festival. Pura Dalem, Kapal (Badung). *Photo Brent Hesselyn.*

4 *Winten* is ultimately derived from the Sanskrit *hira* (via Old Javanese [*h*]*inten*), which also means diamond, but which apparently is not generally used in ritual contexts (cf. *vajra*).

of a *pemangku*, called *mawinten*, is thought to be necessary to anyone coming into contact with the *niskala* world, and that even includes the reading of *lontar* religious texts. Among those who acknowledge the authority of the Brahman priest (and that does not include everyone), the ceremony is carried out by a *pedanda* (fig. 5); but there are other forms of *mawinten* through rituals at certain shrines and temples. The term itself is derived from the word *winten*, which means "diamond," but it is not certain if this is connected with the concept of "diamond" in Tantric thought.[4] *Pemangku* are most commonly addressed as Jero Mangku, *jero* being an honorific of respect.

Sulinggih is a term that has come into currency quite recently to describe the category of "high priest," a category that is the subject of considerable debate and even crisis within Hindu circles in Bali. Traditionally, the Brahman high priest, the *pedanda*, had a virtual monopoly on the function of high priest, on the grounds of belonging to the Brahman (*brahmana*) "caste" (*warna*), the priestly caste, the highest and purest of the four Hindu castes. And, in terms of numbers, Brahman high priests still retain a dominant position. Only Brahman high priests carry the title *pedanda;* of these, there are two groups, the *pedanda siwa* (fig. 6) and *pedanda buda* (fig. 7), who claim descent from the same ancestor prior to their arrival in Bali from neighboring Java. The differences between these two kinds of *pedanda* lie most importantly in their rituals; those of the *pedanda buda* are more properly a Buddhist-Siva cult, incorporating Saivite hymns and mantras along with those from Tantric or Vajrayana Buddhism. But there are also visible differences; for example, the

pedanda buda wears his hair long, and he has additional cult implements. Consecration is undertaken as a married couple, though it is possible for an unmarried *brahmana* woman to become a priestess, known as *pedanda istri kania*.

Other high priest titles depend on caste and descent group. The title Rsi is used by priests from the Ksatria and Wesia castes, and from the *bhujangga waisnawa* group, now considered Sudra (or *jaba*). Priests from other Sudra groups take titles consisting of an honorific (such as *sri* or *jero*) and a descent group name, as in *sri mpu pande* (figs. 9–10), *sri mpu pasek*, *jero dukuh*, *jero sengguhu*.

It is the rite of consecration that gives the clearest indication of ritual status and ritual exclusiveness, and thus the relationship among priests. Until quite recently, with the exception of that for a *rsi bhujangga*, all consecration rites for high priests were conducted by the Brahman high priest, the *pedanda*. Within the Brahman priesthood, this ritual is called *madiksa* (from Sanskrit *diksa*) or *nuhun pada* (literally "to lower the foot"), referring to the consecratory act of the guru placing his foot on the head of the candidate. In this consecration ritual, the candidate even touches the big toe of the guru with his or her tongue, a sign of absolute deference. Through consecration, the guru passes on ritual power and authority to the candidate or pupil (*sisia*), forming a succession of teachers that has its own "genealogy." Rsi from the Ksatria and Wesia castes, *jero dukuh*, and *jero sengguhu* continue to receive consecration from a *pedanda*. *Sri mpu pande* and *sri mpu pasek*, the high priests from the Pande and Pasek kin groups, now conduct consecration rituals by their

Left: Fig. 5. The late Pedanda Wayan Datah, a Buda high priest (*pedanda buda*), pours holy water through a rice steamer over the head of a candidate priest, a purificatory rite during a *mawinten* ceremony to consecrate a *pemangku*. Budakeling (Karangasem). *Photo David Stuart-Fox.*

Right: Fig. 6. A Siwa high priestess (*pedanda istri siwa*) sprinkles holy water over her miter before putting it on her head. Sanur (Denpasar). *Photo David Stuart-Fox.*

Left: Fig. 7. The late Pedanda Wayan Datah, a Buda high priest (*pedanda buda*). Budakeling (Karangasem). Photo David Stuart-Fox.

Right: Fig. 8. Sitting on the ground, an unusual position for high priests, a group of Buda high priests and priestesses perform their rituals while villagers dance the *pendet* dance. Pura Dalem, Budakeling (Karangasem). Photo David Stuart-Fox.

own high priests, and no longer require the services of a *pedanda*. Indeed they consider themselves of equal ritual status as *pedanda*, and claim the right to conduct public rituals at such major temples as Pura Besakih.[5]

The priestly succession of the *rsi bhujangga* has a long independent tradition in which a special kind of bell, called *bajra uter*, is used in the key rite of consecration, equivalent to the *nuhun pada* of the *pedanda*. The status and role of the *rsi bhujangga* remains an unresolved problem. Certain major rituals require three priests (known in the texts as the *trisadaka*): *pedanda siwa*, *pedanda buda*, and a priest who conducts netherworld rites for demonic forces. This priest is the *sengguhu*, who sits at a lower level than the two *pedanda*. The *rsi bhujangga* believes that he is rightly this third priest, but refuses to participate with the Brahman priests who demand that the *rsi bhujangga* also sit at a lower level. Many Balinese do not realize the difference between *sengguhu* and *rsi bhujangga*, regarding them as equivalent. The difference lies in consecration ritual: *sengguhu* receive it from a *pedanda* and acknowledge difference in ritual status, whereas *rsi bhujangga* have their own independent succession.[6]

CULT IMPLEMENTS

The rituals of Balinese Hinduism are traditionally divided into five groups: *dewa yadnya* rituals directed to deities, *buta yadnya* directed to demonic forces, *manusa yadnya* directed to the human being from conception, *pitra yadnya* directed to the human being from death to purification, and *rsi yadnya* directed to priests. Rituals within each group have special requirements, offerings, and prayers, which are often extremely complicated. However, beyond the specifics of ritual, certain ritual acts and procedures can be seen as basic to priestly

5 At Pura Besakih there is an important subsidiary temple dedicated to Ratu Gede Pande, the gods of the smiths, who at Pura Besakih's major yearly ritual must lead the gods in processions. Rituals at Pura Ratu Pande used to be conducted by *pedanda*, but the smiths' own high priests demanded, and won, the right to conduct the rituals. Similarly, the Pasek high priests won the right to conduct rituals at their own temple. But neither has yet won the right to conduct rituals, together with *pedanda*, in the main temple.

6 On the *sengguhu*, see C. Hooykaas, "The Balinese Sengguhu-priest, a Shaman but not a Sufi, a Saiva, and a Vaisnava," in ed. John Bastian and R. Roolvink, *Malayan and Indonesian Studies: Essays Presented to Sir Richard Winstedt on His Eighty-Fifth Birthday*

ritual generally, and comprise the phases of purification of priest and implements, invitation to unseen forces (gods and demons), presentation of worship, counterprestation from deity to devotee, and finally dispersion. These involve notions of the divine guest and of asymmetrical exchange between deity and devotee. Essential to these rituals is the making of holy water (*tirta*), of which there are various kinds, for which the officiating priest requires a number of ritual implements.

I shall begin with the cult implements of the *pedanda siwa*.[7] Dressed in a priest's white clothing (which I shall not discuss here), he (or she) sits cross-legged on a cushion behind a low table or (usually) two footed trays (*dulang*) made from wood (cat. no. 37) or brass, on which his cult implements have been laid out, under a large hemispherical cover made of pandanus leaves (*saab*, *saguan*), by his wife (*pedanda istri*) or an assistant. There is a water vessel (*swamba*), with a water sprinkler (*panyiratan*) resting on its tripod (*tripada*), an oil lamp (*padipaan*), a sandlewood brazier (*padupaan*), the bell (*genta*), and small containers for incense, flowers, and grains of rice. These utensils are usually made of brass (see cat. nos. 32, 33, and 34). Accompanied by specific mantras and actions at each stage, the priest purifies himself and the cult implements, and so begins his intricate ritual in which the god Siwa-soul (*Siva-atma*) descends into the priest, who consecrates the water, which becomes *tirta* or holy water.[8] For the consecration of the bell, the priest takes it in his left hand, sprinkles it with holy water, and utters this Sanskrit hymn:

> The syllable OM is resting in Eternal Siwa,
> Accomplishing the benefit of the Lord of the World;
> It is manifested as the sound of the bell,
> To be rung in reverential salutation.
> The sound of the bell is the utmost good,
> It is loudly proclaimed as being the syllable OM;
> It represents *ardha-candra, bindu,* [*nada* and] *nadanta,*
> It is the spark of fire and it has the quality of Siwa.
> The life of the bell is (deserves to be?) worshipped like a god(?),
> In the case of works that will be done or will not be done;
> The granter of boons who has obtained what is to be united,
> Without doubt [the bell] is the accomplishment of the boon.

Fig. 9. A high priest from the smiths' descent group, bearing the title Sri Empu Pande, performs his ritual. His choice of red clothing, although fitting for members of a craft utilizing fire, is nevertheless unusual. Tonja (Denpasar). *Photo David Stuart-Fox.*

(Oxford: Clarendon Press, 1964), 267–281. The *bhujangga* of Bali are probably related to the *bhujangga* of ancient Java, though the term itself appears to have a range of meanings.

7 For drawings of *pedanda siwa* and implements, see Tyra de Kleen and P. de Kat Angelino, *Mudra's op Bali: Handhoudingen der priesters* ('s Gravenhage: Adi-Poestaka, 1922), figs. 29–48.

8 C. Hooykaas has translated and explained this ritual in detail in his scholarly study *Surya-sevana: The Way to God of a Balinese Siva Priest* (Amsterdam: Noord-Hollandsche Uitgevers Maatschappij, 1966).

RITUAL ARTS AND IMPLEMENTS OF BALINESE PRIESTS   41

And then the bell is held over the brazier, the clapper is touched to the rim, and the bell is sounded.[9]

Besides these cult implements of the *pedanda siwa*, the Buda high priest, or *pedanda buda*, makes use of two additional cult implements: the double-ended *bajra* and the *santi*.[10] Originally the weapon of the Hindu god Indra, the *bajra* (Sanskrit *vajra*), or thunderbolt, was adopted by Vajrayana Buddhism as its distinctive cult implement, identified with the diamond, and symbolizing enlightenment. At either end of the round central section is a finial with a protruding central prong and four surrounding prongs that curve sharply inwards. The *santi* is an enigmatic implement whose purpose, and origin, are not entirely clear; it is sometimes called a "direction-finder," since in certain rituals it is turned to the cardinal directions.[11]

Among the other high priests, the *rsi bhujangga* (and *sengguhu*) himself has cult implements similar to those of the *pedanda siwa*, but there are four additional noise-making cult implements, wielded by the priest and his assistants. They comprise a conch shell, a small clapper drum, a frame of little bells, and a "rubbing" bell (for want of a better expression); if the priest's bell is added the whole group is five in number (fig. 11). The conch shell (*sungu, sangka*) is the attribute of Wisnu, and is one reason why the *bhujangga* are thought to be the inheritors of an old Vaisnava cult. The little drum (*ketipluk*) is a kind of clapper drum mounted on a stick, where the pellets, not inside the drum but attached on cords to the outside, strike the drum heads when the stick is rolled between the palms of the hands, or otherwise shaken.[12] The frame of little bells, called a *genta orag* (*gentorag*), is just that, a wooden conical, tree- or pagoda-shaped frame with a dozen or more little bells attached to it. Shaking the instrument makes the bells ring. It is occasionally found in certain old gamelan ensembles in Bali and Java.[13] Finally, the "rubbing" bell (*bajra uter*) is the most important of these implements, for it plays a crucial role in the consecration ritual of the *bhujangga*, being placed on the head of the candidate priest. The sound itself, perhaps best described as a rich penetrating hum, is produced by rubbing the outside rim of the bell round and round with a stick. Probably no more than five *bajra uter* exist on Bali, and like the other cult instruments they are not used at smaller kin group rituals, only at larger rituals with elaborate netherwold offerings. The origin of this kind of bell is probably India; it is found among cult instruments of Tibetan Buddhism.[14] The role of sound-making cult instruments in certain rituals of the *bhujangga* and *sengguhu* is said to be related to the fact that these rituals are directed to demonic beings, while the conch is used to call the gods to witness the demons receiving the netherworld (*caru*) offerings.

---

9 C. Hooykaas, *Surya-sevana: The Way to God of a Balinese Siva Priest* (Amsterdam: Noord-Hollandsche Uitgevers Maatschappij, 1966), 86–89.

10 For drawings of *pedanda buda* and implements, see Tyra de Kleen and P. de Kat Angelino, *Mudra's op Bali: Handhoudingen der priesters* ('s Gravenhage: Adi-Poestaka, 1922), figs. 4–23.

11 C. Hooykaas, "Santi: A Ritualistic Object from Bali," *Asia Major*, new series, 11, no. 1 (1964), 78–83. See further C. Hooykaas, *Balinese Bauddha Brahmans* (Amsterdam: North-Holland Publishing Company, 1973), 110–113, where it is called a "curse-averter." The word *santi* means "peace" in Sanskrit.

12 One such drum is depicted on a Bhairava statue from East Java, dated c. 1250. See Jaap Kunst, *Hindu-Javanese Musical Instruments* (The Hague: Nijhoff, 1968), 36, figs. 48–48a. It would seem to be similar to the *damaru* (Sanskrit), a word apparently unknown in Java or Bali.

13 Kunst, *Hindu-Javanese Musical Instruments*, 56.

14 A *bajra uter* can have a clapper, but it is not sounded using the clapper. One would expect that it was formerly known in ancient Java, but I have been unable to find any references to it. I am unable to say whether it was made from a special kind of alloy.

Left: Fig. 10. Bell, water vessel, lamp—typical ritual utensils of a high priest, in this case in use by a high priest from the smiths' descent group. Tonja (Denpasar). *Photo David Stuart-Fox.*

Right: Fig. 11. A *sengguhu* priest and his assistants wield their distinctive sound-producing instruments during an exorcistic ritual at Pura Besakih's annual festival. Besakih (Karangasem). *Photo David Stuart-Fox.*

The other major grouping of priests, the *pemangku,* makes no use of cult implements other than the priest's bell, and a vessel for holy water. One passage in their ritual clearly indicates the role of the bell:

OM bell with thy loud voice,
Great Leader, thou art a token
That Gods descend, caused by the bell.
OM, let there be success and homage.[15]

Many *pemangku* do not even use a bell, but perform their rituals with flowers, incense, and water.

Besides the usual water vessels, *swamba* and the *sangku*, other special kinds of containers for holy water are used for specific kinds of rituals. For example, when a ritual requires holy water (*tirta*) from an important spring or from one of the great temples of Bali, the water is placed in a piece of bamboo that is decorated appropriately with cloth. This vessel is then afforded the dignity of a deity, which indeed it is, and called Ida Bhatara Tirta, literally Lord God Holy Water.

Another unusual water vessel is sometimes used for making the holy water of exorcism (*panawar* or *panglukatan* or *pamugpugan*, depending on the level of ritual elaboration). A *balian* or healer with whom I studied, Mangku Ketut Liyer of Pengosekan (fig. 12), makes holy water of exorcism in a vessel fashioned from the inner shell of a coconut with a small hole cut at the top. This vessel, called *sibuh cemeng*, is made from a special coconut that,

15 C. Hooykaas, *A Balinese Temple Festival* (The Hague: Nijhoff, 1977), 34.

Left: Fig. 12. Healer-priest Mangku Ketut Liyer (of *Eat, Pray, Love* fame) blesses a basket of offerings during a healing ritual. Pengosekan (Gianyar). *Photo David Stuart-Fox.*

Right: Fig. 13. Holding a special coconut vessel close to his mouth, a young Mangku Ketut Liyer utters a mantra to create holy water of exorcism. Pengosekan (Gianyar). *Photo David Stuart-Fox.*

instead of the usual two eyes and three veins, has three eyes and four veins. Such coconuts are rare, and considered a charm. When making this holy water, the *balian* sits crosslegged in his work pavilion, facing east—the footed stand covered with offerings and burning incense set in front of him. He always puts a few flowers into the coconut-shell vessel, and if he feels that an evil spirit possesses the patient, he adds a few grains of *beras kuning*, uncooked rice made yellow by mixing it with turmeric. Then, taking the vessel in his hands, he holds it so that his mouth is right over the hole, so close that the mantra is somewhat muffled and indistinct (fig. 13).

> ONG,
> Affliction that comes from the east, return to the east.
> Affliction that comes from the south, return to the south.
> Affliction that comes from the west, return to the west.
> Affliction that comes from the north, return to the north.
> Affliction that comes from the center, return to the center.
> Let Sanghyang Bayu (God of Strength) penetrate the body of this person,
> Emanating multi-colored fire.
> ANG, vanish all machinations of male *leyaks*, female *leyaks*, and hermaphrodites.
> Vanish, vanish, vanish.[16]

He often uses this mantra when preparing *panawar*, but he usually adds several more mantras to ensure the potency of the water. To prepare the next levels of holy water, *panglukatan* and *pamugpugan*, the main mantra is the long and complicated *Astupungku*.

16 Author's translation.

PRIESTS AND THEIR RITUAL ARTS

With this brief introduction to the different priests of Bali and to their cult implements, I turn now to one particular aspect of their professions: what I call their ritual arts. I should define at the outset what I mean, in the context of this essay, by the ritual arts of Balinese priests. I use the term to encompass material objects that are used directly as important elements of ritual, and that are generally made by one or other of the several kinds of Balinese priests, or under their supervision. Excluded in this definition are objects that are employed in the context of a ritual, but not directly in the ritual itself — for example, traditional paintings hung on a pavilion at the time of a ceremony, or the mask worn by a dancer in the context of a ritual.

Ritual objects are made of a wide variety of materials, both permanent and ephemeral, such as paper, cloth, thread, metals, bamboo, palm leaf, or other less common materials. And they are made for all sorts of rituals, perhaps none more so than for the rite of cremation (fig. 14). Offerings are a special group of ritual objects, and are of the utmost importance in Balinese ritual. Offerings are among Bali's most distinctive ritual arts.[17] They are often of great beauty, and their variety and complexity are quite extraordinary, though not without structure.[18] In major rituals involving high priests, the *pedanda istri* (or her equivalent) plays the leading role in preparation of offerings.

Within this definition, however, I limit the discussion in this essay to painted or drawn objects on paper or cloth or other, less usual media, and in particular to two kinds of drawings of special interest: the cremation "shroud" (*kajang*) associated with the high priest, and power drawings (*rerajahan*, *tumbal*) associated especially with the *balian*, the healer-priest. Important elements of many of these drawings are power syllables (*bijaksara*) and weapons (*sanjata*) that are related to three intertwined doctrinal concepts of the utmost significance: the concepts of cosmic space, the number-based system of sacred syllables, and macrocosm-microcosm correspondence.

The concept of cosmic space, the *nawa sanga* system, comprises the eight directions and center, each of which has its own guardian or deity, with corresponding weapon, power syllable, color, and number (among other attributes). When the zenith and nadir are added, there are eleven directions in all; in the most elaborate ritual in Balinese Hinduism, the Ekadasa Rudra held once a century at Pura Besakih, ritual attention is paid to all eleven directions.[19]

In the second of these concepts, sacred syllables are grouped into number-based groupings, the important ones being those based on the numerals ten, five, three, two, and finally the

17 See Francine Brinkgreve and David Stuart-Fox, *Offerings: The Ritual Art of Bali* (Sanur: Image Network Indonesia, 1992).

18 For some thoughts on the structure of offerings and their named groups, in the context of rituals at Pura Besakih, Bali's largest temple, see David J. Stuart-Fox, *Pura Besakih: Temple, Religion and Society in Bali* (Leiden: KITLV Press, 2002), 143–158.

19 See David J. Stuart-Fox, *Once a Century: Pura Besakih and the Eka Dasa Rudra Festival* (Jakarta: Penerbit Sinar Harapan and Citra Indonesia, 1982).

Top: Fig 14. *Angenan,* a symbol of light, a ritual utensil placed by the deceased during a cremation ceremony. *Photo David Stuart-Fox.*

Bottom: Fig. 15. A Siwa high priest (*pedanda siwa*) inscribes sacred syllables on an "ivory" coconut, during the course of a death ritual. Besakih (Karangasem). *Photo David Stuart-Fox.*

center. In ritual and in meditation practice, and in doctrines underpinning them, there is a process in which the groups dissolve into one another in a linear process. Although the naming of groups can vary in the texts, the commonest groups are as follows. *Dasaksara* comprises two groups of five, the *pancabrahma* (Sang, Bang, Tang, Ang, Ing, corresponding to the first syllables of five names of Siwa), and the *pancaksara or pancatirta* (Nang, Mang, Sing, Wang, Yang, with the meaning Nama Siwaya, Honor to Siwa). These ten dissolve into the five syllables of the *pancakasara* (as above, or Mang, Ang, Ong, Ung, Yang), then the *triaksara* (Ang, Ung, Mang), then the *dwiaksara* or *rwabhineda* (Ang, Ah) and finally the central ONG. These sacred syllables lie at the heart of Balinese Hinduism (and Buddhism), whether the syllables are in written form on *rerajahan* and *kajang* and other ritual paraphernalia, or in spoken mantra form in the rituals of Balinese priests. The sacred syllables and their groupings show close similarity to Indian textual and ritual traditions, and in Bali, as elsewhere in the Indic world, they are central to that indivisible whole that encompasses mysticism, medicine, and magic.

The third of these concepts is that of the correspondence between macrocosm and microcosm, what the Balinese call the *buana agung* (great world) and *buana alit* (small world). In this system, macrocosmic powers or energies, related to the deities of the cosmic directions, find their correspondences within the microcosmic human body. For example, the syllable Sang of the *pancabrahma* is located in the east (macrocosm) and in the heart (microcosm), and so on. These correspondences play an important role in traditional Balinese healing.

With regard to the ritual arts, these syllables and weapons are utilized in various rituals and in various media. Sacred syllables are scratched with a knife on a ritual "ivory" coconut (*nyuh gading;* fig. 15), or written with the fingers on the head of a candidate priest or whoever is the focus of a ritual. The weapons of the directions are drawn in rice flour on the ground in connection with major exorcistic rituals (such as Ekadasa Rudra), or building foundation rituals (figs. 16–17). Syllables and weapons are drawn on paper and cloth and hung on buildings at the times of their purification rites or as general protection. The list can go on.

Divine or human figures, too, play an important role in the ritual arts of Balinese priests. Such figures appear made of Chinese coins in certain rice rituals (fig. 18) and in the cremation ritual. Simply drawn in black and white or elaborately painted in

color on little slabs of sandalwood, faces portray the deceased during certain death rituals or represent deities in temple rituals (figs. 19–20). They are drawn on cremation shrouds and magic drawings, as we shall see, both of which are represented in the exhibition.

KAJANG, THE CREMATION "SHROUD"

Among the ritual drawings necessary for the proper performance of death rituals, the most elaborate is the *kajang* (sometimes also called *rerajahan kajang* or *kakereb sari*).[20] It is a special kind of cremation "shroud," placed over the body but not wrapped around it. It is inscribed with a series of sacred syllables (*bijaksara*) with mystical significance in esoteric doctrines of Tantric Hinduism (or Buddhism). Sometimes the syllables are depicted in conjunction with a human figure, representing the deceased, and with figures of deities and mythological animals. It is used during the cremation ritual and is always burned with the body. At the present time the shroud is made of white cloth (occasionally still handwoven), but in the past it may sometimes have been made of bark cloth, such as the "sampler" *kajang* in the present exhibition.

The *kajang* is prepared by a high priest (*sulinggih*), or by a member of a high priest's family under his or her supervision, usually at the priest's residence. A small ritual must precede the preparation itself. I am uncertain whether there is a prescribed size or length for the *kajang*; one source gives the length as three *asta*, the distance from outside of the elbow to tip of the fingers.[21] Attached to the *kajang* is a long piece of white cloth that can

Left: Fig. 16. A *pemangku* makes a "Yamaraja" drawing, consisting of the weapons of the eight directions and center, in readiness for the enormous exorcistic ritual Ekadasa Rudra, held once a century at Pura Besakih. Besakih (Karangasem). *Photo David Stuart-Fox.*

Right: Fig. 17. Two Buda high priests (*pedanda buda*) "enliven" the "Yamaraja" drawing for the village's *taur* cleansing ritual. Budakeling (Karangasem). *Photo David Stuart-Fox.*

20 The word *kajang* is found in Old Javanese and Balinese texts and inscriptions, but it has a broader meaning in the sense of a piece of cloth or cushion used underneath something (P.J. Zoetmulder (with S.O. Robson), *Old Javanese-English Dictionary* ('s-Gravenhage: Nijhoff, 1982) I, 765); it is also apparently sometimes associated with matting made of woven bamboo or palm leaf. Only in Balinese texts dealing with death rituals does it have the specific meaning of "death shroud."

21 I Gusti Ketut Kaler, *Ngaben: Mengapa mayat dibakar?* (Denpasar: Yayasan Dharma Naradha, 1997), 58.

RITUAL ARTS AND IMPLEMENTS OF BALINESE PRIESTS 47

Fig. 18. Human figures created from Chinese coins, eggs, and other materials form part of rituals to bless rice to be used in offerings. Besakih (Karangasem). *Photo David Stuart-Fox.*

be tens of meters long, called the *lancingan*, the same word as that used for the end of the hip cloth (*kain*) that hangs down between the legs.

Cremation involves a long sequence of rituals, too complicated to discuss in detail in the context of this essay.[22] The *kajang* makes its appearance in that part of the ritual called *pabresihan* or *pasucian*, meaning purification, which takes place at the home of the deceased (fig. 21). At this point, the body (or just the dug-up bones of someone previously buried, or occasionally just a body symbol), wrapped in white cloth, has been placed on the pavilion called *bale dangin*. Before the *kajang* is placed on the body, it is empowered or enlivened by the high priest in a ritual called *mlaspas kajang*. Placed on top of the *kajang* is another ritual object, called *ukur*, which usually consists of Chinese coins tied together with cotton thread in such a manner as to form a human figure, representing the deceased.[23]

After the ritual at the home of the deceased, the body, placed on the cremation tower, is carried to the cremation ground. Walking in front of the tower and holding onto the long piece of white cloth, the *lancingan*, attached to the *kajang*, are family members (fig. 22). At the cremation ground (just outside the temple to the dead, the *pura dalem*), the body is burned, the *kajang* along with it (the *ukur* may be removed).

The syllables and figures inscribed on a shroud vary with caste (*warna*) and kin group, and with level of ritual elaboration. There are thus scores of different shrouds. How this variation arose, and when, is uncertain, but there is little doubt it occurred in Bali itself.[24] In Bali, kin groups play a very important role in religion and society, and honoring one's parents, forefathers, and ancestors is a religious duty, the basic motivation for the complex funerary rites that children perform for their parents in the expectation that they in turn will be similarly honored by their children. Reincarnation is generally believed to take place within the kin group.

Democratizing tendencies over the last hundred years have transformed Balinese society in many respects, but its hierarchic tendency remains strong. Traditional Balinese society was strongly hierarchic, built upon the Hindu *wangsa* (or caste) system of Brahman, Ksatria, Wesia, and Sudra. In Bali, the three higher castes, essentially the ruling elite, became known as the *triwangsa*, while the remainder of the population (generally said to

---

22 There is no fully satisfactory study of Balinese death rituals (*pitra yadnya*), the only attempt in a Western language being that in German by Paul Wirz, *Der Totenkult auf Bali* (Stuttgart: Strecker und Schröder, 1928). There are, however, a large number of book(let)s in Indonesian and Balinese dealing with this subject (see titles listed in David J. Stuart-Fox, *Bibliography of Bali: Publications from 1920 to 1990* [Leiden: KITLV Press, 1992]). I Gusti Ketut Kaler, *Ngaben: Mengapa mayat dibakar?* (Denpasar: Yayasan Dharma Naradha, 1997) gives a reliable account.

23 For royal cremations, the *ukur* is sometimes made of gold. A fine example was found in the palace of the ruler of Denpasar after the Puputan Badung, now in the Museum Nasional Indonesia. See Helen Ibbitson Jessup, *Court Arts of Indonesia* (New York: Asia Society Galleries in association with Harry N. Abrams, 1990), 227 (pl. 265, no. 154), where it is mistakenly said to come from Lombok.

24 Considering the relationships between Hindu-Buddhist Java and Bali, it seems likely that *kajang* of some sort were also known there, but I know of no unequivocal references.

be about 90 percent), those outside the courts, are the *jaba* or Sudra. In a status system flexible enough to allow a certain mobility both upward and downward, kin groups were ranked within the basic *wangsa* structure. Genealogy played a crucial role, leading sometimes to differing interpretations of family histories. The possession of a genealogy and the ancestral chronicle (*babad*) belonging to it were much sought after, and were generally obtained, in written form on *lontar*-palm leaves, from a court or high priest. The raja, advised by the *purohita*, the Brahman high priest attached to the court, was the dominant figure in such a political system based on patronage and charisma, where power was often challenged. Often bearing the title Prasasti (inscription) followed by the name of the kin group, these chronicles were generally considered sacred. Attached to them, and likewise dependent on status and *warna*, were certain religious rights, particularly associated with death rites — among them, for example, the number of roofs on the cremation tower, and the nature of the *kajang*.

Genealogy and kin groups' rights are very sensitive issues in Bali, so a critical examination of their development can easily offend. They are a matter of belief. Yet there is evidence that the flourishing of kin group genealogies and ritual rights, particularly in written form, was a relatively late development. The existence of such a large variety of *kajang* is associated with this development. The correct *kajang* as given to a kin group is of great importance. In the past *kajang* were generally a closely guarded secret, but within the last decade or two, *kajang* are often included in published kin group histories and in booklets dealing with death rituals; and, as with other forms of sacred drawing, compilations of *kajang* have been made, based on traditional kinds of "sampler" compilations in *lontar* form.

Although *kajang* themselves are more in the public domain in recent years, the meaning behind them remains guarded knowledge; worshipers at large have little understanding of them. They have yet to receive serious study, and the comments that follow must be taken as preliminary.

In a general sense, the *kajang* is regarded as a symbol of (the body of) the deceased, while the sacred letters inscribed on it symbolize parts of the body. The body symbolism is most obvious, of course, in those *kajang* that besides sacred letters depict a drawing of a human figure. The presence, or not, of the figure does not seem to be related directly to "caste," for there are examples of figural *kajang*

Top: Fig 19. Body symbol (*pangawak*), for use at a cremation ritual. Buleleng (North Bali). Height 52 cm. Collected by W. O. J. Nieuwenkamp in 1906. Collection National Museum of Ethnology, Leiden, inv. no. 1586-69. *Photo Ben Grishaaver.*

Bottom: Fig. 20. Detail of fig. 19.

RITUAL ARTS AND IMPLEMENTS OF BALINESE PRIESTS 49

Left: fig. 21. Family and friends lay out the *kajang* death "shroud" and sacred cloths as part of death rites. Tonja (Denpasar). *Photo David Stuart-Fox.*

Right: Fig. 22. Participants help carry the many tens of meters of white cloth, which are attached to a sacred object carried by a boy in a litter during death rites. Tonja (Denpasar). *Photo David Stuart-Fox.*

25 For example, for *brahmana:* Lontar "Kajang" (Museum Bali 351n/116), HKS 6669:49; *satria:* HKS 6669:49.

26 Swastika 2008:xi-xiv; Jro Mangku Pulasari, *Pangastawa pitra yajña lan gambar-gambar* (Surabaya: Paramita, 2007), 74–75, 80–81.

27 Ngurah Nala, *Aksara Bali dalam usada* (Surabaya: Paramita, 2006), 149–150.

for all four main castes.[25] Adding to the difficulty are the many differences between *kajang* illustrated in the *lontar*s, and their association with particular groups, a state of affairs that possibly reflects different priestly traditions, but may also result from faulty transmission and priestly "creativity." Even so, there does seem to be some agreement. *Kajang* for Pasek kin groups, for instance, frequently depict a human figure.[26]

Besides the human figure, the turtle and the *naga* (serpent) are quite often depicted. These are cosmic symbols, the turtle being the foundation of the world, around which the *nagas* are entwined. They play an important role in the story, in the first book of the *Mahabharata,* of the churning of the milky ocean to produce the elixir of life, desired both by gods and demons. However, in the context of the *kajang,* they probably also serve as symbols of earth and water respectively, two of the five basic elements (*panca mahabhuta*) of material existence. The cremation is intended to release the deceased from these material elements, in a process that guides the soul towards release (*moksa*) or reincarnation.

Sacred syllables are a major element of all *kajang*. The best known (to Westerners) of these syllables is the OM or ONG, in Bali called the Ongkara. The Ongkara itself is said to consist of seven parts (*sapta ongkara*): the three syllables ANG, UNG, MANG dissolving into unity, ONG, together with its nasalization (*ulu candra*), this last element made up of *nada* (triangle), *windu* (circle), and *ardhacandra* (crescent moon). This sevenfold concept is linked with other sevenfold concepts.[27] The Ongkara itself has different written forms, the commonest being the "standing" Ongkara (*Ongkara ngadeg*). More complex forms, although calligraphic in outward form, retain an intrinsic magic component. Certain *kajang* consist entirely of Ongkara. Ongkara are not infrequently found in pairs, facing one another in either vertical (*Ongkara sumungsang*) or horizontal (*Ongkara pasah*) positions.

Among the sacred syllables, the *dwiaksara*, the two syllables ANG and AH, are directly associated with life and death. According to medical treatises (*usada*) as explained by Ngurah Nala,[28] during life the syllable AH is located at the fontanel, in mystic terms associated with the Father and with the purifying water of life (*amerta*); while the syllable ANG is located at the navel, is associated with the Mother and with purifying secret fire (*agni*). When approaching death, these syllables exchange places, a movement that is believed to be the secret of mystic release whereby the soul leaves the material body, through the fontanel, the door of Siwa (*siwadwara*). In accordance with this doctrine, on many *kajang*, the AH is located at the bottom of the drawing and the ANG at the top, indicating the state of the deceased at death and the direction the soul must take.

Another group of sacred syllables frequently found on *kajang* is the *dasaksara*, the ten-syllables. These are generally written in the standard compasslike structure, SANG, BANG, TANG, and ANG at the main directions; NANG, MANG, SANG (SING) and WANG at the intermediate directions; and ING and YANG at the center, sometimes in conjunction with the Ongkara.

A line of sacred designs bearing mystic syllables is sometimes depicted down the center of the cloth or down the center of a figure. If a figure is depicted, the symbols may appear from above the head down to the feet, or below the figure. These symbols are related to the *cakra* system of yoga doctrines, for some are explicitly said to be *cakras;* but their greater number than that of the classic *cakra* system indicates that other doctrines are playing a role. Because *cakras,* and the Kundalini doctrine from which they originate, delineate both the psychic structure of the person and the means to spiritual development, and since cremation serves to help the deceased along the pathway to release from material ties and unification with the divine essence, it seems that the *kajang* too serves to help the deceased reach this goal.

RERAJAHAN, OR "POWER" DRAWINGS

Rerajahan are "drawings" that, with appropriate rituals, have supernatural power that can be directed by the practitioner toward particular goals.[29] The term is used to describe an extraordinary range of drawings on a variety of materials, including drawings of a pictorial nature, as well as drawings consisting of sacred syllables in complicated forms akin to calligraphy, or very often a combination of the two. The commonest materials are white cotton cloth and paper. Two categories are of particular importance.

The first, called *ulap-ulap*, is a small piece of cloth with a figure and/or sacred letters drawn on it, hung on a building that has just undergone the rite of dedication or

---

28 Ngurah Nala, *Aksara Bali dalam usada,* 135.

29 The word is derived from the root *rajah*, which would appear to be an Austronesian root. Zoetmulder, in his Old Javanese dictionary, distinguishes between the *rajah* derived from Sanskrit *rajas*, and a second *rajah* which he translates as "lines and figures (esp. with magic significance)?".

Top: Fig 23. Drawing of the god Samburiding on a tiger, from a paper manuscript of magic drawings. Collection National Museum of Ethnology, Leiden, inv.no. 4844-1. *Photo Ben Grishaaver.*

Bottom: Fig. 24. Drawing of the god Iswara, god of the east, riding on a bull, from a paper manuscript of magic drawings. Collection National Museum of Ethnology, Leiden, inv. no. 4844-1. *Photo Ben Grishaaver.*

consecration (*mlaspas*), or reconsecration after mishap or repair. The *ulap-ulap* both signifies that the ceremony has taken place and serves as protection against malevolent forces. It is left hanging until destroyed by time and weather. As with so many things in Bali, Balinese creativity and prolific production have led to a very large number of these cloths, some that may be used for any building but many specific to a particular kind of building. A recent photocopy publication comprises more than one hundred *ulap-ulap*.[30] Common motifs among them are the lotus (*padma*), the *naga* serpent, the weapons and sacred letters of the directions, and the figure of Cintia (Acintya), a form of the supreme Godhead in Balinese Hinduism. Cintia is depicted in frontal stance, knees wide apart, rounded head, without clothing, a figural style discussed subsequently. *Ulap-ulap* are often made by priests, but not necessarily so; anyone with the skill may make them.

The second important category of *rerajahan* is what I call "magic drawings," what are sometimes called *rerajahan tumbal* in Balinese. *Tumbal* has a rather broad meaning, equivalent to charm, talisman, or amulet. Magic drawings or *rerajahan* in this sense are the work of the *balian*, the healer, a profession available to people of any caste. Generally consecrated as *pemangku*, the *balian* practices meditation, prepares holy water, utters mantras, and presents offerings. He calls upon spiritual powers to aid him in his work, and utilizes powers available through his own "birth brethren" (*kanda empat*) and, occasionally, even "lower" supernatural beings. He diagnoses illnesses according to a traditional classification of symptoms, prescribing a wide range of herbal medicines to effect a cure. He is a psychologist. He is an astrologer, since some afflictions and a person's destiny are believed to be associated with time of birth. He makes amulets or magic objects (*tumbal*) to exorcise, cure, or protect individual clients from various dangers, particularly black magic. Though one can isolate certain aspects of a *balian*'s practice and call them medical—prescribing a herbal cure; or priestly—preparing holy water; or magical—making an amulet, these are merely aspects of an integral and integrated practice through which he treats his patients.

The distinction between magic and religion, of course, is a Western one rooted in Christian thinking. No such clear distinction is made in Balinese thought, nor indeed in Hinduism generally. From the time of the earliest Vedic texts, practices that might be categorized as magical in Western thought, such as overcoming one's enemies, controlling weather, and defeating epidemics, are found together with speculations of a philosophical nature and directives for performing rituals. In later Tantric thought and practice, so-called magical aspects became even more prominent. The achievement of supranormal or magic powers was one result of progress in yogic meditation, but could also be gained through the recitation of mantras and special hymns to divinities. Achieving such magical powers was not regarded as an honorable aim in itself.

Balinese distinguish between two kinds of magic: "magic of the right" and "magic of the left." "Magic of the right" (*panengen*, from the word *tengen* or "right") and "magic of the left" (*pangiwa*, from *kiwa* or "left"), considering the impact of Tantric thought and practice in ancient Indonesia, including Bali, are almost certainly related to the well-known distinction between right-hand Tantra and left-hand Tantra. Their relationship to morality and ethics is a complex issue. At the present time, under the influence of Western ways of thinking, magic of the right is roughly equivalent to "white magic," or magic that is socially "approved" and normally beneficial to those who use it, while magic of the left is equivalent to "black magic," which is not socially approved and is usually deleterious. The expression "black magic" has entered the Indonesian vocabulary. It is a common explanation for a variety of ailments and misfortunes, and the victim seeks help from the *balian* who employs his magic of the right to counteract the magic afflicting his patients. Accusations are sometimes made, but violence against a presumed practitioner of black magic is rare.

White magic in Bali is essentially protective—to guard property, avert misfortune, cure sickness, harmonize personal relationships, and repulse black magic, either after an affliction has struck or beforehand as a precautionary measure. Black magic causes sickness or death or misfortune to befall the victim out of a feeling of malice or jealousy or for profit. At the same time it is believed that if the intended victim has truly done no wrong, the black magic will be ineffectual or even strike the sorcerer as punishment. However, the distinction between the two kinds of magic is not always clear. For example, if someone steals from a field protected by Demon Sempengot, he will fall sick. Some Balinese question the ethics of using such magic, but others say that the victim was a thief and deserved to be punished. Magic mantras or drawings are sometimes essentially neutral and their use for good or bad depends on the intent of the practitioner. A magic object "to make someone lazy" can bring only misfortune to an ordinary householder, but for someone with two wives and who is intent on further affairs it may be just what is needed.

Rerajahan or magic drawings are not part of the practice of all *balian*, or even of all *balian usada*, healers whose knowledge is based upon the written tradition, as found in palm leaf *lontar* books. Despite this reliance on the written word, the knowledge possessed

30 This publication, under the name *Sehananing Ulap Ulap*, which might be glossed as "the complete *upal-ulap* book," was compiled by I. N. Sukada. I would like to express my thanks to Dr. Hedi Hinzler for bringing this publication to my attention.

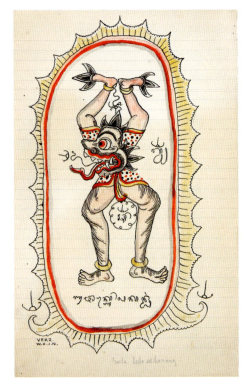

Top: Fig 25. Drawing of Buta Kebo Sakandang. Former collection W. O. J. Nieuwenkamp. Before 1913. Collection National Museum of Ethnology, Leiden, inv.no. 1865-16. *Photo Ben Grishaaver.*

Bottom: Fig. 26. Drawing of Buta Curegah. Former collection W. O. J. Nieuwenkamp. Before 1913. Collection National Museum of Ethnology, Leiden, inv. no. 1865-17. *Photo Ben Grishaaver.*

by a *balian usada* is not mere book learning. The *lontar* books are adjuncts to a healing practice, and the practice is learned from a teacher, often within the family, who is as much the product of an oral practical tradition as of a written tradition.

Among the *lontar* books of a *balian usada*, some usually contain magic drawings (cat. no. 43). The quality of these drawings varies considerably. Considering the space available and the difficulty of drawing on *lontar* leaf, the best of these drawings are sophisticated works of art. In quality they are comparable to the secular drawings on *lontar* leaf, called *prasi*, which illustrate works of Old Javanese and Balinese literature, in a style related to the traditional *wayang* style of painting. When paper, a medium much easier to use for drawings, became readily available, collections of drawings were copied into exercise books or ledgers. When the copyist was an artist, superb and fascinating manuscripts were produced. Several such books are found in private libraries of *balian*s and priests in Bali, and at least two have made their way into Dutch collections (figs. 23–24).[31]

In the manuscripts, both palm leaf and paper, every drawing is accompanied by a brief text giving pertinent information necessary for its use: the name of the drawing, the means (*sarana*, always abbreviated as "sa") by which it is to be used, the afflictions it guards against, and in a few cases the offerings or specific mantra required. Drawings are copied for patients on diverse materials, including white cloth, paper, various kinds of metal foils, and sometimes more esoteric substances. Many are either kept in a magic sash or wrapped as a small separate amulet and used to protect the individual; others are buried or placed in specific places, usually as protection for a house compound and the family members that live there. The drawings depict gods, holy men, and demons. Although some have names of Sanskrit derivation (such as Hindu deities), most are Old Javanese or Balinese names whose etymology is sometimes obscure. With the exception of a few animal forms, *rerajahan* are based on human (or humanlike) figures, of which there are two main styles— the well-known *wayang* style and what I have called the Cintia style.

A common use of power drawings is in a protective, literally "white" sash (*sabuk putih*), given to a client or patient whose illness or misfortunes are diagnosed to be the result of black magic. From the outside, there is nothing to see in such a sash: it is just a length of white cotton cloth some three centimeters wide and long enough to go around the waist, with little sewn-up compartments containing a number of drawings and formulas. Their number can vary from just a few to as many as seventy or more.

In one case handled by a *balian* I was studying with, Mangku Ketut Liyer of

Pengosekan,[32] two young men came saying they were dogged by a monkey-like apparition, which they and my *balian* friend interpreted as black magic. For each man, the *balian* made a sash comprising three drawings on pieces of cloth, and four formulas of sacred letters, two on paper, one on cloth, and one on copper foil. These drawings and formulas all had their own names. One of the drawings, for example, was called "Essence of Wisnu Murti," and the accompanying text read as follows: "This is called the Essence of Wisnu Murti. It may be used in a sash. Guardian of souls, object of homage for all magic powers, bestower of calm on the world. This protection is excellent, and is like a living hood over the head. Even without uttering a mantra, it is alive." This is a drawing the *balian* often uses, for it provides protection against all kinds of malevolence, and besides, Wisnu is one of the major Hindu gods, he explained. The other drawings were called Sanghyang Brahmana Rare Putus (Divine Pure Brahmana Child), to whom leyaks or witches made obeisance, and Sanghyang Gana Esaka (Divine Ganesha Esaka), who neutralizes a whole list of afflictions caused by demons, black magic, *leyak*s, poison, misfortune, and plague (Gana or Ganesha is known as the deity with the power to remove all obstacles and misfortune).

When the two men came to collect their sashes, each was already made up. Before handing the sashes over, Mangku Liyer first took them in his hands and meditated briefly: "I must do that," he explained. "It is said that demons will 'eat' the mantras, so to guard against that I request help from goddess Saraswati." Then he uttered several mantras to empower or give life to the sashes. Such mantras are called *pasupati* mantras, this one among them:

> ONG, imagine I am Sanghyang Siwa, Sada Siwa, Parama Siwa.
> Give life to mantras, all writings, all magic drawings.
> Let them all live, let them live with effect,
> May they all truly exist,
> Come life, come life, come life,
> ONG, honor to all teachings.

After saying the mantras he incensed the sashes, replaced them on the stand with the offerings, and sprinkled everything with holy water while saying a mantra to Saraswati. Again he incensed the sashes, and then gave them to the young men. He told them what offerings they had to give on such holy days as full moon and new moon and the day called *kajeng-kliwon* (every fifteen days). He told them what might happen when they wore the sashes.

"Usually when a patient wears a magic sash he feels his body become very hot, " he explained later. "That is a sign that some form of black magic has entered the body, something

31 Both are in Leiden, one in the collection of the Rijksmuseum voor Volkenkunde, the other in the collection of the Koninklijk Instituut voor Taal-, Land- en Volkenkunde (KITLV). They are published in C. Hooykaas, *Tovenarij op Bali: Magische tekeningen uit twee Leidse collecties* (Amsterdam, Meulenhoff, 1980).

32 I wish to thank Mangku Liyer for his friendship over many years and his willingness to explain his practice. The account that follows, and the quotations, are based on this research.

'dirty' within the body opposing the sash, which is 'clean.' That's good. If the black magic is at all strong it will fight back, and so the body feels hot or there is an unpleasant feeling for a while. Not for long, just an hour or so. Sometimes it can last for a long time and even cause the patient to vomit. But he must continue to wear it. He will get better finally. At times I have forgotten to warn the patient who, frightened, has thrown the sash away."

In answer to a question about how long the patient must wear the sash, he replied, "No, not all the time. Only when it is necessary. Depending on how he feels he wears it when he is going out and at night. If he is not wearing it he must place it in a holy place, usually on the little shrine above the bed. It is specially to repel black magic and everything that is evil. The sash is wholly white magic. Nothing that it contains pertains to black magic."

A protective sash is generally worn under the clothing, or it can be placed on a bedside shrine. An amulet for a women is often in a small package format, easier to hide in the clothing, for if a woman is found with a magic sash she may be accused of witchcraft.

Besides use in a protective sash, power drawings can be used for a number of other purposes. Common among these are protection for a house compound or some other place, to counteract what is called a "hot" compound. This undesirable condition is caused by a number of reasons, such as incorrect placement of a building within the courtyard, a position too close to a graveyard or a temple or a water channel, or a courtyard "speared by a path" (*tumbak rurung*) when a path heads straight at the house before turning aside at the last minute. The text Aji Bangbungalan cites, among these causes, "struck by lightning, struck by fire, struck by a falling tree or branch of a tree that snaps by itself, a papaya tree that grows no top, a branching coconut palm, a branching sugar palm, a branching areca palm, a branching banana tree," and still more. Drawings for this purpose are often done on copper or other metal foil, and then placed on the entrance gate or buried in front of it. Sometimes a drawing will have its own mantra, such as this:

> UNG Sayamadi (name of figure?), I order you to guard this place.
> With your discus you will guard the road.
> Turn back the deeds of evil men, aches and pains of the limbs, and black
> Magic (*teluh, tranjana*), as if turning around a spinning wheel.
> Turn back all evil deeds, send them back to the east, to the south, to the west,
> To the north, and turn upside down those at the center.
> In such a way is the evil turned back towards he who committed the evil …
> Let there always be good health, let danger strike whoever committed the evil deeds.

There are also drawings to protect specific places, such as rice fields or dry fields, a stall for a cow or buffalo, or a watering point; or protection for people going to such places as the forest, which in the past, when tigers still roamed, could be dangerous.

Some drawings have a potential double purpose, good and bad. A drawing to bring about sleep can be used to make a child sleep soundly, but can also be used by a thief to make the occupants of the house sleep soundly. A drawing to keep a fire burning well can be used by brick makers to keep the furnace burning, but can also be used to burn down a house. A drawing for bringing about love can be used by a boy to attract a girl or a married woman to keep the love of her husband, but can also be used by a married man to attract a lover.

The range of purposes for which drawings can be used, and the number of these drawings, is quite remarkable. Equally astonishing is their iconography.

STYLES OF *RERAJAHAN* DRAWINGS, AND POSSIBLE EXTERNAL RELATIONSHIPS

With regard to iconography, the simplest classification of *rerajahan* is the distinction between *rerajahan* that are composed entirely of sacred letters and those that are pictorial, at least in part. Within the pictorial group, one possible classification is that into kinds of figures: deities, priests, demons, animals. But there appears to be no significant correlation between kind of figure and the intention to which the drawings are put; at best there is a partial correlation: for example, demon figures are often used to repel black magic. Of more interest, at least in connection with possible parallels elsewhere, is that within the group of drawings based on the human figure, two main styles can be distinguished: the *wayang* style and what I call the Cintia style.

Wayang refers to various forms of theater, most importantly the shadow play (*wayang kulit*). The influence of the forms of shadow-play puppets on painting and stone relief has given the name *wayang* to this broad artistic tradition and style. It first appeared in East Java during the thirteenth century (Singasari period), and soon spread to Bali. Stone reliefs in *wayang* style are carved on temples throughout Bali, and traditional *wayang* polychrome painting still flourishes at the village of Kamasan near Klungkung. Paintings, sometimes in a folk variation, decorate wooden shrines, ritual cradles, and other prized objects in many parts of the island.

A distictive feature of the *wayang* style is the manner in which it distinguishes figures iconographically on a scale from refinement to coarseness, from divine to demonic.[33] A refined deity, for example, is depicted in three-quarter view; the shoulders are frontal, and

33 An excellent introduction to this style in painting is that of Anthony Forge, *Balinese Traditional Paintings* (Sydney: Australian Museum, 1978).

both feet (usually) point in one direction. Above all the facial features portray refined character: slit eyes, straight nose, even teeth, and lack of facial hair. Such a character is richly dressed and wears the high crown of the gods. Showing certain coarser features are the figures of priests, their hair usually coiled up in a distinctive turban-like headdress (*ketu*). Their eyes are less regular, and wrinkled, and the nose is bulbous. If the coarseness is taken further, the eyes are rounded, there is a fine growth of hair, and fangs signify demonic origin. Less human and more animal-like are the demon figures, with their round eyes, bulbous snoutlike noses, massive teeth, and large fangs, and with hair all over the body and face. Skin is often like that of animals or patterned as if diseased. Clothing is scanty. The *parekan*, those grotesque clownlike characters so popular in the shadow theater and in paintings illustrating the classic mythological tales, are rare among magic drawings.

The Cintia style, the other basic style used for magic drawings, I have named after Sanghyang Cintia, who is often depicted on *ulap-ulap* cloths, as we have seen, and in relief on "lotus seats" (*padmasana*) in temples. The frontal stance is the distinguishing feature of this style. The legs are wide apart, the knees being more widely spread than the feet, which point in opposite directions. The torso tends often to be triangular, ending in broad straight shoulders. Joints are marked by flamelike motifs called *kembang bajra* (literally "*vajra* flower"), signifying active power. The head is roundish. Facial features parallel those of the *wayang* style, and show a gradation from the refined to the coarse or animal-like, perhaps under the influence of *wayang* conventions. The figure is often unclothed. Among demonic figures based on this style, a noteworthy feature is the frequency with which the figure is cut up into component parts, as it were, then reassembled into unnatural freakish forms. Variation in the position of the head is most common; sometimes it is placed over the loins and sometimes over the body. One leg is often raised in a common Balinese dance position, signifying action. Hands may be held in front of the body in a *mudra* position, or raised in the air, or not shown at all. Besides their appearance among power drawings, the frontal face of the Cintia figure is drawn on little slabs of sandalwood, where gods dwell during festival time or the spirits of the dead during funerary rites. The human figure depicted on the cremation shroud would seem to be part of this same, or a related, tradition.

The origins of the style are obscure. It was not a style used in the monumental sculptural tradition, for it does not appear on the reliefs of ancient Java, and in Bali it appears only in the form of the Cintia figure itself. It appears to be a style of drawing largely restricted to a manuscript tradition. Its presence in Javanese books of magic is strong evidence of a common ancestry at least as old as the fifteenth or sixteenth century, when cultural ties between Java and Bali were largely severed; texts accompanying such drawings are quite similar to those accompanying Balinese *rerajahan*.[34] Within Indonesia and the Malay world, the style finds echoes in drawings in Batak (Sumatra) and in Malay books of magic.[35]

Further afield, there are suggestive parallels as far away as China, Cambodia, Thailand, Burma, Sri Lanka, and the Indian subcontinent, often also associated with magic and related to the tradition of the *yantra*. Presumably the Cintia style reflects an ancient Indic tradition. Despite the vast literature on Indian and Indian-influenced art, there seems to be no comprehensive comparative study of this, essentially, manuscript tradition of magic drawings, just as there is no comprehensive study of Indic ephemeral arts like offerings and cremation furniture. Such studies might also throw light on whether this drawing tradition is essentially Tantric in origin, as would seem likely, judging from the strong Tantric aspects of so much of the Balinese healing traditions. Whether it also reflects or incorporates in some way an old Indonesian style of figural depiction is unlikely.

The *kajang* or cremation shroud, whose style in my opinion is associated with the Cintia style, also has remarkably similar Indian parallels. Indian drawings and paintings of the cosmic man or the yogic body, with its *cakras* or psychic centers, are manifestations of an ancient Tantric tradition.[36] Despite the lack of evidence, such drawings were surely once known in ancient Java and Bali, for how else could such imagery and symbolism survive in the Balinese *kajang*?

RERAJAHAN AND MODERN PAINTING

It is hardly surprising that the *rerajahan* tradition in its enormous variety and sheer strangeness has attracted the attention of artists beyond those who actually make and use the drawings. In the first decade of the twentieth century, the Dutch artist W. O. J. Nieuwenkamp collected a number of colored *rerajahan* paintings, two of which are illustrated here (figs. 25, 26). A colored *rerajahan* drawing is itself most unusual; there is no evidence that *rerajahan* were in traditional practice ever colored, though the possibility cannot be completely ruled out.[37] Whether Nieuwenkamp commissioned these drawings or bought them already made is not certain. Probably they are from North Bali, where modernizing developments in all the arts were already apparent from the early 1900s. Whatever their history, other than the use of color, these are typical *rerajahan* drawings.

When new styles of painting emerged in South Bali at the end of the 1920s and beginning of the 1930s, some artists found inspiration in the *rerajahan* tradition. But unlike the traditional *wayang* style of painting, from which much of the new painting sprang

34 In general, there is a dearth of good studies into the continuation in post-Majapahit Java of elements of Hindu-Buddhist traditions, with the exception of Hinduism in Tengger (East Java). The Indic mantra tradition as well as the tradition of magic drawings both left their mark on later Javanist traditions. See, for example, the Javanese magic drawings in Theodore G. Th. Pigeaud, *Literature of Java: Catalogue Raisonné of Javanese Manuscripts in the Library of the University of Leiden and other Public Collections in the Netherlands*, vol. 3 (The Hague: Nijhoff, 1970), figs. 4–5, and accompanying explanations (pp. 40–41).

35 Hindu elements in Batak religion come from two directions: from the Javo-Malayu tradition and from the South Indian Tamil tradition. See Harry Parkin, *Batak Fruit of Hindu Thought* (Madras: Christian Literature Society, 1978), especially chapter 8.

36 Examples are scattered through numerous books on Indian art. See, for example, Ajit Mookerjee and Madhu Khanna, *The Tantric Way: Art, Science, Ritual* (London: Thames and Hudson, 1977), 67.

37 The one exception known to me is the exorcistic cloth in the collection of the National Gallery of Australia, illustrated in Robyn Maxwell, *Sari to Sarong: Five Hundred Years of Indian and Indonesian Textile Exchange* (Canberra: Australian National Gallery, 2003), 40. It is unclear what function a cloth of this size might have had.

Fig. 27. A painting by Mangku Ketut Liyer, illustrating meditating figure, spirit siblings, and cosmic figures. Photographed at healer's home (present whereabouts unknown). Photo David Stuart-Fox.

38 Helena Spanjaard, *Pioneers of Balinese Painting: The Rudolf Bonnet Collection* (Amsterdam: KIT Publishers, 2007), pl. 16.

39 Abby C. Ruddick (ed. with introd.), *Selected Paintings from the Collection of the Agung Rai Fine Art Gallery* (Peliatan: Agung Rai Fine Art Gallery, 1992), 54–55.

40 See *I Ketut Budiana: Illusory View from the Balinese Spiritual Cosmos* (Tokyo: Tokyo Station Gallery, 2003), 51, 83, 85, 102. Alison Taylor, *Living Traditions in Balinese Painting* (Peliatan: Agung Rai Gallery of Fine Art, 1991), 57.

and which continued to exert a strong impact, the influence of *rerajahan* was limited. Their lack of narrative was too limiting for most artists. Those who did paint "modern" *rerajahan* figures tended to glorify the design with decorative flourishes. A fine example is the 1931 work by Anak Agung Gede Sobrat (1912–1992), one of the early Ubud masters.[38] In a later work from 1974, another well-known Ubud painter, Ida Bagus Made Poleng (1915–1999), returned to an almost classic *rerajahan* figure.[39]

One painter who has genuinely interiorized the *rerajahan*, and made it part of his mystical vision of the Balinese cosmos and supernatural world, is I Ketut Budiana (born 1950). In some paintings, the form of the *rerajahan* is clear to see, as in, for example, *Padma* (2000), *Angkus Prana* (1998), or one simply titled *Rarajahan* (1999), but in others little more than an attenuated impression remains, as in a work like *The Dream*.[40]

Mangku Ketut Liyer, mentioned earlier, is perhaps a unique figure in being both *balian* and painter. As a *balian usada*, who followed his father in the profession, he frequently draws *rerajahan* and gives them to his patients when he considers it useful or necessary to do so. But from the time he was a young man, he has been a painter, specializing at first in rice field scenes, but then later painting *rerajahan* and other "*balian*" paintings of the four spirit brethren (*kanda empat*), or figures in meditation (fig. 27).

Whether in the practice of the present-day *balian*, or in publications in the bookshops, or in paintings in the art shops, the extraordinary world of the *rerajahan* is still very much alive. In Bali, where ritual life is thriving and becoming even more elaborate, the priests are as busy as ever.

FRANCINE BRINKGREVE
PALM LEAF AND SILKSCREEN: BALINESE *LAMAK* IN TRANSITION

LAMAK SABLON

In the summer of 2001, I visited Bali for the first time in seven years. During this relatively brief visit, I noticed large numbers of a new variety of *lamak,* the beautiful ritual decorations that I had been studying for several years. A *lamak* is a rectangular-shaped hanging, decorated in various ways. It is used in a multitude of rituals, and has a double function: as a base for offerings and as decoration for altars or shrines to which deities and spirits are invited (fig. 1). More symbolically, a *lamak* is interpreted as a path between heaven and earth, connecting the worlds of deities and human beings. Usually *lamak* are made from palm leaves, and so they have an ephemeral character. After a ritual is over, they are left to wither away, and must be created again for the next occasion. They are often strikingly beautiful, part of the rich transitory art traditions of Balinese Hinduism.[1] However, because the ritual function of the *lamak* is not intentionally transitory, *lamak* are not exclusively made of palm leaf, but can also be made of permanent materials.

Lamak are either made by Balinese housewives, made to order by specialists, or sold at the markets. In the last twenty years or so, there has been a growing tendency to buy permanent *lamak*, rather than to make new *lamak* for every ritual, especially on the part of women with jobs or careers outside their own homes. The *toko yadnya,* shops selling ritual objects, have increasing supplies of a range of permanent *lamak*. Most are textiles decorated in various ways, and some consist of Chinese coins and wood, similar to other kinds of Balinese ritual decorations. But on this visit I noticed for the first time large numbers of a new type of permanent *lamak* at the markets, called *lamak sablon* (fig. 2). The name is derived from the technique, since these *lamak* are mass-produced by patterning pieces of cloth by means of a silkscreen, called *sablon* in Indonesian (from the Dutch word *sjabloon*, meaning stencil). These *lamak* were cheap, and I have seen them with only a limited range of motifs, which at first sight imitate the palm leaf varieties. The colors, too, seem to be chosen in imitation of the palm leaf *lamak* (fig. 3). Whereas traditionally every district, every village, and sometimes even every ward within a village in Bali has its own style of *lamak*, these imitation *lamak* with their limited range of motifs were sold and used all over Bali.

In this article I compare this type of ritual decoration, the *lamak sablon,* with

This article is one of the results of a doctoral research project financed by the Programme of Indonesian Studies, the Netherlands, and was carried out in Indonesia under the auspices of LIPI and Universitas Udayana, Denpasar. I would like to thank Hedi Hinzler for drawing my attention to the discussion on the lamak sablon in SARAD magazine, Lexa Jaffe-Klusman for her generous gift of many lamak sablon, David Stuart-Fox for helpful comments and editorial assistance.

1 See photographs in, for example, Francine Brinkgreve and David Stuart-Fox, *Offerings: The Ritual Art of Bali* (Sanur, Bali: Image Network Indonesia, 1992); Garrett Kam, *Perceptions of Paradise: Images of Bali in the Arts* (Ubud: Yayasan Dharma Seni Museum Neka, 1993); Urs Ramseyer, *The Art and Culture of Bali,* new ed., with pictorial emendations. (Basel: Museum der Kulturen Basel, 2002).

Fig. 1. Three palm leaf *lamak* decorate a shrine and serve as base for offerings in a family temple in Sanur (Denpasar). Galungan 2010. *Photo Francine Brinkgreve.*

Opposite page left: Fig. 2. Ritual decorations, including *lamak sablon* with Dewi Saraswati motif, for sale at the market of Denpasar, 2005. *Photo Francine Brinkgreve.*

Opposite page right: Fig. 3. A *lamak sablon* with a *cili* and a mountain motif decorates a shrine on the beach in Sanur (Denpasar), 2005. *Photo Francine Brinkgreve.*

more traditional forms of *lamak*. I am interested in investigating the main reasons for the development of the *lamak sablon*, whether the *lamak sablon* has the same symbolic meaning as the palm leaf *lamak*, and whether these new varieties fit within the system of regional variation of the *lamak*. But first it is interesting to see what the Balinese themselves thought about this new development.

LOCAL VIEWS OF THE *LAMAK SABLON*

Although *lamak* of nonperishable materials such as textiles have always existed along with the palm leaf varieties, admittedly in relatively small numbers, there was never a difference of opinion about the religious value of the nonperishable *lamak*. However, probably because the *lamak sablon* appeared in such large quantities compared with other permanent *lamak*, and because they were so clearly designed as imitations of the palm leaf ones, they have given rise to an interesting exchange of views about whether they can be regarded as acceptable substitutes for the originals.

In January 2000 an article appeared in *SARAD: Majalah gumi Bali*, a Balinese magazine about the Hindu-Balinese religion, entitled "Who likes the silkscreen *lamak*?" ("*Siapa suka lamak sablon?*"). The author, Ni Made Wawi Adini, collected various then current opinions about the numerous *lamak sablon* or "*lamak palsu*," "false" *lamak*, which were "flooding" the markets of Bali. This inquiry resulted in accounts of a fascinating range of opinions and life experiences, offering a glimpse of transitions occurring in this very traditional society. One woman interviewed, who had a full-time job, stated that it saved her a lot of time during the ritual seasons not to have to make the palm leaf *lamak* herself, but rather instead to buy the *lamak sablon*, which were cheap and could be kept until the next ritual. Moreover, she used the *lamak sablon* on an everyday basis "to give the shrines a festive appearance" ("*biar palinggih tampak meriah*"). However, deep down, she would prefer to keep the traditional ways of the village where she grew up, and not only use palm leaf *lamak* but even make them herself. But she simply did not have the time anymore for doing this. In contrast, another woman suggested that one shouldn't try to be too frugal in front of the deities. Moreover, she liked to make *lamak* herself, since for her working with palm leaves was a good way to relax, to put her mind at rest.

The author of many booklets about offerings and especially about *jejaitan,* palm leaf constructions, specialist Ida Ayu Putu Surayin, also preferred to make the *lamak* herself, not only because it is her personal hobby, but also because she liked to offer the deities something beautiful and attractive. She had not found any restrictions against the use of *lamak sablon* in the religious manuals she knew about. Essentially she left it up to the religious feelings of the individual people themselves, since their intentions form the essence of the offerings.

From the official religious perspective, according to I Gusti Ngurah Oka Supartha, head of Parisada Hindu Dharma Indonesia (the official organization for Hindu affairs) in the district of Badung, the use of imitation *lamak* is not forbidden, and the Hindu congregation is allowed to follow recent developments. But he reminds the Balinese that anything that is offered to the deities must contain leaves, flowers, fruits, and water. According to this high-ranking religious leader, these basic requirements for devotional offerings must be items from nature, and in principle such items should not be imitated. He stresses the religious significance of the *lamak* as a bridge between the human world and the deities, and the symbolism of the motifs, representing the contents of the world. He is concerned that with the increase in the use of the *lamak sablon,* the symbolism of the decorative motifs on the *lamak* will eventually disappear.

In a reaction to this article, in a later issue of SARAD, one of the makers of *lamak sablon,* the son of a temple priest from Sukawati in Gianyar, gives his opinion. Because the palm leaf *lamak* sold at the markets are so expensive, he started his own business. He learned about the materials and techniques of the silkscreen method from a Javanese craftsman in Denpasar, and in making his silkscreen he copied motifs from an original

2 One reader wondered why some people thought that the *lamak sablon* should be forbidden, whereas other new developments, such as offering the deities bottled soft drinks instead of glasses of coffee, were allowed. And again the answer was that a *lamak* must be made from leaves, because of the symbolic value of the natural elements: leaves, flowers, and fruits are symbols of birth, life, and death, of the cycles of life of all creation. According to this opinion, although the ornaments on the new medium are the same as on the palm leaf *lamak*, their symbolic meaning cannot be accepted, because the material lacks religious value.

lamak. He received many orders, and many other producers in Sukawati and the neighboring village of Batuan have followed his example. In his opinion, the use of cloth as decoration for a shrine is no different from the use of other types of textile decorations, such as the long cloths along the eaves of buildings (*ider-ider*). Additionally, textiles are used as parts of offerings. For him, the *lamak sablon* is just a more practical and cheaper way, which does not deviate at all from existing religious values.[2]

But what exactly is the relationship between the palm leaf *lamak*, the *lamak sablon*, and other varieties of textile *lamak*? How can they be compared? The discussion in *SARAD* seems to be mainly about the change in material, but what can be said about the motifs and their ordering within the structure of the *lamak sablon*?

First I will describe the palm leaf *lamak*, their varieties, functions, meanings of their motifs, and regional variations; and in the second part of this article I compare the *lamak sablon* with the traditional forms.

VARIETIES OF *LAMAK*

With intense cultural importance attached to decorating ritual space, the Balinese make the places where they present offerings to deities and demons as attractive as possible. Moreover, it is regarded as a matter of purity to separate the offering from the place where it is offered. Only the smallest offerings that are used everyday, such as little pieces of banana leaf with some rice (*banten jotan* or *saiban*), do not require an extra offering base. Underneath the numerous small palm leaf containers with flowers and betel chewing ingredients (*banten canang*), which are also regularly presented, one usually places the special flower called in English the globe amaranth (Balinese: *bunga ratna*, L. *Gomphrena globosa*). The shrines in a house temple usually have a permanent little mat or rectangular piece of ordinary cloth that serves as a base for the daily offerings. When more offerings are required on regularly recurring festival days, a piece of leaf is put between the offerings and the shrine, or between the offerings and the ground. Such a leaf in general is called *plawa*, and it can be the tip of a banana leaf or a leaf of some other plant (fig. 4).

For more elaborate rituals, however, special decorations are fashioned to serve as the base for the offerings. By making attractive and inviting altars or shrines

Top: Fig 4. A leaf used as a base for *canang sari* and *canang raka* offerings. Sanur (Denpasar), 2005. *Photo Francine Brinkgreve.*

Bottom: Fig. 5. A palm leaf *ceniga* is hung on top of a *lamak sablon*. Peliatan (Gianyar), Galungan 2010. *Photo Francine Brinkgreve.*

where the invisible powers are invited to receive their offerings, even greater reverence is shown on the part of devotees.

The smallest variety of such a specially made offering base is called *terujungan* (from the root *ujung*, point) and is usually a simple palm leaf construction (*jejaitan*) in the form of a long triangle. It is made from light green young leaves (*busung*) of the coconut palm (*Cocos nucifera*) with a border of the dark green older leaves (*slepan*), or vice versa, and fastened together with little bamboo pins (*semat*). It usually does not have special decorative motifs. This kind of offering base can be used on a shrine, but more often it serves as a base for offerings that are placed on the ground for the demonic spirits, the *buta* and *kala*.

Fig. 6. **An offering maker fastens a *cili* motif onto the base of a palm leaf *lamak*. Kerambitan (Tabanan), 1982. Photo Francine Brinkgreve.**

The second type is more elaborate and is called *ceniga*.[3] This is fashioned by pinning together strips of young coconut leaf in such a way that openings are formed between the strips (fig. 5). The leaves are sometimes dyed with yellow and red water-based dyes. A *ceniga* often receives its more specific name from the manner of the patterning of the leaves. When the leaves are folded and fastened together into the fern (*paku pidpid*) or bamboo staircase (*banggul*) patterns, the *ceniga* is called *ceniga paku pidpid* or *ceniga banggul*.

The third category is called *lamak*, the type of ritual decoration that is the focus of this article. The main difference between the *lamak* and other offering bases is that a *lamak* is always ornamented, and is often made from the leaves of the sugar palm (*Arenga pinnata*).[4] A *lamak* usually consists of two layers. The base layer is made by pinning together horizontally strips of the same length of either light green young coconut leaves (*busung*) or yellowish young leaves (*ambu*) of the sugar palm (fig. 6). Ornaments, cut from contrasting dark green leaves of the coconut palm (*slepan*) or of the sugar palm (*ron*) or from dyed leaves, are attached to the base of the *lamak* with bamboo pins (*semat*). These motifs can vary from very simple to extremely complicated designs, both geometric and representational.

A *lamak* always has a rectangular form. It is rather narrow (15 to 40 centimeters), but can vary in length from about 30 centimeters to more than ten meters, depending

3 The National Museum of Ethnology in Leiden has an example of a *ceniga*, no. 5258-110. In the district of Tabanan in West Bali, a *lamak* is called *ceniga gede*, large *ceniga*.

4 In other parts of Indonesia, the sugar palm often has a special sacred connotation. Balinese informants did not specifically mention this, but they said they preferred to use these leaves, because they were softer and easier to work with. The mature leaves of the sugar palm are used for complicated offerings like *pering* and *bebangkit*. The two sides of these leaves, which differ considerably in their intensity of green color, are associated with light and dark, male and female.

Left: Fig. 7. Three cloth *lamak* decorate the shrine of origin in a house temple in Budakeling (Karangasem), 2006. The colours refer to the Hindu Trinity: white for Siwa, red for Brahma, and black for Wisnu. *Photo Francine Brinkgreve.*

Right: Fig. 8. A permanent *lamak* of wood, mirrors, and Chinese coins with a *cili* motif, next to a palm leaf *lamak* with the motif of the tree of life (*kekayonan*). PuraMertasari, Sanur (Depasar), 2006. *Photo Francine Brinkgreve.*

on its purpose and the kind of ritual for which it is used. The enormous variety of *lamak* makes the tradition particularly fascinating.[5]

A *lamak* is not always made from ephemeral palm leaf because the *lamak* is not inherently impermanent like some other important ritual art forms in Bali. For example, particular offerings and objects made for death rituals are always ephemeral. The gift of such offerings cannot be given twice, and the cremation towers and sarcophagi are created to be burned together with the body of the deceased. Although palm leaf *lamak*, from the very nature of their ephemeral material, can be used only once, permanent varieties of *lamak* can be kept and used again for other rituals. Materials used for permanent *lamak* include the more durable leaves of the *lontar* palm (*Borassus flabellifer*)[6]; cloth that is decorated in various ways (fig. 7), for example painted, embroidered (see cat. no. 10), or appliqué (see cat. no 9); woven colored paper or plastic (fig. 17); and combinations of wood, little mirrors, and Chinese coins (*kepeng;* fig. 8).[7] These permanent varieties have always been produced only in small numbers compared to the more common palm leaf types. Some required time-consuming techniques, and are no longer made. One of the newest varieties of permanent *lamak* is the mass-produced *lamak sablon,* with dark green patterns printed on a base of yellowish cloth, by means of a silkscreen.

FUNCTION AND MEANING

All varieties of *lamak*, regardless of their size, motifs, or materials, have two main functions, which are usually combined. First, the upper part of a *lamak* serves as a base for offerings, as an artistic substitute for the flowers or leaves that are otherwise placed underneath offerings. Second, the lower and larger part of the *lamak* hangs down to decorate any construction that acts as a seat for invisible beings, like a fine mat that is laid out for an honored guest. It is a sign that a ritual is being held and that deities and ancestors are invited. For example, at temple festivals, all the places where the deities and ancestors are invited to receive offerings are decorated with *lamak*. These can be permanent shrines or pavilions, or temporary bamboo altars, but also other places ready to receive spiritual essence can be decorated with *lamak*, even if offerings are not always placed upon them. For instance on Tumpek Landep, the day dedicated to honoring metal and metalworking, cars and motorbikes have a festive appearance on account of the *lamak* and other decorative palm leaf constructions attached to them.

The kinds and numbers of *lamak* that are made and used for a particular ritual depend on many factors. Essential considerations are the type of ritual and the level of ritual elaboration, the importance and the position of the shrines or altars they hang from, economic factors such as availability of materials or costs of making or buying the *lamak*, and also individual styles and regional traditions.

On a daily basis, many women tend to decorate only the offering places that are visible to outsiders, such as the shrines in front of gateways and the wooden altars (*plangkiran*) hanging from the walls in shops (fig. 20). They receive simple, small cloth *lamak*, which are left permanently on these shrines or altars.

A small (*nista*) ceremony requires only a couple of *ceniga*, whereas for a ritual at the medium (*madia*) level, *lamak* are always used. For rituals carried out at the highest (*utama*) level of ritual ceremony, large bamboo triple shrines (*sanggar tawang*) are decorated with long, ornate *lamak* with varied motifs. The longest and most elaborate *lamak* are usually hung from the highest shrines, like the *padmasana* (lotus seat for the highest deity) inside the temple, and from the *bale kulkul* (a high structure for the temple drums) (fig. 9) in the outer courtyard, and beside the gateways. Expensive permanent *lamak*, such as those made of old Chinese coins, are of course well protected and not suspended outside gateways. During family rituals, only the shrines of the house-temple that are actually in use, such as the *sanggar kemulan* (shrine of origin; fig. 7), are completed with a *lamak*, the others receiving a *ceniga* or just an offertory leaf (*plawa*), or flowers as a base for the offerings.

5 In the National Museum of Ethnology in Leiden is the oldest registered *lamak* (no. 1586-99), made from *lontar* leaves, cotton, and colored and gold paper, collected by Nieuwenkamp in 1907 (H. H. Juynboll, *Catalogus van 's Rijks Ethnographisch Museum 7, Bali en Lombok* (Leiden: Brill, 1912:151, plate XV, fig.4).

6 The *lontar* palm is an important tree. When the leaves dry, they become white, and they are often used in offerings. Sometimes a ritual requires a white *lamak*, for example suspended from a white-and-yellow tower in a postcremation ceremony. For these *lamak*, the motifs are created by means of cutting away parts of the leaves rather than by adding ornaments to them.

7 A well-known variety of permanent *lamak* is the nowadays very rare blue textile with white motifs in supplementary warp, found in several museum collections and still in use in a couple of temples in the Badung area (Francine Brinkgreve and David Stuart-Fox, *Offerings: The Ritual Art of Bali* (Sanur, Bali: Image Network Indonesia, 1992); Laurens Langewis, "A Woven Balinese *Lamak*," in *Lamak and Malat in Bali and A Sumba Loom* (Amsterdam: Royal Tropical Institute, 1956), 31–47; Ch. Pelras, "*Lamak* et tissus sacres de Bali," *Objets et Mondes* 8, no. 4 (1967): 255–278.) Also other permanent *lamak* are now part of private and museum collections, for example rare appliqué *lamak* (see cat. no. 9) and embroidered *lamak* (cat. no. 10).

Top: Fig 9. A palm leaf *lamak* with sun and tree of life motifs on the southern side of the *bale kulkul* in Pura Bale Agung, Sanur (Denpasar), 1987. *Photo Francine Brinkgreve.*

Bottom: Fig. 10. Lines of *penjor* with *lamak* decorate a street in Pujung (Gianyar) for the Galungan festival, 1985. *Photo Francine Brinkgreve.*

The largest range of different *lamak* can be seen every 210 days during the Galungan and Kuningan festivals. For this great holiday period lasting more than ten days, throughout Bali the ancestral spirits come down to the house-temples of their descendents and the entire island is decorated.[8] This is the best period to observe and compare the regional variations of the *lamak*, since they are visible in front of every courtyard (figs. 11 and 12). In front of their homes, every family erects a *penjor,* a long bamboo pole whose upper end curves gracefully down (fig. 10). From the top hangs an elaborate palm leaf construction called *sampian,* and on the pole itself are attached all kinds of decorations, rice cookies, fruits, sheaths of rice, and pieces of cloth, symbols of the harvest from a fertile earth. Every *penjor* has an offering altar with a *lamak* hanging from it, and sometimes also a *lamak* is directly attached to the *penjor* itself. Although these *lamak* are seldom longer than one meter, the district of Gianyar has its own elaborate variation. In front of houses where a wedding has taken place during the previous months, tall altars are erected from which beautiful *lamak* are hung, five to eight meters long. They serve as a kind of invitation to all members of the neighborhood to come and visit the newlywed couple to present offerings and take home special sweets. These special *lamak* are called *lamak nganten,* wedding *lamak* (figs. 13 and 16).

Many of my Balinese informants shared the opinion that the main functions of the *lamak* are to act as a base for offerings and to decorate shrines and altars as invitations to the invisible spiritual powers. No ritual is complete without *lamak*. Some people however, such as priests who have access to more esoteric knowledge, mentioned a more symbolic significance for *lamak*. According to them, a *lamak* is essentially a medium between the gods and humankind, between the creator and the creation. Since creation is represented by the motifs of the *lamak*, pictured on an empty background (symbolic of the empty earth), a *lamak* functions as a kind of meditation medium, serving to remember the creator by means of his works.

Stemming from its very shape as a long, narrow runner, the *lamak* is also seen as a path or a bridge between this world and the upperworld, which is represented by the shrine or altar. For human worshipers it is the "staircase" to the shrine; it is also the path the gods take when they descend from the heavens to the world of human beings to receive offerings and to bestow upon humankind everything that is necessary for life on earth.⁹ By representing the different manifestations of creation in the motifs, and through the effort put into its beautification, the *lamak* can be regarded as an offering in itself, as a way for the Balinese to worship the gods and ancestors. Finally, the combination of the lighter-colored young and the darker-colored old leaves of the coconut and sugar palms corresponds to the various stages of life cycles, of young and old in general. Light and dark are also sometimes related to the dual opposition male and female, especially when both sides of the mature leaves of the sugar palm, which differ considerably in color, are used in combination.

In this symbolic interpretation, the *lamak* is essentially a connection between macro- and microcosmos, *buana agung* and *buana alit*, universe and human being. This meaning of the *lamak* as a whole is reflected in the meaning of the decorative motifs pictured on it, especially in their hierarchical ordering.

MEANING OF THE MOTIFS

The motifs decorating the base (*dasar*) of a palm leaf *lamak* can be divided into two main categories: geometric patterns called *ringgitan*, and single designs, either representational or natural, called *raka*. *Ringgitan* means something that is cut out, so the term can, for example, also be used to refer to *wayang kulit* figures which are cut out from leather; *raka* means fruits used in offerings, in other words, content. A smaller *lamak* contains only a geometric pattern, or a combination of a geometrical and a representational design, but never just the latter. On a small *lamak* the representational motif is placed at the top and the geometric one at the bottom. On a larger *lamak* these different kinds of motifs alternate, but one of the geometric patterns is always placed in the lower field. The structure of most of the more elaborate permanent textile *lamak* does not differ essentially from the palm leaf ones. Usually in larger or regular-sized *lamak*s, a representational motif is placed above a geometric one.

This geometric pattern on the bottom end of the *lamak* is usually called *kamben* or *bebatikan*. A *kamben* is a long unsewn cloth, worn as a wraparound cloth, whereas *bebatikan* refers to the batik cloth produced in Java but widely used in Bali as well. Sometimes between the various representational motifs only narrow bands of geometric patterns are fastened. These are called *penyelak*. *Menyelak* means to push something aside, so *penyelak* is something in between the representational motifs. The very bottom of a *lamak* shows a special pattern, usually called *cracap* (something with a sharp point) and the sides and ends of the *lamak*, called *sebeh* (frame), are decorated with little motifs as well. The most

8 I Gusti Bagus Sugriwa, *Hari raya Bali Hindu* (Denpasar: Dewan Pemerintah Daerah Bali, 1957).

9 For a comparison with similar structures, ladders, or runners from altars in other parts of Indonesia and Asia, see Francine Brinkgreve, *De lamak als loper van bergtop naar mensenwereld: betekenis van regionale verschillen in materialen, kleuren en motieven van rituele decoraties op Bali* (Leiden: Oosters Genootschap in Nederland, 1996).

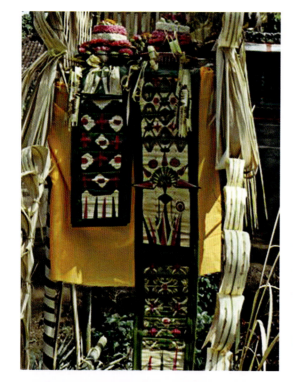

Top: Fig 11. *Lamak* with *batikan* and *cili* motifs on a shrine in front of a house in Jasan (Gianyar), Galungan 1987. *Photo Francine Brinkgreve.*

Bottom: Fig. 12. *Lamak* with *cili* and flower motifs on a *penjorin* front of a house in Sulahan (Gianyar), Galungan 1988. *Photo David Stuart-Fox.*

common of these side motifs is a pattern of small triangles, called *gigin barong*, the teeth of a mythical protective animal. The upper end of a *lamak*, the part on which the offerings are placed, sometimes has the shape of a triangle, and is called *umpal*. This term is also used for a long, narrow piece of cloth, used to tie a wraparound cloth around the upper part of the body.

Many Balinese consider all the motifs on a *lamak* together as a representation of the universe. The base of each *lamak* is said to be the empty earth on which creation is depicted in the form of the various motifs. Within this general concept, the motifs are all related to one another, following the hierarchical ordering of the Balinese worldview into three main divisions: the upper world, dwelling place of deities and ancestors; the middle world where human beings live; and the underworld or base of the earth. Thus, on long *lamak* the representational ornaments at the top and in the center visualize the upper world and the human world, and the geometric pattern at the bottom the base of the earth. The single representational motif on a smaller *lamak* represents either the upper or the middle world, always above the geometric pattern as base. The universe as a whole and the life forces flowing within it are protected by the motif of the sharp points (*cracap*) at the bottom, and the teeth of the protective *barong* along the side borders. The *umpal*, the top of the *lamak*, which is in direct contact with the offerings, is likened to the opening, and does not have a protective pattern above it.

When several *lamak* are hung from one larger shrine, either next to one another as from the triple bamboo *sanggar tawang*, or from the four sides of a structure such as the *bale kulkul*, the motifs of these *lamak* as a group often represent the world as a totality. For example, on the three *lamak* hanging from a *sanggar tawang* I once saw in Karangasem, east Bali, the middle one represented all kinds of creatures living on the mountains and in the sea, the right one showed the motif of the rising sun, the beginning of the day, and the left one visualized the moon or the night.

Of the twelve or so representational motifs that I have found on both palm leaf and permanent *lamak*, in the present article I discuss only those three motifs that are also most commonly copied on the *lamak sablon:* the mountain, the sun and moon, and the female figure.

The *gunung*, mountain (fig. 14), is a triangular-shaped motif consisting of rows of progressively fewer small triangles on top of one another. Sometimes the mountain has a rather tree-like shape, but it is still called *gunung*. Another name for the same motif is *bebukitan*, or *bukit*, meaning hill. The *gunung* or mountain motif is usually explained by the Balinese themselves as being the sacred Gunung Agung, Bali's highest and most sacred volcano, the top of which is the dwelling place of deities and ancestors. The offerings on the shrine from which the *lamak* hangs are essentially presented to the deities on the Gunung Agung. But also other mountains have an important significance for the Balinese. From the mountains flows the water that fertilizes the rice fields, and the rich fertile soil, of volcanic origin, nourishes the plants and woods as sources of human life on earth. Through its crater, a volcano is also directly connected with the powerful forces in the underworld. So it is regarded as a cosmic axis, connecting upper world, human world, and underworld. Because the water flows down from the higher slopes of the mountain and the top is regarded as sacred, the mountain is one of the upper motifs on a *lamak*.

Either the sun (*matanai*) or the moon (*bulan*), or both sun and moon, are often depicted on a *lamak* in the form of a disc composed of several little elements around a center. The sun and the moon are accompanied by stars, *bintang-bintangan*, in a square structure around them (fig. 15). Both the sun and the moon as cosmic objects have a strong influence on the development of life on earth. Representing day and night, they form a complementary opposition that symbolizes the totality of life itself. The rays of the sun, Surya, fertilize the earth, Ibu Pertiwi, so that plants can grow. The god of the sun and the goddess of the earth are both invited as important witnesses at ceremonies marking the different phases of the human life cycle. Sun and Earth are related to each other as male and female, and so too are sun and moon. Moreover, the moon is the dwelling place of Dewi Ratih, goddess of love, and so is associated with the continuity of human life. Two half-circles, instead of full circles, can represent the sun and the moon. This type of representation is said to depict sun and moon as they just arise in the east and set in the west, or when they are just visible from behind the mountain. Two halves forming one totality are also a symbol of marriage, of unification of two opposites, which makes life possible. If depicted on a single *lamak*, the sun and the moon are placed at the top, also above the mountain, since they belong to the sky or the upper world. If four *lamak* are hung from the four sides of, for

Top: Fig 13. *Lamak nganten* with *cili nganten*, sun or moon, and *kekayonan* motifs. Pliatan (Gianyar), Galungan 1987. *Photo Francine Brinkgreve.*

Bottom: Fig. 14. Mountain and *batikan* motifs on a *lamak* in Muncan (Karangasem), 2010. *Photo Francine Brinkgreve.*

PALM LEAF AND SILKSCREEN: LAMAK IN TRANSITION   71

10 Urs Ramseyer, *The Art and Culture of Bali* (Oxford: Oxford University Press, 1977), 35, and L. Langewis, "A Woven Balinese *Lamak*," in Th. P. Galestin, L. Langewis, and R. Bolland, *Lamak and Malat in Bali and a Sumba Loom* (Amsterdam: Royal Tropical Institute, 1956), 40.

11 Francine Brinkgreve, "The Woven Balinese *Lamak* Reconsidered," in ed. M.-L. Nabholz-Kartaschoff, R. Barnes, and D.J. Stuart-Fox, *Weaving patterns of life: Indonesian Textile Symposium 1991* (Basel: Museum of Ethnography, 1993), 141.

example, a *bale kulkul* (high structure for temple drums), the motifs of the sun and the moon are placed on the *lamak* on the east and west sides respectively.

A *cili* (figs.11, 12, 15, 16, 17; see also cat. no. 9 and cat. nos. 6, 7, 8) is a beautiful stylized slender female figure with an elongated triangular body, long arms, a fan-shaped headdress and big cylindrical ear ornaments. The *cili* is not only a very common *lamak* motif, but she appears in many other forms of ritual art in Bali. *Cili* means something like "little puppet," and the same motif is sometimes called *deling*, girl or maiden. Usually one *cili* is depicted, but on a *lamak nganten*, the so-called wedding *lamak*, the long *lamak* found in the Gianyar area in front of houses where a marriage has taken place, two *cili* form the main motif. These *cili nganten* or *cili kembar*, wedding or twin *cili*, are depicted next to one another, usually in the same style as the one large *cili* (fig. 16). In west Bali especially a double *cili* motif is often used without any relationship to a specific marriage.

Most Balinese share the opinion that the *cili* is a representation of humankind, women and men, and that this is the reason why the *cili* is usually placed in the center or middle section of a *lamak*, in the world of life on earth. When a family has recently buried a deceased relative it may not use a *cili* on a *lamak*, because the *cili* is associated with human life. Despite its feminine beauty, the *cili* is an ungendered human figure, neither specifically male nor female. The *cili nganten*, representing the newlywed bride and groom, both have an identical feminine form; the left one is the bride, the right one the groom. According to my informants, it does not really matter whether the form is male or female, because the essence of human life is depicted, and man and woman together form one whole or totality. The *cili nganten* often have flowers on their heads, a symbol of fertility. Another opinion is that the *cili* itself, sometimes depicted with leaves sprouting from her arms, is related to living plants and trees, since human life is dependent on vegetative life.

In the existing literature about Bali the *cili* is often called the symbol of the goddess of rice and fertility, Dewi Sri.[10] As I have argued before, in rituals of the rice-growing cycle, which are often compared with the life cycle of a woman, Dewi Sri sometimes is represented as a *cili*, but not every *cili* is per definition a representation of Dewi Sri, and certainly not on the *lamak*. One could say that a *cili* essentially represents life and fertility, and whether she is mainly giving or receiving it depends on the context.[11]

The geometric motifs occur in endless variety, and more often than not they have no specific name, being called only by the general terms *ringgitan* (something that is cut out) or *bebatikan* (*batik* cloth). Sometimes different designs have the same name, or one pattern has different names. When compared with the actual form of the object after which the motif is named, it is apparent that there rarely seems to be a direct correspondence between name and representation. Most names of these motifs are related to plants and refer to fruits, seeds, flowers, or leaves. Examples include *batu nangka*: seed of the jackfruit; *kembang kopi*: flower of the coffee plant; *kapu-kapu kambang*: an aquatic plant whose leaves float on the water (L. *Pistia stratiotes*); *candigara* or *kanigara*: a kind of tree with yellow flowers (*Pterospermum acerifolium*); and *batu ketimun*: seed of the cucumber, a motif also found on temple reliefs.

In general the geometric patterns are said to represent vegetative life, especially plants that grow in water (although in fact the names of the motifs also refer to other kinds of plants). Seeds represent the fruitfulness of the earth. This connotation of geometric patterns with the base of the earth or the basic conditions for life is the rationale for placing a geometric pattern underneath a representational one, and always at the bottom of a *lamak* (figs. 11, 13, 14).

Apart from the association with plants, geometric *lamak* patterns relate most closely to textiles and textile designs. They are either in general called *bebatikan* or *kain batik*, or only the bottom (usually longer) pattern is called *bebatikan*, *kain batik*, or *kamben*. This wrap-around cloth is said to belong either to the *cili*, wrapped around her legs, or it indicates the lowest part of the human body. Since in Balinese cosmology the universe (*buana agung*) is often compared with the elements and the structure of the human body or microcosmos (*buana alit*), a *lamak* as a whole is also sometimes thought of as a human body, which has a *kamben* (*batik*) around the lower part.

LAMAK MAKERS

Many Balinese housewives can make their own palm leaf *lamak*, using materials from their own fields or gardens, or those bought at the markets. They learn the skill from other women in the household, just as they learn how to make offerings. But when groups of women gather in a temple to prepare the offerings and ritual decorations for a ritual or festival, there are usually some women especially skillful at making *lamak*, whereas others are more talented in the making of other types of palm leaf constructions (*jejaitan*). Even at home not every woman makes her own *lamak*. For example Sagung Putu Alit, a creative woman from the village of Kerambitan who is gifted at making *jejaitan* and often experiments with new creations from palm leaf, prefers to buy ready-made *lamak* at the market for major festival days. Some women have more time or are more talented than others, and choose to make *lamak* for relatives and friends.

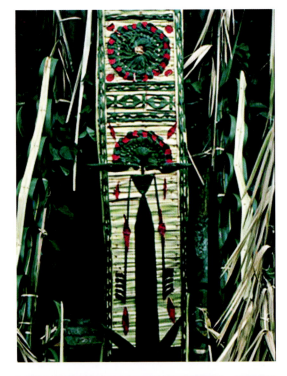

Top: Fig 15. Sun or moon and *cili* motifs on a *lamak* in Pujung (Gianyar). Galungan 1977. *Photo David Stuart-Fox.*

Bottom: Fig. 16. *Cili* and *cili nganten* (the bride and groom, with flowers on their heads) motifs on a *lamak nganten*. Pliatan (Gianyar), Galungan 1987. *Photo Francine Brinkgreve.*

At markets, palm leaf *lamak* are usually sold only just prior to festival times, such as Galungan and Kuningan. They can be found in the vicinity of the stalls of offering sellers, women who sell ready-made small offerings of fresh flowers on palm leaf bases for everyday use. In the *toko yadnya,* shops with ritual utensils, a range of small permanent *lamak* is always available. Who produces these permanent *lamak* has not yet been fully researched.

Traditionally, only women specialists, probably mainly from Brahman households, made permanent *lamak* requiring special decorating techniques, including embroidery, appliqué, or supplementary weft (together with other textiles for ceremonial use), whereas men specialized in making ritual objects from Chinese coins. They were made to order, together with other textiles or ritual objects. However, Men Nis from Kesiman (near Denpasar), the maker of the well-known cloth *lamak* with white motifs in supplementary warp over a blue ground found in several museum collections, was not of Brahman origin.[12] She was active in the 1920s, but no one has followed her example (see cat. no. 10 for developments in embroidered *lamak*).

Generally palm leaf *lamak* available at markets are relatively small. Longer, more elaborate *lamak* are the work of skilled craftsmen (*tukang*), men sometimes as well as women, who are acknowledged in the community as *tukang lamak* (*lamak* maker), and who usually work to order. The long *lamak nganten* (wedding *lamak*) in the Gianyar area are often ordered by the meter from *tukang lamak*, who, besides receiving the raw material, are paid a certain price per meter in return. In Padangtegal in the neighborhood of Ubud, in the heart of central Bali, live several *tukang lamak*. Bapak I Putu Nonderan, an elderly farmer, regularly received requests and orders for *lamak nganten* before the start of every Galungan period. Fifty years ago he learned to make *lamak*, together with the arts of sculpture and carving, from the famous artist I Gusti Nyoman Lempad. He used to work with him whenever Lempad received requests from the palaces in Ubud to prepare cremation towers and other requirements for royal death rituals. From Lempad he also learned specialized knowledge about the meaning of the motifs and ornaments he was creating. The son of Pak Nonderan, I Gusti Putu Taman, started to paint *lamak* motifs on canvas, and created his own variety of *lamak*.[13]

REGIONAL VARIATIONS [14]

Although the individual style of each *lamak* maker is important in the design of a *lamak*, the material from which a *lamak* is made and the ornaments and colors decorating it are largely determined by regional style differences. Motifs especially show the full range of styles. Travelling through Bali during the Galungan festival period, when there is a *lamak* hanging in front of almost every house, makes one aware of this enormous variety. Every region, every village, and sometimes even every street shows its own preference not only for the use of different motifs but also for the styles and colors of the motifs. A woman who, upon marriage, has moved to a different village or another district in Bali, usually learns the style of her new place of residence.

The *cili,* the figure representing human life and fertility, shows this variation in its fullest extent. In the district of Tabanan, west Bali, for example, the *cili* differ considerably from the *cili* in Gianyar, central Bali. The *cili* in Tabanan have rather elongated forms, with ornamented long skirts, long, upright hairstyles or headdresses, and arms that are bent upward at the elbow (fig. 17). *Cili* on some examples of permanent, textile *lamak* from the Tabanan area also show these features (see cat. no. 9).[15] In Gianyar the *cili* are somewhat shorter, their headdresses have the form of a half-circle, their arms are directed downward, often almost reaching the ground, and botanical elements sometimes sprout from their bodies (figs. 11, 16). But within Gianyar itself the different styles of *cili* vary considerably. For instance, while in Pujung (north of Ubud), the *cili* are always very elongated, with small hairdos (fig. 15), the *cili* in Padangtegal (immediately south of Ubud) are shorter, but with a rather wide, elaborate fan-shaped headdress (fig. 13).

The choice of leaves depends partly on environmental conditions. In dry areas like east Karangasem or along the north coast of the island, *lontar* palms grow more easily than do other varieties of palms, so there is a tendency to use more *lontar* leaves in these areas. And since there are more sugar palms in central Bali than in Badung (south Bali), the *lamak* (especially the *lamak nganten*) in Gianyar are more often made from *ambu* and *ron* (younger and older leaves of the sugar palm) than, for example, in Sanur and Denpasar, where coconut palm leaf is more commonly used.

Regarding colors, in central Bali small elements from dyed red leaves are often combined with the green leaves, while in Tabanan this is always the case and red is often quite dominant. In Tabanan and Jembrana yellow is often used as a fourth color, and sometimes even purple elements are added.

The regional differentiation of the palm leaf *lamak* is most visible in the motifs. In

12 Ch. Pelras, "Lamak et tissus sacrés de Bali," *Objets et Mondes* 7, 4 (1967), 255–278.

13 In 1983 Bapak I Putu Nonderan made two *lamak* for the National Museum of Ethnology in Leiden, nos. 5258-96 and 5258-97, from painted *lontar* leaves.

14 A more elaborate interpretation of the symbolic meaning of regional differences in materials, techniques, colors, and motifs of *lamak* was published in Francine Brinkgreve, *De lamak als loper van bergtop naar mensenwereld: betekenis van regionale verschillen in materialen, kleuren en motieven van rituele decoraties op Bali* (Leiden: Oosters Genootschap in Nederland, 1996).

15 *Cili* are not only found on *lamak*, but they are an essential part of many offerings, for instance in the form of figurines made from rice dough. In the offering *pulagembal* in Tabanan the head of a *cili* has a central position. This face has also an elongated, upright headdress, just as on the *lamak*.

Karangasem, where the Gunung Agung is situated, and in Klungkung, both in the eastern part of the island, the mountain is the most common motif. Towards the west, in Bangli and parts of Gianyar, trees are often the main motif.[16] In Gianyar and Badung, more toward the southwest, human figures (*cili*) including the *cili nganten* (wedding *cili*) make their appearance, while the *cili* is the dominant motif in Tabanan, west Bali. In Jembrana in the far west and in the northern coastal region of Buleleng, the motifs of the palm leaf *lamak* are often geometric, or depict flower motifs.

My Balinese informants did not consider such regional style differences as parts of a meaningful encompassing structure or system. They were usually of the opinion that the style of their own village was the best or most complete or beautiful.

However, the regional differences in the motifs show certain relationships that might have a deeper significance.[17] In Balinese cosmology, the island of Bali is regarded as a structured totality. In many places the surrounding sea and the centrally located mountains are a pair of visibly contrasting realities. The tops of the mountains, in particular of the highest volcano, Gunung Agung, are the dwelling places of the deities and deified ancestors. From the mountains the water that fertilizes the rice fields flows toward the purifying salty waters of the ocean. Therefore, in the topographical classification system, upstream or the direction toward the mountains (*kaja*) is more sacred, more related to the upper world than the direction toward the sea, downstream (*kelod*), which is more earthly and profane.

Left: Fig. 17. Plastic *lamak* from Kerambitan with *cili, mas-masan,* and *cracap* motifs. Collection National Museum of Ethnology, inv.no. 5258-52. Photo Ben Grishaaver.

Right: Fig. 18. *Lamak* of painted canvas from Padang tegal with *gebogan* (an offering), *mas-masan,* and *ceracap* motifs. Collection National Museum of Ethnology, inv.no. 5258-50. Photo Ben Grishaaver.

The *kaja-kelod* antithesis is not only a horizontal one, but also an important vertical dimension.[18] Well-known examples of the use of this topographical classification include the layouts of villages and temples. In the village temple system, the temple of the dead (*pura dalem*) is located *kelod* of the village center, and the temple of the deified ancestors of the village people (*pura puseh*) has a *kaja* position. The assembly hall temple (*pura bale agung*) of the village community is situated in the center. The so-called inner court of a temple, situated in the most *kaja* position, is the most sacred part of a temple, where the seats and shrines for the deities are located. The more *kelod*-situated gateways of a temple are richly decorated with plant motifs, representing a more earthly atmosphere.[19]

An examination of the variation of *lamak* motifs also suggests a correspondence with this topographical classification. The regional transformation from mountain motif via tree and human motifs to plant or "hipcloth" (geometric) motifs corresponds to a gradual descent from *kaja* to *kelod*, from the holy mountain Gunung Agung through the fertile plains of central Bali toward the coastal areas. The greater the distance from the top of the sacred mountain, dwelling place of the deities, the more one is present in the world of human and vegetative life.

This regional variation of motifs has, interestingly, the same vertical order as the motifs on one single large *lamak*, where often a mountain is depicted at the top, then a tree, in the middle a *cili,* and at the bottom geometric vegetative ornaments.

Taken as a whole, it is possible to interpret the regional variations of the motifs of all the different *lamak* together in the same way as the ordering of the motifs on one *lamak*, being a connection, runner, or ladder between the world of the deities and of human beings.

Although these regional tendencies are still visible in Bali, due to social and economic developments they are becoming less clear. The different regions are less isolated than they used to be, and improved transport facilities enhance mutual influences. For example, *lontar* leaves originating from the dry Karangasem area are now often used in Denpasar (Badung) because of their durability, while various multicolored permanent *lamak*, fabricated in other parts of the island, appear on shrines in front of houses in east Bali.

CHANGES AND DEVELOPMENTS

Social and economic developments in the past decades have brought about major changes in the preparation and practice of rituals in Bali. As women's occupations outside the home increase, especially in the cities and tourist regions of the island, women have less time to prepare for rituals themselves, or to help other people in this way. This results in an increasing demand for complete sets of ready-made offerings and ritual decorations that specialists produce in their own homes, and which are then taken to the temple or the household concerned just before or on the day of the ritual.

Similarly, the big transitory objects required for cremation rituals are nowadays made to order. Whereas formerly it was mainly the large palm leaf *lamak nganten* (wedding *lamak*) that were ordered from specialist *lamak* makers (*tukang lamak*),

16 The motif of the tree (*kekayonan*) is often used on *lamak* because trees are thought of as a source of human life. All parts of a tree can be used: wood, leaves, flowers, and fruits. In Balinese cosmology, like the holy mountain, the tree functions both as cosmic axis and as a symbol of the unity and totality of all existing phenomena. On a large *lamak*, the tree is placed underneath the mountain motif.

17 Symbolic meaning of regional differentiation is also discussed at length by Rens Heringa ("Tilling the Cloth and Weaving the Land: Textiles, Land and Regeneration in an East Javanese Area," in *Weaving Patterns of Life: Indonesian Textile Symposium 1991,* ed. Marie-Louise Nabholz-Kartaschoff, Ruth Barnes, and David J. Stuart-Fox [Basel: Museum of Ethnography, 1993], 155–176.). She analyzes the manufacturing, formats, colors, and motifs of textiles in a specific area in northeast Java as part of a meaningful structure or totality.

18 J. L. Swellengrebel, "Introduction," in *Bali:Studies in Life, Thought and Ritual* (The Hague and Bandung: Van Hoeve, 1960), 38–39.

19 Swellengrebel, "Introduction," in *Bali: Studies in Life, Thought and Ritual,* 43–44, and Urs Ramseyer, *The Art and Culture of Bali* (Oxford: Oxford University Press, 1977), 132.

recently more and more ordinary palm leaf *lamak* are for sale. Particularly during the few days before the Galungan-Kuningan festival period, piles of ready-made palm leaf *lamak* are sold at the markets in villages and towns.

Traditionally, permanent *lamak* requiring special decorating techniques must have been rather expensive because of the time-consuming techniques, or the cost of coins. But nowadays small, cheap versions of permanent *lamak*, and *lamak* made of simple textiles or of newly fabricated "fake" coins, are increasingly available at the markets and in ritual shops. For people who buy *lamak* rather than make them, these cheaper permanent *lamak* provide a good alternative to palm leaf *lamak*, since they can be used more than once.

Not only for economic reasons but also because the Balinese like to experiment and try out new things, changes in material of ritual decorations have always occurred, provided the religious contents of the objects did not change. In one notable example of problematic change, in the late 1970s in the district of Tabanan it was fashionable to make *lamak* with motifs from brightly colored plastic (fig. 17). Although these *lamak* showed fine craftmanship and many temples used them, after a few years religious authorities gave notice that they should not be used because the material was not regarded as ritually suitable.

On most permanent *lamak*, the decorative motifs and the overall structure correspond to those of the palm leaf varieties, although they are never exact copies. In the mid-1980s, however, especially in the region of Ubud in Gianyar, which is well known for its painting traditions, some *tukang lamak* who made palm leaf *lamak* to order started to paint *lamak* motifs on canvas. Bapak Tantri from Padangtegal created an example for the collection of the National Museum of Ethnology (fig. 18).

The size of these *lamak* is similar to the palm leaf versions, and the colors chosen are as close to the traditional ones as possible. The canvas is painted a light yellow shade, and the ornaments in a contrasting dark green, just like the colors of *ambu* and *ron*, the young and older leaves of the sugar palm respectively. The motifs are handpainted, and in some cases the *tukang* makes use of small carton stencils for certain parts of patterns. The patterns are so similar in style to those of the palm leaf *lamak* in the Ubud area that from a distance almost no difference can be seen. The whole range of existing motifs from this area is copied, since the craftsmen, who are usually specialists in the palm leaf type, are well acquainted with them. These *lamak* can be made to order, but they are rather expensive because of all the work involved, and are mainly used within the families of the *tukang lamak* themselves. Painted large *lamak nganten* are generally too expensive to buy, but they are rented out for special occasions. Related to the painted *lamak* are the *lamak sablon*.

PRODUCTION AND USE OF *LAMAK SABLON*

In contrast to the hand-painted *lamak*, *lamak sablon* are very cheap, since they are mass-produced. One craftsman who lives in Banjar Tebuana, Sukawati (district of Gianyar) worked with two silkscreens, each the size of a *lamak*, one for the main patterns and one for the accents that were added afterwards. The base was a bright yellow piece of cloth, the paint for the main patterns was a dark green color, and red paint was used for the accents.

This *tukang*, I Ketut Lantur, who was already an experienced painter of patterns on dance costumes and cloth fans, began in the early 1990s with the less time-consuming silkscreen technique of decoration. Since this appeared to be a success, he then also started producing silkscreen *lamak*. Lantur bought the silkscreens in Denpasar, where they were made, but he designed the motifs on the screens himself (fig. 19). His *lamak sablon* were about 70 centimeters long and 19 centimeters wide. For a longer *lamak* the silkscreen was used twice, on a piece of cloth twice as long, so that the motifs and structure of a small *lamak* were simply repeated or doubled. Ketut Lantur worked only to order, and for a cheap price. He received his orders mainly from a middleman who sold his *lamak sablon* at the market in Klungkung. He did not make *lamak sablon* every day, and he did not have any for sale in his small household workshop, but once he had received a new order, his production could be up to a hundred pieces a day.

Fig. 19. A screen to make a *lamak sablon,* in the workshop of I Ketut Lantur in Sukawati (Gianyar), 2001. *Photo Francine Brinkgreve.*

According to I Ketut Lantur, he was the first in the area to start producing *lamak sablon*, whereas in Sukawati there were many other *lamak sablon* workshops following his example. I do not have any historical or economic data or figures on this matter, but at the main market in Sukawati I was told that the main centers of production were in Banjar Babakan of Sukawati. At such major markets as those of Denpasar (the capital of Bali) and of Bebandem, in Karangasem, East Bali, the vendors also said that their *lamak sablon* were all made in Sukawati.

While driving and walking the roads of Bali in the summer of 2001, I found that the use of *lamak sablon* was very visible. Many shrines outside the gateways of homesteads in villages and towns used the *lamak sablon* on an everyday basis. Formerly these shrines would have had either a simple textile *lamak* or an ordinary white or yellow cloth as decoration or "clothing," and a little mat and some flowers or leaves as base for the daily offerings. Also the small wooden shrines hanging on walls, for example inside shops, were now often decorated with a *lamak sablon* (fig. 20).

Like the woman quoted in the article in *SARAD* magazine, people told me that they used the *lamak sablon* to make these "daily" shrines, which are in permanent use, more decorative, and the *lamak sablon* were also cheaper than other types of textile *lamak*. In the long run they were even cheaper than the palm leaf *lamak*, for which the material must be bought time and again, especially for people who do not own or have access to coconut or sugar palms.

An important factor is the increasing shortage of the natural materials necessary for ritual objects in Bali, as a result of ever-increasing building activities on the island. Ten years ago the sugar palm was already getting scarce, but today even leaves of the coconut palm are imported from Java and even from as far as Lampung, South Sumatra, by the truckload. The latest development is the use of the leaves of the oil palm (*Elaeis guineensis Jac.*), called in Bali *busung Sulawesi*, since it is imported from Sulawesi; these leaves are not strong enough to be used for *lamak*. In making *lamak*, women prefer to work with the softer and broader sugar palm leaf, but it is expensive.[20] At the market in Ubud in 2001, a small *lamak sablon* cost the same price as a ready-made palm leaf *lamak*. A *lamak sablon* one meter long was about twice that price. The *lamak sablon* clearly was a response to a growing economic need, although in fact much more palm leaf is needed for offerings (which do not have alternative permanent forms) than for ritual decorations.

It was interesting to see large numbers of *lamak sablon* not only at the market in Denpasar but also at the market in Bebandem, a traditional town in Karangasem. In the former, lack of time to make one's own ritual decorations and the lack of sufficient palm leaf appear to be sufficient explanations for the popularity of the new medium, whereas in rural areas these arguments in favor of the *lamak sablon* seem to be less relevant. Probably in this Karangasem case, sensitivity to the latest fashion with regard to ritual objects has been more important in this phenomenon, though economic factors cannot be entirely ruled out. The fact that once remote places are now easily accessible by transportation means that new features spread quickly all over Bali.

Besides mentioning the use of *lamak sablon* at the shrines outside courtyards and in shops and workshops, people also told me that they use *lamak sablon* at the shrines in their house-temples. However, they also noted that during rituals or on special festival days, this alone was not sufficient: they would add the small *terujungan* (offering base) or a small *ceniga* or just some leaves or flowers on top of the *lamak sablon*, directly underneath the offerings, so that the natural realm is still present as a base for offerings (fig. 5). Just like other types of permanent *lamak*, *lamak sablon* are not made from natural material and are therefore not part of the large category of *jejaitan*, palm leaf constructions made for ritual purposes. And although a *lamak* is not an offering itself, whose ingredients must be taken from the natural realm, many Balinese feel that ritual decorations should contain at least some natural elements.

During two short visits to Bali in May and July 2010, I was interested in the latest

20 Made Sajana, "Busung Bali sulit dicari," *SARAD: Majalahgumi Bali,* 1, 2 (2000), 58–59.

developments in the use of *lamak sablon*. Although lacking time for proper research and the opportunity to visit all parts of the island, I noticed a considerable decrease in the use of *lamak sablon* on shrines outside courtyards, along the roads. They were still present, but looked rather old and damaged by sun and rain. However, hanging from shrines inside shops, hotel lobbies and restaurants were still many *lamak sablon* of the same types I had seen in 2001 and still in good shape. Only in and around the town of Sukawati, the previous center of production of *lamak sablon*, were there still new ones hanging outside homes along the roads. In the market and ritual shops of Sanur, where I had earlier bought a collection of different *lamak sablon*, there was not a single *lamak sablon* for sale. But in the markets of Tabanan, Negara, and Bebandem (Karangasem), *lamak sablon* were still for sale.

My visit in May coincided with the Galungan festival period. *Penjors* were still erected everywhere and palm leaf *lamak* were abundant, still produced in the traditional styles of the respective villages. Especially in the area around Ubud, Tegallalang and Sukawati, I noticed several *lamak sablon*, but they were always accompanied by a smaller palm leaf *lamak*, next to or on top of the *lamak sablon* (fig. 5).

MOTIFS AND REPRESENTATION

Although one might expect that the overall design of a *lamak sablon* is meant to imitate a palm leaf *lamak*, a closer examination of the motifs tells a different story. The general impression of a *lamak sablon* in comparison with a palm leaf one is that the former is much more ornate, with empty spaces around the main motifs filled in with small decorative elements. And in fact, many details of the motifs are not physically possible to produce in the medium of palm leaves. Regarding motif designs, the silkscreen method does not have technical limitations to the same extent as does working with palm leaves. Many decorations on the *lamak sablon* are simply too small or too ornate to cut out and to fasten with bamboo needles onto the base layer of leaves. Moreover, whereas a palm leaf *lamak* of equivalent size might contain only one representational and one geometrical pattern, a *lamak sablon* always has two or three representational ornaments and a relatively small geometrical motif.

The main motif on the *lamak sablon* of I Ketut Lantur is a female figure in a long dress, wearing a very large headdress (fig. 19). She is less stylized than the *cili* on many palm leaf *lamak*; she has a realistic face, for example, but she also has such features of a *cili* as long arms, without hands, reaching almost to the ground, and leaflike ornaments sprouting from her dress. The *tukang* called this motif a *cili*, which according to him was a woman, who must be depicted as beautifully (*cantik*) as possible. A circular motif above her head, similar to the sun or moon on palm leaf *lamak*, he called a *padma* (lotus) or *gumi* (world). The pattern

Fig. 20. *Lamak sablon* with Dewi Saraswati, mountain, and *padma* motifs on a shrine at the market of Denpasar, 2005. *Photo Francine Brinkgreve.*

underneath the *cili* consists of six separate flowers, more or less arranged like the geometric pattern *kapu-kapu* on a palm leaf *lamak*, but surrounded by ornamental leaves and petals. I Ketut Lantur called this pattern *bunga mitir*, the yellow marigold flower, which is not a water plant like the *kapu-kapu* (although the *bunga mitir* is not a traditional *lamak* motif it resembles the traditional *kapu-kapu*). The bottom of his *lamak sablon* consists of four long sharp triangles, like the *cracap* (sharp pointed forms) on palm leaf *lamak*, and along the sides and bottom a triangular pattern like the *gigin barong* (teeth of a mythical protective animal) is depicted. On the whole, his *lamak sablon* are more ornate than palm leaf *lamak*, with otherwise empty space being filled with flowery, vegetative ornaments.

On the numerous *lamak sablon* that I have seen for sale at various markets and in use on shrines along the roadside or in shops all over Bali, the female figure is the main, central motif in all cases (figs. 3 and 20). These figures are depicted in three different forms (fig. 21). Many are traditional, stylized *cili* figures, of a kind that reminds one of the Ubud-Tegallalang regional style (fig. 3). But there are also several other female forms, less stylized than the *cili* on palm leaf *lamak*. One type portrays a beautiful woman with a real face, with eyes, nose, and mouth, a long elegant dress depicted as though the woman is moving, and an ornate headdress like that of a bride or a dancer (fig. 19).

Another female type clearly shows the features of a goddess, Dewi Saraswati (fig. 20). This important Hindu goddess is in Bali worshipped as the consort of the creator Brahma, and as goddess of learning, knowledge, and writing, especially regarding *lontar* manuscripts. On the holy day dedicated to her, the last day of the Javano-Balinese *wuku* year, *lontar* manuscripts are ritually purified and honored. Now students and schoolchildren also have their books purified on this day, on which nobody is permitted to read or write. On the *lamak sablon*, Dewi Saraswati is represented with all her attributes, which she holds in her four arms and hands. With one hand and arm she holds a musical instrument that she plays with her corresponding second hand, and in the two other hands she holds a *lontar* manuscript and a rosary (fig. 23). At her feet are two geese, which act as her vehicle, and on her head she wears a kind of crown with an aura around it, a development of the ornate headdress of the traditional *cili*.

This representation is probably influenced by illustrations in modern schoolbooks and religious magazines, which show a tendency to represent deities in a somewhat more realistic Indian style.[21] In a photo essay, Rama Surya shows a street trader with a painting of such an Indian-style Saraswati, and Dewi Saraswati as religious icon in a department store in Denpasar.[22] Furthermore, the day dedicated to Dewi Saraswati is nowadays widely celebrated, not only at schools but also at special ceremonies held at some major temples such as Pura Besakih. In any case, Dewi Saraswati was never depicted on a palm leaf *lamak*, so she is a completely new element in *lamak* iconography.

Another motif always appears above the the female figures. Sometimes this is a circular motif, as on the *lamak sablon* of I Ketut Lantur, which he and other informants called a *padma,* lotus flower, an important cosmic symbol (figs. 19 and 20). In the so-called *nawa sanga* system of cosmological order, the *padma* with its eight petals represents the center of the universe, and the totality and unity of the whole cosmos, represented by the eight points of the compass or wind rose. Although an important Balinese concept, this is a different interpretation from the circular motifs on palm leaf *lamak* that were always associated with the sun or moon. Presumably this more strictly Hindu interpretation reflects a tendency of Balinese religion to integrate more orthodox Hindu elements. Motifs on the textile *lamak* in the exhibition (see cat. nos. 9 and 10), however, can already be interpreted as *padma.*

Fig. 21. Three different kinds of *lamak sablon,* with three different kinds of female figure. Collection Francine Brinkgreve. *Photo Francine Brinkgreve.*

On *lamak sablon* in most cases the top motif is the well-known triangular form, consisting of small triangles, which as on palm leaf *lamak* is said to represent the holy mountain (*gunung*). While on longer palm leaf *lamak* the sun or moon motifs, being celestial ornaments, are usually placed above the mountain motif, on the *lamak sablon* the circular ornament is always placed underneath the mountain (fig. 20).

A pattern consisting of flowers is always placed underneath the *cili*. On the *lamak sablon* of I Ketut Lantur for example, these patterns have a certain relationship with the geometric patterns on palm leaf *lamak*, but they are more ornate, and the elements of the pattern are not connected with one another. Whereas on the painted *lamak* in the Ubud area the geometric patterns were a close copy of the geometric patterns on the palm leaf ones, on the *lamak sablon* these patterns give only a general impression of imitation. Only the triangular side and sharp end motifs are similar to those on palm leaf *lamak*.

The overall hierarchical structure of the palm leaf *lamak*, with representational motifs placed above a more geometric one, does still exist on the *lamak sablon*. However, the meaning of this hierarchy, the relationship among the motifs, seems to have been lost in some cases, because different meanings have been given to the various separate motifs. Traditionally, the structure of longer palm leaf *lamak* is said to be a representation of the vertical tripartition of

21 Fischer and Cooper (Joseph Fischer and Thomas L. Cooper, *The Folk Art of Bali: The Narrative Tradition* [Kuala Lumpur; New York: Oxford University Press, 1998] chapter 4, fig. 2) illustrate a contemporary painting of Dewi Saraswati, which also is not in traditional Balinese wayang style. Similar Indian influence is noticeable in stone sculpture.

22 Rama Surya, "Photo Essay," in ed. Urs Ramseyer and I Gusti Raka Panji Tisna, *Bali:Living in Two Worlds* (Basel: Museum of Ethnography, 2001), 76, 79.

the cosmos. The upper world is represented by the mountain or the sun or moon, the human world by the *cili* or tree, and the base of the world by the geometric patterns of water plants or textiles. On the new *lamak sablon*, however, it is especially the position of the Hindu goddess Saraswati in the middle world of human life that breaks with previous tradition. Not only is it unorthodox to place a goddess underneath the mountain (the top of which is regarded as the dwelling place of deities), but also as the goddess of learning and knowledge she has little connection with the concepts of life and fertility that dominate the traditional *lamak*.

Moreover, the heavenly sphere, represented by sun and moon, is replaced by the symbol of the totality of the cosmos, the *padma*, underneath the mountain. While the position of the motifs on the palm leaf *lamak* as a path from heaven to earth symbolizes the flow of life, the divine gift, down from the sun or moon or the water-giving mountain, this arrangement and meaning are not found with the *lamak sablon*. Here the religious value of the motifs on the *lamak* is still present, but their interrelationships are less clear. Especially on the long *lamak sablon*, where the structure of a smaller version is simply doubled, the meaning of the structure is totally lost, since here the bottom pattern of the top *lamak* (the protective sharp *cracap* pattern) is placed above the more sacred top pattern of the lower one. According to basic Balinese symbolism, this is certainly the wrong arrangement.

In a broader comparison of the two types of *lamak*, one finds that only a limited range of different motifs has been used on the *lamak sablon*, and a far smaller variety of geometric patterns. For example, one motif often found on the traditional *lamak*, the *kekayonan* or tree of life (figs. 8 and 13), is not depicted on the *lamak sablon*, despite its important symbolic significance. The *lamak sablon* are one specific iconographic type. Because they were produced in such a limited area of Bali, in Sukawati (Gianyar, central Bali) and surroundings, but were transported and used all over the island, they did not correspond with the meaningful system of rich regional and local variations of the traditional *lamak*. This means that *cili* were now seen on *lamak sablon* in areas where the mountain used to be the dominant motif on palm leaf *lamak*, as in Karangasem, east Bali; whereas the mountain was shown in areas where the *cili* traditionally is dominant, as in Tabanan, west Bali. Whereas the regional variation of many palm leaf *lamak* fits into the meaningful *kaja-kelod* (mountainward-seaward) topographical classification system, the *lamak sablon* does not fit into this system.

Moreover, all *lamak sablon* have the same colors, which again do not correspond with the regional variations of the palm leaf *lamak*. While the yellow background and green motifs imitate the light and dark green leaves used for any *lamak*, the red accents used on all *lamak sablon* are not used on the palm leaf *lamak* of, for instance, the eastern part of Bali.

CONCLUSION

It is interesting to see how the Balinese solved the problems of the growing lack of natural materials and lack of time with regard to religious requirements, in this case the palm leaf *lamak*, by using cheap imitations in a permanent form. The mass-produced *lamak sablon* was a practical solution for many people. In discussion in *SARAD* magazine, the main issue was whether the natural leaves of the traditional *lamak* could be replaced by an imitation. In fact, permanent *lamak* have existed for a long time alongside their natural counterparts. Moreover, the loss of the religious value of natural materials is mitigated by adding leaves or flowers on top of the *lamak sablon*, directly underneath the offerings. On the other hand, such values as the concept of the life cycle represented by the combination of older and younger leaves is lost in the cloth imitations. And finally, since the meaning of the motifs shows major change, Hindu official I Gusti Ngurah Oka Supartha was right to be concerned about the disappearance of symbolism.

Fig. 22. A statue of Dewi Saraswati with her vehicle the goose, in the garden of Museum Bali in Denpasar, 2006. *Photo Francine Brinkgreve.*

The representational and geometric motifs on the *lamak sablon* still carry religious meanings, although some of them are different from those of the palm leaf *lamak*, but it is especially their meaningful ordering that has often changed. In these cases, the interpretation of the totality of the motifs as representing the vertical cosmological order, in direct relationship to the meaning of the *lamak* as a bridge or path between heaven and earth, does not exist anymore. Moreover, *lamak sablon* do not fit into the system of regional variation of *lamak* motifs, which corresponds with the *kaja-kelod* topographical classification system.

Lamak sablon do not show the rich variation, creativity, and meanings of the palm leaf *lamak* they were meant to imitate. During my recent visit I noticed that they have not at all replaced their palm leaf antecedents. For festivals, palm leaf *lamak* are still produced. Although a single palm leaf *lamak* has a shorter lifespan and is more ephemeral than a *lamak sablon*, the palm leaf *lamak* as a category has proved to be more permanent and has outlasted the *lamak sablon*. Other varieties of permanent *lamak*, such as the *songket* (decorated in the supplementary-weft technique) *lamak* from Negara, and the plastic ones from Tabanan, for various reasons are not produced anymore. And the decrease in numbers of *lamak sablon* shows that this type is transitory, and will probably cease to be made as soon as better alternatives appear on the market. But as long as offerings are made in Bali and palm leaf remains available, the ritual art of the transitory palm leaf *lamak* will continue to exist.

GARRETT KAM
OFFERINGS IN BALI: RITUAL REQUESTS, REDEMPTION, AND REWARDS

Balinese arts such as painting and carving are tangible and enduring forms of craftsmanship and aesthetic production. Most ritual art, however, is temporary and used only once, then consumed, intentionally destroyed, or left to naturally decay (fig. 1). The ephemeral is the essence of *banten* (offerings). Fragrant flowers and trimmed palm leaves quickly wilt under the tropical sun; artistically arranged foods are eaten by worshipers after a ceremony, while dogs devour biscuits and meat on the ground. Any remaining bits and pieces are unceremoniously gathered up and tossed into a nearby river or trash heap where they are burned, buried, or left to return to nature (fig. 2). Ceremonial offerings must be created again every time that they are needed; this ongoing need for production guarantees the survival of the form. Due to constant ceremonial needs, a great number of Balinese are involved in this from the household level to communities to teams of ritual experts. All this transient beauty and all these time-consuming activities are at their core concerned with religious needs. At the peak of their freshness the ingredients, shapes, colors, and fragrances appeal to all of the human senses in hope of satisfying unseen forces.

Garrett Kam studied ritual art in Bali on a Fulbright Grant from 1987 to 1988 and has lived on the island since then. He is the only non-Balinese temple assistant at one of the most important temples in Bali and specializes in offerings. This essay is based exclusively on his research, conversations, interviews, observations, and participation; all photos are by the author.

Left: Fig. 1. Holding a *peras* offering and incense burner, women waft the essence of offerings in shrines toward divine spirits. Natural pigments on asbestos board, 20th century, Bale Kambang pavilion ceiling, Semarapura, Klungkung.

Opposite page: Fig. 2. After a small household temple ceremony, used offerings are placed on the ground outside the gate. Bedahulu, Gianyar.

Left: Fig. 3. Elaborate *penjor* and a banner sway over a temple during a ceremony. Pura Petilan Agung, Kesiman, Denpasar.

Right: Fig. 4. A *canang* on the dashboard is reflected in the windshield of a public transportation vehicle. Gianyar.

FORM AND FUNCTION

Offerings generally consist of set forms with little room for personal or individual expression; to deviate too much would lead to losses in meaning and function. A lion, for example, must be red with wings and a black mane; it should not look like the real animal. To do otherwise opens the door to criticism, ridicule, and embarrassment of the offending person, perhaps even the loss of future opportunities to participate. In many instances, offerings are like edible art installations that a contemporary artist can only dream of creating. Offerings can be public for everyone to enjoy, such as *penjor*, gracefully arching bamboo poles adorned with palm leaf ornaments that line roadsides on certain holy days or are erected in front of temple entrances during an *odalan* (temple anniversary) celebration (fig. 3). *Lamak* (banners) hanging from shrines and altars are fashioned from trimmed leaves pinned onto long panels with symbols of the sun and moon, cosmic mountains and trees, *cili* (fertility figures), teeth of the lionlike *barong* guardian, geometric patterns representing cultivated land, and patterns symbolizing rain dripping from a roof.

At the same time, offerings are personal expressions of faith. The *jotan* or *saiban* consists of a few grains of the first cooked rice of the day, before anyone has taken any for a meal, mixed with a pinch of salt. Placed on small squares of banana leaves, these smallest and simplest offerings are presented daily to all of the household spirits, including to the well where the cooking water is taken, and to every structure and shrine. Slightly more elaborate is the *canang*, a flower-filled leaf tray. In another typical daily event a driver, or a female member of his family, or a market woman puts a *canang* on the dashboard or behind the license plate of a motorized vehicle in the morning to ensure everyone's safety in the chaotic and hazardous traffic (fig. 4). A shop owner arranges the same type of offering on the ground outside his or her doorway to keep harmful spirits away and to ensure that customers come in.

What, then, is the reason for an offering? At the very heart is a unique religion practiced by the Balinese that is called Agama Hindu Dharma, a blend of animism, indigenous beliefs, ancestral worship, Buddhism, and Hinduism into a complex and colorful ceremonial life. The Balinese universe is populated by countless spirits of nature, demons, deified ancestors, and Indic gods and goddesses who must be appeased and indulged. Through offerings, rituals, and ceremonies the Balinese communicate with these unseen beings, who sometimes manifest themselves in a variety of physical forms to certain individuals. There are five categories of *yadnya* (sacrificial rites): *manusa* (human), *dewa* (deity), *buta* (demon), *pitra* (ancestor) and *rsi* (holy person). With the right thoughts, speech, and actions, a person's prayers will be answered and the invisible made visible or manifested in tangible ways. Every offering has a specific name that indicates its function and communicates through a symbolic language of physical objects; a *pejati* offering is made to inform the deities of a new member of a temple, or the deified ancestors that a marriage has just taken place. An offering is a gift, often a request for something in return that can include anything from good health, increased wealth, success in school, or being blessed with children. A polite appeal with a promise in return is made with prayers and presents of food. If the wish is granted, then gifts of thanks are necessary, and so an eternal relationship is established. To forget or intentionally neglect this obligation may bring danger or disaster that can be removed only by more complicated rituals and offerings.

In spite of the enormous range of forms and functions in offerings, some basic elements are common to most of them. Ingredients for chewing betel—areca nut (*Areca catechu*), betel leaf (*Piper betle*), limestone paste, tannin—are essential in the small, flower-filled offerings called *canang*, a refined Balinese word for the betel quid. The quid is represented by a *porosan*: a bit of betel leaf smeared with lime and areca nut that is inserted in a small, lozenge-shaped piece of coconut palm leaf (fig. 5). Guests, whether human, divine, or demonic, are presented betel chew as a sign of welcome and respect.

The presentation must be made visually pleasing with decorative elements of fastened-together palm leaves. These ornaments are called *jajaitan*, derived from the word *jait* (to sew), because the process resembles sewing together leaves with small bamboo slivers. Beautiful patterns are cut into the leaves and then they are assembled into circular, triangular, square, hourglass, fan, and fringed shapes. Different-colored flowers topped by finely shredded fragrant screwpine leaves along with a sprinkling of perfumed water complete the *canang* (fig. 6).

PROPER PRESENTATION

All of the ingredients for offerings must be properly presented in suitable containers. Young yellow-green and mature dark green coconut leaves, sugar palm leaves with green tops and pale undersides, and papery fan palm leaves left naturally pale or dyed in brilliant hues are cut and pinned together with thin bamboo pins to form fanciful shapes. These are often placed in decorative metal bowls, pedestals, baskets, and trays as bases upon which the food is arranged. Other palm leaf ornaments containing betel chew ingredients and flowers are placed on the very top. The overall form of most offerings is a conical shape, which is believed to represent the cosmic mountain Meru where the deities and ancestors dwell. Whatever the interpretation, it is a shape that evolves naturally when things are placed upon each other, and stability is an important consideration. Even when a soft banana tree stem is used as a vertical axis for inserting skewers attached to fruits and cakes, the basic conical form is maintained.

A small amount of money or *sesari* (*sari* = essence), depending on one's financial situation, is included in most offerings. The money is placed at the very top where it can be easily removed by a priest or temple attendant, who usually puts it into a large, locked box through a slot at the top. Worshipers may also spontaneously donate cash. Later, the box is opened and the contents counted, with amounts going to the priest who conducted the ceremony, to pay for the materials for the offerings, and to maintain the temple. If dancers, musicians, or puppeteers are performing, then some of this money may also be used to pay them (fig. 7).

Top: Fig 5. A girl puts together the simple *porosan*, which will be put in larger offerings. Bedahulu, Gianyar.

Bottom: Fig. 6. Women present *canang* and pray at a market temple. Pura Melanting, Ubud, Gianyar.

When offerings are carried to a ritual locale, they are covered with a decorative lid, piece of banana leaf, or even a sheet of paper for more informal events. Women carry offerings on their heads, and men carry offerings on their shoulders (fig. 8). During large temple ceremonies, the women of a *banjar*

(village neighborhood) wear uniform outfits and bring their families' offerings in a long procession with gamelan music (fig. 9). Inside a temple, offerings for the deities are placed on a raised platform or in a pavilion. Covers are removed, fragrant sticks of burning incense inserted, and then the offerings are ritually cleansed with holy water. Even the washing of fruits and flowers is not enough to remove spiritual impurities caused by someone stepping over a basket of fruits unloaded from a truck, or blossoms knocked off a tall tree onto the dirty ground. More sprinkling of holy water and libations accompany the priest's incantations; while he rings a small bell in the left hand, he uses his right hand to perform *ngayab* by gently wafting the essence of the offerings to the deities with a ritual implement or flower. For rites of passage, the invisible essence is wafted toward a person celebrating his or her *otonan* (210-day birthday) or toward a newlywed couple, who receive the essence with open palms of the hands facing the body (fig. 10). *Canang* offerings can also be held in the hands and offered by priests and worshipers before the shrines with an improvised or set dance called *pendet* or *gabor* when performed in pairs (fig. 11). These actions all carry the intangible essence of the food to invisible forces, so offerings can be used only once and must be newly created each time.

The physical leftovers of the offerings are consumed after worshipers pray with incense and flowers, receive sprinkles and sips of holy water, and press some *bija* (raw grains of rice

Left: Fig. 7. A *peras-daksina* (acknowledgment and payment) offering with strings of Chinese coins and a jar of holy water are presented for a performance of *wayang kulit* (leather puppets) at a temple. Pura Goa Gajah, Bedahulu, Gianyar.

Right: Fig. 8. Several *tegtegan* with pork, rice cakes, and fruits are carried by men on their shoulders and placed in a temple. Pura Sri, Jasan, Gianyar.

OFFERINGS: RITUAL REQUESTS, REDEMPTION, AND REWARDS 91

Top left: Fig. 9. Uniformly dressed women from one neighborhood bring tall *banten prani* (festive offerings) in a procession to a temple. Pura Samuan Tiga, Bedahulu, Gianyar.

Top right: Fig. 10. A mother helps her young son, who was born on an inauspicious day, to receive the essence of a *sorohan bebangkit* offering to ensure his health and well-being. Klungkung.

Bottom left: Fig. 11. Unwed women in elaborate costumes hold offerings while performing a group *pendet* dance at a temple. Pura Bale Agung, Asak, Karangasem.

Bottom right: Fig. 12. Temple assistants use *sampian* from their offerings as weapons for a ritual battle. Pura Samuan Tiga, Bedahulu, Gianyar.

soaked in water and usually colored yellow with turmeric) at the center of their foreheads, both sides of the forehead, and the throat before swallowing some as signs of life and thanks. (Nowadays most worshipers no longer place *bija* at the sides of their foreheads.)

At least half of a household's income is used for offerings, although most offerings are consumed as food after being presented. Offerings thus serve religious, physical, and economic purposes. Most families put aside enough money for offerings or begin saving for larger ceremonies. Many Balinese are involved in various aspects of the economy, such as farming, produce selling, and animal raising, so there is a constant flow of cash in the making of offerings. Offerings for the dead are meant for the deceased only and are burned during the cremation, although some parts of certain offerings may be eaten by the family as acknowledgment of their ties. The leaf and flower components are left at the temple or taken back home, where they may be placed on a wall near the gate as a sign of having prayed and presented an offering. In a few temples — Bedahulu, Pejeng, and Buruan in Gianyar — the coconut leaf ornaments (*sampian*) are used as weapons during ritual battles (fig. 12). After a ritual, leftovers from demon offerings are never eaten and are discarded as soon as possible by burial, burning, or being unceremoniously tossed into the nearest river. Very few modern landfills have been opened in Bali, and they are rapidly filling up with discarded offerings and other ritual paraphernalia, much of which is organic and could be properly composted into fertilizer.

POWER POINTS

Offerings are presented daily in Bali according to two different systems of time. The 210-day *pawukon* cycle, with concurrently running weeks of one to ten days, is unique to Java and Bali and probably originated in the growth cycle of indigenous rice from seeding to harvesting. This system has the most permutations of holy days every fifteen and thirty-five days, the latter of which is a *bulan* (month); over forty different combinations occur within a complete cycle, and most ceremonies happen at these times. Days called *tumpek* occur when the final days of the five- and seven-day periods coincide. On these days offerings are presented to specific things: during the weeks of Landep (to metal objects such as weapons, except for gamelan instruments, but including transportation vehicles and electronic gadgets), Wariga (to fruiting trees), Kuningan (to household and occupational tools), Krulut (to song birds and gamelan), Uye (to domesticated animals), and Wayang (to puppets and masks) (fig. 13). An important period for larger and more specific offerings occurs during Galungan in honor of deified ancestors, who visit their descendants for

Top: Fig 13. Offerings are presented to the sacred masks of the widow-witch Rangda and the protective lionlike Barong with a body of crow feathers. Bedahulu, Gianyar.

Bottom: Fig. 14. Worshipers sit on the sand with baskets and bowls of offerings for a *melasti* (purification at a source of water) on a beach. Lebih, Gianyar.

five days. The fifteen weeks before Kuningan are inward looking, with most ceremonies taking place in households; the following fifteen weeks are focused on public temple rituals and especially on trance ceremonies. The final day of the cycle honors Saraswati, the Hindu goddess of learning, knowledge, speech, and music; the first day of a new cycle is for purifying oneself with *banyu pinaruh* (water of knowledge). *Pawukon* cycles are not numbered like calendar years, however; they come and go endlessly.

The other system of time, which follows the lunar-solar cycle, is known as the Saka year and originated in India. This calendar is seventy-eight years behind the Common Era. The Saka New Year begins on the day after the new moon closest to the equinox in March, which is the tenth lunar month instead of the first. Each of the twelve lunar months is thirty days long, but every nine weeks one day is lost because the actual lunar cycle is slightly shorter. To make up for the difference between the 355 days of the lunar and 365 days of the solar cycles, an additional month is added every thirty lunar months for a leap year, which happens in 2011 or Saka 1933. Holy days occur only on the full moon and new moon, and again major temple ceremonies take place during these times. When *pawukon* holy days happen to coincide with those of the Saka calendar, which often happens, more offerings are made to cover both auspicious days at the same time.

Offerings are presented at specific places and times of the day. A place of power is where positive and negative elements connect, such as the threshold of a gate, bridge, crossroads, or a beach—transitional or meeting points of inner and outer, high and low, opposite directions, land and sea (fig. 14). These sites of convergence literally are like battle zones between opposing forces. Likewise, junctions of time, such as at sunrise, noon, and sunset, are dangerous and require offerings and prayers. It is common for offerings to demonic forces to be made at sunset outside household gates during the new moon of the particularly dangerous sixth lunar month, in December.

RITUAL RANKS

There are several levels of ritual, with increasingly elaborate offerings needed for more important ceremonies. Simple offerings are prepared by a family, but larger ones involve experts from within the community or even brought in from a priestly household. One of the first offerings made for any ceremony is called *jaja* or

Left: Fig 15. Yellow rice dough is shaped into *simbar madu* (honey fern) for the *suci* offering. Bedahulu, Gianyar.

Right: Fig. 16. A large *pula gembal* stands in a temple pavilion. Pura Alas Arum, Baha, Mengwi.

sanganan Saraswati, for the goddess Saraswati bestows the knowledge for making everything. A mixture of regular and glutinous rice flour is kneaded with water into a soft dough. It is then rolled, pinched, and shaped into small *cecak* (house lizards) with eyes of purple-black glutinous rice grains; the clicking voice of this reptile indicates the presence of Saraswati. Four of these creatures representing the four compass points are placed on a dough disk. This disk has a cap containing a small letter in black rice dough representing the sacred sound ONG, the Balinese equivalent of the more widely known Sanskrit OM, which roughly means "Hail." After the Saraswati offerings are finished, dozens of small rice-dough figures that comprise the *suci* (pure) offering come next. These figures are abstract representations of plants and animals, and geometric shapes in white and turmeric yellow for basic ceremonies; natural purple and red rice figures are added for larger rituals (fig. 15).

The next level of ceremony requires a *pula gembal* offering. Dozens of different-colored rice dough figures represent the ribcage, trees, birds, ocean, rainbow, plants, miniature offerings, people, and structures such as a rice granary and marketplace. They are skewered and placed vertically around three sides of a square made from banana tree layers, tied on a vertical frame, or arranged around the edge of a circular tray made of palm leaves. Figures are arranged according to colors of the directions in a square tray, but the east or north side, depending on how the offering is placed in the shrine, is left open for a bunch of bananas

OFFERINGS: RITUAL REQUESTS, REDEMPTION, AND REWARDS 95

Left: Fig 17. A *sorohan bebangkit guling* with roast suckling pig for a wedding includes many smaller offerings. Kamasan, Klungkung.

Right: Fig. 18. A *sambutan* (welcoming) offering for a child's birthday includes several rice cones and a special plaited rice container. Bedahulu, Gianyar.

and layers of rice biscuits. In the center are placed even more figures to fill the offering, which is crowned by palm leaf decorations (fig. 16).

Larger rituals, including purifications of buildings and cremation structures, demand a *bebangkit,* a wood or bamboo box with open top and bottom. The four vertical sides are covered with as many as thirty-three or more different rice dough figures representing such things as the sun and moon, mountain and sea, prosperity and frugality. They are placed on opposite sides corresponding to their cosmic directions: day and night are tied on the east and west, door and road on the north and south (fig. 17). The center of the box is filled with many corresponding *ketipat* figures that are steamed, empty, on top of the rice being cooked; this fills them with the essence of the steaming rice, and then a few cooked grains are stuffed inside each one. The top of the box may be crowned with a *sampian*.

Larger rituals at this ceremonial level also include a spit-roasted suckling pig or duck along with the rice offering, making this offering a combination of rice and meat. A couple of cylindrical *jerimpen* offerings, the sides covered with geometric rice-dough figures and topped by *sampian*, rise from small baskets and together represent legs. All of these often are arranged in a large platform with raised sides to include many other component parts of the offering.

The highest or fourth level of a ceremony is called *catur* (four) and includes large offerings of the same name, which have hundreds of single colored rice-dough figures of the major compass points and center made in dozens of different shapes and in quantities matching the numbers of the directions. All of the component parts including cloths, skeins of yarn, strings of perforated Chinese coins, and rice biscuits are placed in a large

round bamboo tray with the rim extended by palm leaves. Many other offerings are added to increase the overall complexity of this ritual level. This would be done for a rededication or major ritual purification of a temple.

Left: Fig. 19. Holy women at a temple assemble *sayut pengambean* (request to summon) offerings. Pura Samuan Tiga, Bedahulu, Gianyar.

Right: Fig. 20. An assortment of *ketipat* is made for a *sorohan bebangkit*. Bedahulu, Gianyar.

RICE REALM

If an invisible guest is especially esteemed or even feared, then a more substantial offering is necessary. In Balinese terms, this means fruits and snacks along with rice and accompanying side dishes of meat and vegetables for the most important visitors. Rice, staple food of the human and supernatural worlds, is therefore essential and is usually shaped into several forms such as the conical *tumpeng* to symbolize the cosmic mountain Meru where the deities and ancestors dwell (fig. 18). Two common offerings are called *ajuman* and *peras*. An *ajuman* offering consists of a pair of small, flattened rice mounds, two small triangular coconut leaf cups of spiced grated coconut with fried beans, a couple of pieces of rice biscuits and banana slices or fruits, a *canang*, and a fan-shaped *sampian* (offering ornament) of trimmed coconut leaves, containing a betel *porosan* and flower petals. The *peras*, a companion offering, includes small, pointed rice mounds rather than flat ones, two pieces of sugar cane instead of banana slices, a *canang*, an hourglass-shaped *sampian*, and a base made of five folded coconut leaves pinned together, the pleats of which are pulled out at the end of the ceremony. Teams of women form, cut, pin, shape, and put together the most numerous offerings, each person putting a specific component in its proper place as on an assembly line (fig. 19).

OFFERINGS: RITUAL REQUESTS, REDEMPTION, AND REWARDS

Rice can be cooked into a rather solid starchy mass in *ketipat* or *anaman*, a small enclosed packet plaited from young coconut leaves. These are ideal for taking to ceremonies located a great distance away and have over a hundred different shapes including geometric forms, astronomical bodies, birds, mammals, and musical instruments of the Balinese gamelan, such as gongs and metallophones (fig. 20). *Ketipat* have male and female shapes; the larger and fuller ones with an even number of points on them are usually identified as female, although sometimes the distinctions appear to be rather arbitrary. But as offerings maker Jero Made Sampreg from Bedahulu village in Gianyar once commented, "Well, it doesn't really matter which one is which, just as long as they're different, right?"

Rice, especially the glutinous or sticky kind, is mixed with grated coconut and palm sugar for making all kinds of *jaja* or *sanganan* (snacks); like humans, deities are fond of sweets. Whether fried, steamed, or baked, these are delicious, and their attractive colors and shapes have important symbolic functions in offerings. The natural colors of different kinds of rice are associated with Hindu deities and the cosmic directions that they inhabit. The Balinese believe that there once was natural yellow rice, but the bird bringing these seeds as a divine gift to humans was attacked by a demoness and the grains were lost. Every direction has a number, sound, and symbolic attribute of the presiding god, as indicated in the following table:

Direction	Deity	Number	Materials	Sacred Syllable	Attribute
East	the lord Iswara	5	white rice and flowers	SANG	*genta/bajra* (bell)
South	the creator god Brahma	9	red rice	BANG	*gada* (club)
West	the great god Mahadewa	7	yellow turmeric rice and flowers	TANG	*nagapasa* (serpent arrow)
North	the god of life Wisnu (Vishnu)	4	purple glutinous rice; purple or dark blue flowers	ANG	*cakra* (discus)
Center	the destroyer-reincarnater Siwa (Shiva)	8	all four colors of rice and flowers	ING and YANG	*padma* (lotus)

Larger ceremonies that include the intermediate directions use combinations of two adjacent colors with flowers and fruits placed according to the same color-direction scheme.

Direction	Deity	Number	Materials	Sound	Attribute
Southeast	the great lord Maheswara	2 or 8	pink flowers and fruits	NANG	*pasepan* (incense burner)
Southwest	the howler, Rudra	3	orange flowers and fruits	MANG	*moksala* (mace)
Northwest	the lord who bestows joy, Sangkara	1	cucumbers and green flowers and fruits	SING	*angkus* (flagstaff/ elephant goad)
Northeast	the benevolent god of joy, Sambu	6	mixed white and black rice, both colors of fruits, light blue flowers	WANG	*trisula* (trident)

ANIMAL ASSOCIATIONS

Offerings known as *caru* that include some kind of animal are placed on the ground to appease a dangerous or offending spirit in order to avoid harm. Such offerings are also given to remove ritual pollution that comes with the death of a member of the family or community. These offerings usually range from the sacrifice of selected chickens on the smallest and most common level, to large-scale ritual slaughter of a whole menagerie of animals on rare occasions. Included in this category are *tajen* (cockfights), for negative demonic forces take delight in the spilling of fresh blood in addition to the breaking of raw eggs and husked coconuts, and libations of locally brewed hard liquor; these are suitable food and drink for their rough and wild character. Blood is particularly enjoyed by demons, which explains why animal sacrifice is necessary. Spilling blood through three rounds of paired roosters is enough for demons, but humans need more to satisfy their addiction to gambling. While limited rounds of cockfights are necessary for these rituals, they can also become extended sessions that may lead to the loss of rice fields to pay for large debts incurred through addictive gambling. (fig. 21).

In some villages of Karangasem in East Bali, human blood is considered to be the ultimate self-sacrifice to demonic forces and is allowed to flow in small amounts by pairs of men in ritual battles using thorny screwpine (*Pandanus moschatus*) leaves, rattan wands, or by intentionally wounding one's own body with a *kris* (dagger) (fig. 22). However, uncontrolled bleeding that occurs during menstruation, up to forty-two days after giving birth, and from accidental injuries is viewed as ritually polluting, and persons

Top left: Fig. 21. Specially dressed men prepare their roosters for a ritual cockfight. Pura Hyang Tiba, Sakah, Gianyar.

Top right: Fig. 22. Bare-chested men draw blood from each other using thorny pandanus leaves during a ritual battle. Tenganan Dauh Tukad, Karangasem.

Above: Fig. 23. Men use large knives on wooden blocks to mince meat for a communal feast. Tenganan Pageringsingan, Karangasem.

Left: Fig. 24. A towering *sate tungguh* stands before shrines with *dangsil* (thunderbolt) offerings at a temple. Pura Samuan Tiga, Bedahulu, Gianyar.

in such conditions are not allowed to enter a holy place to pray or present offerings. Likewise, any death prevents community and family from carrying out any ritual activities.

Meat is complementary to rice, for together they represent plant and animal life, farming and hunting, female and male. The rhythmic sounds of large knives on wooden chopping blocks mincing meat and spices, and the grating of coconut flesh and vegetables, are ubiquitous at ceremonies (fig. 23). Pork is most common, although chicken and duck are also used for making *lawar* (minced meats, grated vegetables, and spices, usually eaten raw or partially cooked), which is placed on squares of banana leaves, pinned-together palm leaves, or parchment paper. Mincemeat is colored by mixing with the animal's fresh blood blanched edible leaves or green beans, chopped, boiled, and grated young papaya, or jackfruit mixed with coconut or colored with turmeric. All four are mixed together for the multicolored center of an offering. Great quantities are prepared for both the demonic and the human participants of the ritual.

Meat is also pounded into a paste with spices and molded onto skewers as small kebabs (*sate*) that are used in larger offerings. For more complex constructions, thick layers of white pork fat are cut and trimmed into delicate flowerlike forms adorned with bright red chili peppers; lacy stomach linings are stretched on bamboo frames into parasols and banners; intestines are inflated like long balloons and tied off in short sections resembling big beads to form necklaces (fig. 24). These, along with different kinds of *sate* and inner organs formed into symbolic attributes of the nine realms, plus the boiled head, feet, and tail of the pig, are inserted into a tall pole covered with a thick layer of dried *lalang* (elephant grass) to form a treelike shape. In October 1989, during a rededication of the important Pura Er Jeruk irrigation temple in Sukawati, Gianyar, the pork was replaced by freshwater shrimps, eels, and crabs from the rice fields, all skewered and cleverly arranged into the same tree shape with symbols of the directions (fig. 25).

The symbolism of colors is important for rituals. For demon offerings the color of the fur, feathers, or skin of the animal matches the associated direction as closely as possible; intact skins with feathers or fur are laid on the ground. Even the internal organs are associated with different directions, so those of the sacrificed animals are placed accordingly in the offering called *gelar sanga* (formation of nine) for the demonic aspects of the deities (fig. 26).

Top: Fig 25. Freshwater shrimps, crabs, eels, and catfish are assembled into a tree for an irrigation temple ceremony. The flowerlike shape is a lotus, which symbolizes the center. Pura Er Jeruk, Sukawati, Gianyar.

Bottom: Fig. 26. Colored rice circles of the nine directions and a *nasi wong-wongan* (human rice figure) with a *canang* are included in a demon appeasement offering. Denpasar.

OFFERINGS: RITUAL REQUESTS, REDEMPTION, AND REWARDS

Direction	Animal Offering	Internal Organ Offering
East	white-feathered goose	heart
Southeast	white duck with a dark band around its neck	lung
South	calf with red-brown fur	liver
Southwest	dog with brown fur and black paws	large intestine
West	goat with cream-colored fur	small intestine
Northwest	black goat	spleen
North	black pig	gall bladder
Northeast	duck with gray, black, and white feathers	diaphragm
Center	water buffalo	kidney
All Directions	chicken with red, black, and white feathers	

In very large *caru* sacrifices to the nine directions, nine different coconuts with skins close to the colors of the compass points each have matching colored yarn, with perforated Chinese coins strung between small bamboo spouts in the number associated with the direction. The coconuts are put in their proper places on the ground with the other offerings, and the water in them is shaken out through the openings during the peak of the ritual. (fig. 27).

Some offerings placed on the ground, called *segehan,* are made before a deity enters or leaves a temple, or when a couple about to be married or a family enters a house for the first time. In large ceremonies this includes breaking open a raw egg and cleaned coconut, their contents are sprinkled over small portions of cooked rice. A live chicken and duck are sacrificed, with the birds' blood dripped into open halves of a coconut and libations of alcoholic liquids onto the ground. The sacred images then are carried inside, or, alternatively, humans walk over the offering and enter the temple or house, in one of the few cases of offerings created to be stepped on. No specific thing needs to be tread upon, as long as some part of the offering is stepped over. For the Balinese, the feet are the lowest part of the body and thus unclean, but the *segehan* offering is meant to distract demons, which inhabit the lower realm. A larger version called *titi mamah* (swaying bridge) has a slaughtered goat or bull in it for deities to ride upon into a temple or specific shrine. Such offerings are distractions for any negative forces that were attached to the deities or humans (fig. 28).

Deities and demons are flip sides of the same coin; appeasing the negative aspect turns

it into positive energy, but offending the benevolent force transforms it into malevolence. In some large offerings, this is symbolically shown with flora and fauna taking on each other's characteristics: rice or fruits are formed into all kinds of living creatures, while animal flesh is transformed into floral arrangements (figs. 29, 30). This represents an important Balinese philosophical-religious concept known as *rwa bhineda*, complementary opposites that share something in common, their unity symbolic of completeness: male-female, light-dark, hot-cold, dry-wet, positive-negative.

BODY BUILDING

Some of the most complex offerings are made for a *pengabenan* or *palebon* (cremation). Not only must the body and soul be taken care of, but deities and demons of the underworld must also be given offerings to grant the soul's passage into their realm, and the family and community need to be protected from harmful forces. Even the towerlike *wadah* or *bade* (bier) and animal-shaped *patulangan* (sarcophagus) must be blessed and purified with major offerings before they can be used (fig. 31). All kinds of holy waters are obtained from every temple where the deceased was a member. Death shrouds with magical symbols, effigies, and other ritual artifacts are made by teams of specialists. Food and refreshments are served to anyone who assists, participates, or comes to pay respects.

Left: Fig. 27. Nine coconuts with bamboo spouts wound by colored yarns and Chinese coins are prepared for a major demon appeasement; a pale coconut on the left is east, with the other directions arrayed clockwise around the center. Bedahulu, Gianyar.

Right: Fig. 28. Boxes containing sacred relics are carried over a *segehan agung* (great distraction) before entering the inner courtyard of a temple. Pura Samuan Tiga, Bedahulu, Gianyar.

 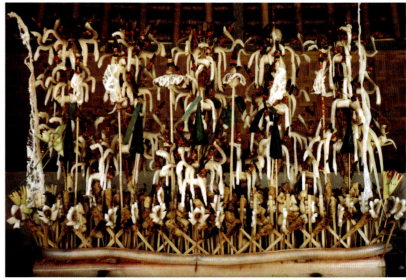

Left: Fig. 29. An enormous animal made of *salaran* (products of the earth) dominates the enclosure for a royal soul deification ceremony. Puri Kawan, Karangasem.

Right: Fig. 30. Pork skewers, fat, and entrails are lined up like puppets on a horizontal banana tree for a temple ceremony. Pura Kehen, Bangli.

Among the many offerings made for the soul is the *uriga*, which contains more than a hundred separate elements called *tetukon*. These specific natural and produced items not only represent, but are made in exchange for, different parts of the body because of their similar shapes, colors, or other qualities: two eggs are eyeballs, a flower bud the nose, a mangosteen the mouth, garlic cloves and kernels of corn the canines and molars, sugar cane stalks the arms, ten rolls of betel chew the fingers, a bunch of bananas the ribcage, a banana bud the heart, two bitter gourds the lungs, a solid mound of coconut sugar the liver, skeins of white and yellow threads the stomach, taro the large intestine, two cucumbers the legs, ten ginger knobs the toes, and strips of metal the skeleton. Many people search the village on a scavenger hunt to find these diverse objects, which cannot be substituted by other things. All of these items, along with leaves, flowers, sweets, incense burners, cloths, strings of perforated Chinese coins, and many other things, are put into a large round bamboo tray with an extended rim made of dried *lontar* leaves trimmed to look like ribs, which explains the name of the offering (*uriga* = behind the ribs). This is accompanied by a pair of smaller offerings called *pisang jati*, which represent the sensory organs and intangible aspects of the body, with a smaller number of similar objects in the *uriga*, such as rice porridge for speech and medicinal spices for the soul. These are placed in coconut leaf baskets with dozens of different *ketipat* hanging outside. All of these offerings are burned with the body, along with many other provisions for the soul on its journey to the netherworld (fig. 32).

COSMIC COOKIES

For elaborate ceremonies, complex offerings known as *sarad*, composed of dozens up to hundreds of different figures made from colored rice dough, are fixed to a vertical bamboo frame that can be several meters tall. The word *sarad* means cosmos, and the many individual figures and symbolic shapes represent the cosmos. Experts specialize in creating these enormous constructions, which take a week or more to create. There are many variations in shapes, colors, and sizes of *sarad*. Mass media and ease of transportation in Bali have led to these offerings being made in places where they never were used before; however, certain regional stylistic features have emerged. In Gianyar, the style tends toward more decorative elements with many floral figures and sculptures of deities, demons, or a newlywed couple, depending on the intended ritual (fig. 33). The Badung style has fewer figures, making the background more visible; contrastingly, in Klungkung the constructions are crowded with miniature scenes. Karangasem has a unique and distinctive type, with three-dimensional funnel-shaped *sarad* containing symbolic figures, and translucent rice cakes painted with *cili* (fertility figures) representing the Balinese rice goddess Dewi Sri (fig. 34). In very rare ceremonies in the mountain village of Sibetan, five to eleven such funnels are stacked upon each other to incredible heights (fig. 35).

In the Bangli region, the *sarad* has some of the most complex symbolic meanings. Its overall shape is based on the *kakayonan*, the Cosmic Tree of Life in *wayang kulit* (leather puppet) theater. While the etymology of *kakayonan* is commonly believed to derive from *kayu* (tree), a more learned and philosophical interpretation of the Balinese identifies the root as *hyun* (thought, desire, affection, will of the mind), from which comes the words *kahyun* (force of creativity and imagination) and *kayun* (right thoughts and desires to be creative and imaginative). These words may even be related to *ayu* (beautiful) and its affixed forms *kahayun* (beauty, happiness), *ayun* (development of skills), *ayunan* (swaying and shaking of the *kakayonan* at the start of a puppet performance, signaling creation; a wooden Ferris wheel representing the sun and the fertile union of heaven with the earth) and *payu* (accomplishment). All of these concepts apply to offerings (fig. 36).

The Balinese universe comprises upper, middle and lower worlds; these three realms are represented in the *sarad* from Bangli. The individual figures around the edge are called *ceracap* (jagged, pointed). The similar *cerapcap*, from the root *capcap* (to drip), describes "a waterline on the ground made by rain dripping from a roof." The next row of figures

Top: Fig 31. A *sorohan bebangkit* and a large *pula gembal* are used to purify a cremation tower. Abianbase, Mengwi.

Bottom: Fig. 32. An *uriga* and smaller *pisang jati* are bartered for the body of a deceased person. Camenggaon, Gianyar.

OFFERINGS: RITUAL REQUESTS, REDEMPTION, AND REWARDS   105

Top left: Fig. 33. Rice dough demons in the colors of the four directions stand at the base of a *sarad* for a temple. Pura Er Jeruk, Sukawati, Gianyar.

Top right: Fig. 34. A cornucopia-shaped *sarad* includes rice cakes painted with images of the rice goddess Dewi Sri at the top for a royal soul deification ritual. Puri Kawan, Karangasem.

Bottom right: Fig. 35. Towering *dangsil* (thunderbolts) dominate a temple during a rare ceremony. Pura Puseh, Sibetan, Karangasem.

Bottom left: Fig. 36. A *sarad* for a temple is full of cosmic symbols. Pura Kehen, Bangli.

on both sides contains the symbols of the four cardinal and four intermediate cosmic directions, represented by different divine weapons along with male and female attendants in specific colors. Crowning the *sarad* is a rainbow, below which is the supreme Hindu god of death and reincarnation, Siwa, who stands below a lotus with eight different-colored petals representing the eight directions converging in the center. Just below Siwa's feet is a tree of life that is flanked by Kama and Ratih, the god and goddess of love; nearby them are figures of the sun and moon, symbols of this divine pair who make the physical world possible. Beneath these is a *garuda* sunbird with two or four circular shield shapes at his sides, which symbolize protection of the offering against harmful forces, or chariot wheels that represent the solar disc and the journey of the Hindu sun god Surya in his daily chariot ride across the sky. A pair of birds of paradise hover close by, completing the upper divine realm.

The central figure in the *sarad* is the face of Boma, demonic son of the earth goddess Pertiwi when the god of life, Wisnu, in the form of a monstrous boar, sexually assaulted her while he was digging into the ground trying to find the base of an enormous *lingga* (phallic representation of Siwa). Boma represents natural and uncultivated fertility; his terrifying face with bulging eyes and fanged mouth is often carved above temple gates in order to prevent evil forces from entering the sacred inner courtyard. On the open palms of his outstretched hands are a *cakra* (discus) and *trisula* (trident), weapons that keep evil away. Boma occupies the middle world, earth.

In the underworld at the base of the *sarad* are the head and at the corners the four feet of Bedawang Nala, the fire-breathing cosmic tortoise who dwells at the bottom of the sea and supports the cosmic mountain Meru, and hence the whole universe, on its back, as represented by the *sarad* itself. She (for the tortoise is believed to be female) is entwined by two cosmic serpents: green Naga Basuki, who represents rivers and surface water, and red Naga Anantaboga, who symbolizes underground water and magma. The serpents keep the tortoise from moving; if they slip, Bedawang Nala shifts and causes earthquakes, with the appearance of Anantaboga as red-hot molten lava oozing from volcanoes in the world above.

Sometimes puppet-style figures in rice dough showing the *penasar* (clown servant-advisors) Twalen (or Malen) and Merdah as the protagonists on the right, and Delem and Sangut as the antagonists on the left, are placed near the base. Other mythological figures, such as the monkey general Hanoman and an ogre from the *Ramayana* epic, may also be included on a larger *sarad*. Miniature water buffalos and dogs stand on the wooden base of the frame. On the back of the *sarad*, which is generally not visible, any remaining rice dough figures along with seasonal fruits are casually tied, in marked contrast to the careful arrangements on the front.

Ornaments cut from young coconut leaves, especially ones shaped like long and spiky *paku pipit* (tiny ferns), are inserted at various places on the *sarad*. The edges are often decorated with fan-shaped cutouts made from dried *lontar* fan-palm leaves, a form identified as the headdress of Dewi Sri and the radiance of the rising sun that is associated with life and fertility. These may be replaced by pointed wooden shapes called *gigin barong* (teeth of the lionlike guardian) to provide protection from harm. In its entirety, the *sarad* illustrates that sunlight and water, two complementary elements in the *rwa bhineda* religious philosophy of Bali, are necessary for life in the universe, which includes male and female, upper and lower, positive and negative.

During closing rituals of ceremonies in Bangli, a *pemangku* (temple priest) brings to life the face of Boma with prayers and offerings. To the accompaniment of *gamelan* music and singing of *kidung* (sacred poems) at Pura Kehen, the terraced state temple of Bangli, the main priest, Jero Gede, takes the temple's sacred *kris* (dagger) named Betara Kawitan (God of Origins) from its shrine and unsheathes the blade. Holding burning incense sticks and the dagger above his head, he circles three times counterclockwise (the direction of death) around the Pelinggih Ibu Pertiwi, a shrine for the mother earth goddess, where the *sarad* stands. He advances toward the *sarad*, steps up on the raised base, and stabs Boma three times to ceremonially kill him, acting out the mythological story of Wisnu killing his son (fig. 37). If a sacred dagger is not available at other places, the officiating priest tosses three flowers at Boma instead, since the *Garuda* sunbird that Wisnu rides upon had to pluck out the magical flower that Boma wore in his hair as the secret of his power before Wisnu could decapitate him. This action with a dagger or flowers is called *nebek* (to stab, wound). The derivative *tatebek* (fixed time to begin planting in the rice fields) describes an important belief and practice. After the ritual death of Boma that closes the ceremony, the *sarad* figures are removed from the frame but are not eaten. Instead, they are buried in the rice fields of the village to ensure the continuing fertility of the earth, a symbolic act of sympathetic magic in which things taken from nature are returned to their source.

Fig. 37. The main temple priest uses a sacred dagger to symbolically kill the figure of Boma on a *sarad*. Pura Kehen, Bangli.

EXPERT EXPRESSIONS

In Bangli, Jero Made Renten is one of the most sought-after *tukang banten* (offerings expert) and especially as a *sarad* maker; she is even asked to go to other places on the island because of her skills. "I started when I was a young girl by copying the older women," she remembers. "I've been doing this for over thirty years now. I volunteer my skills for temples in the Bangli area, but also make *sarad* for ceremonies far away when others ask me to." Her husband, I Nyoman Sudirman, assists with kneading and rolling the rice dough, making some of the forms, carefully frying them so that they do not burn, and tying them onto the frames that he constructs. "The figures must be in their correct positions because the *sarad* has meaning," he says. "Every figure symbolizes something, so each piece has its place in the *sarad* and the universe" (fig. 38).

When told that most *sarad* makers use wooden carvings and even cut plywood forms as bases to mold their figures upon, Jero Made expressed surprise, shock, and even disgust. Her husband just laughed and shook his head, especially when he heard that these pieces are nailed onto the frames. The stiffness of the plywood causes the shrinking rice dough layer to crack and fall off in large pieces, leaving unsightly empty spaces in such *sarad*. For Jero Made and Sudirman, the rice dough figures must be structurally sound and not come apart. "I would never do something like that!" Jero Made commented. "The figures must only be made of rice dough, coloring, and oil; nothing else should be in these edible parts of the offering. Who would want to deep fry wood in oil anyway? That can't be eaten!" she exclaimed. It was not clear whether she was aware that poisonous chemicals such as formaldehyde are used to manufacture plywood.

In a widespread incident that affected many parts of Indonesia in October 1989, packets of inedible dyes were mistakenly labeled as edible food coloring that some people consumed, causing them to fall ill and even die. All coloring powders were removed from the markets and destroyed because there was no way of knowing which ones were safe, and subsequently for a brief period of time offerings were colored only with natural materials: turmeric, purple-black glutinous rice, red and brown rice, blue and red flowers, fresh leaves, ash from burned dried *lalang* (elephant grass), and brewed or powdered coffee. For about a month when commercial dyes of any kind were not available, rice dough offerings took on a beautiful, natural, and pastel appearance (fig. 39). Jero Nyoman Suli, an offerings expert from Bedahulu in Gianyar who was making rice dough figures then, commented that it did take more time and effort than using artificial dyes, but admitted that the colors were more harmonious and beautiful. She explained, "Of course it's absolutely forbidden to put poisonous things into offerings. The gods would get angry, and that would lead to dangerous consequences for us." Indeed, insecticide used to be sprayed onto huge *sate tungguh* or *gayah utuh* to keep flies away; now, only vinegar or *arak* (alcohol distilled from rice) can be used although the pork, fat, and pig parts do spoil very quickly after standing

Fig. 38. Jero Made Renten adds finishing touches to the rice dough face of Boma for a *sarad*. Bangli.

Top: Fig 39. Natural colors were used for this *pula gembal* when artificial dyes were not available. Pura Telangu, Bedahulu, Gianyar.

Bottom: Fig. 40. The Garuda Pancasila national symbol of Indonesia appears instead of a traditional-style bird in this *sarad*. Puri Saraswati, Semarapura, Klungkung.

for a day in the tropical heat. Edible food dyes continue to be used today and the incident of mislabeling seems to have been forgotten by most people.

Jero Made has also seen some enormous *sarad* that can be the height of a two-story structure, and she is very critical of them. "When a *sarad* gets that large, a lot of decorative figures without any meaning need to be added to fill up the big empty spaces, and they're not very beautiful because so many pieces have to be made by a lot of people with different levels of skills," she observes. "Those people are just trying to make things so big without knowing how to create them only of rice dough, so they need to have a structure of some sort in order to hold things together," she observed. "I take care to make my figures look as nice as possible but strong enough so that they do not break apart." She and her husband expressed surprise when told that the Indonesian coat-of-arms Garuda symbol sometimes appears on *sarad* instead of the more traditional form. "That's getting too political and should be separate from religion," Surdirman commented (fig. 40).

Sudirman agrees with his wife, saying that the making of huge *sarad* as well as large meat offerings is more about people competing against one another for personal glory than making an offering within their economic means as beautiful as possible for a ritual. "It's really a contest to see who can make the biggest and tallest offering without really understanding the symbolism," he comments. Today, many inexperienced people do not know how make rice dough figures, so they easily break apart. In addition to a lack of knowledge about making proper figures, this problem of breaking also results from inadequate amounts of more expensive glutinous rice flour in the dough, which acts as a natural adhesive. Some people keep the different elements of a rice dough figure together by inserting *semat* (small bamboo slivers), which are normally used to pin together leaves for offerings. In order to prevent poorly made rice dough figures from crumbling into pieces, they are put into small, clear plastic bags and then tied, stapled, or nailed onto the frames. However, many Balinese feel that this is incorrect, because they believe that the plastic bags prevent the purifying holy water from reaching the figures inside. Some Balinese even wonder if this kind of packaging may prevent the invisible essence from being consumed by the spirit for whom the offering is intended.

AESTHETICS AND ECONOMICS

Many variations in offerings occur across Bali, among Hindu communities on other islands of Indonesia, in districts, and even within a village. This is due to the hands-on tradition of learning how to make offerings, which is mostly done by females of all ages; meat offerings are handled by males, who also adhere to regional styles of ingredients and shaping of forms. A woman who marries into another village adopts the patterns that are used in her new place of residence, no matter how simple or complex they may be in comparison with what she knows. Designs are fashioned from memory, and from constant practice with a sharp paring knife rather than from precut or printed patterns with scissors. Ingredients depend on the fruits and flowers in season or what grows in the household garden, a convenient and freely available source. Of course, social-economic status plays an important role as in most situations in Bali, and wealthy families often purchase imported fruits along with fancy cakes from supermarkets and bakeries to use in offerings. Product name brand stickers, plastic or foam protective nets, Styrofoam trays, and clear plastic wrap are left on the items as status symbols, creating a different kind of aesthetic (fig. 41).

In spite of many guidelines, the Balinese are flexible enough to allow some space for individual creativity in the creation of offerings, as long as this does not stray too far from their specific symbolic meanings. There have been attempts in the past to simplify offerings or even standardize them in books and mass media, but the trend today seems to be going in the opposite direction, with increased complexity as religious ceremonies get larger and occur more frequently. Some offerings such as the tall bamboo poles (*penjor)* but without the accompanying *sanggah* (place for offerings) are used for official government functions. *Canang* appear as centerpieces on restaurant tables, but do not include the essential but inconspicuous betel chew ingredients and thus are considered to be decorations, although they resemble the real thing (fig. 42). Such offerings that have been secularized for ornamental use have been controversial. In 1997 an advertisement for the opening of a new golf course in Bali showed a golf ball in what looked like a *canang*. Local religious authorities and many Balinese were very offended by this degradation of an offering and took legal action. However, in court the promoters claimed that the *canang* that was used did not have a *porosan* in it, so it was not really an offering. This could not be proved since the actual *canang* in the advertisement was not available as evidence, although if it were presented before the court then the *porosan* could have been easily first extracted to support their allegation. In the end, the business was reprimanded and fined for misusing a religious symbol, and stricter rules governing these icons were mandated by the Hindu council. Another more common dilemma are *penjor* made for government functions and village competitions; these are often much better quality and more elaborate than those for religious events, in order to impress visiting officials, gain recognition, or win prizes.

Similar problems occur with *ogoh-ogoh*, large demonic figures made of wood, bamboo,

Left: Fig. 41. Fruits in their supermarket packages appear as status symbols in some *banten prani* (festive offerings). Bedahulu, Gianyar.

Right: Fig. 42. A restaurant table centerpiece resembles a *canang*. Ubud, Gianyar.

paper, and cloth to exorcise evil forces on the eve of Nyepi, the Balinese lunar-solar New Year. Although not offerings in the strictest sense, they do have a ritual function. They began to appear during the early 1980s, and were based on smaller figures that were used for other ceremonies and cremations in some areas of Bali. *Ogoh-ogoh* are carried throughout the streets in noisy, torchlit parades with *gamelan* marching music, and are then burned in the cemeteries after having served their purpose. Today many of the figures are not immediately destroyed, but rather displayed near the meeting halls of the community associations that made them; some of them have even been sold. In addition, increasingly complex figures require metal frames for support, and *ogoh-ogoh* are made for other events such as temple ceremonies, when they take on the form of gods and goddesses instead, or for secular government functions (fig. 43).

In 1991 during the first Gulf War against Iraq, an *ogoh-ogoh* in Denpasar was in the form of two skeletons riding a Scud ballistic missile, even as real ones were being launched by Iraq against Israel. This Balinese attempt at a creative response to an international crisis was heavily criticized, however, as not falling within the meaning of the ritual, which led local religious authorities to set guidelines for these figures. However, in the aftermath of the terrorist bombings of nightclubs in Kuta that killed more than two hundred people in October 2002, an *ogoh-ogoh* again in Denpasar in March 2003 featured the terrifying Balinese goddess of black magic, Rangda, trampling upon a human figure, labeled with the name of one of the main suspects, who had just been apprehended by special police investigators. This image, a modern interpretation of the Hindu goddess Durga subduing the buffalo demon Maesasura (Mahishasura), was not criticized because unlike the Gulf War, the tragedy took place in Bali with devastating consequences.

A growing number of young Balinese, many of whom are followers of strict vegetarian Hindu sects, do not include meat or eggs in their offerings. They are also questioning the increase in live animal sacrifices, especially after the terrorist bombings in 2002. An enormous ceremony held at the bombing site used hundreds of animals to dispel negative energies there, and after the 2004 earthquake and tsunami, many animals were sacrificed at sea to appease the destructive forces. Questions were raised about taking more innocent lives after the tragedies. Putu Semiada, a young Balinese political scientist, wrote in *Hello Bali* magazine (November 2002, page 12),

> From what I note, many Balinese believe that the Kuta blast has a relation to what happened in Klungkung, A giant turtle was found by the seashore in Klungkung several months ago [June 2002]. Usually when Balinese see something strange, they ask the priests first before taking any actions. Instead, they killed it. The question is why they didn't think that the turtle was a 'sign'. Why did they kill it? It was believed that the turtle was 'Ratu Pantai Selatan' (Lord of the South Sea) who was searching for two-hundred *panjaks* (devotees). Unfortunately, she was killed before she found the *panjaks*. Many people believed that she would take revenge. And as we can see around two-hundred people were killed during the bombings. Does it really have a connection? You never know.

Fig 43. An *ogoh-ogoh* of the monkey hero Hanoman (Hanuman) from the Ramayana epic rides a motorcycle while giving the finger. Bedahulu, Gianyar.

Balinese who have read ritual texts say that only the blood of animals needs to be spilled for sacrifices: their actual death is unnecessary. They have called for wounding animals and then releasing them. In 1990 a rare freshwater leatherback turtle, a live representation of the underworld tortoise Bedawang Nala, was symbolically sacrificed for a ritual at Pura Er Jeruk in Sukawati, Gianyar, and then put back into the stream where it was found. In 1996, tiger hairs and a small *ketipat* figure of the animal plaited from coconut leaves were used to symbolize the actual beast in a large demon appeasement at Pura Samuan Tiga in Bedahulu, Gianyar. But when asked why the same could not be done for the other animals, especially water buffalos and cattle, traditional village headman I Gusti Putu Tjenik merely replied, "We'd be embarrassed to do that and such animals are not rare anyway." In 2009, central authorities in Jakarta refused the Balinese government's request for a huge quota of endangered sea turtles to be sacrificed for ceremonial purposes. The number could not be justified and was seen as being mostly for commercial needs, and also threatened the existence of the animals. Yet some Balinese leaders regarded the decision as being insensitive to their religion and culture, even though a number of Brahman high priests have advocated using a drawing on cloth or a rice dough figure of a turtle as a substitute instead. In addition, numerous attempts by the government over the past decades to make cockfighting illegal have met with strong

Left: Fig 44. A motorcycle is protected with a *canang, ceniga* (small hanging) and pair of *ter* (arrows). Gianyar.

Right: Fig. 45. A market vendor sells all kinds of ritual necessities. Gianyar.

resistance from Balinese men, who seem to be more concerned with gambling than ritual. Such bans have proved difficult to enforce anyway, with clandestine matches occurring and law enforcement officials given another kind of offering to look the other way.

RITUAL REALITY

Balinese ceremonies are ways of communicating with the forces of the universe. The religious devotion of the Balinese captures the imagination of observers, because the sights, sounds, and smells of a ritual offer a total sensory experience. Most outsiders, however, do not see the preparations for ceremonies. For many Balinese, a ritual event often means having to find enough money and resources, even selling off the family's rice fields or getting themselves into huge debts to cover the costs of attending large ceremonies all over the island involving very long distances of travel. Hours of sitting and laboring over several days or even weeks can take a toll on health; consuming large quantities of sweets and meat may also lead to obesity, diabetes, heart disease, and stroke. The risks do not end there; physical exhaustion from lengthy ceremonies over long distances has led to inattention and resulted in traffic accidents. Palm leaf ornaments tied to trucks, cars, and motorcycles on Tumpek Landep, the holy day for metal objects, fly up against windshields and mirrors, which obstructs vision and may lead to accidents. (For obvious safety reasons, daily offerings made at petrol stations do not have burning incense put in them [fig. 44].)

Offering contests for the "most beautiful *banten*" have become so common, even for religious events, that village councils often limit the heights of *banten tegeh* (tall offerings)

to discourage showing off and spending more than a family can afford. Nevertheless, there is great pressure to compete even when a person's financial situation and status do not make it possible without creating other problems. After a ceremony there are piles of trash, including plastic bags for flowers and disposable drinking bottles, which are burned or thrown into the nearest stream. Small, clear plastic bags filled with holy water for taking home from temples are more efficient and convenient than bringing one's own containers for that purpose, but they do contribute to the ever growing problem of plastic waste. Very few visitors are aware of such great environmental problems created by increasingly elaborate religious events; most of them see only the beautiful processions, presentations, and performances.

Coconut leaves are in such high demand that truckloads of fronds from Java arrive every day in Bali, resulting in unsightly denuded trees. Although cheaper, the imported fronds tend to be thinner and shorter, and tend to wilt more quickly than locally grown leaves. The Balinese often complain about how difficult the leaves are to work with, but have no cheaper alternative or plentiful supply of better leaves.

These days, as more Balinese hold full-time jobs, they have less time to make their own offerings. As a result, commonly used offerings can be purchased ready-made at most marketplaces every day, and more complicated ones can be ordered in advance from a specialist (fig. 45; see also the preceding essay by Francine Brinkgreve). Some families even choose to purchase their offerings for large ceremonies held at home, because they find that this is more convenient and cheaper than having to feed relatives, visitors, and members of the *banjar* who would normally come over to help. They then do not need

Left: Fig. 46. Men cover carved wooden forms of *naga* with rice dough for a temple *sarad*. Pura Desa, Sayan, Gianyar.

Right: Fig. 47. Small pieces of natural and dyed palm leaves are stapled to create an intricate *sampian* on an offering. Bedahulu, Gianyar.

OFFERINGS: RITUAL REQUESTS, REDEMPTION, AND REWARDS 115

Fig. 48. Men scrape tree trunks with large knives for a temporary temple structure. Pura Samuan Tiga, Bedahulu, Gianyar.

to clean up the household compound several times a day over an extended period and deal with piles of trash. This trend has resulted in a booming business, with followers of other faiths participating purely for economic gain, but has led to criticism from some Balinese religious authorities. Men are making elaborate and enormous *sarad*, because many of them are traditional carvers or architects (fig. 46). Women have not yet become involved in making *sate tungguh*, however, since meat is still a ritual privilege reserved for males.

Artificial materials such as Styrofoam, metal staples, and plastic cord are frequently used these days (fig. 47). It is now common for a high-caste offering specialist to bring a stapler and a box of refills along with small knives to temples, which enables quicker assembling of more intricate trimmed leaves without tearing that often occurs when using bamboo slivers. During the Pancawalikrama (Ritual of Five Superiors) ceremony, which only occurs once a decade and was most recently held in March 2009, Balinese religious authorities forbade the use of plastic cord in the bamboo *penjor* but still allowed staples in the more essential *sampian* offering component hanging from the *penjor's* tip. Purists may disapprove of these trends, but they are signs of the times; it is better for this to take place, as with what happened with the ease of using artificial dyes instead of natural ingredients to color rice dough, than for offerings to dwindle in use or wind up in the hands of a few specialists.

Offerings can be works of art, but most of them are mass-produced and would probably not qualify as "art" in the modern Western definition of the word, since limited creativity or originality is involved where religious symbolism and ritual function need to be maintained. More important, however, is the Balinese concept of *ngayah*, which means volunteering one's time and skills as an expression of faith and community spirit for a religious event at a temple (fig. 48). Young and old, male and female all take part, refining their abilities or learning new ones; this is how traditional education occurs, through observation and repetition by working in a group led by an expert. Participants may not understand the actual meaning, and often the leader withholds the knowledge until the proper time comes. Sometimes the meaning will reveal itself through divine means. But whatever the case may be, the creation and presentation of offerings will always be important and integral to Balinese religion.

FRANCINE BRINKGREVE
W. O. J. NIEUWENKAMP AND HIS ROYAL LION OFFERING-BOX

This exhibition presents many palace treasures from South Bali, lent by museums in the Netherlands. These objects were collected after colonial conflict, including that against the kingdom of Klungkung in 1908, or collected by lovers of Balinese art and crafts, such as the painter W. O. J. Nieuwenkamp (1874–1950). One of the most outstanding objects is borrowed from the Department of Asiatic Art at the Rijksmuseum in Amsterdam, where it is on permanent loan from the Society of Friends of Asiatic Art (Vereniging van Vrienden der Aziatische Kunst). The object (cat. no. 26) is an ivory container collected by Nieuwenkamp, and probably originating from the palace of Klungkung, South Bali. The container or box is fashioned from a single piece of ivory, finely worked into the form of a winged lion (fig. 1).[1] A small four-sided lid has been carved out of the long mane that flows over the lion's back. The animal is 11 centimeters in height and 17 centimeters in length. It rests on a low base of painted wood. It probably dates to the nineteenth century.

In this article I will examine the collection history and provenance of this container: who originally owned this object, and how did it come to be in the Asian art collection of the Rijksmuseum? I will also discuss the function and significance of this artwork: how can we understand its use and symbolism, and to what degree is the container comparable with present-day forms of ritual art in Bali?

ART COLLECTOR W. O. J. NIEUWENKAMP

In 1925 Wijnand Otto Jan Nieuwenkamp (fig. 2), the famous "artistic centipede" (*artistieke duizendpoot*, multitalented or many-sided) as he was known, travelled to Bali. It was in fact his fourth trip to this Indonesian island, which he had first come to know in 1904 and to which he remained extraordinarily attached throughout the rest of his life. As an artist with multiple talents, he had a unique eye for the cultural richness of Bali, and he appreciated the fine craftsmanship with which so many objects were made. During his first trip he began to collect, both for his own collection but also on commission from museums. In the foreword to the book *Bali en Lombok*, which Nieuwenkamp illustrated and published, G. P. Rouffaer, the preeminent scholar of Indonesian arts and crafts, praised in lyric terms both the quality of the objects that Nieuwenkamp had collected and Nieuwenkamp's own art.[2]

This essay is an extended version of Francine Brinkgreve's "W. O. J. Nieuwenkamp en zijn vorstelijke leeuwendoosje," Aziatische kunst 36, no. 3 (September 2006), 2–15.

Thanks to: Cary Venselaar of the Stichting Museum Nieuwenkamp for permission to use unpublished material of W. O. J. Nieuwenkamp; to the National Museum of Ethnology in Leiden and the Museum Nasional Indonesia in Jakarta for photographs of objects from their collections; and to Dr Hedi Hinzler, Pauline Lunsingh Scheurleer, and Dr. David Stuart-Fox for additional material and comments on an earlier version of this article. Translations from the Dutch were done by David Stuart-Fox and Francine Brinkgreve.

1 See also Pauline Lunsingh Scheurleer (ed.), *Asiatic Art in the Rijksmuseum, Amsterdam* (Amsterdam: Meulenhoff/Landshoff, 1985), 189, and "Tentoonstelling van de Vereeniging "Oost en West" van de verzameling W. O. J. Nieuwenkamp in het Stedelijk Museum te Amsterdam," *Nederlandsch-Indië Oud en Nieuw* 11 (1926/1927), 347–352.

2 W. O. J. Nieuwenkamp, *Bali en Lombok* (Edam: De Zwerver, 1906–1910), I–VII.

Left: Fig. 1. Cat. no. 26, offering-box in the form of a winged lion. *Collection Rijksmuseum, Amsterdam.*

Right: Fig. 2. Portrait of W. O. J. Nieuwenkamp, by Nico Jungmann, 1909. *Photo Stichting Museum Nieuwenkamp.*

Just as Nieuwenkamp had during earlier trips, during his 1925 journey he sketched and drew endlessly, he collected art objects, and he made copious notes in his diaries, which he later reworked into articles and travel accounts. These diaries reveal not only the enormous interest and admiration Nieuwenkamp had for the art and culture of Bali, but also the manner in which he formed his collections. The quotations that follow are from these unpublished travel diaries, kindly made available to me by the Stichting Museum Nieuwenkamp in Edam. On June 6, 1925, Nieuwenkamp arrived in Klungkung from North Bali:

DAY TRAVELERS AND A CURIO MARKET

The hostel (*pasanggrahan*) was full of day travelers, tourists from the K.P.M. [Koninklijke Paketvaart Maatschappij, the Dutch shipping line] making use of the place for lunch, and on whose forecourt numerous sellers had their wares on display, spread out on the ground, all sorts of knick-knacks, mostly new things, especially for foreigners. The tourists left around 3 [p.m.], in many cars; the sellers also vanished from the scene. Only I remained behind as guest of the hostel [...] It was located near the remains of the demolished palace of the last Dewa Agoeng, opposite the controleur's residence.

MY COLLECTION INCREASES IN SIZE

[…] It was not long before the forecourt was again full of textiles, basketry, woodcarving, copper and silver wares, *kris,* a bit of everything; mostly new things, made for tourists. But tourists were not present this day and I was the only person at the market. Quickly I discovered that among all that new stuff there were some attractive older Balinese pieces to be found […] I have great admiration for these simple agriculturalists who are such capable artists and craftsmen. […]

A BEAUTIFUL IVORY OFFERING-BOX

The most beautiful acquisition is a valuable ivory offering-box, in the form of a winged lion or *singa,* a very rare piece, of which there are but few to be found on Bali. According to tradition, on great festive occasions, it was in this box that the king—the Dewa Agoeng—of Klungkung brought his offerings, consisting of gold coins, to the Poera Bale Agoeng.

STILL MORE IMPORTANT ACQUISITIONS

The rumor that a Dutchman was now staying at the hostel, who bought all sorts of things, provided they were old, spread quickly through the village, and today in the forecourt it is busier than yesterday with sellers hopefully spreading out their wares in front of them on the gravel.[3]

Nieuwenkamp was persuaded to make further purchases, but he could rightly be proud of his "most beautiful acquisition," indeed a rare piece. He kept it for almost ten years in his own collection, until in November 1934 he sold it for 300 guilders to the Society of Friends of Asiatic Art in Amsterdam. In the meantime he had published the object in one of his books,[4] and it had been exhibited in several exhibitions of Indonesian art.[5] This piece, together with a similar box, also depicting a lion but made entirely of wood, is illustrated in the book that Nieuwenkamp wrote about his Florentine villa, which he bought in 1926 and where he displayed many of the treasures from his collection.[6]

PALACE TREASURES FROM KLUNGKUNG

The Balinese seller of the box had told Nieuwenkamp that the former king of Klungkung, the Dewa Agung, had previously owned the piece. Specific proof of this is lacking, but considering the value of the material and the refined workmanship of its ornamentation,

[3] These quotes were taken from Nieuwenkamp's handwritten diaries, in the possession of the Stichting Museum Nieuwenkamp.

[4] W. O. J. Nieuwenkamp, *Inlandse Kunst in Nederlandsch Oost Indië, II Beeldhouwkunst van Bali* ('s-Gravenhage: Leopold, 1928), 11, pl. 34.

[5] See Tentoonstelling van de Vereeniging "'Oost en West' van de verzameling W.O.J. Nieuwenkamp in het Stedelijk Museum te Amsterdam," *Nederlandsch-Indië Oud en Nieuw,* 11 (1926-27), 347–352 and "Recente tentoonstellingen van Indonesische Kunst te Amsterdam, Parijs, Hagen en München," *Nederlandsch-Indië Oud en Nieuw,* 13 (1928–29), 125–128.

[6] W. O. J. Nieuwenkamp, *Een florentijnsche villa* ('s-Gravenhage: Leopold, 1938), 44. This was an illustration of one of the vitrines in the exhibition "Indonesische Kunst, Sammlung Nieuwenkamp" in Westfalen, 1928 ("Recente tentoonstellingen van Indonesische kunst te Amsterdam, Parijs, Hagen en Munchen," *Nederlandsch Indië Oud en Nieuw* 13 [1928–1929], 125–128).

it is indeed very likely that the ivory box was part of the palace collection of Klungkung before the Dutch conquered the kingdom in April 1908. This battle led to the death of the king and his family in a dramatic "fight to the finish" (*puputan;* derived from the Balinese *puput,* meaning "end," the word describes a final suicidal attack by a ruler in the face of overwhelming odds, bringing virtually certain defeat and death), and the total destruction of the palace. Although Nieuwenkamp was not in Bali at that time, in 1909 he wrote about this event in his book *Bali en Lombok*:[7]

> A brief word over the demise of this once powerful kingdom of Klungkung. [...] Shortly after the introduction of the opium monopoly throughout Bali, Klungkung rebelled. [...] 17 April 1908. Our force was too small (just 200 men) to be able to attack Klungklung and retreated to Lebih. The warships came quickly into action again and salvos of shells were again fired inland. [...] But it did not lead to any fighting. On 29 April,[8] with the arrival in the meantime of troop reinforcements, and after the capital was again thoroughly bombarded, our force advanced towards Gelgel and then toward the palace in the capital. And again the tragic events of Den-Pasar and Pemetjoetan repeated themselves; the Dewa Agoeng also, realizing that his rule was coming to a definite end, decided upon a *puputan*. He and his faithful followers, and many women and children, let themselves be riddled by our bullets; also his son, whom I had met on a previous occasion, and the Tjokorda of Gelgel were killed. [...] The capital was occupied without further resistance and therewith the kingdom of Klungkung ceased to exist.

After the *puputan* some 500 valuable objects were seized. They were first examined on the spot by Assistant Resident H. J. E. F. Schwartz, and later sent to Batavia, where a special commission of the Batavian Society of Arts and Sciences (Bataviaasch Genootschap van Kunsten en Wetenschappen) was given the task of dividing them among various museums. The Rijks Ethnograpisch Museum (the present National Museum of Ethnology) in Leiden, which had expressed an interest in a portion of these valuable objects, received 133 pieces, while the Museum of the Batavian Society retained 157 of them.[9] The remaining objects were sent to other ethnographic museums in the Netherlands, such as those in Rotterdam and Breda.

Among the treasures were objects that had functions in Balinese rituals. There were golden offering bowls, a silver holy water vessel, and silver lamps used by priests in carrying out their rituals. According to Schwartz, who in 1915 became assistant curator at the Museum of the Batavian Society, a number of statues fashioned from Chinese coins originated from the royal ancestor temple located within the palace walls. It is possible

---

[7] W. O. J. Nieuwenkamp, *Bali en Lombok* (Edam: De Zwerver, 1906–1910), 203.

[8] Nieuwenkamp made a mistake here, since the *puputan* was on April 28, 1908.

[9] See also Francine Brinkgreve, "Balinese Rulers and Colonial Rule," in ed. Endang Sri Hardiati and Pieter ter Keurs, *Indonesia: The Discovery of the Past* (Amsterdam: KIT Publishers, 2005), 122–146.

that the ivory box, which tradition claimed was used in rituals, was likewise an item in the collection of temple treasures. In any case it is known that crafting of precious ivory (*danta*) objects, such as ceremonial dagger (*kris*) hilts and parts of sheaths, was one of the court arts that flourished in Klungkung before the colonial period.[10]

But how did this box escape Schwartz's attention so that it was not included among the treasures sent by the Dutch authorities to Batavia? We will never know for certain, but it is possible that someone Balinese took the box from the palace before Dutch forces had full control over the site and its environs. A correspondent from the newspaper *De Locomotief* wrote to his editor on May 1, 1908: "When on the day after the *puputan* I visited the royal residence it presented a sad sight of fallen greatness. [...] Everywhere in the palace stood sentries to prevent looting, a measure that was very necessary."[11]

Two years earlier, on September 20, 1906, Nieuwenkamp had seen with his own eyes similar pillage and plunder by the Balinese population when the palace of Denpasar (capital of the kingdom of Badung) was defeated by the Dutch, following another a suicidal *puputan* by its reigning king (see cat. nos. 45 and 57). At that time the artist could collect little himself, since according to colonial law the spoils belonged to the Dutch authorities, but he did observe that, right under the eyes of the officers, the Balinese themselves took away many treasures from the palace. Something similar could have happened with the ivory box prior to its being offered for sale seventeen years later to Nieuwenkamp. On the other hand, the seller may also have fabricated the account of its royal provenance in order to increase the value of the object. What is certain is that the costly material and fine craftsmanship of the carving of this rare object make it something fitting for a palace. The use of ivory is especially unusual, for this material was mostly used only for smaller *kris* hilts.[12]

THE LION AS OFFERING-BOX

Another function attributed to this box is its use by the king as a container for carrying golden coins at temple rituals, specifically at the Pura Bale Agung temple in Klungkung, located at the center of the town. This account of golden coins as offerings is perhaps just another sales story, but it is well known that Balinese royal houses prior to Dutch subjugation had large amounts of coins at their disposal. The descriptions of the war booty from Lombok, Badung, and Klungkung mention thousands of gold and silver coins, along with jewelry and other valuables. According to eyewitnesses at the *puputan* of Badung, women from the palace of Denpasar threw handfuls of golden coins at the feet of the Dutch soldiers, offered as payment for the soldiers to kill them.

---

10 Tjokorde Gdé Rake Soekawati, "Nijverheid en kunstnijverheid op Bali," *Mededeelingen van de Kirtya Liefrinck-van der Tuuk* 15 (1941), 34.

11 Quote from an article in the Dutch newspaper *De Locomotief* by an unnamed correspondent.

12 For example, RMV inv. 214-7, published in Hans-Werner Hegemann, *Schnitzkunst und Plastik aus Indonesien aus dem Reichsmuseum für Völkerkunde, Leiden, Holland* (Erbach/Odenwald: Deutschen Elfenbeinmuseum, 1977). See also J. A. Loebèr Jr., *Been-, hoorn- en schildpadbewerking en het vlechtwerk in Nederlandsch-Indië.* (Amsterdam: Koloniaal Instituut, 1916). The prince of Gianyar owns a richly worked elephant tusk, illustrated in Leonard Lueras, *Fire: A Balinese Journey of the Soul* (Gianyar, 1994), 63.

Fig. 3. Statue of a winged lion at a ritual in Pura Segara, Sanur (Denpasar), 2006. *Photo Francine Brinkgreve.*

Whether or not golden offering coins were carried in the box, boxes in the shape of animals are still used in Bali for religious rituals. I observed this recently during a short visit to Sanur, South Bali. It was a full moon, and a temple festival was held at Pura Segara, near the beach. The temple was beautifully decorated, for the gods of the temple were visiting, and had descended into small gold statues. Known as *arca, arca lingga,* or *pratima,* these serve as temporary receptacles for the temple gods during festivals. They stood in a high open pavilion, affixed to the boxes where they were kept during the rest of the year; these were decorated with colorful textiles and many flowers. Next to them but somewhat lower was a red-winged lion with round eyes and sharp canine teeth, a rose-colored shawl around its neck, and golden flowers on its head (fig. 3) On its back it carried a *banten canang*, a small offering. According to the *pemangku,* or temple priest, this lion is a *palinggih Ida Batara,* a seat for a deity. It belongs with the statues of the gods of this temple, who look after it as their pet. In return, the winged lion takes care of the gods' transportation and protects them. Most temples in Sanur have their own animals to carry the gods. In one of these temples, when gods from other temples were paying a visit for a festival, I saw fantastic creatures — a winged deer, a winged bull, and an animal with the body of a fish, wings, and the head of a goose (fig. 4). They were all finely decorated and carried small offerings on their backs, the *banten canang* among them. Some of the worshipers present called these animals *pacanangan*.

The word *canang* means both "betel quid" and also "the small offering of which betel quid is the most essential element." To present a betel quid, a mild stimulant, especially in earlier times in Bali (and in other parts of Indonesia), was considered a mark of hospitality and the affirmation of relationship, particularly in ritual contexts. The betel quid consists of the leaf of the betel vine (*Piper betle*), the nut of the areca palm (*Areca catechu*), and a little lime. To this might be added some tobacco and *gambir*, a plant extract (*Uncaria gambir*).

A betel box with compartments for the various ingredients of the betel quid is in Bali, besides other terms, also called a *pacanangan* (in Indonesian, *penginangan* or *kinangan*). In the National Museum of Ethnology in Leiden is a painted wooden betel box from Lombok in the form of a crowned lion, which according to its collector,

13 Finely worked betel sets, wherein all the containers and utensils connected with the ingredients of the betel quid are placed together on an often gold, oval-shaped vessel on a stand (*lelancang*), are among a ruler's possessions kept always in his vicinity. Sometimes they even had special names, and were numbered among the family's heirloom possessions, *pusaka*. In the last known photograph of the king of Klungkung, taken shortly before the *puputan* in April 1908, next to him on the ground is Cokorda Putu Plodot with the betel set called I Kawotan (Margaret J. Wiener, *Visible and Invisible Realms: Power, Magic and Colonial Conquest in Bali* [Chicago: University of Chicago Press, 1995], 319). Among the objects looted following the *puputan* are two beautiful *lelancang* (e.g. MNI 14830/ E 749) and other utensils from betel sets, such as a *kacip*, with beautiful gold-inlaid blade to chop the nuts of the areca palm. See Francine Brinkgreve, "Balinese Rulers and Colonial Rule," in ed. Endang Sri Hardiati and Pieter ter Keurs, *Indonesia: The Discovery of the Past* (Amsterdam: KIT Publishers, 2005), 138–139.

J. P. Kleiweg de Zwaan, is called *penginang*, the Sasak equivalent of the Balinese *pacananган*. This box has a movable lid on its back, covering a space divided into two compartments, which probably were intended for the ingredients, though possibly for the betel quid itself (fig. 5).[13]

These Balinese animal carvings, though used in temple rituals and sometimes called *pacanangan*, have more to do with the *canang* as offering than with the separate ingredients of the betel quid. The *banten canang* is one of the commonest offerings on Bali, the only island in Indonesia with a predominantly Hindu population.[14] Not only is the offering of betel important; the color combination of the offering's ingredients is also significant. The green color of the betel leaf is associated with the god Wisnu, the red of the areca nut with Brahma, and the white of the lime with Siwa.[15] Besides an offering, the *banten canang* is also a manifestation or representation of the gods, a sign of the gods' presence. A *pedanda*, or Brahman priest, explained that the animal figures could be called *pacanangan* because the *canang* offerings on their backs during times of ritual indicate the presence of the gods. The function of the animals as attendants, vehicles, or seats of the gods is thereby affirmed.

ANIMALS AS BEARERS

In the Museum Bali in Denpasar, a great variety of ritual wooden animal figures is displayed. Some have statues on their backs, others just a removable lid, still others solid backs, with

Left: Fig. 4. Statue of a winged creature in Pura Segara, Sanur (Denpasar), 2006. *Photo Francine Brinkgreve.*

Right: Fig. 5. Betel box in the form of a lion from Sewela, Lombok. Collection National Museum of Ethnology, inv. no. 2407-405. *Photo Ben Grishaaver.*

14 Every day and everywhere on Bali, offerings are made to deities, ancestors, and demons, to maintain the proper relationships between the visible (*sekala*) and invisible (*niskala*) worlds. In Bali there exist hundreds of different kinds of offerings, whose names, forms, and ingredients vary by region and sometimes even by village, but the *banten canang*, as one of the basic offerings, appears everywhere. It consists of a small palm leaf container that holds a little food in the form of rice, small pieces of banana and sugarcane, and rice cakes. On top are placed flowers of different colors and a betel quid, from which the name of the offering is derived. See Francine Brinkgreve and David Stuart-Fox, *Offerings: The Ritual Art of Bali* (Sanur: Image Network Indonesia, 1992).

15 Ny. I. Gst. Ag. Mas Putra, *Upakara Yadnya* (Denpasar, 1982), 19.

Left: Fig. 6. Animal vehicles of the gods are carried to visit a temple on its festival day. Pura Agung, Sanur (Denpasar), 1982. *Photo Francine Brinkgreve.*

Right: Fig. 7. A god figure on top of his animal vehicle. Padang Galak (Denpasar), 1977. *Photo David Stuart-Fox.*

16 Museum Bali, *Pameran patung singa koleksi Museum Bali* (Denpasar: Museum Bali, 1978). The inv. nos. 195, 1084, and 2381 are called *pacanangan singa*.

17 The Museum Nasional Indonesia in Jakarta has a similar lion, inv. no. 24068. A. N. J. Th. à Th. van der Hoop, "De ethnografische verzameling," *Jaarboek Koninklijk Bataviaasch Genootschap van Kunsten en Wetenschappen* 8 (1941), 185, in translation: "Woodcarving, depicting a winged lion with flaming mane and tail; standing loose on its back are two small god figures [...], bought in 1940 from the liquidated art business of the Neuhaus brothers of Sanur, South Bali."

18 Compare P. J. Zoetmulder (with S. O. Robson), *Old Javanese-English dictionary* ('s-Gravenhage: Nijhoff, 1982), 1319: "*patarana* = (ceremonial) cushion or mat to sit on."

or without a space for affixing god figures. Although in a catalogue of representations of the lion in Balinese carving these figures were called *pacanangan*,[16] the present labels call them *palinggih*, "seat," or in Indonesian *kendaraan dewa*, "vehicle of the gods." The figure most similar to the Klungkung box is a red wooden lion (no. 1081) with similar bent forelegs, and with a square lid in its back. The label calls it a *pelinggihan singa* (lion).[17] The Brahman priest with whom I discussed these figures described it also as a seat for the god, but used yet another term, *patarana*.[18] Usually these kinds of figures are carried on the head in ritual processions and are placed next to the god figures during rituals (figs. 6, 7, 8). In other cases the god statues are placed on the backs of the animal figures. The National Museum of Ethnology in Leiden has in its possession a beautiful winged lion figure, with the two god statues fitted into a kind of saddle that can be placed on the animal's back (fig. 9). Originating from the same collector is another winged animal, a crowned serpent or *naga*, with two wooden statues of deities fastened into holes on its back (inv. no. 2407-9), like cat. no. 28. In some cases the animal figure itself is considered the representation of a deity, where godlike power can manifest itself. In Kerambitan, West Bali, similar kinds of boxes carried in processions together with the gods are called *ampilan*.[19] Here the boxes, when in use, are filled with the many various ingredients that one finds also in offerings, reinforcing their spiritual essence. These kinds of figures are regarded as symbolic bearers of the gods, or as their attendants.

As bearers of the gods, the function of these animal figures is comparable to that of

Left: Fig. 8. An animal vehicle next to a god figure in Pura Mertasari, Sanur (Denpasar), 2006. *Photo Francine Brinkgreve.*

Right: Fig. 9. A pair of deity figures on top of their animal mount. *Collection National Museum of Ethnology, inv.no. 2407-1.*

other animals that function as vehicles. In classical Hindu mythology in India, and also in its Balinese form, the most important gods have specific vehicles or mounts, *wahana*. The best-known examples are the bull Nandi, Siwa's mount; the eagle Garuda for Wisnu; and the goose Angsa for Brahma. Although these animals are first and foremost vehicles for their divine masters (and also iconographic clues to their identification), they are also animals whose function as bearers is predominantly supportive in nature, providing stability. Indeed, the tortoise Bedawangnala supports nothing less than the whole cosmos on his back. Furthermore, the ritual art of Bali employs a range of winged animals, which often show a combination of characteristics of different animals but which do not have a direct mythic background.[20]

Animals as bearers play all manner of roles in Balinese ritual art. The god statues that are borne by animals are carried on their backs in the same way that the gods are carried in the mythic tales. During a cremation ritual the body of the deceased is cremated in a *patulangan*, a sarcophagus in the form of an animal, whereby the soul is released. Here also the animal has a carrying function, not on the back but in the belly. Ttwo animal boxes in the Museum für Völkerkunde in Berlin, collected by C. M. Pleyte in 1901, are registered as models for cremation sarcophagi, not as offering boxes. Here it is striking that the wooden box with inventory number IC 31825, with regard to its form, is similar to the ivory lion, the materials being the sole difference between the two objects.

A Balinese family of my acquaintance has in its possession a wooden lion perceived as

19 Pers. comm. Hedi Hinzler. In Bali it happens often that an object has different names in different regions. Compare Th. Pigeaud, *Javaans-Nederlands handwoordenboek* (Groningen, Batavia, 1938), 8: "Ampilan = waardigheidstekenen (met iemand meegedragen; insignia/regalia (when carried with someone)." In the Central Javanese royal courts, this is the name of the state or royal insignia of the sultan, which accompany him during royal processions. See I. Groneman, *In den kedaton te Jogjakarta; oepatjara, ampilan en toneeldansen* (Leiden, 1888), 44–46 and K. P. Hadiwidjoyo, "De Rijkssieraden van het Mangkoenagaransche vorstenhuis," *Djawa* 4 (1924), 10–12.

Left: Fig. 10. Right: Fig. 11. Wooden *singa* as container for the clan chronicle (*prasasti*) of a family in Sanur (Denpasar), 2010. *Photos Francine Brinkgreve.*

both box and bearer. In it is kept the *prasasti*, or charter, of the family, a text on *lontar* leaves relating that the family is ultimately descended from the royal house of Klungkung (figs. 10 and 11). For this reason this lion, besides being a container, is at the same time considered a seat for the divine ancestors.

Particularly interesting are three silver animals in the collection of the Museum Nasional Indonesia: a crowned serpent, a bird, and a small duck, each with a lid on its back. They belonged to the state treasures of the former Sultanate of Banjarmasin in Kalimantan, which in 1865 were confiscated by the Dutch government and placed in the Museum of the Batavian Society (the present-day Museum Nasional Indonesia). They closely resemble the regalia, the *upacara*, of the Sultan of Yogyakarta. These regalia consist of five golden animals (but no lion), the majority with lids on their backs, each of which represents an aspect of the character of the sultan as representative of the divine authority on earth. These *pusaka,* or sacred heirlooms, originate from the royal ancestors.[21]

All these animals carry, on their backs, or in their bellies, or just symbolically, something that is in contact with the divine higher world. As animal bearer or mediator, they create a connection between this higher world and the human world, and during rituals they even represent the divine itself. The fact that many of the wooden animal figures have wings indicates their ability to carry the deities efficiently from heaven to earth and back through the sky. With wings, they can also better overcome obstacles.

20 An example is the beautiful golden tobacco container (also from the palace of Klungkung) in the collection of the Museum Nasional Indonesia (inv. 14837 / E 786) that was exhibited in the Nieuwe Kerk. It has the body of a fish, legs and wings of a bird, and a forbidding monster head with bulging eyes, sharp protruding fangs, and extended tongue. See Francine Brinkgreve, "Balinese Rulers and Colonial Rule," in ed. Endang Sri Hardiati and Pieter ter Keurs, *Indonesia: The Discovery of the Past* (Amsterdam: KIT Publishers, 2005), 138.

21 I. Groneman, *In den kedaton te Jogjakarta; oepatjara, ampilan en toneeldansen* (Leiden: Brill, 1888), 40–41. The Central Javanese courts, the Balinese kingdoms, and the Sultanate of Banjarmasin have a common historical background in the fourteenth-century Hindu-Buddhist kingdom of Majapahit.

THE LION

The lion is called *singa* in Bali. The *singa* often, but not always, has wings. A winged *singa* is called *singa ambara* or *singambara*, from the word *ambara,* meaning "sky." In Balinese art, he can be depicted in various postures: standing with all four legs on the ground, standing on the hind legs with raised forefeet, sitting on the haunches with both forefeet (or just one) stretched out in front, or, as with the Nieuwenkamp ivory lion, half-lying with the belly almost on the ground and with curled tail, the head held high with expectation, the ears laid back, and the front legs seemingly ready to pounce. This impression is reinforced by the fact that the back part of the body is higher than the head. The forelegs of the ivory lion rest on a pair of rock motifs. Just as do most Indonesian monster heads, the head of the lion has an open mouth with sharp protruding fangs, and bulging wide-open eyes with eyebrows that extend outward into hornlike protuberances. He has a long curly mane that covers the whole back, and even the wings appear to have curled hair. His hind legs and parts of his back are decorated with small sun motifs.

Like many other animals in the ritual art of Bali, the *singa* has a predominantly transportational function. He makes his appearance especially as the *palinggih* or seat of deities and as *patulangan* (sarcophagus) at cremations (fig. 12). In this role, he has a red color and traditionally carries the body of a member of the Wesia caste, the third caste, of noble line but lower in status than the second caste, the Ksatria. However, the lion appears most frequently in architecture as the base or socle for a pillar, called *sendi* in Balinese,[22] or for the vertical post or *tugeh* supporting the main horizontal roof beam of a building, usually in a palace or temple.[23] A fine example is the large *singa* on the roof beam of the Kerta Ghosa, the court of justice of the Klungkung palace (fig. 20). In Bali the (winged) lion, besides its carrying role, has a supportive, stabilizing role. Furthermore, he can also serve simply as a decorative element independently or in a building (fig. 13),[24] as the stopper for a bamboo container, water vessel, or bottle (fig. 14),[25] or as a decorative figure in relief on temple walls or palace doors — for example in Denpasar (fig. 15) and Amlapura (fig. 16) — and as bases for musical instruments (fig. 17).[26]

Never indigenous anywhere in Indonesia, the lion, as king of the animals, was well known as one of the main characters in the stories of the Old Javanese Tantri Kamandaka, which is popular in Bali. Lions are also represented on temple reliefs and paintings.[27] The lion was native to India, and the word *singa* is derived from Sanskrit *singha*, meaning lion. Illustrating the popularity of the term, one of the larger cities in Bali is Singaraja, meaning "lion king." In terms of iconography, however, in Bali the *singa* is not the vehicle of the

22 Arne and Eva Eggebrecht, *Versunkene Königreiche Indonesiens* (Mainz: Von Zabern, 1995), fig. 249; Made Wijaya, *Architecture of Bali: A Sourcebook of Traditional and Modern Forms* (London: Thames & Hudson, 2003).

23 A. N. J. Th. à Th. van der Hoop, *Indonesische siermotieven* (Batavia: Koninklijk Bataviaasch Genootschap van Kunsten en Wetenschappen, 1949), 154–155; Helen Ibbitson Jessup, *Court Arts of Indonesia* (New York: Asia Society Galleries in association with Harry N. Abrams, 1990), 104.

24 In 1887, O. J. H. Graaf van Limburg Stirum noted in his "Reisindrukken van Bali, meer in het bijzonder van Boeleleng en Bangli," *Tijdschrift van het Nederlandsch Aardrijkskundig Genootschap*, 2e serie, 4 (1987), 12, an impressive *singa* figure decorating the otherwise simple residence of a Brahman priest in Bangli.

25 For example, RMV inv. 214-6 and RMV 3557-24. See also Tibor Bodrogi, *Kunst van Indonesië* (Den Haag, 1971), fig. 147.

26 For example MNI inv. 17853, H.J.E.F. Schwartz, *Gids voor den bezoeker van de ethnographische verzameling, Zaal B Bali en Lombok* (Batavia: Bataviaasch Genootschap van Kunsten en Wetenschappen, 1920), fig. III; RMV 1586-32, H.H. Juynboll, *Catalogus van 's Rijks Ethnographisch Museum. Deel VII Bali en Lombok* (Leiden: Brill, 1912), fig. IX; RMV 1586-31, Francine Brinkgreve, "Balinese Rulers and Colonial Rule*,*" in ed. Endang Sri Hardiati and Pieter ter Keurs, *Indonesia: The Discovery of the Past* (Amsterdam: KIT Publishers, 2005), 132. Many drawings of *singa* and *singa* motifs can be found in H. I. R. Hinzler, *Catalogue of Balinese Manuscripts in the Library of the University of Leiden and other Collections in the Netherlands. Pt. 1: Reproductions of the Balinese Drawings from the Van der Tuuk Collection, Pt .II: Description of the Balinese Drawings from the Van der Tuuk Collection* (Leiden: Brill, 1986–1987).

goddess Durga as he is in India.[28] In Bali he plays a more independent role. Noticeable too is the similarity between the facial form of some *singa*, including that found on the ivory box, and that of a specifically Indonesian type of monster head that is portrayed above the gateways in Hindu-Javanese temple complexes. Besides the round protruding eyes and the fangs, the extension of the eyebrows into hornlike protuberances is similar to that found on monster heads at, for example, Candi Singasari in East Java.[29]

Besides this possible connection with the Hindu-Javanese past, it also appears that the Balinese *singa* has been influenced by the form of the Chinese lion. The form of the ivory lion is similar to that of lions used as Chinese roof decorations.[30] For at least a millennium, indeed probably since early historic times, there has been contact between China and Bali, particularly in connection with trade. Also the mythic protective *barong,* a lionlike figure that plays a role in certain Balinese rituals, is influenced by or derived from the Chinese lion that dances in the street during the New Year feast to chase away evil and to bring good fortune.[31] Especially in Balinese temple and palace architecture, traces of Chinese influence can still be found. One of the most frequently used decorative ("rock") motifs (*karang*) is called *karang saé* — the word *saé* means lion in southern Chinese dialects.[32] Nieuwenkamp himself, writing about the main gateway to the palace of Klungkung (which survived the *puputan* of 1908), remarked: "Both the carving and the form of the doors point strongly to Chinese influence,

Opposite top left: Fig. 12. Red-winged lion as sarcophagus for painter Rudolf Bonnet at a royal cremation ceremony in Ubud (Gianyar), 1979. *Photo Francine Brinkgreve.*

Opposite top right: Fig. 13. Winged lion as decoration. Collection National Museum of Ethnology, inv. no. 1216-7. *Photo Ben Grishaaver.*

Opposite bottom right: Fig. 14. Winged lion as a stopper for a container. Collection National Museum of Ethnology, inv.no. 3557-24. *Photo Ben Grishaaver.*

Opposite bottom left: Fig. 15. Winged lion in relief on the wooden doors of the former palace of Denpasar (catalogue no.45), drawing by W. O. J. Nieuwenkamp. *Photo Stichting Museum Nieuwenkamp.*

Above left: Fig. 16. A sculpture of a lion and a relief of a winged *singa* decorate the entrance to the palace of the former ruler of Karangasem in Amlapura, 2010. *Photo Francine Brinkgreve.*

Above right: Fig. 17. A winged lion supporting a musical instrument, drawing by W. O. J. Nieuwenkamp. *Photo Stichting Museum Nieuwenkamp.*

Top: Fig. 18. Lions as supports of the palanquin of the ruler of Pamacutan, Badung. Collection National Museum of Indonesia, inv. no. 13180. *Photo Francine Brinkgreve.*

Bottom: Fig. 19. Lion as support of the palanquin of the ruler of Badung, drawing by W. O. J. Nieuwenkamp. *Photo Stichting Museum Nieuwenkamp.*

Opposite: Fig. 20. *Singa* on the roof beam of the Kerta Ghosa in Klungkung, 2010. *Photo Francine Brinkgreve.*

and were surely made by Chinese workmen."[33] It is known that Chinese craftsmen had been employed at the palaces of Denpasar, Karangasem, Bangli, and Mengwi since the end of the eighteenth century.[34]

In Asia, as in African and European cultures, the lion as king of the beasts is associated with the power of the ruler (see, for example, fig. 16).[35] The National Museum of Ethnology has in its collection a gilded seat from Klungkung that probably once belonged to the Kerta Council, the law court attached to the palace. Its armrests consist of two lions, their posture similar to that of the ivory lion (cat. no. 50).

In the Museum Nasional Indonesia in Jakarta, four gilded wooden lions act as supports for the sedan chair of the last ruler of Pamecutan, Badung. It was in this chair that the king was carried to his death in the suicidal *puputan* of September 20, 1906 (fig. 18). Nieuwenkamp was also able to obtain two similar lions for his private collection. They are reported to have come from the sedan chair of the last king of Denpasar, who was killed earlier that same day in the *puputan* of Badung (fig. 19). Perhaps Chinese woodcarvers had also made these lions, since Nieuwenkamp remarks: "This is no Balinese *singa*, but a Chinese lion, *saé* or *singa Tjina*. These have no wings, unlike the *singa* on the previous plate [the ivory lion]; besides, this is recognizable from the tendril with leaves and flowers that the animal holds in its mouth."[36]

Whoever the craftsman may have been, the royal lion box collected by the artist W. O. J. Nieuwenkamp in Klungkung in 1925 is an exquisitely decorated example in ivory. It is indeed "an extremely rare piece, of which there are but few to be found on Bali."

27 Marijke J. Klokke, *The Tantri reliefs on Ancient Javanese Candi* (Leiden: KITLV Press, 1993).

28 Heinrich Zimmer, *Myths and Symbols in Indian Art and Civilization* (New York, 1962).

29 Thanks to Pauline Lunsingh Scheurleer for this suggestion. See also E. B. Vogler, *De monsterkop uit het omlijstingsornament van tempeldoorgangen en–nissen in de Hindoe-Javaanse bouwkunst* (Leiden, 1949), 38: " dat [...] de monsterkop van het omlijstingsornament, voor zover deze samengaat met een makara-boog, steeds een echte singha-kop is [...]"("... the monster head of a framing ornament, to the extent that this accompanies a makara arch, is still a real lion's head.")

30 Katherine M. Ball, *Animal Motifs in Asian Art* (New York: Dover, 2004), 64–65.

31 Ong Hean-Tatt, *Chinese Animal Symbolisms* (Malaysia, 1993), 2352–40; Wolfram Eberhard, *Dictionary of Chinese Symbols* (Singapore, 1983), 164–165.

32 Pers. comm. Hedi Hinzler. See also H. N. van der Tuuk, *Kawi-Balineesch-Nederlandsch woordenboek* (Batavia: Landsdrukkerij, 1897–1912), II, 6.

33 W. O. J. Nieuwenkamp, *Bouwkunst en beeldhouwkunst van Bali* ('s-Gravenhage, 1947), 13.

34 Made Sulistyawati, "Integrasi arsitektur Tiongkok ke dalam arsitektur Puri Agung Karangasem," in Made Sulistyawati, ed., *Integrasi Budaya Tionghoa ke dalam Budaya Bali* (Denpasar: Penerbit Universitas Udayana 2008), 85–105.

35 Margaret and James Stutley, *A Dictionary of Hinduism* (London, 1977), 277.

36 W. O. J. Nieuwenkamp, *Bouwkunst en beeldhouwkunst van Bali* ('s-Gravenhage, 1947), 30. The branch in its mouth probably is connected with the lion dance that takes place during New Year celebrations (pers. comm. Hedi Hinzler).

CATALOGUE

This tympanum from a bronze drum, the iconic object par excellence of the metal age of Southeast Asia, is of unknown provenance (though most probably from Java).[1] Surrounding the central eight-pointed star, decorated with four small knobs, is a set of three concentric rings, with a similar set toward the outer rim. Between these sets of concentric rings is a broad band containing four knob-and-loop (or knob-and-braid) motifs whose meaning or significance is uncertain. Possibly this design is connected with the way that the membrane of a premetal prototype was fastened,[2] although it may ultimately be derived from the four stylized birds moving counterclockwise around the star, as found on the commonest type of drum. The flowing design left no trace in later Balinese art, but the four-part structure remains to this day an important element in many aspects of Balinese culture.

The intricate pattern on the tympanum's surface relates it to a distinct regional type of drum, the Pejeng type, which is directly associated with Bali.[3] The name derives from the famous Moon of Pejeng, the largest of all known bronze drums, with a tympanum diameter of 160 centimeters and a height of 185 centimeters. Still virtually intact, it is housed high on a shrine in the temple Pura Panataran Sasih in Pejeng (Gianyar). Besides the tympanum design, other characteristics of the Pejeng-style drum include the high-waisted body, which may reflect an autochthonous *tifa*-like drum (as on Timor); a protruding tympanum; (pairs of) heads or masks on the body of the mantle; and, from a technical point of view, the "positive" nature of the decoration. As the ancestor of the much smaller *moko* drums valued especially on the island of Alor (near Timor), the Pejeng type is also known as the *moko* type.

Besides the Pejeng drum, other drums of varying sizes, all fragmentary in varying degrees, have been found in several parts of Bali: Bebitra (Gianyar), Peguyangan (Badung), Panek/Ban (Buleleng), Pacung (Buleleng), Ularan (Buleleng), Basangbe (Tabanan), and most recently Manikliyu (Bangli).[4] The tympanums of the Bebitra, Ban, and Basangbe drums carry designs rather similar to that shown here, while that from Pacung, reconstructed from fragments, with its 11-pointed star, is markedly different. Both the Basangbe and Ban drums are quite small, in style much closer to the later *moko*. The Manikliyu drum is of special significance, for it was found in situ during excavations in close proximity to a stone sarcophagus, and contained the bones of a person buried in flexed position. That a valuable bronze drum was used for such a purpose surely signifies a burial of someone of high status. There is also a stone carving in a temple at Carangsari (Badung) showing the remains of a figure sitting on a Pejeng-type drum. It is likely that the drums had various ritual functions, as seat and as burial vessel, and certainly as a marker of social status.

1 Tympanum of a bronze drum, approx. 1–200 CE

Perhaps Java

Bronze

Diam: 22¾ in; H: 2⅜ in

National Museum of Ethnology, Leiden, the Netherlands, 1403-2885

---

1 Originally in the collection of the Royal Cabinet of Rarities (Koninklijk Kabinet van Zeldzaamheden), transferred to the National Museum of Antiquities (Rijksmuseum van Oudheden) in Leiden in 1883, before finally entering the collection of the Rijksmuseum voor Volkenkunde in 1903.

2 See A.J. Bernet Kempers, *The Kettledrums of Southeast Asia* (Rotterdam: Balkema, 1988), especially the chapter on the Pejeng type (327–340), and A.J. Bernet Kempers, *Monumental Bali* (Berkeley: Periplus, 1991), 16–31.

3 Among the now extensive literature on bronze drums, two books are of special importance with regard to Pejeng-style drums: A.J. Bernet Kempers, *The Kettledrums of Southeast Asia* (Rotterdam: Balkema, 1988) and Ambra Calò, *The Distribution of Bronze Drums in Early Southeast Asia: Trade Routes and Cultural Spheres* (Oxford: Archaeopress, 2009); see also the references cited in these two works (several Indonesian-language sources are not available to the author of this catalogue entry).

4 For list with sources, see Ambra Calò, *The Distribution of Bronze Drums in Early Southeast Asia: Trade Routes and Cultural Spheres* (Oxford: Archaeopress, 2009), 157. On the drums from Basangbe and Ban, see D. D. Bintarti, "Hasil penelitian benda-benda perunggu dan besi di Indonesia," *Rapat evaluasi hasil penelitian arkeologi I, Cisarua, 8–13 Maret 1982* (Jakarta: Pusat Penelitian Arkeologi Nasional, 1983), 85–86; for Ban drums, see also an unpublished report by I Wayan Widia, *Temuan nekara perunggu Banjar Panek Desa Ban Kecamatan Kubu Kabupaten Daerah Tingkat II Karangasem Bali* (Denpasar: Museum Bali, 1980). The drum from Manikliyu is also the subject of a short article by I Made Sutaba, "Discovery of Late Prehistoric Burial Systems in Bali," *SPAFA Journal* 9, no. 1 (1999); diameter of tympanum 30.3 in, height 47.2 in, without illustrations of tympanum. The Ban find is said to date from about 1939, but it came to the attention of the authorities only in 1980; in a newspaper article that reported the find, there is mention of a second, larger drum which had disappeared some time earlier. The Pacung drum is now in a private London collection.

All the drums found in Bali are of the Pejeng type. Indeed, no Heger I–type drum, the commonest kind, has been found in Bali, although they have been found on the neighboring islands of Java and Lombok. Outside Bali, Pejeng-type drums have been found only in East and Central Java. In East Java at least three are known, one excavated at Kradenanrejo (Lamongan), one in a private collection said to come from Lumajang, and a third, also in a private collection, said to come from the south coast of East Java (sold by Spinks in London in 1989). From Central Java, drums are known from Tanurejo (Kedu), Kendal, and Traji. The Lamongan drum was found in conjunction with a Heger I–type drum, also in connection with a burial. The design on the tympanum of the Lumajang drum shows a possible transitional form from the four stylized birds moving counterclockwise around the star, as found on Heger I–type drums, and the knob-and-loop (or –braid) motifs of most Pejeng-type drums. Almost as tall as the Moon of Pejeng, though somewhat slimmer, are the Spink drum and the drum, said to come from East Java, that is now in the collection of the Asian Civilisations Museum in Singapore.[5] The Leiden tympanum shown here is also presumed to come from Java. In all, sixteen Pejeng drums are now known, eight from Bali and eight from Java.

The Pejeng-type drum is clearly a regional type. Furthermore, the discovery of fragments of "printing molds," or stamps for impressing the decoration onto the wax during the manufacturing process, have been found in a temple at Manuaba (Bangli), first noticed by Walter Spies in 1931, and during recent excavations at Sembiran (Buleleng). It seems certain then that Pejeng-type drums were made in Bali, possibly somewhere on the northeast coast, but possibly also in Java. Various other distinctive bronze objects found in Bali confirm the existence of skilled metalworking there during the early centuries of the first millennium CE.[6] Heger I–type drums, the so-called Dong Son drums, were probably all imported as prestige goods via an Asian trading network that already, by the beginning of the first millennium, linked China to India. Bali was part of this network. Pottery from the Philippines and Vietnam, and pottery and beads from India, have been found in Bali at sites such as Gilimanuk, Pacung, and Sembiran. Indeed, the metals needed to craft the wonderful Pejeng-type drums must also have been imported along trade networks, since these metals are not found on Bali. It is possible that the drums found in Java were made in Bali and then traded along this same network.

The story of the Pejeng-style drums does not end with the Balinese metal age, for there is a traceable stylistic development from the oldest form, such as the Moon of Pejeng, via intermediate forms, to the nineteenth- and early-twentieth-century *moko* made in Gresik,

East Java. The latest in the series show influence of European decorative elements. However, at the present state of research, the chronology of this development is unclear. On Alor, moko drums served as items of traditional wealth in social exchange networks. *Moko*-style drums have also been found on Borneo, and the famous Pejeng mask design is even more widespread.

DSF

Moon of Pejeng, Pura Panataran Sasih, Pejeng. *Photo Martha Hertelendy.*

5 On the Lamongan drum, see D. D. Bintarti, "Analisis fungsional nekara perunggu dari Lamongan, Jawa Timur," *Pertemuan ilmiah arkeologi III (PIA III), Ciloto, 23–28 Mei 1983* (Jakarta: Proyek Penelitian Purbakala Jakarta, Departemen Pendidikan dan Kebudayaan, 1985). The drums were found on top of one another, base to base, the Pejeng drum below and the Heger I drum above. It remains speculative, but might the Pejeng-type drum have female connotations in respect to the Heger drum, reminding one that the great Pejeng drum of Bali bears the nickname "moon," which also has female connotations? The Lumajang drum is discussed by Nerina de Silva, "The Analysis and Conservation of a Newly-Found Bronze Drum from Lumajang, Java, " in ed. Ian Glover, *Southeast Asian archaeology 1990* (Hull: Centre for South-East Asian Studies, University of Hull, 1992), 227–232. For the Spink drum, see the auction house's magazine, *Octagon 26,* no. 2 (autumn 1989), 32–33. De Silva says that "many" Pejeng-type drums are known to be in private collections, but specifically cites only the Spink drum. The Singapore drum is illustrated in *The Asian Civilisations Museum A–Z guide to Its Collections* (Singapore: Asian Civilisations Museum, 2003), 49.

6 The remarkable Bronze Weaver from Flores, recently acquired by the National Gallery of Australia and dated to the sixth century CE, besides several other bronzes from that general area, suggests that there were possibly other metalworking centers in Indonesia's eastern islands.

As in many Asian countries, in Bali rice is the divinely given staple food. For centuries, rice cultivation on irrigated fields (*sawah*) and dry land (*tegalan*) has been accompanied by many beliefs and ritual practices. Rice is so important in Balinese culture that tools and implements used in various stages of the agricultural cycle were not always plain, simple utilitarian objects. They were decorated by the farmers themselves or by specialists in the village communities.

These two hand-held rice-harvesting knives, *anggapan,* contrast stylistically: one is plain with a handsome shape, the other has elaborate surface patterning. Both were used to cut the ears of rice at harvesting, the most crucial period of the cycle of labor. The ears of ripe grain, *padi,* were carefully cut, one by one, in order to lose as few grains as possible. Afterwards they were tied into bundles and transported to the granary. This practice may have developed because many traditional varieties of rice ripen unevenly. But the usual explanation for the use of the hand knife is that it does not hurt the rice and is therefore not offensive to the rice goddess, Batari or Dewi Sri.[3] Moreover, by cutting the ears "mindfully," one at a time, the harvesters expressed their gratitude for the abundance of the fields, presented to them by Dewi Sri.[4]

Nowadays modern varieties of rice are harvested with a sickle, which is more efficient for larger quantities, and threshed on the field prior to storage. But some farmers still have a special corner in their fields reserved for traditional rice plants, the seat of Dewi Sri, which they continue to harvest with a hand knife and keep for special occasions.

The wooden *anggapan* (cat. no. 3) is carved in the form of a cock with a sharp beak and a curved tail. The crescent-shaped iron knife is under his belly, and in the center of his back is a hole for a stick handle, which is not present. Cocks are found everywhere in Bali, and their crowing (together with the barking of dogs and contemporary motorized traffic) is the most common sound in the villages. In rural areas, every household keeps chickens, and men look after their fighting cocks, which make their presence heard every day at sunrise. Cockfighting and the gambling that accompanies it are not only popular pastimes, but as blood offering (*tetabuhan*) cockfighting (*sabungan*) is an indispensable part of certain rituals.

The stick handle of the other *padi* knife (cat. no. 2) is made of bamboo, and the dark-glazed surface is beautifully decorated with carved flower and tendril ornaments that stand out against the lighter, natural color of bamboo. The carver might have found inspiration for his motifs in the abundant plants found close at hand in the *sawahs,*[5] or in varieties of flower (*patra*) ornaments so common in Balinese sculpture, woodcarving, metalwork, and painting. The tip of the stick closest to the knife shows an ornament of sharp triangles, often used in Bali to signify the borderlines of an object.

FB

2 Rice-harvesting knife (*anggapan*), approx. 1900–1930 (top)

Iron, wood, and bamboo
H: 14⅞ in; W: 4⅛ in; D: 2¼ in
Collection, Tropenmuseum, Amsterdam (the Netherlands),
1496-9[1]

3 Rice-harvesting knife (*anggapan*), approx. 1900–1930 (bottom)

Iron and wood
H: 1½ in; W: 6½ in; D: ¼ in
Collection, Tropenmuseum, Amsterdam (the Netherlands),
740-42[2]

1 This knife was a gift in 1941 from E. Bessem.

2 This was a gift to the museum in 1932 from F. James.

3 Roy W. Hamilton et al., *The Art of Rice* (UCLA Fowler Museum of Cultural History, 2003), 55; J. W. van Dapperen, "Het padimesje," *Nederlandsch-Indië oud & nieuw* 15, issue 9 (January 1931), 263.

4 J. W. van Dapperen, "Het padimesje," 259.

5 J. W. van Dapperen, "Het padimesje," 267.

4 Rice sheaf paddle (*panaptapan*)

Kerambitan, Tabanan, South Bali
Wood
H: 13 in; W: 7⅛ in; D: 2 in
National Museum of Ethnology, Leiden, the Netherlands, 4760-28

Early photographs of Bali show farmers walking from the paddy fields to the rice barns: women carrying bundles of newly harvested rice on their heads, and men with bales on either side of a pole carried on the shoulders. This sight is not common today because the introduction of new rice strains into Bali in the late 1960s and early 1970s changed methods of growing and harvesting rice. New hybrid strains are shorter than the "old Bali" rice, and their grains are more loosely held to the stalk. Therefore today most rice is threshed in the fields, rather than stored on the stalk in rice barns as was the practice historically.

Rice paddles were used to even the ends of a sheaf of rice before it was tied and taken from the fields. The paddles are smooth and flat on one side, and sometimes carved on the other with a depiction of a demonic face. A wide variety of demonic deities exist in Bali. On this paddle, it is difficult to determine whether the figure is a specific deity or is meant to more generally represent a guardian. Such an image is often described as the face of Boma, the same monstrous deity who guards over the doorways to many Balinese temple gates (*kori agung*). With bulging eyes, bared upper teeth, and no lower jaw, the face here resembles depictions of Boma in temple architecture. In Balinese mythology, Boma is the son of the god Wishnu and Ibu Pertiwi, the goddess of the earth. His name itself means "of the earth." Such terrestrial connections could explain the popularity of images of him on these agricultural tools.

NR

The Balinese traditionally planted several types of rice, known generically as *padi Bali*. This crop grew over a period of about 150 days to a height of a meter and a half. The rice would be harvested in the fields, with small knives called *anggapan* (see cat. nos. 2, 3). Handful by handful, clusters of rice would be reaped and then collected in large bundles. One farmer would use a tool like this to pound the ends of the accumulated stems to make a uniform sheaf.

Like cat. no. 4, this rice sheaf paddle was used to even the ends of the harvested rice before it was stored in sheaths in the rice barn. The carved portion of this unusual paddle depicts a human face. The oval face has large round eyes, a wide nose, and parted lips exposing the upper teeth. The smooth hairline peaks in the middle of the forehead and is tucked behind the figure's ears. The simplicity of the carving of the face and the lack of a diadem or jewelry give few clues to the figure's identity. Paddles with depictions of the rice goddess Dewi Sri are known, but she is often depicted with a high headdress and earplugs.[1]

NR

5 Rice sheaf paddle (*panaptapan*)

Wood

H: 15⅝ in; W: 4⅝ in; D: 2 in

Private collection

[1] Roy W. Hamilton et al., *The Art of Rice* (UCLA Fowler Museum of Cultural History, 2003), fig. 2.35.

In Bali, as in many Indonesian cultures, rice is sacred and divinely given.[4] According to a myth about the origin of rice in Bali,[5] Batari or Dewi Sri, consort of Batara Wisnu (the sustainer of life), took her seat in the first three different seeds of rice, sent from heaven to give people on earth better food to eat. The seeds consisted of grains of white rice (*padi*) and black glutinous rice (*injin*), both cultivated on wet land (*sawah*), and a red variety (*gaga*) grown on dry fields (*tegalan*). A fourth, yellow seed was stolen before it reached the earth, and was transformed into the turmeric root (*kunir*), which is used as a yellow dye for rice. Ever since, Dewi Sri has remained in rice grains to protect the life principle residing in the germ.

Dewi Sri shares her name with a Hindu goddess, but she very likely incorporates a pre-Hindu rice spirit, the life force of rice plants, which was believed to be related to the soul or life force of human beings.[6] She is not only the rice goddess but also, in a wider sense, a deity of fertility, prosperity, wealth, and beauty.[7] As such, Balinese villagers, especially farmers, feel a closer and more intimate relationship with her than they do with the more distant Hindu gods and goddesses who visit their temples on earth only once a year. For these reasons, in Bali Dewi Sri is represented by a human image that anybody with skills in the making of offerings can fashion, or that can be bought at the markets.

These three female figures made of plaited *lontar* palm leaves are such human images, receptacles of Dewi Sri, and referred to simply as "Sri." They are usually put on small wall shrines in village houses, especially those belonging to farmers with many rice fields.[8] Here, at home like an ancestor spirit, Dewi Sri receives daily offerings and is asked to look after the well-being of the family. The effigy is comparable to a *daksina palinggih*, a kind of offering often placed on wall shrines in shops and workshops, to serve as a temporary residence for a deity who blesses work to be done and brings success and good luck.

Sometimes these figures are called *cau*. In this case, they do not serve as receptacles for the goddess but rather as offerings to her, accompanying harvest rituals in the fields, and afterward placed in the rice barn.[9] According to some accounts, these offerings are burned in the rice fields in the hope that the harvest will be abundant.[10]

Because of their small size and elegant female shape, these figurines are also sometimes called *deling*, or *cili*,[11] which means "small and nice, pretty, cute." H. N. van der Tuuk, who lived in North Bali in the late nineteenth century, calls them *cecilian* or *cili-cilian*, which he translates as "a doll, made of *lontar* leaves, a figure with a headdress extending on either side, sold at the market for five Balinese coins."[12] For a discussion of the meaning of the *cili* motif, see the article on *lamak* by Francine Brinkgreve in this catalogue.

The *lontar* figurines all represent beautiful girls with slim bodies, thin arms, and triangular faces with beauty spots. They wear very large fan-shaped headdresses and big earplugs (*subeng*);

6 *Lontar* **figurine, palm leaf image of Dewi Sri (*cili*), approx. 1920–1950 (opposite page)**

Leaves of the *lontar* palm
H: 16⅞ in; W: 9¾ in
Collection, Tropenmuseum, Amsterdam (the Netherlands),
1100-20[1]

7 *Lontar* **figurine, palm leaf image of Dewi Sri (*cili*), approx. 1920–1950 (following page)**

Leaves of the *lontar* palm, metal, yarn
H: 16⅞ in; W: 11¼ in
Collection, Tropenmuseum, Amsterdam (the Netherlands),
1936-7[2]

8 *Lontar* **figurine, palm leaf image of Dewi Sri (*cili*), approx. 1920–1950 (following page)**

Leaves of the *lontar* palm, beads
H: 16⅞ in; W: 9⅜ in
Collection, Tropenmuseum, Amsterdam (the Netherlands),
3555-10[3]

long skirts cover their feet.. Some of the images have long hair, tied in a knot at the back; some have many kinds of flowers or other decorations in their headdresses. With two of these figurines, additional materials have been used to accentuate eyes or ear ornaments.

The main construction material for the images consists of narrow strips of the leaves of the fan palm, *Borassus flabellifer*, which are also used for making offering ornaments. Before fashioning, the *lontar* leaves are boiled and put in running water in order to obtain a very light color after drying. For the construction of the bodies, a plaitwork technique is used, equivalent to the technique used for making palm leaf containers, *ketipat*, in which rice can be steamed as part of offerings.

Various plaiting and cutting techniques were used to make these figurines' faces and headdresses, with the addition of small beads, and bits of cloth for the *subeng* of cat. no. 8. The different components are sewn together with cotton thread. The facial features of cat. nos. 6 and 8 are a series of dots burned into the leaf with the tip of a burning incense stick. The eyes of cat. no. 7 are thin coins, *kepeng*, fashioned from a copper alloy and enjoying widespread ritual use in Bali.

FB

1   This figurine was a gift from J. H. Mulder and R. A. H. Arntz.

2   This object was purchased by the museum from E. W. Sayers-Stern.

3   This was a gift from E. Lagerweg.

4   Alb. C. Kruyt, "De Rijstmoeder in den Indischen Archipel, " *Verslagen en mededeelingen der Koninklijke Akademie van Wetenschappen, Afdeeking letterkunde*, 4th series, 5 (1903), 409.

5   Tjok. Gde Rake Soekawati, "Legende over den oorsprong van den rijst en godsdienstige gebruiken bij den rijstbouw onder de Baliërs," *Tijdschrift voor Indische Taal-, Land- en Volkenkunde* 66 (1926), 423–434.

6   Alb. C. Kruyt, "De Rijstmoeder in den Indischen Archipel," *Verslagen en mededeelingen der Koninklijke Akademie van Wetenschappen, Afdeeking letterkunde*, 4th series, 5 (1903), 361.

7   Paul Wirz, "Der Reisbau und die Reisbaukulte auf Bali und Lombok," *Tijdschrift voor Indische Taal-, Land- en Volkenkunde* 67 (1927), 289.

8   Paul Wirz, "Der Reisbau und die Reisbaukulte auf Bali und Lombok," 289.

9   R. Goris (text) and P. L. Dronkers (photography), *Bali: Atlas kebudajaan/Cults and customs/Cultuurgeschiedenis in beeld* (Djakarta: Pemerintah Republik Indonesia [1952]), 38.

10 *Ethnographische Kostbarkeiten: Aus den Sammlungen von Alfred Bühler im Basler Museum für Völkerkunde* (Basel: Museum für Völkerkunde, 1970), 44–45.

11 Miguel Covarrubias, *Island of Bali* (New York: Knopf, 1937), 172, 412.

12 H.N. van der Tuuk, *Kawi-Balineesch-Nederlandsch woordenboek* (Batavia: Landsdrukkerij, 1897-1912), I, 633.

7

8

One of the most widely used ritual decorations in Bali is the *lamak*.[1] A *lamak* is a hanging of rectangular form, made of various materials and decorated by various means. It is used in all kinds of rituals, and has a double function. First, the upper part of a *lamak* serves as a base for offerings, as an artistic development of the flowers or leaves that are otherwise placed underneath offerings. Secondly, the lower and larger part of the *lamak* hangs down to decorate any construction that acts as a seat for invisible beings, like a fine mat that is laid out for an honored guest. It is a sign that a ritual is being held and that deities and ancestors are invited. As ritual decoration, a *lamak* is comparable to a festive dress, the clothing of a shrine.

Lamak are usually made of the leaves of the coconut palm or the sugar palm, but can be made of permanent materials as well. Materials used for permanent *lamak* include the more durable leaves of the *lontar* palm (*Borassus flabellifer*), cloth that is decorated in various ways (painted, embroidered, appliqué, woven), colored paper or plastic, and combinations of wood, little mirrors, and Chinese coins (*kepeng*).

This appliqué *lamak* is of a very rare type. Only four published examples are known: a second one is in a private collection, one is in the Australian Museum in Sydney, and one is in the Powerhouse Museum in Sydney.[2] Although the exact provenance of this type of *lamak* is uncertain, the style of its decorations is most similar to the style of Tabanan in West Bali. Nowadays, only very small and rather old appliqué *lamak* sometimes decorate shrines in West Bali (Tabanan and Jembrana).[3]

The motifs of the *lamak* on exhibition are cut from felt in four colors, applied on a white cotton base with small stitches, and additionally decorated with silver thread couchwork, sequins, and pieces of mirror.

As with most permanent textile *lamak*, the structure of this *lamak* does not differ essentially from the palm leaf variety. Representational motifs are placed above geometric ones. The undecorated upper end of the *lamak*, the part on which the offerings are placed, is called *umpal*, a term also used for the long, narrow piece of cloth used to tie a wraparound cloth around the upper body.

The elegant female figure at the top end of this *lamak* is known as a *cili*, motif of life and fertility.[4] Typical of the style of a *cili* in Tabanan, this figure has a rather elongated form, with an ornamented long skirt, a striking, upright hairstyle or headdress made of black cotton and arms that are bent upward from the elbows. She wears cylindrical ear ornaments (*subeng*). Next to her body two vinelike plants with leaves and flowers seem to sprout from the fertile earth.

9 Altar hanging (*lamak*), approx. 1900–1950 (following page)

Cotton, felt, sequins, silver thread, mirror, metal

H: 89 in; W: 12⅝ in

Tabanan or Jembrana

Private collection

[1] For a general discussion of *lamak*, see the article by Francine Brinkgreve in this catalogue.

[2] Francine Brinkgreve, *De lamak als loper van bergtop naar mensenwereld* (Leiden: Oosters Genootschap in Nederland, 1996); Robyn Maxwell, *Textiles of Southeast Asia: Tradition, Trade and Transformation* (Melbourne: Australian National Gallery, Oxford University Press, 1990), 205 and fig. 295; Christina Sumner and Milton Osborne, *Arts of Southeast Asia from the Powerhouse Museum Collection* (Sydney: Powerhouse Museum, 2001), 51.

[3] Joseph Fischer and Thomas Cooper, in *The Folk Art of Bali: The Narrative Tradition* (Kuala Lumpur: Oxford University Press, 1998) illustrate an appliqué *ider-ider* with felt *wayang* figures (fig. 91), said to come from Negara.

[4] For a discussion of the motif of the *cili*, see the article by Francine Brinkgreve on the *lamak* in this catalogue. See also cat. nos. 6, 7, and 8.

Beneath the *cili*, in the center of this *lamak*, is a square, divided into four triangles of different colors. Within the center is a flower motif whose heart is formed by a mirror in disc form, cast in a metal rim. From this central flower, four branches with leaves and flowers emanate toward the four corners of the square. Leaves and flowers are decorated with small pieces of mirror within metal rims. The structure of this motif (a square divided into four triangles) is related to a *lamak* motif known as *ibu*, referring to Ibu Pertiwi, Mother Earth, the four sides representing the cardinal directions. The flower in the center of this fertile earth might then be interpreted as a lotus (*padma*), which in the Balinese system of horizontal cosmological classification is positioned in the center of the universe.

The geometric motifs at the bottom end of a *lamak* are generally known as *kamben* or *bebatikan* motifs. A *kamben* is a long unsewn cloth, worn wrapped around the hips, whereas *bebatikan* refers to the *batik* cloth produced in Java but widely used in Bali as well. The names of these motifs are usually related to plants and refer to fruits, seeds, flowers, or leaves. On this *lamak*, the pattern in the central row of the three vertical rows of motifs is called *batu ketimun*, seeds of the cucumber.

FB

A *lamak* is a rectangular hanging used to decorate shrines and serving also as a base for offerings. While *lamak* are usually made from ephemeral palm-leaves, cloth varieties exist in a range of techniques.[1] Unlike the appliqué *lamak* of cat. no. 9, which is very rare, embroidered *lamak* from Negara, the capital of the district of Jembrana, West Bali, are well known.

Much less common, and in a style different from that of Jembrana, are embroidered *lamak* from Buleleng, North Bali, which show very fine needlework and more precious additional materials.[2]

Embroidered *lamak* and other ritual temple decorations, like *ider-ider* (long narrow cloths hung horizontally from the eaves of temple buildings), are a special form of narrative art. Like *wayang* paintings on cloth, the embroideries illustrate themes and figures from the Indian epics. A *lamak* usually contains one figure, drawn from the many characters in the traditional *wayang* or *kekawin* stories.[3]

Fischer and Cooper describe how in the first half of the twentieth century *songket* weaving (with metallic threads for the main design) of *lamak* in Negara was replaced by less labor-intensive embroidery, using cheaper materials.[4] But since the 1980s embroidered *lamak* are also gradually disappearing, because they too have become too time consuming to make. Increasingly, the old embroideries are sold and become part of private and museum collections.[5]

However, some women in Negara still have needlework skills, and nowadays in Jembrana small embroidered *lamak* can be seen decorating shrines. Woollen yarns, brighter and thicker than embroidery silk, are often used in its place. The embroidery is done with a long needle and the help of a tambour frame, using a continuous chain stitch. It is mainly a women's craft, although men sometimes outline in pencil the characters and motifs to be embroidered.[6]

This embroidered *lamak* has an undecorated *umpal* at the very top and a decorated frame (*sebeh*) with a triangular pattern called *gigin barong*, the teeth of the *barong*, a mythical animal (see cat. nos. 86, 90, 91, 92). The teeth are said to have a protective function. The motifs are all embroidered with silk in subdued colours, on a long rectangular piece of cotton.

A female deity is depicted here; she is identified as Batari Sri,[7] goddess of rice and fertility. Beneath her, taking up most of the space, is a bold floral ornament, also associated with fertility. Separating the two main elements of this *lamak* is a narrow band of geometric patterns called *penyelak*, from *menyelak*, to push something aside. It consists of a row of five swastikas, symbols of the sun.

As is typical of Negara narrative embroidery, Batari or Dewi Sri is portrayed in the same way as on a traditional *wayang* painting, in three-quarter view. She has a refined oval face and

10 Altar hanging (*lamak*), approx. 1920–1950 (following page)

Negara, Jembrana
Cotton, embroidery silk, mirror
H: 10 4/8 in; W: 10 3/8 in
Private collection

1 For a general discussion of *lamak*, see the article by Francine Brinkgreve in this catalogue. See also cat. no. 9.

2 Joseph Fischer and Thomas Cooper, *The Folk Art of Bali: The Narrative Tradition* (Kuala Lumpur: Oxford University Press, 1998), 64.

3 Joseph Fischer, *Story Cloths of Bali* (Berkeley: Ten Speed Press, 2004), 10; Joseph Fischer and Thomas Cooper, *The Folk Art of Bali: The Narrative Tradition* (Kuala Lumpur: Oxford University Press, 1998), 67.

4 Joseph Fischer and Thomas Cooper, *The Folk Art of Bali: The Narrative Tradition* (Kuala Lumpur: Oxford University Press, 1998), 63–64.

5 Joseph Fischer and Thomas Cooper, *The Folk Art of Bali: The Narrative Tradition* (Kuala Lumpur: Oxford University Press, 1998), 90; Joseph Fischer, "Balinese embroideries," *Jurnal seni* 8, 4 (2001), 341.

long hair. She wears the crown or headdress of a female deity, and she is placed in a nimbus. Her name is "written" above her head. In this case, Balinese script and Old Javanese spelling are used, indicating that this *lamak* is an older embroidery, dating from the first half of the twentieth century. More recent embroideries use the Latin alphabet.[8] The representation of Dewi Sri is not the exclusive subject for an embroidered *lamak*; other deities and heroes from the epics, such as Rama, Hanoman, and Arjuna, are depicted just as often.[9]

Characteristically for embroidered *lamak*, the bottom ornament consists of a graceful floral decoration, much like a *patra* design, instead of the geometrical pattern with plant names found on palm leaf varieties. Sprouting from a kind of mountain or hill motif in the form of half a flower, two tendrils with leaves, buds, and flowers spiral upward, ending in a half-open flower. Three big flowers each have a circular mirror in their center, as the heart. Since they have eight petals, they are probably meant to represent lotus flowers (*padma*; see cat no. 84). The floral pattern makes a strong impression.

FB

6 Joseph Fischer, *Story Cloths of Bali* (Berkeley: Ten Speed Press, 2004), 13; Joseph Fischer and Thomas Cooper, *The Folk Art of Bali: The Narrative Tradition* (Kuala Lumpur: Oxford University Press, 1998), 62.

7 See cat. nos. 6, 7, and 8 for a discussion of this important deity.

8 Joseph Fischer and Thomas Cooper, *The Folk Art of Bali*. See also the *lamak* illustrated in Roy W. Hamilton, *The Art of Rice: Spirit and Sustenance in Asia* (Los Angeles: UCLA Fowler Museum of Cultural History, 2003), 256.

9 In their book on Balinese folk art, Fischer and Cooper illustrate four embroidered *lamak* with characters other than Dewi Sri, and in Fischer's book on Balinese embroideries sixteen different characters are represented. Joseph Fischer and Thomas Cooper, *The Folk Art of Bali*; Joseph Fischer, *Story Cloths of Bali* (Berkeley: Ten Speed Press, 2004).

Left: *Lamak* with embroidered figure of Batara Siwa. Yeh Kuning (Jembrana), Galungan 1994. *Photo Francine Brinkgreve.*

Right: *Lamak* with embroidered *cili* figure. Beraban (Tabanan), Galungan 2010. *Photo Francine Brinkgreve.*

In Bali many sacred images are considered repositories, objects not divine in their own right, but vessels into which divine beings may descend. Such vessels can be images made from long-lasting materials, such as metal and wood, or fashioned from easily perishable plant matter. They are entities that enable the interaction of the devotee with the divine. These encounters can occur at any number of ceremonies during the year, including the anniversary of a temple (*odalan*), when the divinities are invited to visit. During the period when an image is inhabited by the deity, it is treated as one would treat a royal guest.[1]

Chinese coins are important elements of many Balinese offerings, as well as components of images of deities. When found in pairs, images made from coins often represent the rice goddess, Dewi Sri, and her consort, Rambut Sedana, the god of wealth. Together the couple is referred to as Sri Sedana. These deities often have side-by-side shrines in a temple where the statues are kept during the year. A particularly important festival at the island's most sacred temple, Besakih, honors these deities every year. In this commemoration of the couple's marriage, images are paraded in palanquins in procession, as the deities visit different temples.[2]

Images of Sri Sedana can have many forms. Sometimes they have bodies made of Chinese coins, with the hands, feet, and faces or heads made from wood. Sometimes a thin metal or wooden plaque with an image of a face is attached to the statue, as in this example. The coins used to make the body are old Chinese coins known in Bali as *pis bolong* (money with a hole in it). Trade with China has ancient roots, and communities of Chinese descent have lived in Bali for centuries.[3] The earliest Chinese coins found on the island date from the Tang dynasty (816–907). Although Chinese coins have not been officially used as money since the early 1900s, they are sold for use in offerings and rituals. While such a coin is not valuable as currency, it symbolizes wealth.

This pair of statues was collected by the Mexican artist Miguel Covarrubias in the 1930s.

NR

11, 12 Coin images of deities (Sri Sedana), approx. 1900–1930

Probably Sanur, South Bali
Copper alloy coins, wood, string, gold leaf
H: 18½ in; W: 8⅞ in; D: 8½ in
H: 19⅛ in; W: 8½ in; D: 8½ in
Fowler Museum at UCLA,
LX74.28 a-d and LX74.27 a-d

1 See chapter three in Hildred Geertz, *The Life of a Balinese Temple: Artistry, Imagination, and History in a Peasant Village* (Honolulu: University of Hawaii Press, 2004).

2 See the description of the Usaba Ngeed ritual in David J. Stuart-Fox, "Sri and Sedana at Pura Besakih, Bali," in *The Art of Rice*, ed. Roy W. Hamilton (Los Angeles: UCLA Fowler Museum of Cultural History, 2003), 276–285.

3 Claudine Salmon and Myra Sidharta, "The Hainanese of Bali: A Little Known Community," *Archipel* 60, no. 4 (2000): 87–124.

Like the figures in cat. nos. 11 and 12, these statues are representations of the deities Dewi Sri, goddess of rice, and her consort, Rambut Sedana, god of material wealth, known collectively as Sri Sedana. In both Java and Bali the rice goddess is called Dewi Sri. The name derives from Indic traditions where Sri Devi (or Lakshmi), the consort of Vishnu, is a goddess of wealth and prosperity. In the Indonesian archipelago there are many names for rice goddesses, and the Hindu deity was undoubtedly adapted to a much older tradition of worship of natural and agricultural spirits.[1] As for her consort, the word *rambut* is an honorific, and *sedana* means wealth.

These images were collected by the American dancer Katharane Mershon (1892–1986), who lived for nine years in Bali, mostly in the southern Balinese village of Sanur.[2]

The statues are carefully dressed in a variety of different textiles and have jewelry, imitation gemstones, and gold leaf decorative elements. Dewi Sri and Rambut Sedana can be worshiped in many forms and are among the most revered deities in Balinese ritual practice. Rice agriculture formed the basis of many aspects of Balinese traditional life, including complex calendrical systems full of rituals and ceremonies.

The terraced rice fields of Bali were and are a major tourist attraction in Bali, even as they are being transformed into tourist accommodations for the very people who come to see them. The romantic image of farmers in the rice fields belies the grueling labor involved in their upkeep. The easier (or at least quicker) money provided by contemporary economic development suggests that, in metaphorical terms, Dewi Sri is presently losing ground to Rambut Sedana.[3]

NR

13, 14 Coin images of deities (Sri Sedana), approx. 1900–1930

Probably Sanur, South Bali
Copper alloy coins, cotton fabric, silk fabric, plant fiber, wood, skin, imitation gemstones, metallic thread, gold leaf, lacquer, paint
H: 17¾ in; W: 8⅛ in; D: 3⅞ in
H: 19 in; W: 9 in; D: 3⅝ in
Fowler Museum at UCLA, The Katharane Mershon Collection of Indonesian Art, X61.77 and X61.78

[1] Roy W. Hamilton et al., *The Art of Rice* (UCLA Fowler Museum of Cultural History, 2003), 257.

[2] Katharane Edson Mershon, *Seven Plus Seven: Mysterious Life Rituals in Bali* (New York: Vantage Press, 1971).

[3] See Graeme MacRae's discussion on land value around Ubud in Graeme MacRae, "The Value of Land in Bali: Land Tenure, Landreform (sic), and Commodification," in *Inequality, Crisis and Social Change in Indonesia: The Muted Worlds of Bali,* ed. Thomas Reuter (London; New York: RoutledgeCurzon, 2003), 143–165.

Most studies of Indonesian bronzes have focused on objects manufactured in Java between the eighth and the sixteenth centuries.[1] One type of object has largely been neglected in these studies: images of human figures found on the island of Bali that are thought to date from the thirteenth to the seventeenth century.[2] One reason for the lack of scholarship on these images is that only a small number of such statues exist in museum collections.[3] Undoubtedly there are undocumented examples, which are still considered sacred and are stored in temples in Bali.[4] These types of statues are particularly interesting because they do not seem to have any sort of counterpart in Javanese art.

Ancient Hindu and Buddhist bronze statues found in Bali are similar to those found in Java. Some, perhaps, are imports from South Asia, while others are very similar in style to bronzes that were produced in Central Java during the eighth to the tenth century.[5] It seems clear that a variety of bronze images were considered sacred, and the collections found in some Balinese villages and temples have been quite diverse.[6] But there are also a number of bronzes that have been found only in Bali and that differ strikingly from Central Javanese images. According to W. F. Stutterheim, these bronzes were considered more sacred by the Balinese than were the older bronzes.[7] These statues have often been described as ancestor figures, and most do not bear a resemblance to, or carry any attributes of, well-known Hindu or Buddhist deities.

All of the bronzes depict male or female figures, standing stiffly upright, and measure between 20 and 50 centimeters in height. As with this pair, male and female figures with similar dress and ornamentation were produced to represent couples. In most cases the arms are lowered, with forearms bent and hands held, both palms facing up, one on top of the other, in front of the chest (a gesture resembling the *mudra* of meditation, *dhyanamudra*). On some of the statues there is an object resting on the open palm. In one case this object appears to be a small *stupa*; another holds a rounded form, perhaps a lotus.[8]

The statues all wear elaborate headdresses. Their eyes are open, and accentuated by incised upper lids and eyebrows. The ears protrude and are either pierced or marked by an indentation for the attachment of an earring. A typical figure wears a wide necklace, with a meandering motif, that comes to a point in the middle of the chest. This point is mirrored by a diamond-shaped ornament at the statue's waist. Decorated bands encircle the very top of the upper arms with ornaments that appear to jut up, forming points above the statue's shoulders. Forearms and ankles (if the statue still has them) also wear bangles.

15 Pair of ancestral figures, 1400–1600

Bronze
A: H: 14 3/4 in; W: 5 in; D: 3 1/2 in
B: H: 15 1/4 in; W: 4 1/2 in; D: 3 3/4 in

Asian Art Museum, Gift of the Connoisseurs' Council and Shawn and Brook Byers; and museum purchase, B86B6.a–.b

1 See, for example, Pauline C. M. Lunsingh Scheurleer, and Marijke J. Klokke, *Ancient Indonesian Bronzes: A Catalogue of the Exhibition in the Rijksmuseum Amsterdam with a General Introduction* (Leiden; New York: E. J. Brill, 1988).

2 Thermoluminescence testing of the core of these two statues produced a date range of 1430–1650 CE.

3 Some examples are in the Museum Bali, MB 3577; Rijksmuseum voor Volkenkunde, Leiden, 1403-2752; Museum of Fine Arts, Boston, 1983.327; National Gallery Australia, NGA71.101.28.A-C, NGA 71.101.29. A-B. Other images can be found in W. F. Stutterheim, "Bronzen beeldjes van Bali," *Mededeelingen van de Kirtya Liefrinck-van der Tuuk* 2 (1930): 3; Urs Ramseyer, *The Art and Culture of Bali* (Basel: Museum der Kulturen: Schwabe & Co., 2002), 43; Wayan Widia, *Arca perunggu koleksi Museum Bali* (Denpasar: Proyek Pengembangan Permuseuman Bali, 1980), 11, 14–19. Also see Oudheidkundig Dienst photos 9333, 9334, 10811-10817, Inter Documentation Company, *Indonesian Archaeological Photographs on Microfiche Photo Collection of the National Research Centre of Archaeology of the Republic of Indonesia 1901–1956 at the Kern Institute, University of Leiden.* (Zug, Switzerland: Inter Documentation Co., 1982) and other photos in the KITLV database.

4 Because of their sacred nature, many of these statues are kept in locked storehouses of temples and have not been available for research.

5 For examples, see Widia and Proyek Pengembangan Permuseuman Bali (Indonesia), *Arca perunggu koleksi Museum Bali.*

6 *Oudheidkundige Dienst in Nederlandsch-Indië* (Batavia: Albrecht and Co, 1927), 107–108; Stutterheim, "Bronzen beeldjes van Bali," 43.

7 Stutterheim, "Bronzen beeldjes van Bali," 47.

8 Stutterheim suggests that similar objects depicted in stone are *pushpalingas*, lingas "made of flowers, which were employed at the *sraddha* ceremony as a temporary receptacle of the soul of the deceased prior to its conveyance to heaven by an officiating priest." W. F. Stutterheim and India Society (Great Britain), *Indian Influences in Old-Balinese Art* (London: India Society, 1935), VII; The *sraddha* ceremony in Majapahit Java is described in the Desawarnana cantos 64–67. Unfortunately the role on statuary in these rituals is not clear. Prapañca and S. O. Robson, *Desawarnana: (Nagarakrtagama)*, Verhandelingen van het

The lower body is wrapped in a cloth, which is sometimes decorated with a diamond checkerboard pattern. Two swathes of fabric loop down from hip to hip, bisected by a long sash that falls straight between the legs. On some images, sashes seem to cascade down the sides of the figure from each hip. A number of figures have small hoops at either hip and at the back of the head; the function of these is not clear. A few statues still stand on openworked double lotus bases. The rest either are broken at the ankle or rest on bare feet.

A number of examples vary from this basic model. A bronze in the Pejeng Museum has a more elaborate headdress and jewelry.[9] This statue lifts its right hand to the middle of its chest, clasping a rosary while the left hand, held palm up at waist level, holds an unidentified object. Another statue, illustrated by Ramseyer, is a large male figure with exaggeratedly broad shoulders that was found with six other bronzes at Pura Gaduh in Blahbatuh. It stands with the right arm raised in front of the chest and the left lowered in front of the waist. The headdress, jewelry, and clothing of this figure are simple. It is difficult to determine what the statue holds. Two of the other statues from this temple also have unusual features. One has a beard, and the other has four faces and raised arms.[10]

As stated earlier, these statues do not have any real precedent in Javanese bronzes of either the Central Javanese or East Javanese periods. One does find in East Javanese stone sculpture depictions of human figures that bear comparison to these Balinese bronzes. These statues, dating mostly from the late East Javanese period (13th to 16th centuries), have been called "portrait statues" and have been discussed extensively by Marijke Klokke.[11] These figures stand stiffly upright, often hold their hands in the *dhyanamudra*, and can be found in paired male-female sets. Unlike the Balinese bronzes, these figures bear four arms and hold attributes of Hindu deities, clearly indicating divine features. Klokke concludes that these images are not portraits of royalty, but "deification images." The *mudras* and downcast eyes of these figures could represent the state of meditation required before unification of a royal figure with a god after death.

Looking to Balinese stone sculpture, one can find objects of even closer comparison.[12] A tenth-century image from Pura Tegeh Koripan (also known as Pura Sukawana), on Gunung Penulisan, portrays a couple separated by a stone divider. Each stands in the same position as the bronze statues, holding a round object in upturned palms. The jewelry and headdress of a fourteenth- or fifteenth-century statue at the same site is even more similar to the bronze images, but its bent arms are held straight out in front of the body rather than folded in front of the waist.[13] A comparison can also be made with a few rare examples of

Balinese wood sculpture that, despite the tropical climate, appear to have survived for centuries.[14]

It is likely that on both islands the standing stone statues were associated with royal ancestor worship, ceremonies consecrating the release of the soul of the deceased ruler into the world of the ancestors. This seems clearly also the case with the bronze sculptures under discussion. A. J. Bernet Kempers writes, "Their stiffness, facial expression, and attributes of flowers in their hands recall the ancestral figurines and puppets nowadays used in certain rituals, of which they may represent an earlier, more costly version."[15] Thus these small images in bronze are most likely continuing a tradition that existed in Bali with stone sculpture  from as early as the eleventh century. For reasons that are still unclear, at some point around four hundred years ago artisans moved from using permanent media like stone and bronze to the ephemeral materials that are used today.

NR

Koninklijk Instituut voor Taal-, Land- en Volkenkunde, 169 (Leiden: KITLV, 1995), 71–74. *Puspasarira* is another term used for a flower effigy used in Balinese contemporary funerary rituals.

9 A. J. Bernet Kempers, *Monumental Bali: Introduction to Balinese Archaeology & Guide to the Monuments* (Berkeley; Jakarta: Periplus Eds.; Java Books, 1991), fig. 27.

10 The bearded figure has been described as a "guru" and the four-faced figure as Brahma. This latter image is one of the few that seems to directly allude to a Hindu deity. See Oudheidkundig Dienst photos 9333, 10815, 10816, and 10817. Other bronzes found at Pura Gaduh can be seen in photos 9334, 10811-10817. For a four-faced figure in stone see the O.D. photo 5672 from Pura Panataran Sasih in Pejeng.

11 Marijke J. Klokke, "The Iconography of the So-Called Portrait Statues in Late East Javanese Art," in *Ancient Indonesian Sculpture*, ed. Marijke J. Klokke and Pauline C. M. Lunsingh Scheurleer, Verhandelingen van het Koninklijk Instituut voor Taal-, Land- en Volkenkunde, 165 (Leiden: KITLV Press, 1994), 178–201.

12 For an in-depth discussion of Balinese stone statuary of this type, see Endang Sri Hardiati Soekatno, *Arca tidak beratribut dewa di Bali: sebuah kajian ikonografis dan fungsional* (Universitas Indonesia, 1993).

13 For another example of this type, see Jane Belo, ed., *Traditional Balinese Culture* (New York: Columbia University Press, 1970), fig. XVIII.

14 A statue in the Basel Museum is given a date between the thirteenth and fourteenth centuries, and although very worn, it has the same basic characteristics as the bronzes under discussion. The example from Museum der Kulturen Basel, IIc, 21157 is illustrated in Ramseyer, *The Art and Culture of Bali*, fig. 38; another example is found in Haags Gemeentemuseum, *De Kunst van Bali,* (Den Haag, 1961), fig. 2.

15 Bernet Kempers, *Monumental Bali*, 68.

16 Ancestral figure, 1400–1600

Bronze
H: 10⅞ in; W: 3 in; D: 2⅜ in
National Museum of Ethnology,
Leiden, the Netherlands,
1403-2752

Mystery surrounds how this statue came to be found during the dredging of the river Waal near the eastern city of Nijmegen in the Netherlands in 1878. It was discovered along with a number of other completely unrelated objects. Even at this early date it was recognized as an object from Asia, although it was described in letters as an image of a Javanese king.

Although it clearly has similarities to other Balinese bronze figures (see cat. no. 15), it has some unusual characteristics. The roughly cast male figure wears a simple headdress that has been broken away in areas. The statue has pierced ears and a necklace with a large pendant, which looks as though it is strung with curving boar tusks. Upper arm ornaments, bracelets, and anklets are simply depicted. The figure holds its hands together in front of the waist, supporting an unidentified object. A unique feature of this bronze is the animal skin wrapped around the waist, with its head falling between the statue's knees. Animal skins are a mark of an ascetic, and were worn by deities such as Siwa.

NR

These two statues appear to have been carved by the same artist and designed as a couple. The pair was bought by the Rijksmuseum voor Volkenkunde, Leiden in 1932. The condition of paint indicates that the sculptures were already quite old when purchased, but it is impossible to precisely specify the date of their manufacture. Many statues of this type are dated to the late nineteenth–early twentieth century, but it is possible that they are much older.

The female figure's deeply lidded eyes stare straight forward. Her red lips are slightly parted to expose her teeth. Her black hair is pulled up behind a gold diadem, rising higher on the left. From the rear one sees her great mass of hair coiled into a loose knot and then cascading down the back to her waist. Masses of red flowers rest at her temples, and red-and-gold floral earplugs fit in her lobes. She wears a red and gold necklace as well as bracelets.

Although the paint depicting the statue's clothing is very worn, it is clear that the artist took notable care to represent a variety of patterned textiles. A gold-edged red breast cloth with meandering vines is wrapped over the statue's chest, then crosses her back and gathers at her hips. She wears a red underskirt beneath a blue lower garment with red flowers. A lighter colored floral sash forms U-shaped folds across the center of her skirt. The patterns on the textiles have a painterly quality that has no immediate counterpart in Balinese textiles. The colors and floral motifs are reminiscent of those on some Indian textiles traded to Indonesia, but also of batik from Java and painting traditions from Kamasan.[1] Both of the statue's arms are held in front of her chest with her hands clasping a sheaf of what might be rice diagonally across her body. The little finger of her right hand extends from her closed palm, displaying a long fingernail.

The male of this couple has a similar countenance, with staring eyes under darkly outlined brows and a slightly open mouth. He too wears a crown, which is decorated in the back with a large *garuda* (eagle) head, a protective motif known as *garuda mungkur*. He wears ornaments on his upper arms near the shoulders. Like his female counterpart, this figure's dress consists of a variety of patterned cloths and sashes. The statue's left arm falls by his side, and the right is bent so the hand rests on the right hip.

These figures do not appear to have been made for a tourist market, like later, "prettier" statues.[2] They both stand on wooden bases that have small square holes cut in the middle, indicating that the statues were at one time attached to something

17 Female figure, approx. 1700–1850 (following page left)

Wood and pigments

H: 24 in; W: 7⅛ in; D: 6⅛ in

National Museum of Ethnology, Leiden, the Netherlands, 2259-7

18 Male figure, approx. 1700–1850 (following page right)

Wood and pigments

H: 24⅞ in; W: 8¼ in; D: 10¾ in

National Museum of Ethnology, Leiden, the Netherlands, 2259-8

---

1 Robyn Maxwell, *Sari to Sarong: Five Hundred Years of Indian and Indonesian Textile Exchange* (Canberra: National Gallery of Australia, 2003), 137, 204.

2 Frans Leidelmeijer, *Art deco beelden van Bali (1930–1970): van souvenir tot kunstobject* (Zwolle: Waanders, 2006), fig. 62 a and b.

else. The crown, upright stance, and arm ornaments are reminiscent of bronze statues (see cat. no. 15) that are thought to be images of deified ancestors. The possibility that the female figure carries a sheaf of rice might point to these images being associated with Sri Sedana images. They seem to bridge some kind of link between early bronzes associated with ancestor worship and contemporary images still used in the worship of deities or deified ancestors.

NR

In 1933, this small statue of a seated woman was loaned to the Tropenmuseum in Amsterdam by the Dutch artist Charles Sayers.[1] Sayers was born in Java in 1901, to a family that had been there since the 1840s. After going to the Netherlands for schooling, Sayers returned to the East Indies, traveling to Bali in 1927–1928. Some of his extensive collection was no doubt acquired during this period, but his paintings made in the 1920s of Balinese objects suggest that he also collected works in Europe before his trip.[2] He returned to Bali in 1932, and remained in the archipelago until the Japanese occupation. He was interned and then sent to work on the Burma Railway, where he died in 1943.

When this object came into the collection it was described as an old image, and the patina and wear confirm this. The figure's right arm is broken and much of the paint is worn away. The woman kneels with her left arm falling by her side, seemingly bent at an impossible angle. The ability to hyperextend the elbow was a hallmark of female beauty and can be seen on images of heroines on fourteenth-century East Javanese temple reliefs (see cat. no 38). The figure's long, attenuated fingers are also emphasized, stretched out on the base beside her knee. Although the right arm is missing, the elongated hand remains resting on the red fabric of her lower garment.

The woman's head is marked by an enormous chignon of black hair piled into an oval on the left side of her head; a smaller projection of hair points out to the left below it. Photographs from the early decades of the 1900s show women with their hair in this style.[3] The figure wears a red diadem with five triangular points. At the edges of this headdress are two large circles that also show traces of red paint. These may represent *gegempolan*, hair ornaments consisting of disc forms attached to a stickpin inserted into the hair. The even larger cylindrical forms below are earplugs (*subeng*).

It is difficult to tell what this small statue was used for. It is unlikely that it was produced as a tourist object, because it was already quite old when Sayers acquired it. A hole on the bottom of the base indicates that it may have once been attached to something. It is likely that it is an image of a deity or deified ancestor.

NR

19 Kneeling woman, approx. 1700–1850

Wood and pigments

H: 6¾ in; W: 2¼ in; D. 2⅝ in

Collection, Tropenmuseum, Amsterdam (the Netherlands), 809-139

1 Koos van Brakel, *Charles Sayers: Pioneer of Art in the Dutch Indies* (Amsterdam: KIT Publishers, 2005).

2 Ibid., 114–115, 132.

3 See, among others, Tropenmuseum photographs number 60049117 and 60052466.

The similarities between this statue and cat. no. 21 indicate that the two are a pair. Paired figures occur regularly in Balinese sculpture (see cat.no. 15). They often represent deities or ancestors, but these two are unusual in a number of ways. The colors used in painting the textiles are more subdued than those found in many old Balinese statues, the facial details are finer, and specific, identifiable textiles are carefully rendered.

The male figure stands with his feet slightly splayed and his bare toes pointing upwards. His knees are bent and his body leans forward. His left hand holds a flat rectangle, and his right grasps a stylus. Unusual features are a row of raised gold dots running above his eyebrows and a series of similar black dots on his reddened lips. The head is covered with a headcloth that rises smooth and high in the back but presents a complex series of folds and points in the front.

The figure wears a blue top with a beige chest cover ornamented by large gilt dots. His lower garment is a yellow cloth decorated with a grid of large black squares with four-petaled flowers at the intersections. The cloth opens at the front, exposing the figure's right knee and the short gray-black trousers worn underneath. The front of the cloth is decorated by rows of triangles filled with stylized floral motifs; these patterns are often found on *kain prada*, textiles decorated with gold leaf or gold powder (see cat. no. 84). The *kain prada* is pulled high up under the arms and secured with a sash, whose ends fall between the figure's feet. A *kris* in its sheath is roughly attached to the figure's back, and may not be the original.

The palette of this image, with its blue, yellow, and gold, differs from the reds, blacks, and whites of other wooden statues collected in the early twentieth century. It is different, too, from the bright colors used on some statues commissioned for foreigners (cat. no. 101) or the later plain wood images made for the tourist market (cat. no. 115). The posture of the figure bending to write is unlike the stiffer poses of images of ancestors or deities. A sticker on the bottom of the base identifies the figure as the hero Prince Panji from a cycle of stories known as Malat in Bali.[1]

A focus of these narratives is the frustrated love of Prince Panji for the Princess Rangkesari. In one episode of the story, full of desire for Rangkesari, whom he believes to be the wife of a friend, the prince wanders into the mountain forests. There he plucks the petals from a pandanus flower and writes a love note. While Balinese texts were traditionally written on the leaves of the *lontar* palm, literature also describes the use of the petals of the pandanus, especially when lovers exchanged poetry.[2] When scratched by a stylus, the white petals immediately turn black. Pandanus leaves are an ephemeral mode of recording verse; the petals quickly wither and blacken. This statue may represent Panji as he writes a love letter for Rangkesari.[3]

NR

20 Prince Panji, hero of the *Malat*, approx. 1900–1930

Wood and pigments
H: 29⅞ in; W: 10¾ in; D: 7⅞ in
Collection, Tropenmuseum, Amsterdam (the Netherlands), 809-112

1 Adrian Vickers, *Journeys of Desire: A Study of the Balinese text Malat* (Leiden: KITLV, 2005).

2 P. Zoetmulder, *Kalangwan: A Survey of Old Javanese Literature* (The Hague: Martinus Nijhoff, 1974), 135–137.

3 Thanks to Adrian Vickers for help in this identification.

21 The princess Rangkesari, approx. 1900–1930

Wood and pigments
H: 31½ in; W: 9⅛ in; D: 8¼ in
Tropenmuseum, Amsterdam,
809-113

1 Koos Van Brakel, *Charles Sayers: Pioneer of Art in the Dutch Indies* (Amsterdam: KIT Publishers, 2005).

This statue of the Princess Rangkesari forms a pair with the image of Prince Panji (cat. no. 20). These characters play important roles in narratives sometimes called Panji tales or Malat stories. These tales describe the adventures of kings and princes in ancient East Java. Rangkesari is a princess, the beloved of the ideal prince Panji.

She is depicted here with her knees bent outward, her feet slightly splayed with toes pointing upward, a stance often found in dance. Her right arm grasps her sash while the left falls at her side. She smiles slightly and stares directly ahead. Like the statue of Panji, this image has small gold raised dots above the eyebrows. She also has two small black dots on her cheeks. In her ears are large earplugs (*subeng*) (see cat. no. 65). Her hair is arranged in two large coils; the right coil is almost rectangular, while the left is more rounded. A long coil of black hair winds down her back. A series of long unpainted wooden sticks radiates from the left hair bun.

Rangkesari wears a reddish short-sleeved shirt with a green and gold breast cloth wrapped tightly around her chest. A sash with a pattern of multicolored zigzags encircles her waist, holding up her lower garment (*kain panjang*). The back of her skirt is patterned with a large vertical zigzag, forming triangles filled with light red foliate motifs. The front is patterned with a basket weave or swastika pattern known as *banji* on the left thigh and a pattern of twisting vines and leaves in the center. Her jewelry consists primarily of large gold disks, which mirror those found on the statue of Panji.

The large, lopsided bun and earplugs are features commonly found in statues of female figures. But, as with the statue of Panji, the colors and details of this image are unusual.

This image and its partner were collected before 1933 by the Dutch artist Charles Sayers.[1]

NR

Gateways are integral to the division of space in Balinese architecture. Temples, palaces, and domestic compounds are all composed of courtyards, or discrete areas divided by function. In a temple compound, a split gateway (*candi bentar*) often forms the initial entrance from the street to the temple grounds, and a large gate (*kori agung* or *pamedal agung*) divides a forecourt from the inner areas of the compound.[1] Boundaries formed by these doorways are not merely geographic partitions: they also signal divisions in sacred space. Most Balinese temples are divided into two or three courtyards, and the last inner compound is considered the holiest. It is in this inner sanctum that the shrines for the gods are located, and where the gods descend to visit on ceremonial occasions.

A Balinese temple is a site rather than a single building. Comprising a number of separate structures, each with a specific ritual purpose, the temple comes alive when the community gathers to welcome and honor the visiting deities. While it may lie empty much of the year, on ritual occasions the temple is the place where gods, ancestors, and humans meet.

The array of structures in a temple can vary widely; there can be dozens of miniature shrines, open altars, and pavilions. Some altars are for storing images that serve as the temporary resting places for deities (*panyimpenan*); others are for the use of deities visiting from other temples (*pasimpangan*). But the most important are the thrones (*palinggih*) where the deities sit during ceremonies.[2] Almost all of these structures are built on high pedestals so that the altars are above the worshipers' heads.

This elaborately carved doorway is similar to another in the Museum Bali Denpasar, which dates from approximately the late eighteenth or early nineteenth century.[3] Although this doorway resembles North Balinese palace architecture, its origin is not a palace. Rather, its source is most likely the Pura Dadia Pande temple in Tejakula, Buleleng. Tejakula is a small northern coastal village, known today for its gamelan, *wayang wong* dance performances, and silversmiths. The temple was dedicated to the *pande* or blacksmith caste. Smiths have long held a special status in Balinese society, and have their own priests, who are not of the highest Brahman caste.

Although much of the paint has worn away, one can still see traces of red throughout, and gold, blue, white, and green hues in the detailed carving. The motifs include a basket weave pattern called *banji* and floral and foliate patterns.[4] The lintel is carved with flowers and leaves growing from a Balinese motif called a *karang bintulu*, a one-eyed monster face. Ferocious winged lions crouch on either side of the lintel, staring downward. Pierced carving in the lintel of doorways such as this often served to allow air to circulate within the room behind it.

22 Temple doors, perhaps 1700–1800 (following page)

Tejakula, Buleleng, North Bali
Painted and gilded wood
W: 104¼ in; H: 102⅜ in; D: 47¼ in
Private collection

---

[1] For an interesting study of one court doorway in Klungkung, see Margaret Wiener, "Doors of Perception: Power and Representation in Bali," *Cultural Anthropology* 10, no. 4 (1995): 478.

[2] Images of deities (images serving as the gods' temporary abodes) are often taken in procession to visit other temples. For a fascinating analysis of the structure and workings of Pura Desa Batuan, see Hildred Geertz, *The Life of a Balinese Temple: Artistry, Imagination, and History in a Peasant Village* (Honolulu: University of Hawaii Press, 2004).

[3] Helen Ibbitson Jessup, *Court Arts of Indonesia* (New York: Asia Society Galleries in association with H. N. Abrams, 1990), fig. 155.

[4] The term *banji* derives from the Chinese word for the swastika pattern, *wan*.

To the sides of the central double doors are rectangular panels that rise to a flaming arch. Little paint remains on the panels, but they show faint images of figures standing in profile, like shadow puppets (*wayang kulit*). Presumably other colors were once painted on the white base that now remains. Photography brings out the detail of the painting, especially in the right panel. In the arch of this panel hovers a bird in midflight. Below it stands a crowned male and female, perhaps Rama and Sita from the *Ramayana*. A servant squats below them. He is painted with the exaggerated and coarse features one often finds in clown/jester types (*parekan*). Traces of paint suggest that other figures may have once been painted behind the male and to the side of the female. Dots of paint indicate a pointed headdress that could have belonged to another male figure. A tall sweeping curve might indicate the raised tail of a monkey — perhaps Hanoman?

On the back of the doorway are two Balinese inscriptions commemorating renovations to the structure in 1979 and 1989.[5] The first inscription mentions a renovation of the doorway and the second thatching of the gateway. The word *pamedal*, used to describe the door in the second inscription, is a term used for the main gateways into a temple's compounds. The beams and pillars that extend from the doorway at one time helped support the thatched roof of the open-air veranda in front of it. At the base (*sendi*) of each of these pillars are two worn carved animals, presumably seated lions. This type of framework is unusual for a temple gateway, but can be seen on structures in a temple's inner compound.[6]

NR

5 First inscription:

*Ngayum duk Rahi-
na, Sukra, Matal, Ti-
thi, Tang, Ping, Solas
Rah Windu, Tenggek
Siki, Saka, Bumi, Su
Nya, Marganing, Widhi
1901* (numerals)

David Stuart-Fox kindly provided the following translation of the inscription:

The repairing [of the gateway] [was completed on] the day Friday of the week Matal, in the moon cycle on the eleventh day after the new moon, of the Saka year 1901 (= 1979 CE).

Second Inscription:

*Ngrabin Pamedal
Budha Pon, Medangkungan,
Tithi, Tang, Ping, Kalih, Rah, Daso
Tenggek, Siki,
I, Saka, Warsa, Siki, Siuh, Siki, Siki
1911* (1989)

David Stuart-Fox's translation:

The thatching of the gateway [was completed on the day] Wednesday Pon [day in the five-day week], [of the week] Medangkungan, in the moon cycle on the second day after the new moon, of the Saka year 1911 [numerals written as words], 1911 [written in ciphers] (= 1989 CE).

6 See, for instance, the Meru Agung illustrated in Geertz, *The Life of a Balinese Temple*, 112.

The terrifying Rangda is often described as a witch or sorceress.¹ But the role of Rangda in Balinese society is much more complex than that definition might imply. She has been seen as a historical figure, an antagonist in a famous dance drama, a denizen of the graveyard and purveyor of black magic, and a manifestation of the Hindu deity Durga. These are but the most well known of her personae; myriad other myths and interpretations exist.²

The word *rangda* means widow in Balinese, and Rangda is associated with the famous eleventh-century queen and widow Mahendradatta. According to the legend, Mahendradatta, the mother of King Airlangga, was banished by her husband for practicing black magic. After her husband's death, she was feared because of her magical powers. Angry because no one would marry her beautiful daughter, she threatened to destroy the kingdom. King Airlangga enlisted a holy man, Mpu Bharadah, to fight her. After gaining the widow's palm leaf (*lontar*) book of black magic, he fought and defeated her.

A similar story is enacted in the exorcistic dance drama Calonarang, but in the case of the drama a different protagonist repels the widow Rangda. A mythical creature called Barong fights Rangda and sends her away but does not defeat her. This battle is said to represent the constant struggle for balance between good and evil, two seemingly opposing forces that can be defined only in relation to one another. Although the drama is performed in abbreviated form for tourists today, it is also performed in village ceremonies of ritual purification.

Masks of Rangda and Barong are considered sacred objects in their own right and are stored in the village temple.³ They are given personal names and, much like statues used in religious ritual, are considered places into which divine spirits can descend. See cat. nos. 85, 86, 87, and 89 for masks and photographs of Barong and Rangda.

With her matted hair, bulging eyes, sharp fangs, and flaming tongue, it is easy to see how Rangda can evoke terror. Graveyards (where bodies are buried before they are exhumed for cremation) are home to dangerous beings (*leyak*), and Rangda is considered queen of these powerful proponents of black magic. Tourist literature describes Rangda as the epitome of evil, who brings illness, destruction, and death, but Balinese interpretations are much more nuanced. In Claire Fossey's interviews with a wide variety of Balinese, Rangda was described as a powerful being capable of both benevolence and malevolence.⁴

Rangda is also associated with the Hindu goddess Durga, the consort of Siwa. One of the earliest statues of the goddess, from Kutri in Gianyar, dates to the late tenth century and shows a Durga quite similar to models found in Central Java or India — a beautiful

23 The widow Rangda, 1800–1900

Wood and pigments

H: 23½ in; W: 16½ in; D: 10 in

Asian Art Museum, Gift of Thomas Murray in memory of his father Eugene T. Murray, 2000.37

---

1 Claire Fossey traces the history of Western interpretations of Rangda, from romantic visions of Rangda representing the "dark side of paradise" to the anthropologist Jane Belo's Freudian view of Rangda as a manifestation of ideas about a neglectful mother, to concepts spread in tourist literature. Fossey also interviews a number of Balinese of different backgrounds for contemporary Balinese views on the subject. Claire Fossey, *Rangda, Bali's Queen of the Witches* (Bangkok: White Lotus, 2008).

2 Barbara Lovric points out Rangda's possible connections to the plague in "Bali: Myth, Magic, and Morbidity," in *Death and Disease in Southeast Asia: Explorations in Social, Medical and Demographic History*, ed. Norman G. Owen (Melbourne: Asian Studies Association of Australia, 1987), 117–141.

3 Unconsecrated masks are not in this category.

4 Fossey, *Rangda, Bali's Queen of the Witches*.

goddess effortlessly fighting a demon. Later depictions of the goddess, both in Java and in Bali, begin to show the goddesss in a wrathful form.[5] In this guise Rangda is seen as the counterpart to Siwa's role as the destroyer.

Stone sculptures of Rangda can often be found in the temple of death (*pura dalem*) of a village. Wooden sculptures of Rangda are less common.[6] It is difficult to tell whether this statue was part of an architectural structure or if it had some other purpose. It appears that the statue's original right arm has been replaced, and there are many chips and paint losses. These losses reveal that the sculpture has been repainted multiple times, and that portions of the statue were once gilded. Assorted iron nails can be found in the hair, around the neck, in the corners of the mouth, and below the waistband of the skirt. Traces of material under these nails suggest that the statue had rawhide decorative embellishments. There is a remnant of what must once have been a long leather tongue nailed inside the statue's mouth.

NR

---

[5] Pauline Lunsingh Scheurleer, "Skulls, Fangs, and Serpents: A New Development in East Javanese Iconography," in *Southeast Asian Archaeology 1998: Proceedings of the 7th International Conference of the European Association of Southeast Asian Archaeologists, Berlin, 31 August–4th September 1998*, ed. Wibke Lobo and Stefanie Reimann (Hull, Berlin: Centre for South-East Asian Studies, University of Hull; Ethnologisches Museum; Staatliche Museen zu Berlin Stiftung Preussischer Kulturbesitz, 2000), 189–204.

[6] While later wood carvings of Rangda were made for the tourist market, statues made for the Balinese are less common. This statue has similarities to a *kris* holder, acquired in 1901, in the Rijksmuseum voor Volkenkunde, Leiden.

Life in Bali is full of rituals. The rites of passage, *manusa yadnya* and *pitra yadnya*, are carried out to help the soul of a person along his path of life, from before birth until well after death. Especially the souls of vulnerable young babies, who, according to Balinese belief, at birth have just arrived on earth from the realm of the gods and deified ancestors, must be well protected.

In Balinese Hinduism, this protection is the task of Sanghyang Raré Kumara, or Dewa Kumara, who is ordered to carry out his protective function by his father Batara Siwa. As was explained to Katherine Mershon when she inquired about a small shrine hanging above a cradle: "'That is Kumara's seat. He is the tiniest deity of them all and the youngest. That's why he guards little children, singing crickets, and fluffy birds. He is lord of the small!' The miniature shrine was indeed a lovely symbol of the ever-young."[1] This interview occurred at a three-months' celebration in Sanur, when the baby was to sleep for the first time in a cradle.

This small shrine or offering altar, known as *plangkiran,* is both a temporary seat for Dewa Kumara and a place for special offerings directed to him. It is hung over the baby's cradle or next to the bed where he sleeps with the parents, after the navel cord has fallen off, for the first year (Balinese year of 210 days) of his life and often even longer.[2] When the infant is twelve days old (*ngerorasin*) it is named, and at the three-months' ceremony (*nelubulanin*) the child is allowed to touch the earth for the first time. These life cycle ceremonies, as periods of transition, require extra protection, so additional offerings for Dewa Kumara are put on his shrine. The Balinese hope that he will request that his divine father, Siwa, grant the child prosperity and a long life.

This seat for Dewa Kumara is made of wood and is decorated with beautiful carvings of high quality. It is possible that it was made for one of the many princely courts in Ubud, probably in the nineteenth century. The two sides are two crowned *naga,* mythical serpents, similar to the *naga* which decorate the armrests of the gilded chairs (cat. nos. 50, 51). Like other animal figures, the *naga* is well known in Bali as *wahana,* mount or carrier of *arca lingga,* small statues of deities (see the article by Francine Brinkgreve in this catalogue). The extra wings of the animals seem to stress their function as carriers of such a hanging shrine, which sometimes even takes the form of a flying animal itself.

As in many other Indonesian cultures, the serpent as symbol of new life and fertility has a function in life cycle rituals in Bali, and both *naga* on the shrine are probably supposed to help the soul of the baby through the first phases of life. In death

24 Suspended offering shrine (*plangkiran*), approx. 1850–1900

Wood and pigments
H: 20½ in; W: 9⅜ in; D: 11⅜ in
Ubud, South Bali
Collection, Tropenmuseum, Amsterdam (the Netherlands), 1330-192

[1] Katharane Edson Mershon, *Seven Plus Seven: Mysterious Life-Rituals in Bali* (New York: Vantage Press, 1971), 105.

[2] Urs Ramseyer, *The Art and Culture of Bali* (Oxford: Oxford University Press, 1977), 175, fig. 239.

rituals of certain high-caste families, a large image of a *naga*, called *naga banda*, is burned at the same time as the cremation of the body, in order to transport the soul of the dead person to heaven. In Bali, the mythical serpent is also strongly influenced by Indic mythology and beliefs. Basuki and Anantabhoga, entwined around a mighty turtle, play an important role in keeping the Balinese universe in balance, and are often represented in sculpture and painting.

The back of this shrine's seat is carved with a protective *karang bintulu*, a demon's head with one eye, surrounded by foliate ornaments. Even the bottom of the hanging shrine is beautifully decorated, with a sun motif and meandering flowers. At least parts of the *plankiran* have been painted, since some traces of white, red, and black paint are still visible.

The object was collected by the same collector as a *barong macan* mask from the Leiden collection (cat. no. 92).[3] J. P. Kleiweg de Zwaan was a medical doctor and anthropologist with deep cultural interests who worked for many years in Bali and Lombok.

FB

3 *Budaya Indonesia: Kunst en cultuur in Indonesië/Arts and Crafts in Indonesia* (Amsterdam: Tropenmuseum/Royal Tropical Institute, 1987), 270.

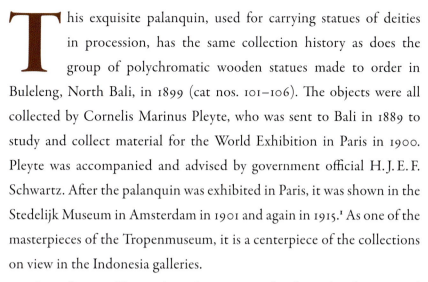

This exquisite palanquin, used for carrying statues of deities in procession, has the same collection history as does the group of polychromatic wooden statues made to order in Buleleng, North Bali, in 1899 (cat nos. 101–106). The objects were all collected by Cornelis Marinus Pleyte, who was sent to Bali in 1889 to study and collect material for the World Exhibition in Paris in 1900. Pleyte was accompanied and advised by government official H. J. E. F. Schwartz. After the palanquin was exhibited in Paris, it was shown in the Stedelijk Museum in Amsterdam in 1901 and again in 1915.[1] As one of the masterpieces of the Tropenmuseum, it is a centerpiece of the collections on view in the Indonesia galleries.

According to Pleyte, the palanquin was "made under the personal auspices of Ida Njoman Karang, District-chief of Savan in the section Buleleng."[2] He probably also supervised the making of the wooden statues of Bhatara Guru (cat. no. 102) and Uma (cat. no. 101), because stone sculptures of these deities stood in front of the main shrine in his house temple.[3]

Decorated palanquins of this size are still used in Bali to carry small god figures, *arca, pratima,* or *pralingga,* into which deities are requested to descend during rituals. Such palanquins are also used in procession (*makiis, melis*) to visit other temples, or as part of purification ceremonies near the seashore. Pleyte gives the following impression of such an event:

> During our stay on the island of Bali we had twice the opportunity of seeing the litter carried in procession, which was in reality a very fine sight. In front went the orchestra, *gamelan,* accompanied by little girls and others somewhat elder, beautifully dressed and carrying on their heads baskets of flowers and fruits, all arranged with a very good effect. Then came the men in their many coloured garments, glittering with gold, then the litter and then again men and women.[4]

It is not quite clear whether Pleyte saw this particular palanquin in use or whether he commissioned it especially to be sent to the Netherlands, as he did with the statues. A similar but plainer palanquin from the same period, in the collection of the Museum of the Batavian Society (the

25 Palanquin (*pengongongan*), approx. 1850–1899

Sawan, North Bali
Painted and gilded wood
H: 39⅜ in; L: 75⅝ in
Collection, Tropenmuseum, Amsterdam (the Netherlands),
15-155

1 *Exposition universelle internationale de 1900 à Paris: Guide à travers la section des Indes Néerlandaises, groupe XVII (colonisation)* (La Haye: Nijhoff, 1900), 227; *Gids voor den bezoeker van de Indische tentoonstelling in het Stedelijk Museum te Amsterdam* (Amsterdam: Stedelijk Museum), 1901, 72. See also J. C. van Eerde, *Gids voor de tentoonstelling betreffende Oud-Javaansch en hedendaagsch Balisch Hindoeïsme* (Amsterdam: Koloniaal Instituut, 1915) and photograph 60040500 KIT in album ALB-0068. It was illustrated in B. M. Goslings, *Gids in het Volkenkundig Museum, II: Bali en Lombok* (Amsterdam: Koninklijke Vereeniging Koloniaal Instituut, 1927), 51, pl. 10, and in *Budaya Indonesia: Kunst en cultuur in Indonesië/Arts and crafts in Indonesia* (Amsterdam: Tropenmuseum/Royal Tropical Institute, 1987), 23.

2 C. M. Pleyte, *Indonesian Art: Selected Specimens of Ancient and Modern Art and Handwork from the Dutch Indian Archipelago* (The Hague: Nijhoff, 1901), 9.

3   C. M. Pleyte, "Herinneringen uit Oost-Indië: Bali," *Tijdschrift van het Koninklijk Nederlandsch Aardrijkskundig Genootschap*, 2nd series, 18 (1901), 43–44.

4   C. M. Pleyte, *Indonesian Art: Selected Specimens of Ancient and Modern Art and Handwork from the Dutch Indian Archipelago* (The Hague: Nijhoff, 1901), 9.

5   MNI 10110 and MNI 17853 respectively. See H. J. E. F. Schwartz, *Gids voor den bezoeker van de ethnographische verzameling, Zaal B Bali en Lombok* (Batavia: Bataviaasch Genootschap van Kunsten en Wetenschappen, 1920), 8, pl. III. The Balinese language has several words for palanquin or sedan-chair, which formerly may have described different forms (certainly they are less common today), such as Schwartz indicates, or which may be regional terms. *Pengogongan*, possibly a North Balinese term, would seem to be restricted to a palanquin for deities (see also H. N. van der Tuuk, *Kawi-Balineesch-Nederlandsch woordenboek* [Batavia: Landsdrukkerij, 1897-1912], I, 445). *Jempana* (originally Sanskrit) is now probably the commonest term, used both for a palanquin for deities and for humans in certain ritual contexts. Other terms are *joli*, *sarad*, and *gayot*.

6   See, for example, a photo of the Pura Bale Agung of Singaraja in C. M. Pleyte, "Herinneringen uit Oost-Indië: Bali," *Tijdschrift van het Koninklijk Nederlandsch Aardrijkskundig Genootschap*, 2nd series, 18 (1901), opp. page 42.

present Museum Nasional in Jakarta), was called by Schwartz a *pengogongan,* in distinction to the palanquin with a closed shrine, which he called a *jempana*.[5]

The palanquin consists of a square shrine-like section and a lower elongated section. The shrine section, with four posts supporting a roof, is partly enclosed on three sides by intricate carving. The construction rests on two cylindrical carrying poles. The carving is partly openwork and partly in very high relief, almost like different sculptures. The highly ornate style of this carving is reminiscent of that found on temples in North Bali.[6] The carving consists mostly of leaves, tendrils, and lotus flowers, *padma*. The *padma,* depicted with eight leaves around the center, is in Balinese cosmology a symbol of the universe (see cat. no. 84), as well as being a symbol of new life and fertility. At the base of the chair are lozenge-shaped motifs called *mas-masan*, from *mas,* meaning gold. The carvings are entirely gilded; the background of the carvings and the inside of the chair are painted red and black.

On the sides, curving from the front of the shrine section to the front of the palanquin, are carvings of two crowned *naga,* mythical serpents, similar to the *naga* that decorate the armrests of the gilded chairs (cat nos. 50, 51) and the sides of the suspended offering shrine (see cat. no. 24). As the main decoration of this palanquin, the *naga* seem to act as carriers of god figures, in the same way as they often function as the mounts or vehicles (*wahana* or *palinggihan*) of *arca lingga*, small statues of deities (see the article by Francine Brinkgreve in this catalogue).

FB

Statues of Dewi Sri (left) and Rambut Sedana (right) on their processional palanquins. *Usaba ngeed,* **Besakih (Karangasem).** *Photo David Stuart-Fox.*

This box was collected in 1925 by W. O. J. Nieuwenkamp. For a description, the collection history, and an analysis of the function and meaning of this object, see the article by Francine Brinkgreve in this catalogue.

FB

26 Offering-box in the form of a winged lion, approx. 1875–1900

Klungkung
Ivory, wood, pigments
H: 4¾ in; W; 2¾ in; D: 3 in
Rijksmuseum, Amsterdam,
AK-MAK-280

This wooden box, like the ivory box from the Rijksmuseum in Amsterdam (cat. no. 26), is shaped in the form of a winged lion. Lions can be seen in many forms in Balinese art. They are found in architectural elements (cat. nos. 22, 46), palm leaf manuscripts, paintings on cloth, shadow puppets (cat. no. 123), and even as sarcophagi for members of the Ksatriya (warrior, aristocracy) caste.

This beautifully carved example shows all the features that were common in depictions of this animal. A series of flamelike spikes rises from the lion's mane and upcurved tail. Smaller, tightly curled ringlets circle his neck. As with Balinese depictions of many other animals, the lion's facial features are fierce, with bulging eyes and an open mouth with exposed fangs. The body is painted red and is covered with four-lobed spots, each with a center of gold surrounded by blue, white, and then black. Lions were not indigenous to Indonesia, but tigers and leopards were, and perhaps the artists who rendered these cats were drawing on familiarity with those beasts in their depictions of the unfamiliar lions. Knowledge of lions must have spread to Bali from India, where lions were a sign of royalty and appeared prominently in both Hindu and Buddhist iconography. Balinese uses of leonine creatures as guardian figures in architectural contexts has parallels in China, and people have compared the Balinese mythical lionlike *barong* to the lion from Chinese lion-dances.

As discussed in Francine Brinkgreve's article in this volume, wooden objects like this are still used today. They are considered seats for the gods and accompany the deities when on procession. Occasionally, as in cat. no. 28, statues that are considered temporary receptacles for the gods are attached to an animal vehicle; in other cases a small offering is placed on the creature's back.

NR

27 Offering-box in the shape of a winged lion, perhaps 1900–1930

Wood and pigments
H: 9 in; W: 6⅜ in; L: 15¾ in
Collection of Anne Kahn and Timothy Kahn

The small male and female figures seen here are known as *arca lingga* or *pratima*; they are considered temporary repositories for deities when they descend from the heavens. Resting places for the gods can be made of gilded wood (often sandalwood) like these figures, or from any number of other materials. The gods may inhabit a figure made of Chinese coins, a mask, a bronze inscription, or a receptacle made of ephemeral flowers and leaves.

For much of the year these images are stored in a temple shrine, but on ritual occasions when the gods are invited to visit, the statues are retrieved, clothed, given offerings, and sometimes taken in procession to the ocean or a holy spring for purification. The figures are always carried aloft, either on top of a worshiper's head, on a specially carved animal mount, or in a palanquin.

This couple is on a mount (*wahana*) or seat (*palinggih*) that is a mythical composite animal with the crowned head of a snake (*naga*), the wings of a bird, and the tail of a fish. A similar type of animal is known as a *naga kang*, or serpent-fish.[1] Similar composite animals are also chosen as the shapes for sarcophagi of certain castes or kin groups.[2]

The animal rests on a rectangular base ornamented with motifs common in Balinese stone and woodcarving. The corners of the base depict the head of a bird with only the upper beak showing, a decoration known as *karang goak*, or crow ornament. On the middle of the base there is an ornamental design of a one-eyed monster, or *karang bintulu*.

Carved animals like this can be found without images on their backs as well (see cat. nos. 26 and 27). For more on the use of these animal figures, see Francine Brinkgreve's essay in this volume, "W. O. J. Niewenkamp and His Royal Lion Offering-Box."

NR

28 Male and female figures on their animal mount, approx. 1900–1940

Wood and pigments
H: 11¾ in; L: 17¼ in; D: 6¾ in
Collection of W. E. Bouwman

1 H. I. R. Hinzler, *Catalogue of Balinese Manuscripts: In the Library of the University of Leiden and Other Collections in the Netherlands* (Leiden: E. J. Brill, 1986), 70.

2 For a photograph of a sarcophagus similar in shape to this winged serpent-fish, see Hinzler, fig. 23.

Among Bali's rich variety of textiles, the *bebali* plays a special role. *Bebali* is a general term for a range of textiles that have ritual functions, which are mostly made with a continuous warp on a backstrap loom, and which traditionally were made of handspun cotton. The majority are striped or checkered cloths, each with its own name (that can vary from region to region), depending on combinations of colors and widths of stripes or checks. They are made in such a way that they can be removed from the loom with the warp intact; hence the expression continuous warp.[1] In some rituals, the act of cutting the warp is an essential element.

To my knowledge, the cloth exhibited here is the only kind of *bebali* cloth that is decorated with a drawing or painting. Made of undyed handspun cotton, the textile has its warp still intact. On one section of the cloth, somewhat less than half its total length, is a highly refined painting of the god and goddess of love, Kama (or Semara) and Ratih, depicted within a nimbus, sign of divinity, and shaded by an umbrella, symbol of high status. The god and goddess are portrayed in intimate loving embrace, her legs around his waist, their arms around each other's necks. Kama stands on a lotus flower growing out of a lotus plant with four broad leaves. The painting is in a style typical of the most refined work of painters from the village of Kamasan, near Klungkung, where traditional Balinese painting has flourished to the present day. The red is typically that of imported Chinese *kencu* paint. Unusual, and certainly contributing to the visual impact of this work, is the thin gold leaf (*prada*) accentuating ornaments and dress. The painting is almost certainly Kamasan work; its dating is conjectural (late nineteenth–early twentieth century).

Bebali cloths with drawings or paintings of Kama and Ratih are used in only two kinds of rituals in Bali: tooth filing and consecration of a high priest. According to Urs Ramseyer, in tooth-filing ceremonies that he witnessed in east Bali, the candidates lie on a plaited mat on which Kama and Ratih are depicted, while during the seclusion period prior to the tooth filing the candidates "take the fringed part of an undyed *wangsul* cloth decorated with a depiction of the love gods between thumb and forefinger, and let Semara and Ratih slip gently over their cheek (*ngusap rai, ngares pipi*)."[2]

I have seen such a cloth used during the consecration of a Brahman high priest and priestess (*pedanda buda*) of the *brahmana buda* descent group at the village of Budakeling (Karangasem region). After various rituals of cleansing, the candidates were asked to sit in front of the consecrating priest (*nabe*), who performed a series of very complicated ritual acts. The candidates then were dressed in two special textile objects: the *paragi* (or *salimpet*), white cloth bands worn across the body, and the *usap rai*, the cloth sash decorated with a

29 Ritual cloth (*usap rai*), with painting of the gods Kama and Ratih, approx. 1875–1925

Cotton, paint, gold leaf

H: 24½ in; W: 9¼ in

Private collection, Netherlands

drawing of Kama and Ratih, worn diagonally across the chest from the left shoulder.[3] Soon thereafter followed the key rite of consecration (*nuhun pada*).

For these, and for other rituals where no drawing is required, special offerings and mantras are directed to Kama and Ratih. Among the Sanskrit hymns of the high priest are some directed to Kama and Ratih. Kama is invoked by the *wayang* puppeteer to enrapture the audience.

Besides the well-known association of Kama and Ratih with love and desire — hence their connection to life-cycle rituals of maturation such as tooth filing — the role of this divine couple in rituals in a broader sense revolves around the idea that desire is necessary for things to come about. In the *paselang* ritual, a part of certain elaborate ceremonies, Semara (Kama) and Ratih are associated with restraining affliction, suffering, and misfortune, and with the bringing of "happiness and good fortune, long life and perfection, youth, and as the pinnacle of the bestowal, increase in virtue."[4] In the *Smaradahana* mythic story of Siwa's fiery destruction of Kama, which is well known in Bali, Kama sacrificed himself for the well-being of the world.

DSF

1 Cloths with continuous warp are also called *wangsul*, a High Balinese word with the same meaning, "return," as *wali* (or *bali*).

2 Urs Ramseyer, "Bebali: Borderlines Between the Sacred and the Profane," in Brigitta Hauser-Schäublin, Marie-Louise Nabholz-Kartaschoff and Urs Ramseyer, *Textiles in Bali* (Berkeley: Periplus, 1991), 70–72. The *bebali* illustrated (fig. 5.13), which he calls *wangsul/gedogan usap rai*, shows a rather rough ink drawing on the white cloth.

3 Another interpretation of these drawings that I heard at that time was that they represented Ardhanareswari, a symbol of the unity of the male (*purusa*) and the active female (*pradhana*) principles, depicted as a half-male, half-female figure (seen in rice dough form in the offering called *bebangkit*).

4 David J. Stuart-Fox, *Pura Besakih: Temple, Religion and Society in Bali* (Leiden: KITLV Press, 2002), 222–225.

These two drawings are part of a larger group of drawings on paper that the artist-collector W. O. J. Nieuwenkamp donated to the National Museum of Ethnology in Leiden in 1913.[1] Nieuwenkamp had collected for the museum during visits to Bali in 1904 and 1906, but objects that he personally found of special interest he kept for his own collection. These bear the notation "Verz. Nieuwenkamp" or "Verz. W.O.J.N."[2]. It is not known where or when he collected these drawings, nor why he decided later to donate them to the museum.

The two drawings exhibited here are similar in structure and theme: at the bottom of each drawing, a deity in the guise of a high priest performs a ritual that is associated with a demon portrayed on the upper part of the drawing. Inscriptions in Balinese script identify the characters; their names in Latin script have been added in pencil.

In the first drawing (1864-8), Begawan Bregu (Sanskrit: Bhagavan Bhrigu), one of the so-called seven holy men (Sanskrit: *saptaresi*), is depicted as a *pedanda* or Brahman high priest. His ritual implements are those of a Siwa priest. He holds a bell in his left hand while sprinkling holy water with a sprinkler held in his right hand. Before him is the vessel containing holy water that he has consecrated, resting on a footed stand (*dulang*). His ritual lamp rests on his lap. Bregu is said to be patron of the cockfight.[3] The demon above his head is Kala Rahu (Rau) who has just bitten a piece out of the moon (or sun). This subject represents an eclipse. In the myth of the churning of the milky ocean, Rahu managed to drink a drop of the elixir of life (*amerta*) before being decapitated by Wisnu. Rahu, depicted only as a head, chases the moon or sun trying to swallow it, causing an eclipse. However, the celestial entities always reappear.

In the second drawing (1864-10), it is the deity Batara Ludra (Rudra) in the guise of a high priest, this time wearing his priest's miter (*ketu*), who performs the ritual. He handles the ritual lamp in his right hand and the bell in his left. The holy water vessel, with sprinkler, is on the footed stand in front of him. Above him is the head of the demon called Gelap, depicted with fangs and lolling tongue, a figure quite common in Balinese painting and sculpture.[4] The word *gelap* is variously translated as "thunder" or "lightning." Ludra or Rudra is the fierce aspect of Siwa.

DSF

30, 31 Drawings of deities in the guise of priests, with demons, before 1913 (following pages)

Perhaps Buleleng, North Bali

Paper, ink

H: 13¾ in; W: 8½ in

National Museum of Ethnology, Leiden, the Netherlands, 1864-8, 1864-10

---

1 On Nieuwenkamp, see the essay by Francine Brinkgreve in this volume.

2 Verz. is an abbreviation for *verzameling*, meaning collection in Dutch.

3 J. C. van Eerde, *Gids voor de tentoonstelling betreffende Oud-Javaansch en hedendaagsch Balisch Hindoeisme* (Amsterdam: Koloniaal Instituut, 1915), 85, though one wonders how many cockfight aficionados know that. Van Eerde lists Bregu among the Balinese pantheon, surprising since he is virtually unknown in Bali, at least at the present time. As one of the seven holy men, see T. Goudriaan and C. Hooykaas, *Stuti and Stava (Bauddha, Saiva and Vaisnava) of Balinese Brahman Priests* (Amsterdam: North-Holland, 1971), nos. 028, 905.

4 See, for early examples, drawings from the Van der Tuuk collection, H. I. R Hinzler, *Catalogue of Balinese Manuscripts in the Library of the University of Leiden and Other Collections in the Netherlands. Pt. 1: Reproductions of the Balinese Drawings from the Van der Tuuk Collection, Pt. II: Description of the Balinese Drawings from the Van der Tuuk Collection* (Leiden: Brill, 1986–1987), 3390-20 and 3390-46.

In the enactment of his ritual, the Balinese *pedanda* or Brahman high priest (or priestess) makes use of a number of ritual or cult implements. For the Siwa high priest, the *pedanda siwa*, these consist of a bell (*genta*), lamp (*padipan* or *padamaran*), brazier (*padupaan*), holy water vessel (*suamba*) resting on a tripod (*tripada*), and small containers for rice and incense. The Buda high priest or *pedanda buda* uses in addition two implements specific to him, the double-ended *bajra* and the *santi*.[2]

In basic form these implements have remained essentially unchanged for more than a thousand years, but the decorative elements can vary considerably. The bell exhibited here is typical of Balinese ritual bells: a plain body, a molded handle, and a finial in the form of a *vajra* (*bajra* in Balinese), with a protruding central prong and four surrounding prongs that curve sharply inward. The bell itself is sometimes called *bajra* after this element. The base of each prong is decorated. The bell is made in two pieces, the bell proper and the handle, joined by a rivet; the clapper is attached to a ring inside the bell proper. Old Javanese bells are sometimes more elaborately decorated or have sculpted finials.[3] Bells are valued according to their ring; the purer and sweeter the note the more valuable it is, and the best bells can command high prices. As one smith remarked, it is just like trading turtledoves, which are kept in Bali for their song; the very best demand high prices.[4]

The lamp also shows decorative variation upon a standard form: a cup-shaped container for oil, rising from a curved supporting frame ending in two legs attached to a flat decorative openwork base. Most variation in these vessels occurs in the animal features of the curved frame. In this example, the front is adorned with the crowned head of a serpent (*naga*), whose body forms the curve of the frame. Resting on the back curve of the frame, behind the *naga*, is the image of a bull, representing Nandi, the god Siwa's animal vehicle, a fitting ornament for a bell used by a *pedanda siwa*.[5]

The third utensil exhibited is a tripod, on which the vessel for holy water would have rested. Elaborately decorated with curvilinear floral designs, its three legs rise from the tails of standing *singa* or lion figures.[6]

All these cult implements are of brass,[7] and it can be presumed that they were all made by smiths in the village of Budaga, just west of Klungkung, who specialize in the working of brass (*kuningan*). When Nieuwenkamp visited Budaga in 1906, there were some twenty smiths making a variety of brass objects, using the lost-wax process. Of these, three specialized in the making of bells and lamps and other necessities used by priests, among whom one, Nang Karang, was famous. He was employed by the Dewa Agung, the king of Klungkung. Nieuwenkamp received permission to have Nang Karang make a set of

Cult implements of a Siwa high priest (*pedanda siwa*), approx. 1900–1930

Originally on loan from Charles E. H. Sayers 1933; purchased 1959[1]

32 Bell (*genta*)

Brass
H: 7⅛ in; D: 3 in
Collection, Tropenmuseum, Amsterdam (the Netherlands), 809-185a

33 Lamp (*padipan* or *padamaran*)

Brass
H: 9⅝ in; W: 2⅜ in; D: 8⅞ in
Collection, Tropenmuseum, Amsterdam (the Netherlands), 809-186

34 Tripod (*tripada*) for a holy water vessel

Brass
H: 5½ in; D: 6¾ in
Collection, Tropenmuseum, Amsterdam (the Netherlands), 809-190

1   The bell and lamp were previously published in *Budaya Indonesia: Kunst en cultuur in Indonesië/Arts and Crafts in Indonesia* (Amsterdam: Tropenmuseum/Royal Tropical Institute, 1987), 206 and 279 (no. 290), 205 and 279 (no. 288) respectively.

2   A discussion of these implements in relation to priests' rituals is discussed further in the essay by David Stuart-Fox in this volume.

3   See for example, Pauline Lunsingh Scheurleer and Marijke J. Klokke, *Ancient Indonesian Bronzes* (Leiden: Brill, 1988), 119–122.

4   *Bali Post,* October 25, 1984.

5   A virtually identical lamp is illustrated in J. E. Jasper and Mas Pirngadie, *De inlandsche kunstnijverheid in Nederlandsch Indië, V. De bewerking van niet-edele metalen (koperbewerking en pamorsmeedkunst* ('s-Gravenhage: Mouton, 1930), 122 (fig. 201). A beautiful lamp (and the water vessel on its tripod), now in the Museum Nasional Indonesia, was among the loot from the palace of Klungkung after the *puputan* of 1908. Illustrated in Francine Brinkgreve, "Balinese Rulers and Colonial Rule," in ed. Endang Sri Hardiati and Pieter ter Keurs, *Indonesia: The Discovery of the Past* (Amsterdam: KIT Publishers, 2005), 139.

6   See Jasper and Pirngadie, *De inlandsche kunstnijverheid in Nederlandsch Indië, V. De bewerking van niet-edele metalen (koperbewerking en pamorsmeedkunst)*, 122 (fig. 203) for a comparable example.

ritual objects for him, which he reproduced in one of his own drawings. This set, illustrated by the well-known artist-collector, is remarkably similar to the Sayers set. According to Nieuwenkamp, at that time Budaga was the only village in Bali making objects of brass.[8] In 1920, when P. de Kat Angelino made his study of Balinese smiths, Nang Karang was still alive and retained his high reputation. By that time, besides producing work for the traditional Balinese market, the Budaga smiths were also selling priest bells and other objects to visiting tourists.[9] Some years later, one of these sets was bought by the Dutch painter Charles Eugène Henry Sayers (1901–1943), whose extensive collection of Balinese artifacts is now in the Tropenmuseum.[10] The industry survives to this day.[11]

DSF

7 I know of no metallurgical analysis of the metal used in these cult implements. In earlier times, at least in ancient Java, they were made of bronze.

8 W. O. J. Nieuwenkamp, *Zwerftochten op Bali* (Amsterdam: Elsevier, 1910), 181–182.

9 P. de Kat Angelino, "Over de smeden en eenige andere ambachtslieden op Bali," *Tijdschrift voor Indische Taal-, Land- en Volkenkunde* 60 (1921), 254–262, gives a good account of the Budaga smiths. He says it was Agerbeek, the Dutch official in Klungkung after the *puputan* of 1908, who encouraged the smiths to enter the tourist market.

10 On Sayers, see Koos van Brakel, *Charles Sayers 1901–1943: Pioneer Painter in the Dutch East Indies* (Amsterdam: KIT, 2004).

11 Ayu Kusumawati, "Catatan tentang tempat pengerjaan logam di Budaga dan hubungannya dengan upacara agama di Bali." *Pertemuan ilmiah arkeologi ke-II, 25-29 Pebruari 1980 di Jakarta* (Jakarta: Proyek Penelitian Purbakala, Dep. P&K, 1982), 749–755.

An unmarried Siwa high priestess (*pedanda istri kania*) and her cult implements — bell, lamp, water vessel on its tripod. Gria Tegal, Denpasar. *Photo Francine Brinkgreve.*

This golden water jar was seized by Dutch troops at the palace of Klungkung, after the so-called *puputan* Klungkung, on April 28, 1908 (see article by Francine Brinkgreve in this catalogue).[1]

Although it is not one of the high priest's implements (see article by David Stuart-Fox in this catalogue), this water vessel from the royal palace of Klungkung could have been used for the holy water that plays such an important role in Balinese religion. But it is also possible that the vessel was used for drinking water at royal banquets.[2] According to the report of Aernoudt Lintgensz, who was in Bali in 1597, golden vessels were used at the court of Gelgel in the sixteenth century.[3] Usually a *caratan* is made of clay and can serve all sorts of purposes in a household. For use as royal gifts, sometimes only the spout or the lid is gold,[4] but this rare example is entirely made of gold.

This vessel was very likely manufactured by the goldsmiths (*pande mas*) who worked to order for the court of the Dewa Agung and for his family in other palaces in Klungkung, and who lived in nearby Banjar Pande Mas in Kamasan.[5] Before the *puputan,* fifteen goldsmiths worked more or less full time at the courts. They were particularly busy at times of major rituals.

For modeling royal vessels and ceremonial boxes, the goldsmiths used a thin sheet of gold called *peripihan*.[6] The sheet was beaten out of a lump of gold. For the water vessel, the sheet was hammered into its basic shape with a rounded hammer and a punch. The surface of the golden *caratan* has been left plain, with the exception of delicately embossed foliate meanders or tendril ornamentation on a rim around the spout and a lotus flower motif on the lid. The decorations in relief, achieved by repoussé technique (embossing from the back), were applied after hammering the vessel into shape. Final touches to the decoration were worked by chasing or chiseling from the front. The different parts, such as the spout, were soldered together later.

FB

35 Water vessel (*caratan, cecepan*), approx. 1850–1900

Klungkung

Gold

H: 8⅞ in; D: 6 in

National Museum of Ethnology, Leiden, the Netherlands, 1684-13

1 H. H. Juynboll, *Catalogus van 's Rijks Ethnographisch Museum, Deel VII Bali en Lombok* (Leiden: Brill, 1912), 40.

2 J. E. Jasper and Mas Pirngadie, *De inlandsche kunstnijverheid in Nederlandsch Indië, IV. De goud- en zilversmeedkunst* ('s-Gravenhage: Mouton, 1927), 240.

3 *De Kunst van Bali: verleden en heden* (Den Haag: Haags Gemeentemuseum, 1961), no. 164.

4 Gift from the Raja Karangasem, published in Francine Brinkgreve, "Balinese Rulers and Colonial Rule," in ed. Endang Sri Hardiati and Pieter ter Keurs, *Indonesia: The Discovery of the Past* (Amsterdam: KIT Publishers, 2005), 125.

5 P. de Kat Angelino, "Over de smeden en eenige andere ambachtslieden op Bali," *Tijdschrift voor Indische Taal-, Land- en Volkenkunde* 61 (1922), 370–381.

6 Jasper and Pirngadie, *De inlandsche kunstnijverheid in Nederlandsch Indië, IV. De goud- en zilversmeedkunst,* 34.

A *bokor* is a round bowl with a low flaring rim, usually made of silver, but in palaces golden ones were not uncommon. They are still widely used in Bali, now mostly produced from much cheaper aluminium. They are commonly used as bases for large offerings, *banten gebogan*, tall, tower-shaped arrangements of fruits and cakes, carried to the temple and presented to gods and deified ancestors. A *bokor* is also used as a container for smaller offerings and gifts brought to a house where a ritual is being held. Sometimes a *bokor* functions as a tray for the various boxes and containers of a betel set.

The upright rim of this golden *bokor* is decorated with three bands of repoussé ornamentation. These motifs are divided, as usual, into *karang* (rock or reef) motifs and floral patterns, *patra*. The narrow top band is filled with small spiral patterns, evocative of snails (*kakul-kakulan*). On the broad central band, four groups of demonic *kala* faces alternate with groups of plain ovals. Each group of *kala* faces consists of a *karang kala* (demon motif) or *karang tapel* (mask motif) in the center, flanked by two outward-facing raven or crow motifs (*karang goak*). The bottom rim is filled by the flower motif called *patra sari*.[1]

This golden offering bowl was looted by Dutch troops from the palace of Klungkung after the *puputan* Klungkung on April 28, 1908 (see article by Francine Brinkgreve in this catalogue).[2]

FB

36 Ceremonial bowl (*bokor*), approx. 1850–1900

Klungkung

Gold

H: 2⅛ in; D: 9½ in

National Museum of Ethnology, Leiden, the Netherlands, 3600-98

1 Urs Ramseyer, *The Art and Culture of Bali* (Oxford: Oxford University Press, 1977), 68–69.

2 Published in Francine Brinkgreve, "Balinese Rulers and Colonial Rule," in ed. Endang Sri Hardiati and Pieter ter Keurs, *Indonesia: The Discovery of the Past* (Amsterdam: KIT Publishers, 2005), 138.

The *dulang*, or footed wooden tray, is a common Balinese wooden artifact found in almost every home. Its diameter varies from about twenty centimeters to more than fifty centimeters, its height in rough proportion to the diameter. The top tray section usually has a slightly raised rim approximately one inch across. The tray always has a flaring foot. It usually is made out of a single piece of wood. The *dulang* exhibited here, of average size, is typical in all these respects. Many *dulang* are made of plain unpainted wood. Some are painted black (especially those from Lombok), while others are painted and decorated with geometric and plant designs. Exceptional *dulang* are decorated with painted animals or human figures illustrating or alluding to a particular story.

This *dulang* is elaborately painted over a red base color. On the upper surface of the tray, there is a central figure of a demonic *kala* head, typically found above temple gateways, with hands making symbolic gestures. Surrounding this head are alternating figures of four fiery demonic heads (often called *gelap*) and four triangular flame ornaments. On the underside of the tray, alternating with pomegranate designs, are four animal figures arranged in two pairs: a lion facing a bull, and a lion facing a dog or jackal (or pig?).[2] The depiction of these animals does not tell a particular story but refers in a general way to the famous group of animal tales known in Bali as Tantri (Panchatantra in India), where these animals play significant roles. Tantri stories are common themes in sculpture and painting.[3]

A *dulang* has various uses. Its original purpose was probably as a vessel for serving food, as is still the case in parts of Bali.[4] In this traditional use, four or more people, their right hands facing inward, sit in a circle around the *dulang*, which is piled high with rice and side dishes.

The *dulang* is currently most often used as a base for food offerings. It also serves as a tray on which a priest places ritual utensils, such as the bell and holy water vessel. The beautifully decorated *dulang* presented here is said to have served such a purpose, and this interpretation is supported not only by its artistic qualities but also by the *mudra*-like hand gestures of the central *kala* head.[5]

DSF

37 Footed wooden tray (*dulang*), approx. 1925–1950

Wood, paint

H. 10¼ in; D: 14⅝ in; Base D: 9⅛ in

Purchased from Freule M. A. de Jonge, 1958

Collection, Tropenmuseum, Amsterdam (the Netherlands), 2733-2[1]

1 Previously published in *De kunst van Bali: verleden en heden* (Den Haag: Haags Gemeentemuseum, 1961), no. 203; and in *Budaya Indonesia: Kunst en cultuur in Indonesië/ Arts and Crafts in Indonesia* (Amsterdam: Tropenmuseum/Royal Tropical Institute, 1987), 136 and 270, no. 124.

2 The identification of this animal is unclear. Judging by the animal's skin it is likely to be a dog or jackal. Earlier catalogues have interpreted these animals as a dog, a bull, and two tigers.

3 Marijke J. Klokke, *The Tantri Reliefs on Ancient Javanese Candi* (Leiden: KITLV Press, 1993), provides interesting information on these stories.

4 In Old Javanese, the derivative *angdulang* or *andulangi* means to feed someone.

5 For a *dulang* with priest's utensils, see H.J. E. F. Schwartz, *Gids voor den bezoeker van de ethnographische verzameling, Zaal B Bali en Lombok* (Batavia: Bataviaasch Genootschap van Kunsten en Wetenschappen, 1920), pl. VIII.

Bali is one of the few places in the world that produces textiles in which both the warp and weft are tie-dyed before weaving, a process known as double ikat. The threads of the warp and weft are strung on a frame, and then small sections are bound tightly with fibers to prevent them absorbing color when dipped in a dye bath. After an initial dyeing, the threads may be rebound to add another color; eventually the entire pattern is dyed into the threads before weaving. This is a very complicated and difficult technique, as the dyeing must be extremely precise in order to produce patterns that are clear. These highly prized textiles are made only in one village in Bali: Tenganan Pegeringsingan. The textiles are worn during ceremonial occasions and used during rites of passage. They are believed to be imbued with protective and magical powers.[1]

Local myths recall the Hindu god Indra's role in teaching the women of the village to weave. Literary evidence suggests that these textiles have been produced for centuries. The chronicle of the fourteenth-century East Javanese king Hayam Wuruk describes the king's cart having curtains made of *geringsing*.[2]

This cloth is a wonderful example of this type of double-ikat textile. The handspun cloth retains its deep colors, obtained from dyes made from the root of the *noni* tree (*Morinda citrifolia*) and the indigo plant.[3] The metal-wrapped embroidery thread on the ends of the cloth is most likely made of ramie that has been wrapped with thin strips of paper coated with a combination of gold and

38 Ceremonial textile (*geringsing*), approx. 1875–1925

Tenganan Pegeringsingan, Karangasem, East Bali

Cotton and metal-wrapped ramie (?) thread

W: 88½ in; H: 20⅞ in

Asian Art Museum, Gift of Diana K. Chace, 2009.24

silver. The presence of this gold embroidery indicates that the piece was probably made as a gift or tribute to a royal court of a neighboring kingdom; the gold embroidery may have been applied at the courts of that neighboring kingdom.[4]

Twenty different motifs have been identified on *geringsing* cloths. The design on this cloth is known as *geringsing wayang kebo*. *Geringsing* means "without sickness"; *wayang* indicates the depiction of figures that have the angular features of *wayang* shadow puppets. In this example, a central four-pointed star divides the main field of the cloth into four semicircular sections. Within each semicircle, six human figures are seated in a row. A turbaned man with a woman to either side of him is mirrored in each of the semicircles and repeated eight times throughout the textile.

One kneeling female figure faces the turbaned man with her hands in a gesture of reverence. He sits slightly higher than the women, one hand in his lap, the other raised in front of him. Behind him the second woman sits with her head turned away, looking downward over her left shoulder. Her position, with her left arm seemingly unnaturally flexed, is also seen on portrayals of women in stone carving and other media. Some scholars have suggested that she is the priest's wife because of her turbanlike headdress. In Bali today, a priest's wife helps her husband and assumes his duties upon his death.

NR

1 Brigitta Hauser-Schaublin, Marie-Louise Nabholz-Kartaschoff, and Urs Ramseyer, *Textiles in Bali* (Berkeley; Singapore: Periplus Editions, 1991), 116–135.

2 Mpu Prapanca, *Desawarnana (Nagarakrtagama)*, trans. S. O. Robson (Leiden: KITLV Press, 1995), 38.

3 These dyes are listed in Balinese charters from as early as the tenth century. Jan Wisseman Christie, "Texts and Textiles in 'Medieval' Java," *Bulletin de l'Ecole française d'Extrême-Orient* 80, no. 1 (1993): 186.

4 Marie-Louise Nabholz-Kartaschoff, "The Textiles of Sembiran," in *Burials, Texts and Rituals* (Universitätsverlag Göttingen, 2008), 101.

Opposite: Relief from Candi Panataran, Blitar, East Java.

Bali has an exceptionally rich written culture, and there are perhaps tens of thousands of *lontar* books in private hands around Bali, in addition to important library collections. A major category of book concerns religion in its broadest sense, and includes works on philosophy and doctrine, mysticism, ritual, divination, and "magic." These Western distinctions are not always very useful in categorizing Balinese texts, and this is especially true regarding the so-called "magical" texts, which often combine aspects of mysticism, magic, and medicine.[1]

The *lontar* exhibited here is typical of this category of text.[2] It is not a single integrated work. Rather, it is a compilation of shorter texts of similar nature, borrowed and copied from various sources, which is often the case with *lontar* books of this category. The first half of this *lontar* contains a variety of magical-mystical texts dealing with the microcosmic aspects of the individual and relationships with divine macrocosmic powers, the development of the individual from conception, and the strengthening of supernatural powers through ritual and meditational practices, involving the use of mantras and power syllables. Among these items is one of the central medical texts, the Usada Sari, and important texts named after the healers Buddhakacapi and Kalimosada-Kalimosadi.

The second half of the *lontar* consists of *rerajahan* or magic drawings used for a variety of purposes; a selection of these is described here.[3] They are drawn on both sides of the leaf. Each drawing is accompanied by a brief text that provides necessary information, such as its name, what it accomplishes, how it is used, required offerings, and sometimes a special mantra. Some have specific names, generally that of the supernatural being invoked; others have simply a generic name.

> 24B This is Yama Raja. Talisman (*tumbal*) for the body, place in the courtyard. Requirements: draw this on copper, use at an irrigation shrine (*badugul*), place at the northwest, bury in the middle of the "mouth" of the shrine; amulet to protect your home, all evil activities against your house are frightened away, as well as *leyak* (witch), *desti*, *teluh*, *taranjana* (all kinds of black magic), that is the result.[4]

> 25B LEFT This is the talisman Kara ... Requirement: draw on a red brick and bury in the courtyard.

> 25B RIGHT The result [of this drawing] is long life, and illness kept away. It is protection for a child; draw this on *lontar* leaf, place on the room shrine (*plangkiran*).

39 *Lontar* book with magic drawings, approx. 1850–1925

Lontar leaves, wood, pigment, string, metal coins (*kepeng*)
W. 16¾ in; H: approx. 22⅜ in
Private collection, Netherlands

1 For a discussion of these texts, see the essay by David Stuart-Fox in this volume.

2 A transcription was made by A. A. Ketut Rai, in 1980, under the title "Kawisesan ring buana alit" (*Proyek Tik* no. 3125). The words of this title are virtually untranslatable. *Kawisesan* means "magical-mystical supernatural power." *Buana alit*, literally "small world," is often translated as "microcosm," with reference to the individual; *buana agung* is the macrocosm. This concept of *buana alit-buana agung* is of major importance in Balinese religious thinking in the broadest sense.

3 *Rerajahan* are also discussed at length in the essay by David Stuart-Fox in this volume.

4   For comparable drawings of Yama or Yama Raja, see C. Hooykaas, *Drawings of Balinese Sorcery* (Leiden: Brill, 1980), 143; C. Hooykaas, *Tovenarij op Bali: Magische tekeningen uit twee Leidse collecties* (Amsterdam, Meulenhoff, 1980), nos. 65, 114, 159. A common feature is the eight-petal lotus over the chest, with an inscription on each petal, and the letter "Ya" in the center. Yama Raja, god of the underworld or afterlife, "lord of judgment" (Hooykaas), is discussed in detail in C. Hooykaas, *Agama Tirtha: Five Studies in Hindu-Balinese Religion* (Amsterdam: Noord-Hollandsche Uitgevers Maatschappij, 1964), chapter 2.

26A   Talisman to be placed to left and right of the entrance, its result is that theft and malevolence do not come near you. Requirement: draw this on a red brick; [use] all kinds of pure offerings. If done on a holy day, the money component is 777 coins....

26B–27A   This is a talisman to protect an animal stall for cow or buffalo, for all kinds of livestock; it is called the demon (*buta*) of changing form. Offerings are one measure (*sapangkon*) of rice, and meat consisting of raw and cooked innards of a pig. Requirement: draw with lime on a black stone, and place in the stall. Mantra: ONG, Sang Danawa-pati, do not destroy my cherished animal.

28B   This is to ward off crop diseases. Requirement: draw this on copper. *Caru* [netherworld offerings, placed on the ground]: *nasi punjung* (a rice offering), meat consisting of fried pig liver, to be made at the irrigation shrine (*badugul*). Place the drawing at the mouth of the *badugul* shrine, its result being the disappearance of all afflictions and obstacles. The drawing is called *Sarwa sarpa buana* (All serpents world, or, All world serpents).

29B   Talisman for a gateway, draw this on a brick. Offerings: *rumbah gile* [pig meat prepared in a special way], a round-shaped measure (*sapulung*) of rice. Its result is that if there is evil it has no power to wage an attack. Its name is Hyang Raja Pangalah (Divine Lord He-who-defeats). It is a protector [of the house].

30A   This is Sanghyang Sungsang-Buana (Divine Upside-down-World). He defeats all *leyak*s, *desti*, *teluh*, *tranjana* [three kinds of black magic or sorcery], and even thieves. Requirements: draw this on white cloth made into a waist sash, one *depa* in length. *Caru*: a roasted reddish multicolored chicken, five measures of rice, money component 1000 coins, offering called *peras*.

30B (not on photo)   This is called Tabceb [Tanceb?] Bhumi (Pole of the World). Iron staff, this is a "man-maker" (*panglanang*). Requirements: A piece (*ros*) of *temu* root (*Curcuma sp.*), the three-spices. Draw this on a betel leaf. Mantra: Tabceb Bhumi, I request that my male organ become large and strong, *poma poma poma* (let it be so). The netherworld offering (*caru*) is yellow rice and fried eel. After saying the mantra, spray it over the male organ three times.

31A This is [a talisman] to separate (*pamasah*) a man and his wife. Requirements: draw this on bark paper, place on the courtyard of the house-temple, and bury it three times (or: bury three of them?), they will quickly separate (*pasah*) as married couple.... Offerings: rice of alternating colors, money component of 227 coins. Carry this out on Pasah (first day of the three-day week).

32A This is called Nahina. A means of prevention against illnesses of the seventh and eighth lunar months. Requirements: offerings of *tumpeng adanan*, a *sanggah cukcuk* shrine outside, draw this on "ivory" bamboo (*pring gading*), make offerings each day for one month, its result is that illness afflicting humans disappears.

33A This is a means of prevention [against affliction] for a former house yard or stall for a buffalo, or all kinds of domestic animals. Requirements: draw this on a red stone. The offerings are all kinds of pure offerings, carried out at the *bedugul* shrine *kaja-kangin* [in South Bali generally northeast] of the house yard, little daily offerings (*banten jotan*) to be given every day, all kinds of impurities disappear.

34A (NOT ON PHOTO) This is a talisman for dry fields or irrigated rice fields suffering from plant epidemic. Requirements: draw this on bamboo of the "ivory *ampel*" variety; Hyang Pretanjala [is its name], and place it by the fields. Offerings are a *cau petik* and five *bubur pirata* [a kind of rice porridge].

DSF

Books in Bali are made from the leaf of the *lontar* palm or Asian palmyra palm (*Borassus flabellifer*). The books themselves are called *lontar* (or sometimes *rontal*).[2] The leaves are processed and cut to size, inscribed using a special knife, and then tied together with string through holes cut in the leaves. Usually the leaves are protected with an outer board of wood or bamboo. Sometimes, though, valuable *lontar* books, such as Old Javanese metrical poems or *kekawin*, are kept in plain closed wooden boxes called *kropak*. These *lontar* boxes, and also storage boxes of other sizes and shapes, are occasionally painted.[3]

This *lontar* box is decorated with paintings from the Ramayana — a fitting subject, since the Ramayana *kekawin* is the most honored of all *kekawin* poems. It is very possible that the box was specially painted for a *lontar* book of this poem. The paintings are in typical traditional *wayang* style, in red, blue, and gold over a white background. The figures have been identified in clumsy Latin script, using unusual spellings, and furthermore are not wholly accurate; very possibly they have been added later.

Each of the two long sides is divided into two scenes by a diagonal divider of triangular motifs. The painter has chosen four early scenes from the famous epic. On one side, the left scene shows Rama and Laksmana, his younger brother, conversing; the latter is presumably informing Rama that his wife Sita has been abducted. The scene on the right depicts Rawana carrying off Sita by force. The two scenes on the other side follow immediately after Sita's abduction. At left is the struggle between the bird Jatayu and Rawana. Jatayu attacks and wounds Rawana (here he is depicted lying on the ground, blood spurting from the wound), and catches Sita as she falls. Jatayu, though, is ultimately no match for Rawana, who cuts off one of his wings. The scene at right shows the mortally wounded Jatayu, one wing drooping, telling Rama and Laksmana what has happened.

The top of the box, painted with a red background, is decorated with lozenge and half-lozenge shapes containing floral motifs and weaponlike designs.

The box is said to come from West Lombok, which was colonized in the seventeenth century by Balinese from the East Balinese state of Karangasem. Virtually nothing is known about traditional painting in Karangasem or Lombok, so where the painting was actually done cannot be determined; it might be Lombok, or Bali itself. Johan Christiaan van Eerde (1871–1936), the donor, may have collected the box during the years 1897–1903 when he worked in Lombok as a civil servant. In 1913 he became director of the Ethnology section of the Colonial Institute, the forerunner of the Royal Institute for the Tropics (KIT). In 1915, he organized an important exhibition on Old Javanese and Balinese Hinduism in the Stedelijk Museum in Amsterdam.[4]

DSF

40 Painted wooden box for *lontar* book, approx. 1850–1900

Perhaps West Lombok
(Balinese people)
Wood and pigments
H: 4½ in; W: 21¼ in; D: 2¾ in
Gift from J. C. van Eerde, 1926
Collection, Tropenmuseum, Amsterdam (the Netherlands), 274-2[1]

1 Published in *Budaya Indonesia: Kunst en cultuur in Indonesië/Arts and Crafts in Indonesia* (Amsterdam: Tropenmuseum/Royal Tropical Institute, 1987), 138 (object no. 128), 270 (text). It also served as the cover illustration for the guidebook to Bali and Lombok published by the Colonial Institute in 1927. See B. M. Goslings, *Gids in het Volkenkundig Museum, II. Bali en Lombok* (Amsterdam: Koninklijke Vereeniging Koloniaal Instituut, 1927).

2 The word *rontal* is derived from *ron*, meaning leaf, and *tal*, the name of the tree, as in some Indian languages. *Lontar* would seem to be derived from *rontal*.

3 See, for example, cat. no. 70, also illustrated in *Archives of Asian Art* 58 (2008), 146–149 (cat. no. 70). Other objects that are sometimes painted include footed stands (*dulang*), water pots of various materials (usually for the tourist trade), etc.

4 Van Eerde, *Gids voor de tentoonstelling betreffende Oud-Javaansch en hedendaagsch Balisch Hindoeïsme* (Amsterdam: Koloniaal Instituut, 1915), 109, no. 492.

Set against a lush landscape is a village scene densely packed with activity. In the background, flooded rice terraces climb the slopes of a sacred volcano. A funerary procession winds its way in the foreground past the brick walls and gates of a temple. On the far left a man scales a tree to beat on the slit drum (*kulkul*), calling the villagers together. Below him a drummer sits, and a pair of men carry a gong in procession. They are following the tall cremation tower (*wadah* or *bade*), which is borne aloft by a group of men laboring to maneuver the wide lattice of bamboo poles at its base. The tower itself has seven pagoda-like roofs reaching high into the sky. The body of the deceased is hidden from view under a white cloth shaded by two parasols. The ornate tower is decorated with the face of the protective deity Boma.

In the center of the panel, a priest in a tall headdress and white lower garment aims an arrow at a mythical dragonlike snake, the *naga banda*. The *naga banda* is used only in rituals for members of royalty, and its symbolic killing aids the release of the soul of the departed. Leading the procession, on the right side of the painting, a boy and girl, relatives of the deceased, are carried in a palanquin toward the cremation grounds. Ahead of them, under a small pavilion, is the bull sarcophagus (*lembu*) in which the body will be placed for the cremation.

The painting teems with other aspects of village life: a farmer leads ducks to the fields; another plays the flute on the back of a water buffalo; women carry offerings.

Shown here are only a few of the many rituals involved in the complicated process that purifies the soul of the deceased and releases it from the bonds of the material world, a series of events that may take years to complete. Like many artists creating paintings for the tourist market, I Made Djata chose to depict one of the most spectacular of these rituals, the procession of the cremation tower, an event that fascinated (and still fascinates) visitors to the island.

I Made Djata was one of a group known as the Batuan artists, painters living in or near the South Bali village of Batuan. Through contact with the prominent European expatriate artists Walter Spies and Rudolf Bonnet, young artists in the village began to explore painting with new mediums and in new styles. Depictions of village life were an especially popular subject for these paintings, which were bought by a tourist clientele. Among the many Western visitors who collected the art of Batuan painters were the anthropologists Margaret Mead and Gregory Bateson (cat. no 117).

NR

41 Funeral procession in Bali, approx. 1960–1970

By I Made Djata (approx. 1920–2001)
Pigments on cotton
H: 34 in; W: 57 in
Asian Art Museum, gift of Judy and Sheldon Greene, 1998.92

The cremation ritual (*ngaben*) is one of Bali's most spectacular Hindu rituals. For those in positions of power, cremation was (and still is) a potlatch-like display of wealth and influence, in which ritual necessities are produced in elaborate fashion. This is no more visible than in the impressive cremation towers (*bade*) and sarcophagi (*patulangan*), and even in the roofed dais or pavilion within which the sarcophagus is placed for burning. Such a pavilion is called *bale gumi* (*gumi* means earth), or *bale pabasmian* (from the High Balinese word *basmi*, meaning burn).

The pavilion exhibited here, together with a bull sarcophagus and a complete cremation tower (now lost), were presumably made especially to order, and then donated to the museum by the Resident of Bali and Lombok in July 1930.[1] In Amsterdam, they were set up temporarily in the main exhibition hall, where they provided a fine backdrop for group photographs, such as for the Balinese dancers who visited the Netherlands in June 1931 as part of their European tour.[2] The artist N. J. Moedelare, otherwise unknown, made an ink drawing of pavilion and sarcophagus, dated January 17, 1930.[3]

This is a typical Balinese four-post pavilion. Each slender post, square in form, is finely carved and painted. The whole pavilion comes apart into many separate pieces; codes in Balinese script facilitate correct reassembly. It stands on a high terraced base. In cremation grounds, such pavilions often stand on raised earthen mounds. For simple cremations, either there is no pavilion or a pavilion is made of bamboo, if wooden ones are too expensive.[4]

DSF

42 Roofed dais for cremation ritual, 1930

Wood and pigments

H: 189 in; L: 133¾ in; W: 112¼ in

Gift from the Resident of Bali and Lombok (H. Beeuwkes), 1930

Tropenmuseum, Amsterdam, 628-2

1 This commission may have been made in connection with planning for the International Colonial Exhibition that was to take place in Paris in 1931, but if so the set of objects was not used for exhibition there.

2 The Tropenmuseum possesses many photographs showing these objects. Photographs TM 60054851-60054852, 60054962-60054969, and 60054996 (with Balinese dance group, dated June 6, 1931).

3 In the collection of the Tropenmuseum, Amsterdam, 628-4.

4 For examples, see Paul Wirz, *Der Totenkult auf Bali* (Stuttgart: Strecker und Schröder, 1928), figs. 69–74, 76, 79.

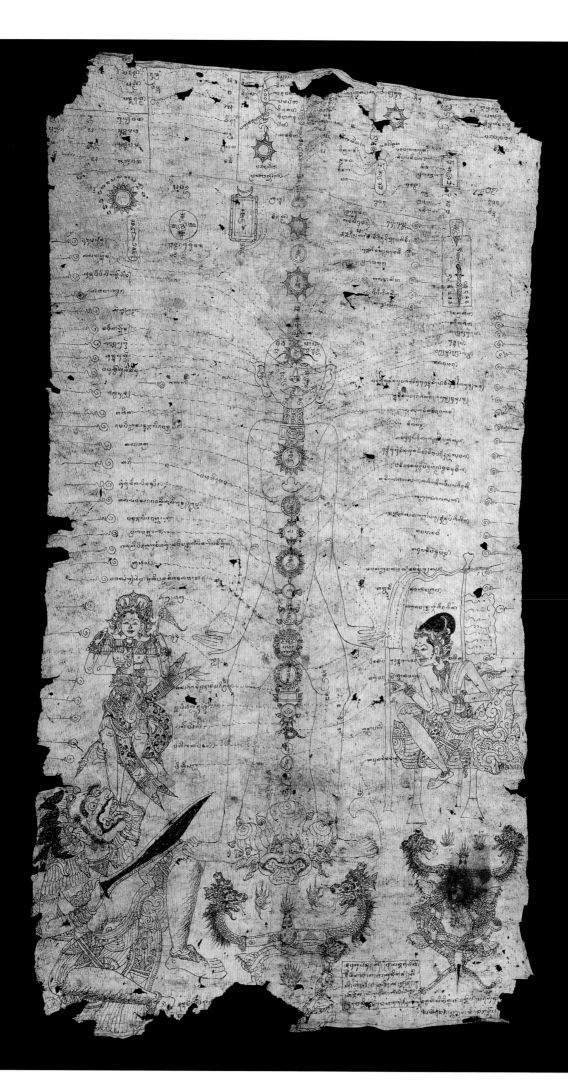

A *kajang* is a special ritual cloth necessary for the proper performance of a Balinese cremation ceremony. It is laid over the body (rather than being a shroud in which to wrap the body), and is burned together with the body. The cloth is inscribed with a series of sacred syllables of mystical significance according to the esoteric doctrines of Tantric Hinduism. Sometimes, as in the case of the cloth exhibited here, the syllables are depicted in conjunction with a human figure representing the deceased, and with figures of deities and mythological animals. The syllables and figures inscribed vary with caste and kin group, and with the level of ritual elaboration; thus there are scores of different *kajang*. A *kajang* is normally created by a high priest, such as a *pedanda*, or by a member of a priestly family under the priest's supervision. The knowledge and creation of *kalang* are often kept secret. (For a further discussion of the *kajang*, see the essay by David Stuart-Fox in this volume.)

This *kajang* is unique in many respects. Firstly, the fact that it exists at all: Why was it not burned during the cremation ceremony? To begin to answer this question, we can further examine some basic characteristics of a *kajang*, and some peculiarities of this *kajang*. The design, syllables, and figures on a typical *kajang* are so complicated, and the number of different shrouds so large, that the design and symbolic elements cannot be committed to memory alone. In priestly households, among the collection of *lontar* books, what might be called "sampler" *lontar*s are often found, giving examples of many different kinds of *kajang*. When a *kajang* is required for a cremation, the priest copies the design from the *lontar* book onto a piece of cotton cloth. The *kajang* exhibited here, however, indicates that samplers were not only found in miniature form in *lontar* books, but also full size on lengths of cloth. This fact is made explicit in the inscription within the outlined rectangle at the bottom.

The inscription on this shroud is in itself most unusual if not entirely unique (but since such objects are kept so secretively, one cannot be certain), for it provides information as to the purpose of the *kajang*, when it was made, and who the owner was. It reads as follows:

> Putus sinurat, polan kajang iki, ring dina, sa, ka, wara kuningan, titi, tang, ping, 8, sasih, ka, 3, rah, 2, tenggek, 9, isaka, 1792. Druwen i[da] made cadug, ring subagan. [*The writing of this* kajang *sampler was completed on Saturday (Saniscara), Kaliwon {a day in the Balinese five-day week}, Kuningan {a week in the Balinese thirty-week* wuku *calendar}, moon cycle, eighth day of the waxing moon, the third month, of the Saka year 1792 {*rah *2 refers to the final numeral of the year number, and* tenggek *9 to the penultimate numeral}. Property of Ida Made Cadug, at Subagan.*]

The inscription explicitly calls this cloth a "*polan kajang*," that is, a sampler (*pola*

43 Ritual cloth for use at a cremation (*kajang*), 1870

Bark paper, ink
H: 56.3 in; W: 29.9 in
Private collection, Netherlands

means design or pattern), which explains why this *kajang* is still in existence. The date on which the drawing or writing of the cloth was completed can be precisely determined from the calendrical information provided: September 3, 1870.[1]

The "owner" of the *kajang*, who presumably is also the maker, is given as Ida Made Cadug of Subagan. The title "Ida" indicates that he is from the Brahman caste; the fact that it is not "Ida Bagus," the title generally carried by a Brahman of a Saiva priestly family, suggests that he may be from a Buddhist family. Subagan is a village just west of Amlapura (Kabupaten Karangasem) where there are priestly households (*griya*) from both Saiva and Buddhist families. The *kajang* itself, however, shows Saiva characteristics, as we shall see.

A further unique aspect of this *kajang* is that it is drawn on finely made bark cloth or bark paper (*dluang*), related to Polynesian *tapa*.[2] Bark cloth was sometimes used for traditional *wayang*-style Balinese paintings, and it is also sometimes prescribed for certain ritual objects, such as for another death ritual object called *ulantaga*, or for magic drawings (*rerajahan*). Bark cloth or paper was made and used in ancient Java; in former times it was used in Bali, but whether it was once produced there is uncertain. At least in more recent times bark cloth was imported from Sulawesi, presumably originating from Toraja peoples who used bark cloth for clothing.[3] Details of this trade are unknown, but such commerce was presumably handled by either Chinese or Bugis traders operating from Buleleng on the north coast of Bali.

The *kajang* is dominated by a somewhat elongated standing human figure, arms down at its sides, in a stance and style related to other figures in the magical-mystical-medical arts of Hindu and Buddhist Asia. Down the center of the figure, from above the head down to the turtle-like image at its feet, is a line of sacred designs bearing mystic syllables. These symbols might seem to be related to the *cakra* system of yoga doctrines, and some such designs are explicitly described as *cakras,* centers located along the central axis of the subtle body along which energy flows. In this case, the number of symbols, greater than the seven *cakras* of the classic *cakra* system, indicates that other doctrines are playing a role. Also important are the number-based sets of sacred syllables (*dasaksara*, etc.) that play such a crucial role in all forms of Balinese ritual. Short texts on either side of the figure run the length of the shroud, with intermittent lines linking each text to a point on the figure. To what extent these texts, which are in a mixture of Kawi (Old Javanese) and Sanskrit, are an integral part of the shroud, or are explicative in nature, is uncertain.

At the bottom of the *kajang* are a number of drawings. Between the figure's feet is

---

[1] This elaborate calendrical information is internally consistent, in the sense that the date reckoned according to the *wuku* calendar is consistent with that from the lunar calendar: September 3, 1870, is indeed the eighth day of a waxing moon, and the third Balinese month does generally fall in or around September.

[2] Another *kajang* drawn on bark cloth, believed to be in a German collection, has parallels with this *kajang* and is likely from the same source. It too bears an inscription that indicates it is a *kajang* of the Pasek Gelgel kin group. It bears the date Saka 1811, equivalent to 1889.

[3] Miguel Covarrubias, *Island of Bali* (New York: Knopf, 1937), 192. Anthony Forge, *Balinese Traditional Paintings* (Sydney: Australian Museum, 1978), 9.

a turtle, and below that a pair of serpents (*naga*), symbols related to the structure of the cosmos. On the right-hand side, at the bottom corner, there is another, partly obscured, figure of two *naga* entwined around a turtle, as indicated by its accompanying text. Above this figure is a human figure seated on a platform, indicated schematically by the bottom of two of its posts. Next to this figure are a flag (*kober*) and a banner (*umbul-umbul*), objects that commonly accompany Balinese rituals. Presumably the figure represents a high priest who is conducting the ritual, and assisting the deceased to reach the goal of liberation from the confines of material matter, the ultimate aim of the cremation ritual.

On the left hand side is a pair of figures depicting the four-armed god Siwa emerging from the mouth of a demonic figure, holding a very large knife, presumably representing Kala. Siwa holds the fly whisk and rosary (*ganitri*) in his back hands. In this context, this image perhaps symbolizes the liberation of the soul from karmic attachments, and its return to divine form. Clearly, the *kajang* as a whole refers to a number of esoteric doctrines, whose full implications have yet to be interpreted by scholars.

To return to the *kajang* itself, unfortunately the surviving inscription does not indicate the kin group for whom it is intended. This is an extremely elaborate *kajang*, drawn with consummate skill. Although *kajang* for a high priest usually consists only of sacred syllables, which may be connected with the higher spiritual status of a priest, this *kajang* may be an exception. The caption accompanying a published photograph of a remarkably similar *kajang* in the possession of a brahmana buda priestly family[4] calls it a "rajah kajang Sutasoma" and indicates that it is to be used at the cremation of a Buda high priest (*pedanda buda*). The Sutasoma is an Old Javanese metrical poem with a strongly Buddhist character. Sutasoma is in fact none other than the Buddha himself. The story ends with Sutasoma, for the sake of the world, offering himself to Kala who tries to kill him with his sword and then tries to swallow him, but without success. Kala realizes Sutasoma's true nature and is initiated into the dharma. This episode, as the publication indicates, offers an alternative (or additional) interpretation of the drawing of Kala and the deity: it represents Kala trying to eat Sutasoma. Since the poem emphasizes the essential oneness of Buddha and Siwa, and since (as far as I know) Sutasoma, as Buddha, has no distinctive iconography in Balinese painting, Sutsoma is represented in the likeness of Siwa. The association of this kind of *kajang* with the *brahmana buda* finds support in the fact that the owner of the *kajang* exhibited was also probably a member of a *brahman buda* family

DSF

4 Ida Wayan Oka Granoka, *Perburuan ke prana jiwa: perburuan seorang Ida Wayan Granoka* (Denpasar: Sanggar Bajra Sandhi, 1998), 75–77. From the photograph it is not clear what kind of material it is made of (paper of some sort?). Is it also a "sampler" *kajang,* or is it possible that special *kajang* were reused and not burned (perhaps in conjunction with one that was)?

44 Ceremonial axe, approx. 1935

Copper/nickel/zinc alloy, steel, wood

L: 23 in; W: 5¼ in

Asian Art Museum, Vicki Baum Bali Collection, Gift of Wolfgang Lert and Ruth Clark Lert, 1992.42

1 Albert G. van Zonneveld, *Traditional Weapons of the Indonesian Archipelago* (C. Zwartenkot Art Books, 2001), figs. 83–85.

2 Van Zonneveld, fig. 644.

3 Christiaan Hooykaas, *Drawings of Balinese Sorcery* (Leiden: E. J. Brill, 1980).

4 Thanks to David Stuart-Fox for deciphering the inscriptions.

This ceremonial axe most likely belongs to a class of Balinese knives used during death rituals. The long round hilt is wrapped with thin sheets of a copper, nickel, and zinc alloy. The blade curves and widens slightly, then flares at the tip into three flame-shaped points. Blades of this type can take a number of forms, some geometric and others anthropomorphic.[1] One side of the blade is decorated with a geometric pattern of inlay resembling basket weave. The same pattern is seen on other Balinese knives, especially the short machetes known as *wedung*, which also have a largely symbolic purpose.[2]

The other side of the axe is inscribed in a number of places. In the three tips of the blade are three sacred syllables, *ang*, *ung*, and *mang*. These syllables are known as the *triaksara* and symbolize the Hindu deities Brahma, Wisnu, and Iswara (Siwa). Letters and syllables are very important in Balinese religious practice, and these three are commonly found on sacred drawings.[3] Also inscribed near the center of the blade are what appear to be the Roman letters I, J, and K. Their meaning is unclear. At the bottom of the blade in Balinese are letters possibly reading "I Ceka," which could be the name of someone associated with the knife (the blacksmith, the patron?).[4]

Unlike some of the other objects collected by the German novelist Vicki Baum (cat. nos. 116 and 117), this ritual weapon was most likely not produced for a tourist market, and it would be interesting to know more about how and why Baum purchased it.

NR

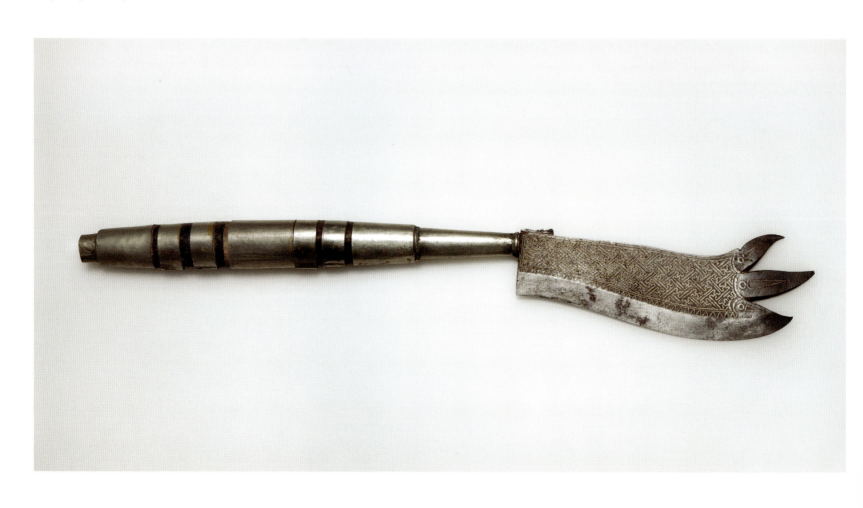

These doors (*jelanan*), from the palace of the raja of Badung, Denpasar, are famous not only because of their huge size and finely carved decorations in high relief, but also because of their dramatic collection history.[1] In 1906, the artist W. O. J. Nieuwenkamp, travelling in Bali to collect Balinese arts and crafts for the National Museum of Ethnology in Leiden (see article in this volume), more or less by chance witnessed the military expedition of the Dutch against the raja of the small kingdom of Badung, I Gusti Ngurah Made Agung. On September 20, 1906, the capital, Denpasar, was taken, followed by the *puputan* ("fight to the finish") of the ruler, his family, and many followers.[2] From the "dreadful mess" and "terrible shambles" of the partly burned palace (*puri*) he "rescued some objects." He also measured the vast palace and made a map of it.

> The whole, 171 meters long and 158 meters wide, consists of twenty-three right-angled spaces ... surrounded by a massive wall, six meters high and one-and-a-half meters thick.... I was able only with great difficulty to save two beautiful doors from the great doorway, which led from the forecourt to the space meant for guests.[3] The men had wanted to use them for making a bridge over a water channel, for the soldiers; happily, they are now safely housed in the Ethnography Museum in Leiden, and find themselves among the most beautiful of the very extensive Bali collection. These massive pieces, each carved out of one enormous piece of *djati* [teak], are 4.37 meters high, 1.46 meters wide taken together, and 6 cm thick, and on one side are entirely carved.[4]

From the invoice Nieuwenkamp sent to Leiden, we learn that forty porters were needed to transport the heavy doors to the coast in Sanur; from there they were shipped to the Netherlands.

In his *Bouwkunst van Bali* Nieuwenkamp published three drawings of details of the carved panels of the doors, which he described as follows:

> "The bottom part of the right door shows a *singa* or winged lion; the center part of the left door shows Sarpamoeka, a serpent with the body of a monkey and the center part of the right door Djatajoe, from the Ramayana."[5]

A winged *singa* is also carved on the bottom part of the left door. Both *singa* or lion figures are depicted with neck ornaments and with their heads bent backward, their mouths wide open, showing their teeth and curled tongues. The wings seem to give them extra power.[6]

At the top of the carved panels, two birds sit among spirals of floral and leaf motifs. It is possible that the large bird with human arms in the center of the right door is meant to be Jatayu, but it might also represent Garuda, the giant eagle (cat. no. 47). The composite

45 Pair of palace doors (*jelanan*), approx. 1800–1900

Denpasar, Badung
Wood
H: 172 in; W: 57½ in (both doors)
National Museum of Ethnology, Leiden, the Netherlands, 1586-31

---

1 Published several times, most recently in Francine Brinkgreve, "Balinese Rulers and Colonial Rule," in ed. Endang Sri Hardiati and Pieter ter Keurs, *Indonesia: The Discovery of the Past* (Amsterdam: KIT Publishers, 2005), 132.

2 Francine Brinkgreve and David Stuart-Fox, "Collecting after Colonial Conflict: Badung and Tabanan 1906–2006," in ed. Pieter ter Keurs, *Colonial Collections Revisited* (Leiden: CNWS Publications, 2007), 146–150.

3 Photograph in H. M. van Weede, *Indische reisherinneringen* (Haarlem: Tjeenk Willink, 1908), 480.

4 W. O. J. Nieuwenkamp, *Zwerftochten op Bali* (Amsterdam: Elsevier, 1910), 135. Author's translation.

5 W. O. J. Nieuwenkamp, *Bouwkunst van Bali* ('s-Gravenhage: Leopold's, 1926), 12, figs. 25–27. Sarpamuka means "with the face of a snake," hence the split tongue of the figure, but I do not know this name as belonging to any character in the Ramayana epic. Author's translation.

figure on the left, a combination of at least three animals, has the tail of a monkey, wears a crown, and has the split tongue of a serpent and the wings of a bird. According to Nieuwenkamp, this is Sarpamuka (literally "serpent face"). But could he also be identified as Sugriwa, the king of the monkeys who helped rescue Sita in the Ramayana epic, as though in conversation with Jatayu (depicted opposite), who as brave messenger also plays a role in this narrative?[7] But whether the subject is Sarpamuka or Sugriwa, the wings of the figures are atypical. It is also possible that both figures, and the two *singa* and birds, have only a decorative function amid the floral motifs.

The identification of the floral design of the carving is uncertain. It could be the lotus flower, a typical Hindu symbol of purity and often represented in Balinese floral ornamentation. But it can also be identified as the flower and fruit, full of seeds, of the *delima* (or *dalima*), the pomegranate (*Punica granatum*),[8] which in Hinduism symbolizes prosperity and fertility. Another possibility is the chrysanthemum flower, which, like the motif of the winged lion, is influenced by Chinese styles, and is called in Bali *patra Cina*, the Chinese ornament. The floral design is probably a combination of all three ornaments, in Bali called *patra sari*, flower ornament.[9]

Nieuwenkamp collected palace doors not only from Badung but also from the palace of Tabanan (see the entries for cat. nos. 48 and 49) and the palace in Klungkung.[10] All these palaces were demolished by the Dutch. The Dutch, in one sense, were no different from indigenous conquerors, for after war among Balinese states themselves, they too carried away parts of palace buildings as spoils.[11] Finely carved doors, used in the gateways of the walls that separated the different courtyards in the palace complex, or in some of the closed buildings of the palace, are among the most beautiful examples of Balinese court art.

FB

6 On the *singa* motif, see also the article by Francine Brinkgreve this volume.

7 In the Javanese *wayang,* a puppet of a monkey with serpent head is called Antareja. See Walter Angst, *Wayang Indonesia: Die phantastische Welt des indonesischen Figurentheaters/The Fantastic World of Indonesian Puppet Theatre* (Konstanz: Stadler, 2007), 150–151, ill. 81.

8 H. H. Juynboll, *Catalogus van 's Rijks Ethnographisch Museum, Deel VII Bali en Lombok* (Leiden: Brill, 1912), 29.

9 About Chinese influence, see the article by Francine Brinkgreve in this catalogue; Helen Ibbitson Jessup, *Court Arts of Indonesia* (New York: Asia Society Galleries in association with Harry N. Abrams, 1990), 242; Urs Ramseyer, *The Art and Culture of Bali* (Oxford: Oxford University Press, 1977), 69; *patra sari*: J. E. Jasper and Mas Pirngadie, *De inlandsche kunstnijverheid in Nederlandsch Indië, IV. De goud- en zilversmeedkunst* ('s-Gravenhage: Mouton, 1927), 53.

10 Now in the Staatliches Museum für Völkerkunde, München, illustrated in ed. Arne and Eva Eggebrecht, *Versunkene Königreiche Indonesiens* (Mainz: Von Zabern, 1995), no. 252.

11 Francine Brinkgreve and David Stuart-Fox, "Collecting after Colonial Conflict: *Badung* and *Tabanan* 1906–2006," in ed. Pieter ter Keurs, *Colonial Collections Revisited* (Leiden: CNWS Publications, 2007), 152.

Ink drawing made on January 19, 1907, by W. O. J. Nieuwenkamp, of the palace gateway with the doors still in situ. The text in translation: "The beautiful wooden doors from this gateway brought to Holland are now in the museum in Leiden." *Photo Stichting Museum Nieuwenkamp.*

T his wood panel presumably once served as a lintel to a doorway of an aristocratic home. The scene depicts two crouching winged lions with spiky manes and bulging eyes. At right, one lion has a paw on the ground, while the other reaches up to grab a crown that forms the apex of the lintel. The left lion's large forepaw seizes the hind leg of a small red deer and pulls it up toward his open jaws. The deer twists his head in panic, looking up at his predator.

This panel's motifs draw on a combination of different cultural sources. The lion as symbol of kingship spread from India throughout much of Southeast Asia. Lions are found on the earliest Hindu and Buddhist temple architecture in Java, and winged lions feature prominently in the decoration of the East Javanese temple of Panataran. The motif of a lion attacking a deer is depicted on various architectural elements in Bali.[1]

Lions were also, of course, a sign of royalty in Europe and were part of the Netherlands coat of arms. The royal emblem of the Dutch nation has a rampant lion on either side of a shield topped by a crown; that crown consists of a golden ring with eight pearl-studded diadems that meet at the center, topped by a golden orb and cross. The crown on the top of this Balinese lintel is clearly modeled after the Netherlands' heraldic crown, which was established in 1815. An open flower tops the Balinese version depicted here, and the round objects studding the sides of the crown have small holes in the center.

In the nineteenth century, images of the Dutch coat of arms and the crown quickly made their way to Indonesia, depicted on coins, colonial architecture, and in paintings of William I, as well as incorporated into the regal emblems of the courts of Central Java.[2] The winged lion became the symbol of the Buleleng regency of northern Bali, whose capital, Singaraja, means "lion king." As the administrative seat of the Dutch colonizers, it makes sense that this mixture of cultural emblems found expression there.

NR

46 Lintel

Singaraja, North Bali
Wood and pigments
H: 23¾ in; W: 34 in; D: 7½ in
Private collection

1 H. I. R Hinzler, *Catalogue of Balinese Manuscripts in the Library of the University of Leiden and Other Collections in the Netherlands* (Leiden: E. J. Brill, 1986), 65–66; Made Wijaya, *Architecture of Bali: A Source Book of Traditional and Modern Forms.* (University of Hawaii Press, 2003), 114e, 171g, 183f.

2 Kees Zandvliet, ed., *The Dutch Encounter with Asia, 1600–1950* (Amsterdam: Rijksmuseum, 2004), figs. 146, 154, 155, 167.

This painted cloth was used as a covering for the ceiling of a pavilion, most likely in one of the South Balinese royal or princely palaces or temples. According to the collector, Th. A. Resink, who worked as an engineer in Bali in the 1930s and who was involved in the founding and development of the Bali Museum in Denpasar, the painting is made in the style of Kamasan. This village is near Klungkung, where the *sangging*, specialists in the art of drawing and painting, lived and worked to order for Klungkung courts.[1]

The painting shows an episode from the *Garudeya*, a part of the *Adiparwa* that tells the story of the giant eagle Garuda, the vehicle of Batara Wisnu and one of Hinduism's best known mythical creatures. The *Adiparwa* is the first book of the Mahabharata, one of the two great classic Hindu epics (the other being the Ramayana), which became a major thematic source for Balinese narrative, visual, and performing arts. The Old Javanese prose version of the *Adiparwa* remains popular in Bali to this day.

The story is as follows:[2] The serpent Winata has become the servant of her sister Kadru, having lost a contest. She now must look after 1000 unruly serpent children of Kadru, and she orders her son Garuda to help her with this onerous job. The only way Garuda can release his mother from this curse is by stealing for the serpents the *amerta*, elixir of life, which is in the possession of the gods. Garuda undertakes this task, but the gods, under the leadership of the god Indra, intend to defend their treasure. There ensues a great battle, which is illustrated by the painting; the text describes it in part:[3]

> The gods aimed their weapons at him; he was struck by spears, discuses, and thunderbolts. The gods fired all kinds of weapons at him, but none of them harmed him. They were powerless and broke off and not a feather of him was injured. In his turn Garuda lashed out at the multitude of gods; they were blown away, thrown about, turned upside down, and knocked over.

Garuda proves himself the stronger and succeeds in obtaining the *amerta*, with which he is able to release his mother. Afterwards he allows the god Wisnu to ask a favor from him and, as a result, becomes Wisnu's vehicle. Eventually the serpents lose the elixir of life again, and it remains from that time in the possession of the gods.

The battle scene is painted in a lively way. The giant figure of Garuda holds in his right hand the winged vase containing the elixir of life. Surrounding him are six gods, each depicted with a separate nimbus, attacking the bird with their arrows. According to the collector Resink, the deities represent the protectors of the four cardinal directions (upper two and lower two), the zenith (left center), and the nadir (right center).

47 Painted canopy (*leluur*), approx. 1875–1925

Cotton, pigments
H: 106¼ in; W: 57⅞ in
National Museum of Ethnology, Leiden, the Netherlands, 4491-65

1 *De Kunst van Bali: verleden en heden* (Den Haag: Haags Gemeentemuseum, 1961), 14; Francine Brinkgreve, "Balinese Rulers and Colonial Rule," in ed. Endang Sri Hardiati and Pieter ter Keurs, *Indonesia: The Discovery of the Past* (Amsterdam: KIT Publishers, 2005), 144.

2 H. H. Juynboll, "De geschiedenis van Garuda," *Koninklijk Instituut voor de Taal-, Land- en Volkenkunde van Nederlandsch-Indië: Gedenkschrift uitgegeven ter gelegenheid van het 75-jarig bestaan op 4 juni 1926* ('s-Gravenhage: Nijhoff, 1926), 156–170; P. J. Zoetmulder, *Kalangwan: A Survey of Old Javanese Literature* (The Hague: Nijhoff, 1974), 69.

3 Adiparwa, H. H. Juynboll, "De geschiedenis van Garuda," *Koninklijk Instituut voor de Taal-, Land- en Volkenkunde van Nederlandsch-Indië: Gedenkschrift uitgegeven ter gelegenheid van het 75-jarig bestaan op 4 juni 1926*, 165.

4 The Old Javanese text of the *Adiparwa* (Section 6) does not single out these four deities, but instead mentions groups of divine beings in the four directions. On the *lokapala*, see J. E. van Lohuizen-de Leeuw, "The Dikpalakas in Ancient Java," *Bijdragen tot de Taal-, Land- en Volkenkunde* 111 (1955), 356–384. They do sometimes make their appearance in traditional wayang painting; see, for example, Anthony Forge, *Balinese Traditional Paintings* (Sydney: Australian Museum, 1978), pl. 46. In the common *nawa-sanga* system, Iswara is in the east, Brahma south, Mahadewa west, and Wisnu north.

5 For the sake of artistic symmetry, the artist has shown the gods on the left side with their bows in their left hands. Only the god of the upper right corner carries a weapon in his other hand. This object appears to be a thunderbolt, the weapon of Indra, rather than of Kuwera. Furthermore, the text states that the north was defended by the twelve Adityas under the leadership of Indra. It would seem that, to fit the text, the artist has exchanged the usual positions of Indra and Kuwera.

6 See cat. nos. 48 and 49.

7 *De Kunst van Bali: verleden en heden* (Den Haag: Haags Gemeentemuseum, 1961), 14.

8 Anthony Forge, *Balinese Traditional Paintings* (Sydney: Australian Museum, 1978), text to pl. 11.

9 Anthony Forge, *Balinese Traditional Paintings*, pl. 11.

Resink identified the four corner deities as Indra, Kuwera, Yama, and Baruna. These are not the typical gods of the cardinal directions, but follow the less common system of the world protectors called *lokapala* or *dikpala(ka)*.[4] Contrary to Resink's identification, these four corner figures seem to represent the following: top right: Indra, god of the north; top left: Kuwera, god of the east; bottom left: Yama, god of the south; and bottom right: Baruna, god of the west. As a ceiling painting, the sides of the painting (but not the ends) are reversed when attaching it to the ceiling; the left side of the painting becomes the right side when looking up at it, and vice versa. Thus Kuwera, god of the east, for example, although left on the painting, would in fact be on the east side of the ceiling, and so on. These deities appear — mostly individually, rarely as a group — in other traditional *wayang* paintings, with their own iconography. Yama for example, as god of the underworld, is always portrayed with demonic features, and Baruna has the rounded eyes of less refined characters. They all carry bows in their hands; Indra also carries in his left hand his own characteristic weapon, the thunderbolt (*vajra,* or *bajra* in Balinese).[5] The god of the zenith is depicted as a *halus* type, with refined characteristics, and the god of the nadir as having certain *kasar* or coarse characteristics.[6]

At the very bottom on the left, the *panakawan* figure Twalen, one of the servant or clown figures of the *wayang,* flees the battle for safety; he wears his usual checked *poleng* waist cloth. It is, however, too late for a *gandharwa,* a celestial follower of the gods, who is crushed beneath the claws of Garuda's left foot.[7] The air is filled with arrows, and the mass of fill motifs suggests a violent, vibrating atmosphere.

According to Anthony Forge, "Balinese artists frequently use this scene to show the Balinese conception of the directions, with the attributes which are attached to each."[8] This painting of the great battle shows Garuda attacked from six directions. In other ceiling paintings of this battle, Garuda is attacked by the eight gods of the four cardinal and four intermediate directions, the common *nawa-sanga* system.[9] The story is also painted in other formats.

FB

One week after the *puputan* (final ritual battle and suicide) in Denpasar (September 20, 1906), the Dutch expeditionary force marched against the neighboring state of Tabanan. As an ally of Badung, Tabanan had refused to close the border during the Dutch blockade of Badung. However, the old ruler, Gusti Ngurah, and his son and heir to the throne, Gusti Ngurah Anom, were compelled to surrender to the Dutch when they arrived in Badung to attempt negotiations. That same night, in shame at their surrender, the king and his son took their own lives. After the Dutch took control, the *puri* or palace of the raja of Tabanan was also organized into an army camp, and a *controleur*, inspector, was installed to enforce Dutch authority.[1]

W. O. J. Nieuwenkamp visited Tabanan, arriving there on January 6, 1907. He wrote:

> A public sale was held of the numerous movables from the *poeri,* because it was simpler to divide up a particular sum of money between the dead prince's heirs than a huge number of different objects. Here I was able to purchase a good many important items on behalf of the R.E.M. [Rijks Ethnographisch Museum] in Leiden. I also succeeded in acquiring a fine set of very fine wooden doors with gilded carving, for this museum, together with two pieces of painted bed compartments, and four ceremonial weapons carried in front of the ruler of Tabanan when he went walking.[2]

This painted panel, called a *parba,* which decorated one of the royal sleeping pavilions in the palace of Tabanan, illustrates extensive and highly detailed episodes from the Ramayana *kakawin* (see also cat. no. 40). It depicts the killing of Rawana and his son, Indrajit, in the final battle between Rama and Rawana and their armies, and the conclusion of the great epic, the fire test of Sita.[3] This subject is one of the great examples of the continuing conflict between good and evil, a theme also often expressed in *wayang* theater. In the conventions of the *wayang,* the good (*halus* or *manis*) figures are on the right of the puppeteer or *dalang,* and the evil ones (*keras, kasar*) on the left. But viewed from the side of the spectators, these directions are reversed. The convention of wayang painting follows the viewpoint of the spectator: the good are on the left and the bad on the right, as in this painting.[4] The fierce battle scenes are separated from one another by flaming rock motifs.

On the lowest panel on the left, Rama, followed by Wibisana, the brother of Rawana who supports Rama, is leading an army of monkeys; the white one at far left is Hanoman. Rama fights an army of demons headed by Indrajit on the right, one of the children of Rawana. Laksmana, Rama's brother (depicted beneath Rama and Wibisana), has just

48 Painted wooden panel (*parba*) from a pavilion, approx. 1800–1900

Tabanan

Painted and gilded wood

H: 62⅝ in; W: 58¼ in; D: 2 in

National Museum of Ethnology, Leiden, the Netherlands, 1586-33

---

1 Francine Brinkgreve and David Stuart-Fox, "Collecting after Colonial Conflict: Badung and Tabanan 1906–2006," in ed. Pieter ter Keurs, *Colonial Collections Revisited* (Leiden: CNWS Publications, 2007); Francine Brinkgreve, "Balinese rulers and colonial rule," in ed. Endang Sri Hardiati and Pieter ter Keurs, *Indonesia: The Discovery of the Past* (Amsterdam: KIT Publishers, 2005).

2 W. O. J. Nieuwenkamp, *Bali en Lombok* (Edam: De Zwerver, 1906–1910), 187. Author's translation.

3 Sarga 23 and 24. P. J. Zoetmulder, *Kalangwan: A Survey of Old Javanese Literature* (The Hague: Nijhoff, 1974), 225–226. See also H. H. Juynboll, *Catalogus van 's Rijks Ethnographisch Museum, Deel VII Bali en Lombok* (Leiden: Brill, 1912), 31 and pl. VII; Francine Brinkgreve, "Balinese Rulers and Colonial Rule*,*" in *Indonesia: The Discovery of the Past*), 132–133.

4 Anthony Forge, *Balinese Traditional Paintings*, 70–74.

shot an arrow into the heart of Indrajit, who is escorted by nine wives (the text mentions seven) who stand behind him, far right. They are all killed by Laksmana's arrows. Blood spurts from their chests, and Indrajit falls backward from a chariot drawn by two horses and decorated with two umbrellas. The characters seem to traverse waters set afire by the battle, and fish peek above the surface to watch the scene. Perhaps this is a representation of the sea between Lengka (Rawana's realm) and Ayodhya (where Rama rules), which was bridged by the monkey army led by Sugriwa and Hanoman.

Next Rawana himself sets out in his golden chariot. In the central panel of the painting, toward the top left, Laksmana is hit by Rawana's arrow Amogha. Blood spouting from his breast, he is healed by Wibisana with the aid of a miraculous herb fetched by Hanoman from the Himalayas. Toward the center, Rama shoots Rawana with the god Indra's arrow. With one shot, Rawana's ten heads are severed from his body. In the painting, Rawana has already lost most of his heads and is falling backward from his carriage, which is decorated with two red umbrellas.

After Rama's victory, Wibisana becomes king of Lengka. Rama and Sita finally meet again, but according to Rama they can no longer live together, because she has been held captive by Rawana. Overcome with grief, Sita calls on the gods to bear witness that she has remained faithful and pure. As shown on the top panel of the painting, Sita descends into the fire as proof of her faithfulness. Rama, Laksmana, Wibisana and many monkeys watch the fire ordeal. Sita is protected by the god Agni; Siwa and all the other gods appear, and the fire changes into a golden lotus. This phenomenon dispels Rama's suspicions, and they all return happily to Ayodhya.

This painting follows both *wayang* theater conventions and *wayang* iconography in the characteristics of the figures. The skin of noble types like Rama is white, beige, or light ochre, while that of demonic ones like Rawana is dark brown or red. Coarse characters like Indrajit are hairy and have fangs and round, bulging eyes, whereas refined types, male and female, remain delicate and graceful, even in the fiercest battle, as illustrated by Laksmana. Head coverings, clothes, and jewelry provide information about sex, rank, and function. For example, Rama and Rawana, both being kings, wear crowns. Other characters wear their princely jewelry and sumptuous textiles even in the midst of epic struggle.

The story of King Rama and his faithful wife, Sita, is very popular throughout Southeast Asia. At the courts of Bali, the rajas identified themselves with Rama, the heroic incarnation of Wisnu. This theme, therefore, seems fitting for the decoration of a royal bedroom. Paintings in palaces were used to enhance the meaning of the buildings they embellished, illustrating

5 Helen Ibbitson Jessup, *Court Arts of Indonesia* (New York: Asia Society Galleries in association with Harry N. Abrams, 1990), 183; Urs Ramseyer, *The Art and Culture of Bali* (Oxford: Oxford University Press, 1977), 61.

6 Urs Ramseyer, *The Art and Culture of Bali*, 63; P. de Kat Angelino, "Over de smeden en eenige andere ambachtslieden op Bali," *Tijdschrift voor Indische Taal-, Land- en Volkenkunde* 61 (1922), 381–424.

the ideas that made the buildings significant. Their main purpose was not only to entertain the viewer, but also to convey the ethical and moral standards of the established order.[5]

The place of origin of these panels' painters (*sangging*) is uncertain. To date there is no evidence that the court of Tabanan itself had painters in residence. Quite possibly the work was done by painters from Kerambitan, some ten kilometers away, where an important court existed belonging to a senior line of the same descent group as that of the Tabanan ruler. A few fine old *parba* paintings still survive in palaces at Kerambitan. What might be called the Kerambitan school of traditional painting continued into the twentieth century in the fine work of the painters I Matjong and I Gusti Wayan Kopang.

The painting on this *parba* includes the colors white, red, black, and brown, accentuated by many thick white dots. Lines are first drawn with charcoal and then with China ink or lampblack ink, and the figures are colored with a brush made from bamboo. Traditional paints are produced from natural materials: white made from burnt and pulverized pig skulls, black made of lampblack, vermilion imported from China, while brown is made by mixing the primary colors. The paints are mixed with water, Chinese fish glue, and lime. Jewelry is enhanced with gold leaf, and corrections and additions are made with China ink.[6]

FB

This *parba* has the same collection history as cat. no. 48. They were collected at the same time by W. O. J. Nieuwenkamp, from the palace of Tabanan, in January 1907.¹

The painting depicts scenes from the *kekawin* Smaradahana, the Burning of Asmara. This is an Old Javanese poem about the eternal love between Asmara, or Kama, and his wife, Ratih.² The following episodes, separated by dividing motifs, are illustrated on the *parba*.³

Heaven is threatened by the demon Nilarudraka, but the god Siwa does not intervene because he is performing penance on Mount Meru. A son of Siwa and Uma could also act as savior, but since Siwa is indifferent even to the charms of his wife, the couple does not have children yet.

On the bottom panel of the painting, at the left Siwa is depicted in a meditative posture, in a rocky landscape under a tree (a *dharsana* tree, according to the text). As usual, his body is white, and in the upper pair of hands he holds two of his usual attributes, a rosary and a fly whisk. The fingers of his other hands are in a *mudra* position.

Wrhaspati, counselor of the gods, determines a solution. Indra asks Kama, the Cupid of the Hindu pantheon, to inflame Siwa's heart with love for Uma, so that she might give birth to a son who will be a savior of the gods. Kama launches various flower weapons against the god, and finally a powerful flower-shaped arrow penetrates his heart. But, disturbed in his meditation, Siwa in great fury emanates all-destroying flames that burn Kama to ashes.

In the upper left corner of the *parba*, three deities appear, all within a gold nimbus. With the god Indra leading the way, the trio visits Kama's widow, Ratih, in her palace, which is represented by a sleeping pavilion with three pillows, to inform her of her husband's death. In despair, Ratih clings to Wrhaspati's leg. Wrhaspati, depicted with the head covering of a sage, assures her that in the future she will be reunited with her husband. The gods are accompanied by their attendants, the servant-clown figures Twalen and Merdah.

Ratih accepts her fate and declares that she will follow Kama in death. To the right we see Ratih on her way to the place where Kama died, accompanied by her two servants, Nanda and Sunanda; all wear head scarves. In the woods and mountains they meet several animals and birds. One of the servants carries a betel bag (a plaited container for betel-chewing ingredients). In the bottom right corner, arriving at the spot where Kama was burned to ashes, Ratih, Nanda, and Sunanda can find only some bones, his skull, and the flowers from his love darts. Siwa causes the fire to flare up, and Ratih throws herself

49 Painted wooden panel (*parba*) from a pavilion, approx. 1800–1900

Tabanan

Painted and gilded wood

H: 59 in.; W: 57⅞ in.

National Museum of Ethnology, Leiden, the Netherlands, 1586-34

1 See also cat. no. 48 for general remarks on *wayang* paintings.

2 P. J. Zoetmulder, *Kalangwan: A Survey of Old Javanese Literature* (The Hague: Nijhoff, 1974), 291–295; see also cat. no. 29.

3 Juynboll's interpretation of this story, in H. H. Juynboll, *Catalogus van 's Rijks Ethnographisch Museum, Deel VII Bali en Lombok* (Leiden: Brill, 1912), 31 and pl. VIII, was later corrected by Galestin, *Cultureel Indië V*, 76. The story is also illustrated in ed. Paul L. F. van Dongen, Matthi Forrer, Willem R. van Gulik, *Topstukken uit het Rijksmuseum voor Volkenkunde/Masterpieces from the National Museum of Ethnology* (Leiden: Rijksmuseum voor Volkenkunde, 1987), 74.

into the flames, together with her two servants. Ratih and Kama are reunited in death, Kama enters the heart of Siwa, and Ratih that of Uma. It seems plausible that the figure of Siwa both begins and ends the story as depicted in the painting.

The story ends (not illustrated on the *parba*) with Siwa finally making love with Uma, the birth of their son, Gana (Sanskrit: Ganesha), who has the head of an elephant, and Gana destroying the demon Nilarudraka. Finally, Kama and Ratih are granted rebirth by Siwa.

Until the beginning of the twentieth century, at some Balinese courts, the widows of a raja who had passed away followed their husband in death by throwing themselves into the fire during his cremation ritual. This so-called *masatia* ritual was a sign of their eternal faithfulness and love, as though they were imitating the burning of Ratih in the Smaradahana. Thus this story is a fitting theme for the decoration of a royal bed. The Dutch colonizers tried to ban ritual suicide, but in 1903, it occurred again in Tabanan. This event was one of the causes of the military expedition against the court of Tabanan in 1906.

The frame of the painting is decorated with a meandering flower motif, *patra sari*. This painting from the Tabanan palace was probably made by an artist from Kerambitan, as in cat. no. 48.

FB

232 CATALOGUE

These gilded and richly decorated wooden chairs are said to originate from the pavilion of the court of justice, Kerta Ghosa, in Klungkung. Kerta Ghosa is situated on the grounds of the main palace, *puri*.[1] The palace was destroyed after the *puputan* of Klungkung in 1908,[2] but the hall remained intact and was still in use during the colonial period.[3] The chairs were purchased by the museum in 1946 from a private individual in The Hague. Whether they are really from the Kerta Ghosa or not, they are similar in design to the Kerta Ghosa chairs visible in old photographs and to those still in the building today. Those chairs are red and gold, whereas the chairs in the exhibition are almost entirely gilded, with some additions in white, black, and red.

Furniture was not particularly important in traditional Balinese craftsmanship. Traditionally, high-caste persons sat on mats or square cushions (*lungka-lungka*)[4] on the floors of elevated pavilions (*bale*), or on elevated platforms within pavilions. Chairs, tables, and thrones in chair form were adopted by the courts in imitation of Dutch colonial practice, and from the late nineteenth and early twentieth centuries became common in palaces, at least partly in order to receive European guests.[5]

These chairs have gilded carvings. The armrests of RMV 2582-1 feature two lion figures. Although the lion is not indigenous to Indonesia, in literature the *singa* is often regarded as ruler of the animals in the forest, and in general as a symbol of power and royalty. The back of this chair is entirely carved with flower, leaf, and fern ornaments, as a representation of the lions' natural surroundings. Apart from the lotus flower, a combination of various *patra* patterns is employed: *patra sari*, *patra samblung*, and *patra cina*. The chairs could well have been made by, or influenced by the work of, Chinese woodcarvers.

The back of the other chair, RMV 2582-2, has a beautifully carved composition of flowers in a vase, lotus buds, and abundant birds on branches. The birds make a fine contrast to the stately crowned and winged *naga* serpents that form the armrests. Because they also have feet, these *naga* appear to take the role of bearers or vehicles, similar to their function as carriers of figures of deities (*wahana* or *palinggihan*), and on palanquins as carriers of statues of deities (cat. no. 15). In many Indonesian cultures, the serpent as symbol of new life and fertility has a function in life cycle rituals (see also cat. no. 24), but it is also sometimes associated with royal power and protection.[6] In Bali the *naga*, like the *singa*, is strongly influenced by Indic mythology and beliefs. Basuki and Anantaboga, serpent royalty, entwined around a mighty turtle, play an important role in keeping the Balinese universe in balance, and are often represented in sculpture and painting.

FB

50, 51 Two chairs, approx. 1875–1925

Klungkung
Gilded and painted wood
H: 44¾ in; W: 22¾ in; D: 20¼ in;
H: 45¼ in; W: 23 in; D: 19⅞ in
National Museum of Ethnology, Leiden, the Netherlands, 2582-1 and 2582-2

1 Published in ed. Arne and Eva Eggebrecht, *Versunkene Königreiche Indonesiens* (Mainz: Von Zabern, 1995), nos. 235–236.

2 *Jaarverslag van het Rijksmuseum voor Volkenkunde 1946*, 4. Unfortunately, precise data on the collection history of these objects is lacking.

3 See, for example, a photo in the collection of the KITLV, nr. 7346, taken around 1915.

4 H. J. E. F. Schwartz, *Gids voor den bezoeker van de ethnographische verzameling, Zaal B Bali en Lombok* (Batavia: Bataviaasch Genootschap van Kunsten en Wetenschappen, 1920), 27.

5 Helen Ibbitson Jessup, *Court Arts of Indonesia* (New York: Asia Society Galleries in association with Harry N. Abrams, 1990), 178.

6 Hari Budiarti and Francine Brinkgreve, "Court arts of the Sumatran sultanates," ed. Francine Brinkgreve and Retno Sulistianingsih, *Sumatra: Crossroads of Cultures* (Leiden: KITLV Press, 2009), 125. As symbols of royal power, *naga* often decorated the prow of the royal boat. As a carrier, the mythical snake plays a role in rituals of transition. On the Lampung ceremonial seat or *pepadon*, the snakes on either side are associated with concepts of power and protection.

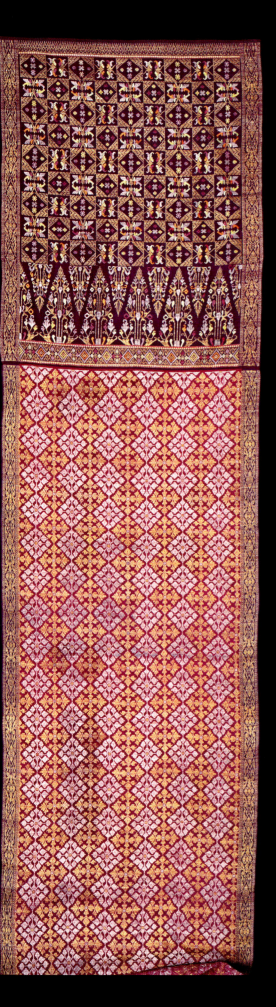

These unusual textiles were collected in Bali in the 1930s by the dancer, choreographer, and ethnologist Katharane Mershon (1892–1986). Mershon lived in Bali from 1931 to 1940, mostly in the coastal village of Sanur. Information provided to the Fowler Museum of Cultural History, to which Mershon donated her collection, states that these textiles were draped over the back of the palanquin of a raja, probably referring to the king of Buleleng in northern Bali.[1]

These two textiles, while exhibiting quite different patterns in the bodies of the cloths, share similar motifs in the end panels, suggesting that they were woven by the same person. Both long cloths are tours de force of weaving, combining intricate patterns, a wide variety of dyes, and a difficult technique. The textiles consist of a very long central panel with separately woven end panels and separately woven borders on one cloth. The color of the body of one cloth is pinkish purple with a deep purple end panel, while the other has a purple body and reddish purple end panels. The technique used to make the complex patterns on the textile, called *songket*, involves the addition of supplementary-weft metallic threads. These threads, comprising a silk core wrapped with thin strips of paper coated with silver or gold, were mostly imported from China.[2] Their use was a mark of the wealth and stature of the owner.

Until the second half of the twentieth century, the production and use of *songket* cloth were largely restricted to the highest castes.[3] But in recent times these cloths have become a sign of status for anyone with the money to purchase them. The technique of making these textiles has been described as "an extremely specialized craft" that often involves a number of assistants or specialists.[4] Before the textile is woven, the pattern is set into the threads of the warp with pattern rods, a complicated process that can take days.

A variety of patterns are used on these textiles. The very long center panels of both cloths display a single repeated pattern arranged in a diagonal grid. The main panel of the purple cloth is decorated with a pattern of eight-pointed stars; the other cloth has a stylized rosette pattern. The star motif was popular on Indian trade textiles found throughout Indonesia, including double-ikat *patola* cloths and cheaper block-printed textiles.[5] The pattern was repeated in a variety of techniques on indigenous textiles from many regions of Indonesia.

The detailed patterns seen in the end panels of these cloths are contained in a checkerboard framework. They include geometric and floral elements, as well as depictions of small birds (on the red end panels). A hallmark of many Indonesian

52 Ceremonial textile, approx. 1900–1930

Possibly Buleleng, North Bali
Silk and metal-wrapped threads
H: 29 1/8 in; W: 215 in
Fowler Museum at UCLA, The Katharane Mershon Collection of Indonesian Art, X61.61

53 Ceremonial textile, approx. 1900–1930

Possibly Buleleng, North Bali
Silk and metal-wrapped threads
H: 28 1/4 in; W: 246 in
Fowler Museum at UCLA, The Katharane Mershon Collection of Indonesian Art, X61.62

1 Roy Hamilton, personal correspondence.

2 Marie-Louise Nabholz-Kartaschoff, "The Textiles of Sembiran," in *Burials, Texts and Rituals* (Universitätsverlag Göttingen, 2008), 101–102.

3 Urs Ramseyer and Marie-Louise Nabholz-Kartaschoff, "Songket: Golden Threads, Caste and Privilege," in *Textiles in Bali* (Berkeley; Singapore: Periplus Editions, 1991), 36–37.

4 Marie-Louise Nabholz-Kartaschoff, "Cepuk: Sacred Textiles from Bali and Nusa Penida," in *Textiles in Bali* (Berkeley; Singapore: Periplus Editions, 1991), 42.

5 Robyn Maxwell, *Textiles of Southeast Asia: Tradition, Trade and Transformation*, revised (Hong Kong: Periplus Editions, 2003), figs. 303, 304.

6 Brigitta Hauser-Schaublin, Marie-Louise Nabholz-Kartaschoff, and Urs Ramseyer, *Textiles in Bali* (Berkeley; Singapore: Periplus Editions, 1991), 45.

textiles is a pattern of interlocking triangles (*tumpal*), forms that evoke both a tree and a mountain, that is often found on the end panels of the cloth. In Bali these motifs are called *tetumpengan*, a term derived from the cone-shaped rice offerings, or *pucuk rebong*, named after the bamboo shoot.⁶

NR

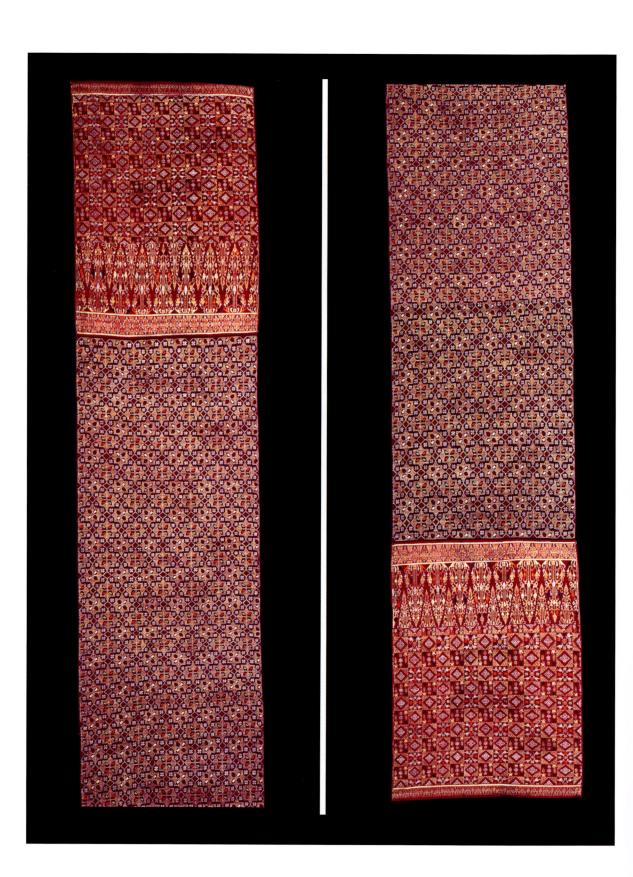

While smaller palanquins of this sort may have been used to carry images of deities during temple ceremonies, this nine-foot-long sedan chair was likely a vehicle for a member of a royal family.[1] Only the elite were allowed to use such sedan chairs, as it was deemed inappropriate for the public to see the feet of a king or queen touch the ground. In certain contexts rulers were referred as "gods on earth," and they deliberately associated themselves with divine imagery. One can still see members of Balinese princely families carried on palanquins during funerary ceremonies. By sponsoring extraordinarily expensive and elaborate rituals, the royalty asserted their status and wealth.

A Dutch army officer donated this palanquin to the Volkenkundig Museum Nusantara in Delft soon after the museum opened in 1864. It is finely carved and decorated with three painted panels. Crowned snakes, a common motif in Balinese art, flank the footrest. They represent *nagaraja,* or snake kings, which are associated with the kingdom of water. *Nagas* are often found around the base of the *padmasana,* a shrine found in many Balinese temples. There they represent Basuki and Anantaboga, two serpents who help churn the ocean of milk in an important Balinese creation myth.

The episodes illustrated on the back and sides of the palanquin come from an eleventh-century Javanese text, the *Arjunawiwaha* (Arjuna's Wedding), which was popular in Bali as well as in eastern Java. The poem describes episodes in the life of Arjuna, the third of the five Pandawa brothers, from the Indian epic the Mahabharata.[2] The story concerns a demon who cannot be defeated by the gods and who is intent on destroying Indra's heaven. Indra decides to ask for Arjuna's help, but first must assess his power. Arjuna has been meditating in a cave on a mountain, and Indra decides to test his readiness by tempting him with seven celestial maidens. Arjuna remains steadfast and convinces Indra of his worthiness. The demon sends a wild boar to kill Arjuna, who takes his bow and arrow and shoots the raging animal. The god Siwa, who has assumed the shape of a hunter, also shoots the boar, and Arjuna and Siwa argue over who has killed it. Almost defeated, Arjuna grabs the hunter's feet, causing Siwa to turn back into his godly form. Arjuna prays before Siwa and is rewarded with a magic weapon, an arrow with magical powers.

The back panel of the palanquin shows Arjuna's temptation. Arjuna sits cross-legged, in the garb of an ascetic, with his hair wrapped in a turban and his hands in a position of meditation. A red arch surrounds him, perhaps indicating the cave where he has retreated to gain spiritual power. Standing at his sides are four female figures, celestial nymphs sent by Indra to distract him, who lean toward him seductively, but

54 Palanquin (*jempana*), approx. 1800–1865

Painted and gilded wood, mica
H: 34⅝ in; W: 26¾; D: 101⅜ in
Volkenkundig Museum Nusantara, Delft, S58-I

1 For another example, see the raja of Pemecutan's palanquin in the Museum Nasional, Indonesia, illustrated in Pieter ter Keurs, *Colonial Collections Revisited* (CNWS Publications, 2007), 149.

2 Mpu Kanwa, *Arjunawiwaha: The Marriage of Arjuna,* trans. S. O. Robson (Leiden: KITLV Press, 2008).

in vain. The placement of Arjuna in the center of the panel aligns the hero with the seated passenger of the palanquin, and implies parallels between the two.

The relief to the rider's left depicts the episode in which Arjuna and the god Siwa, in the guise of a hunter, shoot the same boar. Siwa tries to test Arjuna by interrupting his penance with a demon in the form of a boar. The panel, curiously, shows only Arjuna, holding his bow, standing before the injured animal. Most depictions of this scene include Siwa as well, and show two arrows in the boar.

At first glance the third side of the palanquin (at the rider's right) seems to represent the denouement of this scene, in which Siwa appears before Arjuna, who kneels before him. Arjuna is rewarded by the gift of a magic weapon, the Pasopata. But comparison with versions of the *Arjunawiwaha* in palm leaf manuscripts suggests this actually might be Arjuna meeting Indra again in Indra's heaven. Behind Arjuna we see Twalen, Arjuna's servant and adviser, a god in the guise of a jester. His checked lower garment suggests his semidivinity, while his misshapen body and comical countenance point to his role as a clown. A fourth figure, with misshapen legs and a turban on his head, stands in the corner. This is likely to be Baru, a crippled servant who wears the garb of an ascetic.

The fact that this object was collected in the nineteenth century suggests a provenance from North Bali, where the Dutch had made conquests in middle of the century, but the style of painting on the panels is reminiscent of painting from the village of Kamasan in South Bali.

NR

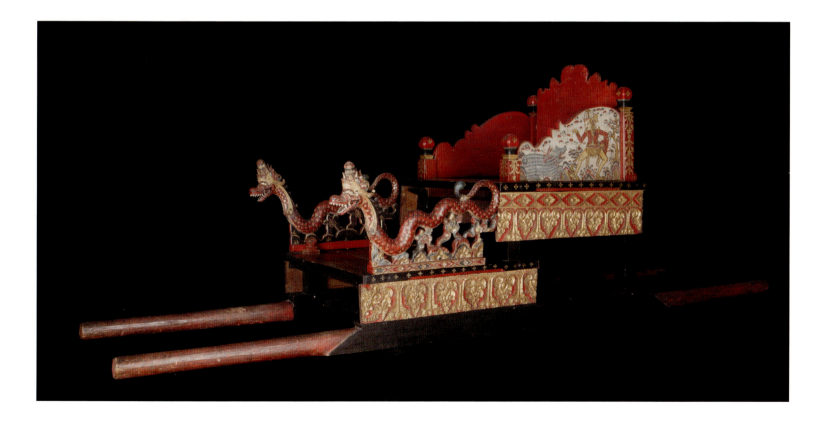

Today in Bali statues of the Hindu deity Wisnu on his mount, the mythical bird Garuda, are commonly produced for both for the tourist and local markets.[1] It is rare, though, to find an example as intricately carved as this one, which most likely dates from the mid-nineteenth to early twentieth century. It is rarer still to find an old statue with its apparent partner (see cat. no. 56), an image of the demon Rawana on his mount, Wilmana.

Wisnu has long been linked with kingship, due in part to two of his avatars, Rama and Krisna, whose exploits are described in the Ramayana and the Mahabharata. Rulers in both Java and Bali were compared to Wisnu and his avatars, or described as being incarnations of them.[2] The connections of rulers to Wisnu were strong in the precolonial Balinese courts, where the deity was associated with water and, through his consort, Dewi Sri, with rice agriculture. The eleventh-century Javanese king Airlangga was associated with Garuda as well. He used a symbol of Garuda as his seal and took a name associated with the mythical bird when retiring to become an ascetic. Stories of Garuda's exploits were popular literary subjects in both Java and Bali.

Some of the earliest Hindu stone sculpture from Indonesia depicts Wisnu on or with his mount, Garuda. Most of these Central Javanese images show Wisnu seated on the shoulders of a cross-legged figure with a human body and a bird face.[3] In the most famous ancient Indonesian image of the pair, a statue long (but perhaps falsely) associated with the East Javanese bathing place of Belahan, Garuda has been transformed.[4] He stands on birdlike feet, with spread wings and demonic facial features. Balinese depictions of Garuda also emphasize his fierce nature, with bulging eyes and sharp teeth and fangs emerging from his beak.

How statues such as this one were used is not known. One of the most common functions of some sculptures of Garuda portrayed alone, or of Wisnu with Garuda, is as an architectural element that served as a base (*sendi*) for the pillars supporting the roof of a pavilion. When used in such a manner, statues often had a space for the beam to attach to Garuda's back. The lack of that feature on these statues (cat. nos. 55 and 56) indicates that they likely stood alone and decorated royal palaces. There is no evidence that they were ever considered sacred objects to be worshipped in their own right.

In this statue Wisnu carries a discus in his right hand and a small, round, lidded jar in the left.[5] He sits on Garuda's shoulders, with the bird's magnificent wings and tail spread around him. Garuda stands with his bird feet splayed, his human hands grasping Wisnu's legs. Both figures wear elaborate crowns and jewelry.

NR

55 Wisnu on Garuda, 1850–1900

North Bali
Wood and pigments
H: 38¼ in; W: 19¾ in
Asian Art Museum, Acquisition made possible by the Connoisseurs' Council and the estate of K. Hart Smith, 2010.18.1

1 The popularity of this image and the extent to which it has become a symbol for Bali can be observed in the controversial plan to erect a 146-meter-high bronze statue of the subject on the Bukit peninsula of southern Bali. Carol Warren, "The Garuda Wisnu Kencana Monument Debate: Environment, Culture and the Discourses of Nationalism in Late New Order Bali," in *Kulturen und Raum; Theoretische Ansätze und empirische Kulturforschung in Indonesien*, ed. W. Benno and W. Samuel (Zürich: Rüegger, 1995), 337–90.

2 Margaret Wiener, *Visible and Invisible Realms: Power, Magic, and Colonial Conquest in Bali* (Chicago: University of Chicago Press, 1995), 117.

3 See images of Wisnu on Garuda from the Dieng plateau in the National Museum in Jakarta: inv. nos. 2, 17.

4 P. Scheurleer, "The Javanese Statue of Garuda Carrying Wisnu and Candi Kidal," *Artibus Asiae* 69, no. 1 (2009): 189–218.

5 Wisnu can manifest in many forms. He is commonly associated with a four-armed form that often holds the attributes of discus, mace, conch, and sometimes lotus. The small covered bowl Wisnu holds here seems to have been popular in depictions of the deity in Bali. It could refer to the container of *amerta* that Garuda stole from the gods in order to rescue his mother.

This statue depicts the demon king Rawana on his mount, Wilmana. The carving, painting, and shape of the base of the statue indicate that it was the partner of the statue of Wisnu on Garuda (cat. no. 55). Statues like the present example have often been misidentified as Wisnu on Garuda.[1] One of the reasons for this misidentification is that within the Indian pantheon of Hindu deities, the god Wisnu is most commonly identified as having a bird mount. Wilmana is not mentioned in the Indian epics. In the Old Javanese Ramayana, Rawana abducts Sita, the wife of the hero, Rama, and takes her away on his chariot or mount (VI: 15–28). According to Hendrik Kern, the name Wilmana results from a corruption of the Sanskrit word *wimana,* which means "vehicle for the gods." In Javanese and Balinese the word *wil* means a demon or evil spirit. The conflation of these words led to the interpretation of Rawana's mount as a winged demon.[2]

Dutch museum collections contain many Balinese images of Rawana and Wilmana, indicating the popularity of the subject.[3] From the 1930s onward statues of Wisnu on Garuda and Rawana on Wilmana became very popular items for tourist purchase. However, the number of these figures dating from the mid-nineteenth century to the early twentieth century suggests that they were important before the advent of major tourist markets.[4]

While most images of Wilmana have the wings and tail of a bird, some lack the birdlike beak seen in this example. When compared to Garuda in its partner statue, the two figures are very similar, differing primarily in the color of their skin and in their ornaments.

Rawana wears the same type of crown as does Wisnu, rising in a boxy shape behind a diadem. The ferocity of his countenance is in stark contrast to the calm visage of Wisnu. Round eyes bulging, mouth open, teeth bared, he seems on the verge of attack. In his raised right hand he holds his weapon Candrahasa (moon-blade), a gift from Siwa, and in his left what appears to be a piece of cloth, perhaps an edge of one of his sashes.

NR

56 Rawana on his mount, Wilmana, 1850–1900

North Bali
Wood and pigments
H: 37⅜ in; W: 18⅞ in

Asian Art Museum, Acquisition made possible by the Connoisseurs' Council and the estate of K. Hart Smith, 2010.18.2

1 *Internationales Archiv für Ethnographie* (P.W.M. Trap, 1897), 160.

2 Occasionally Wilmana is the mount for other deities as well, including Boma and Brahma.

3 For a few statues of Rawana and Wilmana, or Wilmana alone, see Rijksmuseum voor Volkenkunde, Leiden, 2299-84, B134-167, 1964-1; Tropenmuseum, Amsterdam, 1330-25, 2557-2, 809-27a–b. 809-119; and the Art Gallery of South Australia, 20057S10(a–k).

4 An image of Rawana on Wilmana is discussed in 1847: Bataviaasch Genootschap van Kunsten en Wetenschappen, *Verhandelingen van het Bataviaasch Genootschap der Kunsten en Wetenschappen,* vol. 21 (Batavia: Egbert Heemen, 1847), 67. Van Hoevell mentions that images of Rawana as a *kris* holder are not uncommon, but an image of Rawana on Wilmana, given as a gift to the prince of Goa, was worth describing. G. W. W. C. van Hoevell, "Kleine Notizen und Corrspondenz," *Internationales Archiv für Ethnographie* 17 (1905), 221. An image of Rawana holding Sita on Wilmana from the Rijksmuseum voor Volkenkunde, Leiden (RMV 1239-72) is on the cover of an early publication, Rijks Ethnographisch Museum (Netherlands) et al., *Verslag van den Directeur...* (Ministerie van Binnenlandsche Zaken, 1900).

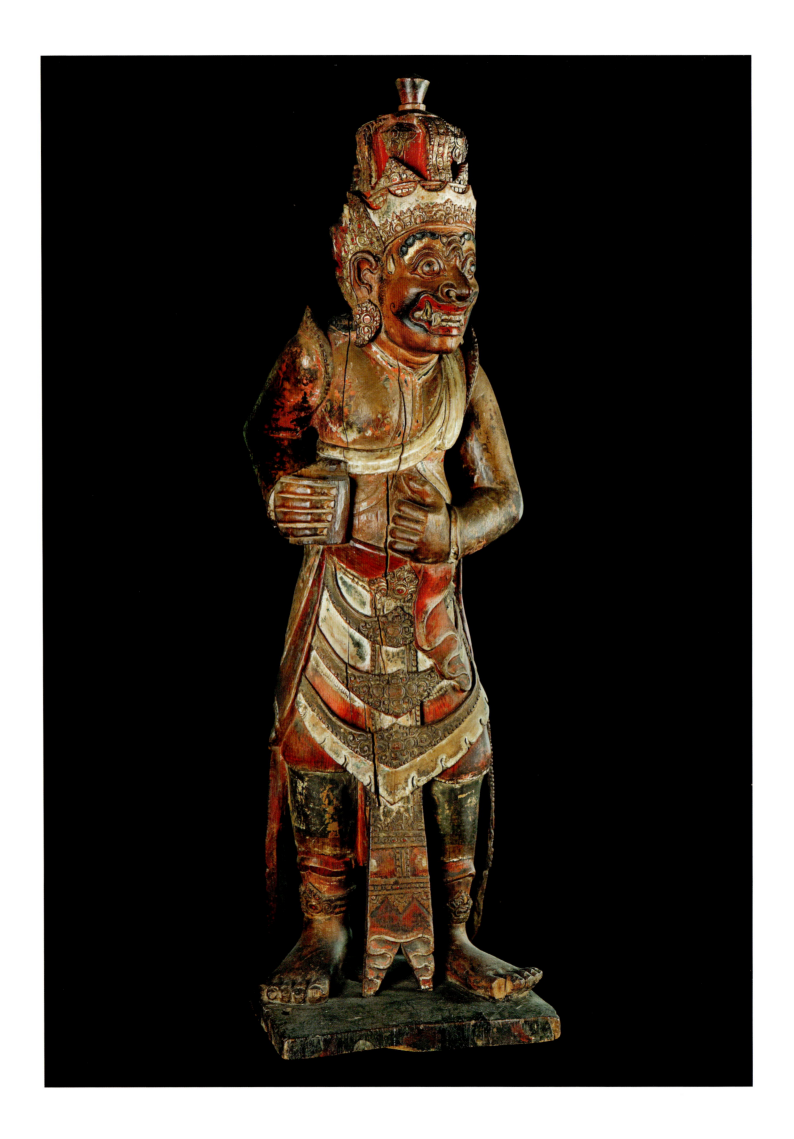

On September 20, 1906, as Dutch forces neared the palace, the raja of Denpasar chose the path of certain death through battle, leading a procession of family, lords, and followers into their final bloody assault against Dutch colonial forces, the so-called *puputan* Badung.

The fall of Denpasar brought the victors spoils ("*krijgsbuit*") in great number. Hundreds of objects were seized by the Dutch and the Balinese themselves. Some of these objects probably originated from palaces elsewhere in Bali, for the Balinese kings also looted extensively when they conquered their neighbors: they took as many weapons and precious objects as they could get and burned their rivals' palaces.[1]

One of the many objects from the palace of Denpasar is this *kris* holder in the form of a painted statue of Rawana, the demon king who fights against Rama in the Ramayana epic. (See also the painting of the final battle in the Ramayana on the *parba* from the palace of Tabanan, cat. no. 48).[2] The statue has a hole in its right hand that served to hold the *kris*.

Balinese etiquette of former times, it is said, required that a man entering a house or palace should take off his *kris*, and place it in a *kris* stand set in readiness by the door.[3] Curiously, clear evidence for this, such as photographs or visitors' accounts, seems to be lacking. A *kris* was regarded as part of a nobleman's costume and not as a weapon one had to take off in ordinary circumstances (unless, perhaps, the visitor was an envoy from a rival kingdom, or was to enter the presence of the king himself). It is quite possible that *kris* holders in a palace were used for holding *kris* of princes or noblemen who did not wear them inside the palace all the time, or as stands for one of the many *kris* of the raja himself.

In addition to the museum in Leiden, the Museum of the Batavian Society in Batavia (the present Museum Nasional in Jakarta) each received three *kris* holders from the Badung palace. W. O. J. Nieuwenkamp bought a Rawana *kris* holder at the auction of treasures from the palace of Tabanan.[4]

Nowadays Balinese men wear *kris* only at ceremonial occasions, but the knives still play an important role in rituals: as receptacles for a deity or ancestor, as replacements for an actual person, or to accompany the gods when they visit a temple. As an animal figure bears the statues of deities, the *kris* holder bears the *kris* when it is placed on a shrine. I have seen *kris* stands in use in the ancestral temple of the former court of Kerambitan, for example.

Although in the Ramayana epic Rawana has ten heads, in sculpture he is usually represented with only one.[5] In accordance with the traditional iconography of a demonic figure, his skin has a reddish-brown color, he has body hair and fangs, and the eyebrows above the round, bulging eyes are thick and black. Indicating his position as a high-caste

57 *Kris* stand in the form of a statue of Rawana, approx. 1800–1900

Denpasar, Badung

Painted wood

H: 34⅝ in; W: 10⅝ in; D: 9⅜ in

National Museum of Ethnology, Leiden, the Netherlands, 1602-185

1 Francine Brinkgreve and David Stuart-Fox, "Collecting after Colonial Conflict: Badung and Tabanan 1906–2006," in ed. Pieter ter Keurs, *Colonial Collections Revisited* (Leiden: CNWS Publications, 2007), 152.

2 H. H. Juynboll, *Catalogus van 's Rijks Ethnographisch Museum, Deel VII Bali en Lombok* (Leiden: Brill, 1912), 116.

3 *Gids voor den bezoeker van de Indische tentoonstelling in het Stedelijk Museum te Amsterdam* (Amsterdam: Stedelijk Museum, 1901), 70; Fred and Margaret Eiseman, *Woodcarvings of Bali* (Berkeley: Periplus, 1988), 28.

4 Published in Francine Brinkgreve, "Balinese Rulers and Colonial Rule," in ed. Endang Sri Hardiati and Pieter ter Keurs, *Indonesia: The Discovery of the Past* (Amsterdam: KIT Publishers, 2005), 133.

5 See, for example, C. M. Pleyte, *Indonesian Art: Selected Specimens of Ancient and Modern Art and Handwork from the Dutch Indian Archipelago* (The Hague: Nijhoff, 1901), pl. XIII, fig 2.

ruler, he wears a crown, *gelung candi*, golden jewelry, including ear pendants, *rumbing* (cat. no. 66), and a caste cord, *upawita*. The Rawana figure (sculpture in the round, *togog* in Balinese) has a very powerful expression and is skillfully made. The carver superbly mastered the technique of gradually chipping bits of a chunk of hard wood with sharp instruments and light taps of a mallet.[6]

Although following a standard iconography, the Rawana *kris* holder from Denpasar is noticeably different in style from the example collected by Nieuwenkamp at Tabanan. Such stylistic differences suggest that, although we have no information about individual carvers, artists were at times able to express creative personal styles.

FB

6 Miguel Covarrubias, *Island of Bali* (New York: Knopf, 1937), 188.

A *kris* in its holder stands guard beside an ancestral deity figure in Pura Batur, the royal temple of the court of Kerambitan (Tabanan), 1982. *Photo Francine Brinkgreve.*

58 *Kris* stand in the form of a frog, approx. 1900–1940

Wood and pigments

H: 13¾ in; W: 10¼ in; D: 10¼ in

Tropenmuseum, Amsterdam, 1772-588

This carving of a frog (*katak*) represents one of the many different forms that a *kris* stand can take, although most are human or mythological figures (see cat. no. 57). In this case, the *kris* would have been placed in the open mouth of the animal, which is looking upward.

The attractively carved and painted animal is more than just an ordinary frog, for it illustrates the Balinese love of composite creatures. It has the body of a frog, a head with long ears, the bulging eyes and fangs of a mythical demonic beast, and hair and nose like a pig's (see cat. no. 91). Such composite creatures have a special fascination to the Balinese.

No symbolic or mythological reason seems to exist for choosing the frog for such a purpose. In visual art, animals often have supernatural symbolism, representing particular deities or serving them by acting as mounts. Animals frequently function as architectural ornaments or features, as containers, or, like this frog, as *kris* stands.[2]

Frogs do not play a role in the great Hindu epics, but they appear in some Balinese

---

[1] Published in *Budaya Indonesia: Kunst en cultuur in Indonesië/Arts and Crafts in Indonesia* (Amsterdam: Tropenmuseum/Royal Tropical Institute, 1987), 262; Koos van Brakel et al., *A Passion for Indonesian Art: The George Tillman (1882–1941) Collection at the Tropenmuseum Amsterdam* (Amsterdam: Royal Tropical Institute, 1996), 22; H. J. Voskuil, "Bij foto's van Indonesische wapens uit de verzameling Wurfbain," *Nederlandsch-Indië Oud en Nieuw*, 15 (1930–31), 386, pl. 20.

[2] According to Koos van Brakel and David van Duuren (Koos van Brakel [et al.], *A Passion for Indonesian Art*, 40 and 44), following a theory of Hindu symbolism of F. D. K. Bosch, the frog as water creature should be seen here as *padmamula*, female principle of life, joined with the male *kris*, with the hilt in the form of a demon as *brahmamula*, together symbolizing life and creation. However, although the complementary opposition of male and female principles is one of the basic Hindu Balinese doctrines (in Bali called *rwa bhineda*), there is no evidence that this particular combination of *kris* stand and *kris*, probably used in a nonreligious context, would have this symbolic meaning.

[3] Marijke J. Klokke, *The Tantri Reliefs on Ancient Javanese Candi* (Leiden: KITLV Press, 1993), 241–242.

4 Ex-collection J. G. Wurfbain, collected by Georg Tillmann, gift of W. G. Tillman.

folktales. In these stories, animals portray wise or foolish characters, and humble or ordinary animals such as frogs are sometimes transformed into more important beings. The so-called Frog Dance recounts the story of a frog turning into a prince after being kissed by a beautiful girl. Stories about animals (including frogs) from the Old Javanese text Tantri Kamandaka were popular in Bali, and were represented on temple reliefs and paintings. One story describes how a snake tries to win a frog's confidence by posing as a saintly person.[3]

The frog sits on a wooden base, whose sides are decorated with various motifs, such as the demonic head with one eye (*karang bintulu*) in the center of the panels.

It is quite possible that this choice of subject for a *kris* stand was simply the whim of the craftsman or of the person who commissioned it. From at least the late nineteenth century, craftsmen, especially in North Bali, were fashioning objects with the foreign market in mind, a kind of early tourist art, and this frog might conceivably be such a piece.

The *kris* stand is from the collection of Georg Tillman (1882–1941), a major collector of Indonesian art and benefactor of the Tropenmuseum.[4]

FB

The history of this ceremonial knife from Buleleng, North Bali,[1] dates to 1864. In that year the ruler of Buleleng, I Gusti Ngurah Ketut Jelantik, visited the governor general L. A. W. J. Baron Sloet van de Beele, in his palace in Buitenzorg. During that audience he presented this beautiful weapon, together with two ceremonial *kris*.[2] The occasion was even photographed, making Gusti Jelantik the first Balinese ruler to have his photograph taken.[3]

Sloet van de Beele, governor general from 1862 to 1866, received many weapons from indigenous rulers, given to him as the highest authority in the Netherlands-Indies. The presentation of beautifully decorated weapons, objects of status and products of excellent craftsmanship, was very common among rulers within the Indonesian archipelago, serving to confirm or maintain political relationships. In 1888 Sloet van de Beele's spectacular collection was inventoried and documented at his request by J. D. E. Schmeltz, curator of the museum in Leiden. After van de Beele's death, part of his collection was bought by the museum from his heirs.[4]

This kind of knife was called *wedung* in Bali, the name of a similarly shaped ceremonial weapon from Java.[5] The word *wedung* is found in Old Javanese inscriptions in both Java and Bali, so it is a weapon of considerable antiquity. Although we know how a Javanese *wedung* was worn as part of ceremonial court dress, we do not know how a Balinese *wedung* was carried. It is also unclear whether a *wedung* was ever part of the ensemble of sacred heirlooms, *pusaka*, as was often the case with a *kris*. In contrast to a *kris*, which has a double-edged blade, the blade of the *wedung* has a straight back and an S-shaped edge. This one might have been used for sacrificial purposes, since there is a groove in the blade, parallel to the back of the knife, probably to facilitate the flow of blood.

The hilt of this weapon is made from dark buffalo horn, beautifully carved with decorative plant motifs and a so-called *garuda mungkur* (the mythical bird Garuda looking backward) ornament. A ring of black stones of unknown provenance circles the hilt, while a silver band fastens the hilt to the blade.

A special part of this object is the beautifully carved small mask on the wooden sheath, which is otherwise decorated with painted leaves and flower motifs. This use of a mask attached to a sheath is comparable to other examples in old European collections, including those in Leiden,[6] in the Tropenmuseum collection,[7] and in two German ethnological collections: one in Munich,[8] published in 1887, and the second in Dresden, dating from before 1861.[9] It is likely that all four weapons originated from Buleleng, which in the second half of the nineteenth century was the only part of Bali experiencing regular contact with Europeans.

59 Ceremonial knife (*wedung*) with sheath, before 1864 (following page)

Knife: iron, silver, buffalo horn
L: 17⅞ in; W: 2¾ in; D: 1⅝ in
Sheath: wood and pigments
L: 19.3 in; W: 2.8 in; D: 3.5 in
National Museum of Ethnology, Leiden, the Netherlands, 1050-2

1 Described and illustrated in J. D. E. Schmeltz, "Indonesische Prunkwaffen," *Internationales Archiv für Ethnographie* 3 (1890), 99 and pl. IX, fig.10; H. H. Juynboll, *Catalogus van 's Rijks Ethnographisch Museum, Deel VII Bali en Lombok* (Leiden: Brill, 1912), 121; Albert G. van Zonneveld, *Traditional Weapons of the Indonesian Archipelago* (Leiden: C. Zwartenkot Art Books, 2001), 74.

2 Francine Brinkgreve, "Balinese Rulers and Colonial Rule," in ed. Endang Sri Hardiati and Pieter ter Keurs, *Indonesia: The Discovery of the Past* (Amsterdam: KIT Publishers, 2005), 123–124.

3 Photographed by Studio Woodbury and Page (KITLV coll. 3512).

4 Francine Brinkgreve, "Java: Gifts, Scholarship and Colonial Rule," in ed. Endang Sri Hardiati and Pieter ter Keurs, *Indonesia: The Discovery of the Past*, 101–104.

The wooden sheaths of all four weapons display a face or mask, carved almost in the round, but they are all different. The mask of this sheath from the National Museum of Ethnology is a beautifully carved head of a demonic figure, called *karang Boma* (Boma motif), amid garlands of lush foliage. The Balinese Boma, related to Kala and Banaspati in Java, is the son of the earth divinity, Ibu Pertiwi. As a protective, evil-repelling force, he also appears, with his protruding tongue and bulging eyes, above the entrance to temples and palaces, and as the main figure on the towers used at cremation rituals. Used on the sheath of this ceremonial knife, Boma is probably meant to protect the owner of the weapon. This use of a mask on a sheath may be influenced by those examples on *kris* sheaths from Madura (see cat. no. 60).

FB

5 Albert G. van Zonneveld, *Traditional Weapons of the Indonesian Archipelago* (Leiden: C. Zwartenkot Art Books, 2001), 152–153.

6 RMV 1289-1.

7 TM 809-109, published in *Budaya Indonesia: Kunst en cultuur in Indonesië/ Arts and Crafts in Indonesia* (Amsterdam: Tropenmuseum/Royal Tropical Institute, 1987), 212, 280 and TM 1772-600a–b, published in Koos van Brakel et al., *A Passion for Indonesian Art: The George Tillman (1882–1941) Collection at the Tropenmuseum Amsterdam* (Amsterdam: Royal Tropical Institute, 1996), 23.

8 Friedrich Ratzel, *Völkerkunde. Zweiter Band: Die Naturvölker Ozeaniens, Amerikas und Asiens* (Leipzig: Verlag des Bibliographischen Instituts, 1886), 391, fig. 9.

9 Petra Martin, "Was die Natur und der Mensch des merkwürdigen Tropenlandes erzeugen … : Wolf Curt von Schierbrand und seine Sammlungen, *Kleine Beiträge aus dem Staatlichen Museum für Völkerkunde Dresden* 17 (1999), 23.

An important object in many Indonesian cultures, the *kris* is a dagger with an asymmetrical double-edged blade that broadens toward the hilt, usually with nickel *pamor* (the effect achieved by forging together layers of ordinary iron and nickel-bearing iron) patterns forged into the iron blade. A *kris* is believed to have a personality, an extra dimension, because of this spiritually charged patterning.[1] *Kris* with elaborate decorative hilts and sheaths of precious materials were intended for state or ceremonial occasions, while simpler ones with wooden handles and scabbards were used for combat. Special *kris* associated with ancestors were preserved as valuable heirlooms, *pusaka*, which brought protection and prosperity. *Kris* were also often part of royal state regalia. They represented the ruler's power, and each *kris* frequently bore an individual name.

Like other ceremonial weapons, *kris* were also favorite royal gifts, such as the precious example given by a North Balinese ruler to a Dutch governor-general in 1864 (cat. no. 59). The *kris* illustrated here, acquired in 1883, was probably such a gift from one of the Nusantara rulers, since the previous owner, Albertus Jacobus Duymaer van Twist (1809–1887), was governor-general in the Netherlands Indies from 1851–1856.[2] On the occasion of that governor-general's visit to the courts of Central Java in 1852, he received a beautiful *kris* from the Susuhunan of Surakarta,[3] and another from the sultan of Yogyakarta, both of which, like this *kris*, he donated to the Tropenmuseum.[4] But it is not known when and where Duymaer van Twist came into the possession of this particular *kris*. His travels in 1853 brought him to Madura and Banyuwangi in East Java (the location from which Bali was administered by the Dutch until 1854), but not to the island of Bali itself.[5]

This *kris*,[6] however, is reported to have come from Bali, and the Tropenmuseum has three other very similar *kris*, which are also of Balinese origin according to their documentation.[7] The sheath has almost exactly the same features as other *kris* in the Tropenmuseum collection, and they originate from Madura.[8] The Museum Nasional Indonesia in Jakarta has at least three of these *kris topengan* (*kris* with a mask on its sheath), all definitely coming from Bangkalan, Madura.[9] According to Hamzuri, who described the Jakarta *kris* collection, the mask (*topeng*) on their sheaths is one of the special features of *kris* from Madura, and has the same protective meaning as demonic Kala or Banaspati figures from East Java.[10] Like the Boma figure on the sheath of the Rijksmuseum ceremonial knife (cat. no. 59), the mask on the sheath of this *kris* is probably meant to protect the owner of the weapon. According to David van Duuren, Madurese *kris* can be found in East Java and Bali because soldiers from Madura, known for their courage, fought in these areas for the Dutch army.[11] Madurese troops helped the Dutch

60 *Kris* with sheath (*kadutan*), approx. 1800–1850

Blade and handle: iron, nickel, gold, diamonds, wood (*kayu pelet*)
L: 8⅛ in
Sheath: wood (*kayu pelet*), gilded silver alloy, diamonds
L: 18½ cm; W: 6¾ in
Tropenmuseum, Amsterdam, H-6

1 Extensive literature on the Indonesian *kris*: David van Duuren, *The Kris: An Earthly Approach to a Cosmic Symbol* (Wijk en Aalburg: Pictures Publishers, 1998); Albert G. van Zonneveld, *Traditional Weapons of the Indonesian Archipelago* (Leiden: C. Zwartenkot Art Books, 2001), 62–68; J. E. Jasper and Mas Pirngadie, *De inlandsche kunstnijverheid in Nederlandsch Indië, V. De bewerking van niet-edele metalen koperbewerking en pamorsmeedkunst* ('s-Gravenhage: Mouton, 1930), 147–247; Hamzuri, *Petunjuk singkat tentang keris* (Jakarta: Proyek Pengembangan Museum Nasional, Departemen Pendidikan and Kebudayaan, 1982–1983), Bambamg Harsrinuksmo, *Ensiklopedi keris* (Jakarta: Gramedia Pustaka Utama, 2004), etc. Especially on the Balinese *kris*: P. de Kat Angelino, "Over de smeden en eenige andere ambachtslieden op Bali," *Tijdschrift voor Indische Taal-, Land- en Volkenkunde* 60 (1921); Urs Ramseyer, *The Art and Culture of Bali* (Oxford: Oxford University Press, 1977). See also the annotated bibliography on *kris* by David van Duuren, *Krisses: A Critical Bibliography* (Wijk en Aalburg: Pictures Publishers, 2002).

2   Encyclopaedie van Nederlandsch-Indië, I, 649; J. C. Smelik, C. M. Hogenstijn, W. J. M. Jansen, *A. J. Duymaer van Twist: Gouverneur-generaal van Nederlands-Indië (1851–1856)* (Zutphen: Walburg Press, 2007). Duymaer van Twist became well known in the Netherlands as the governor-general who played a role in the conflict with Eduard Douwes Dekker in early 1856, which resulted in the famous book and protest against Dutch colonial policy, *Max Havelaar*, written by Multatuli.

3   The receipt of this *kris*, TM H-2a, is described by the wife of Duymaer van Twist; see J. C. Smelik, C. M. Hogenstijn, W. J. M. Jansen, *A. J. Duymaer van Twist*, 52–54. It is also illustrated in Isaäc Groneman (preface and introduction by David van Duuren), *The Javanese Kris* (Leiden: C. Zwartenkot Art Books and KITLV Press, 2009), 196.

4   TM H-5a, illustrated in J. C. Smelik, C. M. Hogenstijn, W. J. M. Jansen, *A. J. Duymaer van Twist*, 114, and David van Duuren, *The Kris: An Earthly Approach to a Cosmic Symbol* (Wijk en Aalburg: Pictures Publishers, 1998), 53.

5   See J. C. Smelik, C. M. Hogenstijn, W. J. M. Jansen, *A. J. Duymaer van Twist*, 55–56. But since North Bali by that time was already under colonial rule, it is also possible that he received the *kris* on the occasion of a visit from one of the North Balinese rulers to Batavia (see cat. no. 59).

6   Also illustrated in TM photograph 60054904 and in Koos van Brakel [et al.], *A Passion for Indonesian Art: The George Tillman (1882–1941) Collection at the Tropenmuseum Amsterdam* (Amsterdam: Royal Tropical Institute, 1996), 4.3.

7   For example: *kris* TM A-5873, A-5993, both acquired in 1889 and like H-6 with a gilded sheath mask and sheath cover, and *kris* TM 1772-587, "state *kris*" with silver sheath and sheath mask, illustrated in H. J. Voskuil, "Bij foto's van Indonesische wapens uit de verzameling Wurfbain," *Nederlandsch-Indië Oud en Nieuw*, 15 (1930–1931), 386, pl. 20 (see also cat. no. 58).

8   For example TM 903-21 and 889-28, 889-29. See also David van Duuren, *The Kris: An Earthly Approach to a Cosmic Symbol*, 49, illustrating a sheath mask from Bali or Madura. Isaäc Groneman (preface and introduction by David van Duuren), *The Javanese Kris*, 36, illustrates a similar *kris* sheath, with origin in East Java.

during the Java War of 1825–1830.[12] In 1831 the sultans of Sumenep and Pamekasan, who were allies of King William I, installed the so-called *korpsen barisan* on Madura, who until 1882 helped the Dutch to fight several colonial wars. In the expeditions against North Bali in 1848 and 1849, the first major Dutch military campaigns against the Balinese, Madurese troops and laborers from Sumenep and Pamekasan formed part of the expeditionary force.[13] So it is possible that *kris topengan*, acquired in Bali, were in fact Madurese *kris* taken from Madurese troops; their quality would suggest that they belonged not to the ordinary soldiers but to their leaders. Or, possibly, they were in fact wrought in (North) Bali, after Madurese examples.

Whether forged in Bali or not, this beautiful *kris*, decorated with precious materials, is a fine example of skilled craftsmanship. The overall shape of the blade is straight, known as *dapur bener*,[14] with an undulating *pamor* pattern. The *ganjah* or separate base of the blade and the blade itself are almost entirely decorated with inlaid gold spiraling flower and leaf motifs. A short double line above the *ganjah* is the blood groove, *sogokan*. The spotted wood of the hilt,[15] *ukiran*, is called *kayu pelet*, a collective name for various precious woods with graduations of color. The ring around the base of the hilt is decorated with small diamonds.

The sheath, also made of *kayu pelet*, is covered with an oversheath (*pendok*) of gilded tin, the front fully decorated with repoussé tendrils and other motifs, the back with engravings of foliate ornaments. The top part or "mouth" (*wrangka*) of the sheath, carved in a kidney shape (*gayaman* type), is largely covered with a repoussé mask, with eyes and eyebrows accentuated by small diamonds. In Bali, evil-repelling faces or masks, carved in wood or hammered in gold or silver, are known as *karang Boma* (see cat. no. 59), *karang kala*, or *karang tapel* (mask).[16] The mask on the gilded oversheath of this *kris* (and other *kris topengan*) differs slightly from these Balinese monster heads: it has no ears, its eyebrows are extended, it has a moustache in the form of two small wings, and there is a clearly marked, oval-shaped border around its face. This monster head also looks less terrifying, because the eyes are less bulging, the nose is longer, and the teeth are less prominent than those of his Balinese counterparts.

FB

9 MNI E658/5841, illustrated in A. N. J. Th. à Th. van der Hoop, *Indonesische siermotieven/ Ragam-ragam perhiasan Indonesia/Indonesian ornamental design* (Batavia: Koninklijk Bataviaasch Genootschap van Kunsten en Wetenschappen, 1949), 110–111, and Hamzuri, *Petunjuk singkat tentang keris* (Jakarta: Proyek Pengembangan Museum Nasional, Departemen Pendidikan and Kebudayaan, 1982/1983), 113 (MNI E706/5859), 111-112 (MNI E707/2137), 110.

10 Hamzuri, *Petunjuk singkat tentang keris*, 99. This Madurese origin is supported by Bambang Harsrinuksmo in his *Ensiklopedi keris* (Jakarta: Gramedia Pustaka Utama, 2004), 269–272.

11 David van Duuren, curator, Tropenmuseum, pers. comm. January 15, 2010.

12 C. C. F. M. Le Roux, "Madoereesche krisheften," *Cultureel Indië* 8 (1946), 166.

13 J. van Swieten, *Krijgsverrigtingen tegen het eiland Bali in 1848* ('s Gravenhage: Erven Doorman, 1849), 36–37, 43. Alfons van der Kraan, *Bali at War: A History of the Dutch-Balinese Conflict of 1846–49* (Clayton: Monash University, 1995), 48, 77. Contact between Bali and Madura has a long history, both military and commercial, so it is conceivable that Madurese *kris* reached Bali at an earlier time. See Zainalfattah, *Sedjarah tjaranja pemerintahan di daerah² di kepulauan Madura* (S.l.: s.n., 1951), 32–34, 42–45, 143–147.

14 Since the *kris* probably originated in Java, most terms to describe the elements/features of a *kris* are in Javanese.

15 Although this type of hilt is also common in Bali, in G. J. F. J. Tammens, *Kris: Magic Relic of Old Indonesia*, dl. 2 (Eelderwolde: Tammens, 1993), 224, pl. 10, a *kris* from East Java is published with exactly the same features as *kris* TM H-6. Several Madurese examples in the Museum Nasional Indonesia also have the same kind of hilt.

16 Urs Ramseyer, *The Art and Culture of Bali* (Oxford: Oxford University Press, 1977).

This exquisitely carved object was once the handle of a Balinese *kris*. *Kris* have long played important roles in Balinese society, and in precolonial Bali most men possessed at least one. Weapons that could be used in hand-to-hand warfare were, and still are, also markers of status, sacred heirlooms, and spiritually powerful objects. The most important part of a *kris* is its blade. Undoubtedly part of the power ascribed to the *kris* derived from the mysteries of its production. Smiths had special status in ancient Indonesia, and in Bali they have their own clan group called *pande*, who claim in their sacred texts a status higher than the highest case of Brahmans.[1]

Royal *kris* would often have handles made of precious materials such as ivory or gold encrusted with gems. In a mid-nineteenth-century account of the visit of a Thai trader to Bali, the king of Klungkung requests that the trader bring him one or two big elephant tusks, whatever the price, if he visited in the future.[2] It is likely the king was requesting the ivory for use as a *kris* hilt, as the material was rarely used for other purposes (cat. no. 26 is a rare exception). These hilts frequently depict a number of hard-to-identify demonic figures. These are sometimes referred to as ogres (*raksasa*), but are also said to depict the wind god Bayu, father of the Pandawa brother Bima from the Mahabharata epic. Bayu plays an important role in the popular Balinese story of Bima's quest for holy water to rescue his earthly parents from death. It is perhaps because of this mythical story that in some images of the deity, he holds a jar of the elixir of immortality in his right hand.

It is difficult to tell what the demonic figure depicted on this handle is holding. His left hand seems to grasp a swath of cloth, perhaps the corner of one of his sashes. His right arm swings across his chest and clasps a small, segmented round object. The orb is framed by the curving, elongated thumbnail of the figure's hand. Long, sharp fingernails (especially thumbnails) are an attribute associated with Bima, who used them as a weapon. They are also seen on Bima's father, the god Bayu, and on Bayu's other son, the monkey Hanoman.

Some aspects of this figure are similar to other Balinese *kris* handles, especially the stance of the figure, and the bulging eyes and exposed fangs. But the figure's delicate beard is quite unusual. Exceptional too, is the intricacy of the deep and detailed carving. The carver of this handle employed motifs commonly found on Balinese temples, including the stylized bird face (*karang goak*) on the clasp at the figure's waist and the one-eyed monster's face (*karang bintulu*) found on the back of his headdress, as well as the overall abundance of floral and plant ornamentation.

NR

61 *Kris* hilt depicting a demonic figure, perhaps 1700–1800

Ivory
H: 5¼ in; D: 1¾ in
Asian Art Museum, Acquisition made possible by William M. Brooks with additional funding from Betty and Bruce Alberts, Fred Levin and Nancy Livingston, Joan and M. Glenn Vinson Jr., Hok Pui and Sally Yu Leung, and an anonymous friend of the Asian Art Museum, 2010.1

1 R. Goris, "The Position of the Blacksmiths," in *Bali: Studies in Life, Thought, and Ritual*, 289–299; Fred B. Eiseman, *Bali, Sekala and Niskala, Vol. 1: Essays on Religion, Ritual, and Art*, 4th ed. (Periplus Editions, 1996), 76–81.

2 Charnvit Kaset-siri, "The Statement of Chinkak on Bali," *Indonesia* 7 (1969): 101.

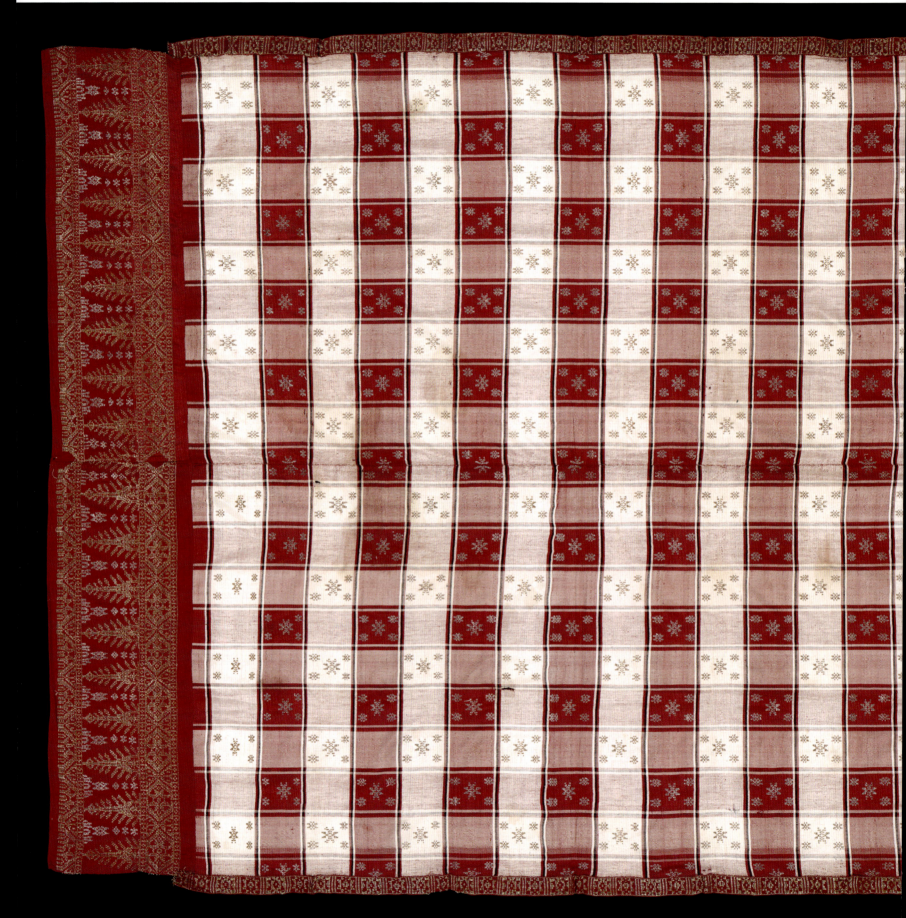

In 1846 a Siamese ship captain, Chinkak, visited Bali, and upon his return made a fascinating report of his experiences trading on the island.¹ While on Bali, Chinkak met with the ruler of the northern Balinese kingdom of Buleleng and the ruler of Mengwi in south central Bali.² He describes both rulers as wearing the same garb: a black-and-white checked silk cloth, with each check four finger-widths square. This type of cloth, called *poleng*, remains an important Balinese textile that is used in a wide variety of ways.³ *Poleng* are not worn by the upper classes today, but are seen adorning guardians, sacred trees, certain shrines and temples, sacred dancers, and particular religious specialists.

Balinese noblemen in the early-twentieth-century photographs are often shown wearing a lower garment with this distinctive checked pattern. Checked textiles can also combine red and white threads to produce a pattern of red, white, and pink squares, with thin lines of black accentuating the pattern; however, these textiles are not considered *poleng*.

The borders of this textile are elaborated with supplementary strands of silver- and gold-wrapped threads. In this example, metallic threads are also used to make a pattern of an eight-pointed star surrounded by four smaller stars on each of the white and red squares. A popular motif in Southeast Asian textiles, the eight-pointed star had particular resonance in Bali, where it was associated with the gods of the points of the compass.⁴ The large garment is actually two separately woven pieces that were carefully joined to produce a single panel.⁵

NR

62 Nobleman's ceremonial lower garment (*saput songket* or *kampuh songket*), 1800–1900

Singaraja, North Bali

Silk, metallic thread, cotton

H: 47¼ in; W: 53 in

Private collection

1 Charnvit Kaset-siri, "The Statement of Chinkak on Bali," *Indonesia* 7 (1969), 83.

2 There is some confusion as to which rulers Chinkak met, for he refers to meeting the raja of Klungkung (an important kingdom in South Bali) while in the north. Charnvit Kaset-siri, "The Statement of Chinkak on Bali," 36.

3 Brigitta Hauser-Schaublin, Marie-Louise Nabholz-Kartaschoff, and Urs Ramseyer, *Textiles in Bali* (Berkeley; Singapore: Periplus Editions, 1991), 80–93.

4 Mattiebelle Gittinger, *To Speak with Cloth: Studies in Indonesian Textiles* (Los Angeles: Museum of Cultural History, University of California, 1989), 197.

5 See similar examples in the National Gallery of Australia, 2000.844, and the Museum of Fine Arts Boston, 43.19.

Bali's famous weft ikat textiles (*endek*) are decorated with various motifs. *Wayang* figures are not uncommon, either as separate figures or in groups. On this textile, however, they are portrayed in unusual numbers and splendor.[1] The cloth consists of two ikat pieces sewn together along their length, with *songket* end pieces sewn on, rather than woven in one piece as is sometimes the case. In the top register, the gods or princes and their entourage march across the cloth from left to right in a procession that would make any Balinese proud. There are ten figures in all. In the center is a group of two noble figures preceded by two attendants; in front of them and behind are groups of two noble figures with a single attendant. The central figures are somewhat larger and seem to suggest a difference in status compared to the smaller figures. It is difficult to determine whether the maker of the cloth had particular figures or a particular story in mind, or whether the imagery was drawn from the general *wayang* puppet theater repertoire.[2] There is a veritable flutter of pennants, some clearly held in the hands of the figures themselves, many others added for good measure. And in the sky above, a variety of filler ornaments leaves no unwanted empty space. Below, in the lower register, a similar assembly of figures is arranged, but this time in groups, facing different directions. This variation gives this spectacular cloth an added distinction.

Endek is the general Balinese term for weft ikat textiles; these are still produced in large quantity, now for the most part on mechanized looms. In the pre–World War II period, from which this cloth dates, three kinds of weft ikat can be distinguished: a loose, gauzelike ritual cloth about which little is known; another kind of ritual cloth called *cepuk*; and what might be called the *endek* proper.[3] Nongeometric figures, such as *wayang* figures, serpents (*naga*), and Garuda, are found only on *endek* proper. These prewar *endek* cloths are predominantly red in color; indeed it is rare to find one that is not red. Against this background the figures show a multitude of hues, these colors being dabbed or painted on. The process normally involved only a single ikat procedure, which produced the basic figures — in the case of so many nonrepeating figures, as seen here, a complicated and exacting process in itself.

63 Outer wrap cloth (*kampuh endek*), before 1940

Silk; silver and gold thread
H: 43¼ in; W: 63 in
Private collection, Netherlands

1 Related *endek* cloths with a row of *wayang* figures are in the collections of the National Gallery of Australia: Robyn Maxwell, *Sari to Sarong: Five Hundred Years of Indian and Indonesian Textile Exchange* (Canberra: Australian National Gallery, 2003, 50) and the Musée Guimet, *Lumières de soie: soieries tissées d'or de la collection Riboud* (Paris: Réunion des Musées Nationaux, 2004, 201). They also appear on supplementary-weft *songket* textiles.

2 It is suggested that the figures on the Musée Guimet cloth represent the heroes of the Ramayana (*Lumières de soie: soieries tissées d'or de la collection Riboud*, 201). *Wayang* figures are also used to decorate *songket* (supplementary-weft) cloths and embroidered cloths.

3 An excellent introduction to Balinese textiles is Brigitta Hauser-Schäublin, Marie-Louise Nabholz-Kartaschoff, and Urs Ramseyer, *Textiles in Bali* (Berkeley: Periplus, 1991), especially 14–30 (on *endek*) and 94–114 (on *cepuk*).

4 W. O. J. Nieuwenkamp, *Bali en Lombok* (Edam: De Zwerver, 1906–1910), 129–130; W. O. J. Nieuwenkamp, *Zwerftochten op Bali* (Amsterdam: Elsevier, 1910), 66, 201; J. J. Fraser, "De weefkunst in de afdeeling Boeleleng (Bali)," *Tijdschrift voor het Binnenlandsch Bestuur* 35 (1908), 324–333. An enigmatic seventeenth-century source refers to colored textiles from northwest Bali, but no place is mentioned, nor is the technique discussed. Fraser's account is technical and mentions no actual places of manufacture.

5 Brigitta Hauser-Schäublin, Marie-Louise Nabholz-Kartaschoff and Urs Ramseyer, *Textiles in Bali* (Berkeley: Periplus, 1991), figs. 2.4 and 2.11.

Although *endek* cloths were already known in the late nineteenth century, accounts by Nieuwenkamp and Fraser date only from the beginning of the following century.[4] Nieuwenkamp, who traveled widely throughout Bali, mentions *endek* being made in Bubunan and surrounding villages in North Bali, and adds that they were made of Chinese silk thread imported via Singapore, using aniline dyes. Because of such written sources, it is often suggested that prewar *endek* all originated from Bubunan. However, figural *endek* were apparently also made later in Klungkung or Karangasem.[5] It is not possible to say with certainty whether the silk *endek* exhibited here was made in or around Bubunan or elsewhere on Bali, but the former is most likely.

This garment is an outer wrap — *saput* in Low Balinese, *kampuh* in High Balinese — worn by a man above the main waist cloth, either tied around the waist or tied around the chest under the armpits with a separate sash. This latter style of tying an outer wrap was common among the noble class. Only a male member of a prestigious noble family would have worn a cloth of such quality.

DSF

Balinese textiles show remarkable diversity in terms of techniques, colors, and patterns. This sash is made with two different techniques of ornamentation. In the first, called *endek*, the weft threads of the textile are bundled and tied so that parts resist absorbing color when the threads are dipped into a dye bath. This technique, also known as ikat, is a complex process that can involve numerous retyings of the threads, depending on the number of colors in the textile, all before the cloth is actually woven.[1] The second technique, known as *songket*, involves the use of supplementary silver or gold threads to ornament the cloth. The northern province of Buleleng was a center for the production of both these types of textiles. According to scholars, *endek* and *songket* were once made only by women of the courts, and the wearing of such textiles was a privilege of the upper classes.[2]

In this sash, a plain red central panel is surrounded by wide, ornamented borders.[3] In the borders small bands of ikat form concentric diamonds of white, green, yellow, orange, and dark reddish purple. Rows of these diamonds are repeated, interspersed with rows of supplementary weft patterns in gold- and silver-covered thread. These metallic patterns are either rows of Vs, formed by groups of five slanting lines at diagonals, or depictions of moths with wings outspread. It is difficult to know the significance of the moth, although it may refer to the insects that produce the silk from which this sash is made.

NR

64 Waist and breast sash (*sabuk*), 1880–1925

Buleleng or Jembrana
Silk, metallic thread
H: 21¼ in; L: 115¾ in

Asian Art Museum, Acquisition made possible by Fred M. and Nancy Livingston Levin, The Shenson Foundation, in memory of Ben and A. Jess Shenson, 2008.33

1 Today the process of making *endek* textiles has been simplified. The threads are tied with a pattern and then dipped into a dye bath to establish the background color. After the ties have been removed, the other colors are dabbed onto the undyed portions of the threads.

2 Brigitta Hauser-Schaublin, Marie-Louise Nabholz-Kartaschoff, and Urs Ramseyer, *Textiles in Bali*, 15, 36–37.

3 See comparable examples in the Art Institute of Chicago, 2002.992 and 2002.958b, the Rautenstrauch-Joest Museum, 51564, and the National Gallery of Australia, 1984.1242.

Above: A small figure of deity wears a pair of *rumbing*. Padang Galak (Denpasar), 1977. *Photo David Stuart-Fox.*

1   The pair of *subeng* is drawn by Nieuwenkamp and published as *gouden oorknop* in his book *Bali en Lombok* (Edam: De Zwerver, 1906–1910), 63. See also H. H. Juynboll, *Catalogus van 's Rijks Ethnographisch Museum, Deel VII Bali en Lombok* (Leiden: Brill, 1912), 13. The ear pendants are also published in Francine Brinkgreve, "Balinese Rulers and Colonial Rule," in ed. Endang Sri Hardiati and Pieter ter Keurs, *Indonesia: The Discovery of the Past* (Amsterdam: KIT Publishers, 2005), 134.

2   Francine Brinkgreve and David Stuart-Fox, "Collecting after Colonial Conflict: Badung and Tabanan 1906–2006," in ed. Pieter ter Keurs, *Colonial Collections Revisited* (Leiden: CNWS Publications, 2007), 154.

3   See, for example, the illustration in J. E. Jasper and Mas Pirngadie, *De inlandsche kunstnijverheid in Nederlandsch Indië, IV. De goud- en zilversmeedkunst* ('s-Gravenhage: Mouton, 1927), 142.

4   J. E. Jasper and Mas Pirngadie, *De inlandsche kunstnijverheid in Nederlandsch Indië, IV. De goud- en zilversmeedkunst*, 141.

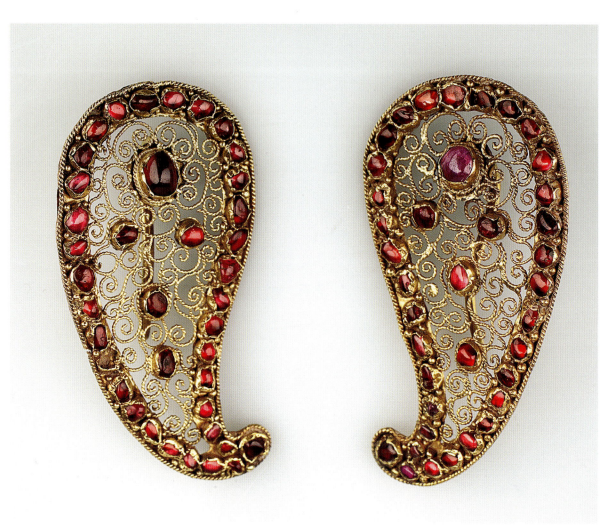

In January 1907 W. O. J. Nieuwenkamp bought these two sets of jewelry[1] at a public sale of treasures from the Tabanan palace, after the raja had surrendered to the Dutch and committed suicide (see cat. nos. 48 and 49). It seems that the Dutch often sold looted objects of lesser value to offset military costs. In the case of Tabanan, however, it was palace treasures that were sold, and for a different reason: "The sale of the *poeri* [palace] possessions of Tabanan served to create a capital sum to offset the costs of maintaining Tabanese exiles on Lombok."[2]

To judge by the representations of ear jewelry on statues and paintings, the cylindrical *subeng* were worn by both male and female deities, nobles, and men and women of the courts, whereas the drop-shaped *rumbing* were exclusively male. For example, both male and female sculptural images are portrayed wearing *subeng* (cat. nos. 17 and 18), whereas the Uma statue (cat. no. 101) wears *subeng* and the Rawana *kris* stand (cat. no. 57) *rumbing*. The bronze statue (cat. no. 16) has big holes in his earlobes, obviously to wear *subeng*. In the paintings from Tabanan (cat. nos. 47 and 48), Rama, Rawana, and the deities wear *rumbing*, and Sita and Ratih wear *subeng*. But also on both *parba*, *subeng* seem to be worn by most of the other characters. Palm leaf images of Dewi Sri (cat. nos. 6, 78) usually have very large *subeng*.

Both of these pairs of ear jewelry were meant for female and male nobles of the court of Tabanan and were probably made by goldsmiths who worked to order at the palace. The jewelery was worn at all kinds of rituals and festive occasions, such as wedding ceremonies or temple festivals. This kind of jewelry, first used exclusively at the courts, over time became more and more fashionable among rich villagers, especially as part of wedding costumes.

Both pairs of ear plugs and ear pendants are made of gold filigree, set with precious stones, which were usually imported from Kalimantan. The pendants have a hook fastened to the ornament, to be put through the earlobes. They have the form of a curled leaf, the Indian palmette motif.[3]

The earplugs are made in the form of cylinders which are pushed through the holes in the earlobes and fastened in the front. Taking the shape of a disk, decorated with a star motif, these *subeng* are called *subeng luwed agung*.[4] When the *subeng* are not worn, the holes in the earlobes are kept open by pieces of rolled-up *lontar* palm leaf, which also serve as ear ornaments. This is illustrated in two Dewi Sri images (cat. nos. 6 and 7).

FB

65 Pair of earplugs (*subeng*), approx. 1850–1900

Tabanan

Gold, precious stones, wing case of a beetle

H: 2⅜ in; D: 3 in (larger pieces); H: 1⅛ in; D: 2¾ in

National Museum of Ethnology, Leiden, the Netherlands, 1586-112

66 Ear pendants (*rumbing*), approx. 1850–1900

Tabanan

Gold, precious stones

H: 2⅜ in; W: 1⅜ in

National Museum of Ethnology, Leiden, the Netherlands, 1586-113

These richly decorated gold and silver boxes (here and overleaf) are parts of betel or *sirih* sets, containers for the various ingredients of the betel quid.[1] They were seized from the palace of Klungkung after the *puputan* Klungkung on April 28, 1908. They were most likely made by gold- and silversmiths, *pande mas*, who lived in Kamasan and worked to order for the Klungkung courts.

The custom of betel chewing, which carries an important role in various social activities and ceremonies, was widespread in Bali. For enjoyment as a stimulant, ingredients for the betel quid were offered to guests as a sign of welcome and token of politeness. Although there has been a marked decrease in its daily use in Bali, the offering of *sirih* is still regarded as a sign of hospitality, and as confirmation of relationships. In a ritual context, betel ingredients are presently mainly used as part of offerings to deities and ancestors.

The basic ingredients for betel chewing are betel (*sirih*) leaf (*Piper bitle*), areca (*pinang* palm) nut (*Areca catechu*), and lime (calcium oxide). *Gambir* (an astringent extract from the leaves of *Uncaria/Uncaria gambir*) and tobacco are potential additions to the basic elements of the betel quid, rendering the whole more fragrant.

Anyone who chewed betel had the basic ingredients at hand, stored in various types of containers. These might be simple compartmented open boxes made of wood, or bags made of bamboo, or, among people of higher social status, in all kinds of little containers, placed together on a beautiful dish or tray. Especially in the context of a royal palace or princely court, containers for the ingredients of the betel quid were usually made of precious materials, such as gold or silver, and decorated with gemstones.[2] In the same way that the accumulated powers of the ancestors are believed to reside in an heirloom *kris*, a betel set was also often one of the most valuable inherited items, the *pusaka,* because of its connection with the presence of the ancestors.[3] Betel sets were even incorporated into the state regalia.

In their portraits, rulers often had themselves shown with a fine *sirih* set close at hand. A complete betel set, or simply some of the containers, was also favored items for presents or diplomatic gifts from one ruler or senior official to another.[4]

Boxes for the ingredients of betel quid, approx. 1850–1900

67 Tobacco box (*lopa-lopa* or *tepak*)

Klungkung

Gold

H: 1.7 in; W: 2¼ in; L: 4⅜ in

National Museum of Ethnology, Leiden, the Netherlands, 1684-17

68 Pair of *sirih* boxes (*kopok*)

Klungkung

Silver

H: 1⅞ in; D: 2¾ in (smaller);

H: 3⅛ in; D: 3¾ in (larger)

National Museum of Ethnology, Leiden, the Netherlands, 1684-83

---

1 H. Juynboll, *Catalogus van 's Rijks Ethnographisch Museum, Deel VII Bali en Lombok* (Leiden: Brill, 1912), 10–11.

2 J. E. Jasper and Mas Pirngadie, *De inlandsche kunstnijverheid in Nederlandsch Indië, IV. De goud- en zilversmeedkunst* ('s-Gravenhage: Mouton, 1927), 251.

3 Henry Brownrigg, *Betel Cutters from the Samuel Eilenberg Collection* (London: Thames and Hudson, 1992), 28; Wahyono 1999: 112.

4 Francine Brinkgreve, "Balinese Rulers and Colonial Rule," in ed. Endang Sri Hardiati and Pieter ter Keurs, *Indonesia: The Discovery of the Past* (Amsterdam: KIT Publishers, 2005), 127.

5 Pienke W. H. Kal, *Yogya Silver: Renewal of a Javanese Handicraft* (Amsterdam: KIT Publishers, 2005), 96.

6 J. E. Jasper and Mas Pirngadie, *De inlandsche kunstnijverheid in Nederlandsch Indië, IV. De goud- en zilversmeedkunst* ('s-Gravenhage: Mouton, 1927), 50–56.

7 H. N. van der Tuuk, *Kawi-Balineesch-Nederlandsch woordenboek* (Batavia: Landsdrukkerij, 1897–1912), III, 738.

8 A. N. J. Th. à Th. van der Hoop, *Indonesische siermotieven/Ragam-ragam perhiasan Indonesia/Indonesian Ornamental Design* (Batavia: Koninklijk Bataviaasch Genootschap van Kunsten en Wetenschappen, 1949), 272.

9 H. N. van der Tuuk, *Kawi-Balineesch-Nederlandsch woordenboek*, II, 295.

These boxes from the Klungkung palace were beaten out of sheets of gold and silver. The various parts were hammered into shape and decorated before soldering.[5] The process of embossing decorations from the back is called repoussé work. Final details in the design are achieved by chasing on the front side.

Like most Balinese gold- and silverwork, the boxes shown here are richly decorated with geometric, foliate, and floral borders, influenced by Indian motifs and by Javanese Hindu temple ornamentation. The general name of these flower motifs is *patra*.[6]

The gold container for tobacco is called *lopa-lopa* or *tepak*.[7] The sides of the box are decorated with rows of triangles and meandering tendril and flower motifs, *patra sari*, also called "recalcitrant spiral," a motif that often occurs as Javanese Hindu temple wall decoration.[8] The lid is decorated with flower borders and a rim of meanders or *banji*, associated with ancient solar symbols.

The pair of round silver containers, connected by a small chain, is called *kopok* (or *klopok* or *copok*).[9] The bigger box was probably used for *gambir*, the smaller one for lime. The central flower motif on the lids is encircled by spirals of leaf ornaments.

FB

SIRIH BOXES 269

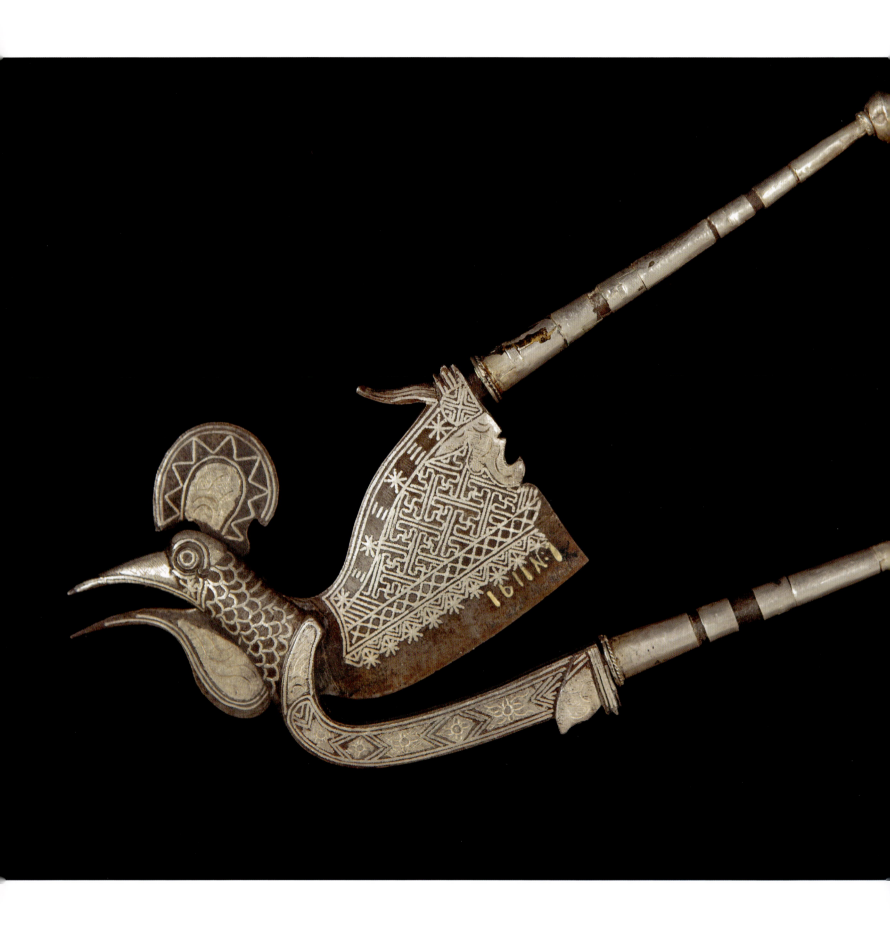

270 CATALOGUE

An indispensable part of the betel quid is the areca nut (*Areca catechu*) (see cat. nos. 67 and 68, illustrating gold and silver containers for the ingredients of the betel quid).

Cutters (*caket*) are used to cut the hard areca nuts into small pieces, and are made of wrought iron, sometimes inlaid in silver or gold. In Bali these cutters often have zoomorphic shapes, especially horses and various kinds of birds.[1] The blade and the base of the cutter are fastened together in such a way that the animal's head seems to make a chewing motion when the scissors are cracking the nut.

This elegant betel cutter is forged in the shape of a bird, possibly a peacock. In Hindu mythology, the peacock is the mount of the war god Skanda or Kartikeya, a son of Siwa and Parwati. The bird is usually identifiable by its crest and the long tail with its numerous eyes.[2] However, although the bird represented on this nut cutter does indeed have a crest, its tail is short. The circular crest is encrusted with a silver star motif, and the body of the bird has silver-encrusted decorations, especially *banji* or swastika motifs. The swastika, an ancient Indian symbol, symbolizes the rotation of the celestial bodies, and more specifically is a symbol of the sun.

In the technique of encrusting, deep lines or grooves are engraved in a dark-colored metal (usually iron), and silver wire is hammered into the grooves. In Balinese this technique is called *tetatahan* or *gegayaman*.[3] The handles of the cutter are covered with silver. Occasionally gold is used.

Although the use of silver and the refined craftsmanship of this *caket* suggest a provenance from one of the Balinese courts, the object was bought in 1907 in The Hague, at a shop called Boeatan, which was set up to deal in Indonesian handicrafts and decorative arts. Boeatan (from the Balinese *buatan,* meaning manufactured, crafted, made), an endeavor of the East and West Association, was formed after the Dutch National Exhibition of Women's Labour in 1898. In accord with Dutch Ethical Policy, which was formally established around 1900, the goals of the founders of the East and West Association were to help develop Indonesian handicrafts and to sell decorative arts in the Netherlands.[4]

FB

69 Betel cutter (*caket*), approx. 1850–1900

Iron with silver inlay
H: 3¼ in; W: 10½ in x D: ¼ in
National Museum of Ethnology, Leiden, the Netherlands, 1611-1

[1] Henry Brownrigg, *Betel Cutters from the Samuel Eilenberg Collection* (London: Thames and Hudson, 1992). H. H. Juynboll, *Catalogus van 's Rijks Ethnographisch Museum, Deel VII Bali en Lombok* (Leiden: Brill, 1912), 9.

[2] A. N. J. Th. à Th. van der Hoop, *Indonesische siermotieven/Ragam-ragam perhiasan Indonesia/ Indonesian Ornamental Design* (Batavia: Koninklijk Bataviaasch Genootschap van Kunsten en Wetenschappen, 1949), 194.

[3] J. E. Jasper and Mas Pirngadie, *De inlandsche kunstnijverheid in Nederlandsch Indië, IV. De goud- en zilversmeedkunst* ('s-Gravenhage: Mouton, 1927), 85–86, 254.

[4] Pienke W. H. Kal, *Yogya Silver: Renewal of a Javanese Handicraft* (Amsterdam: KIT Publishers, 2005), 27.

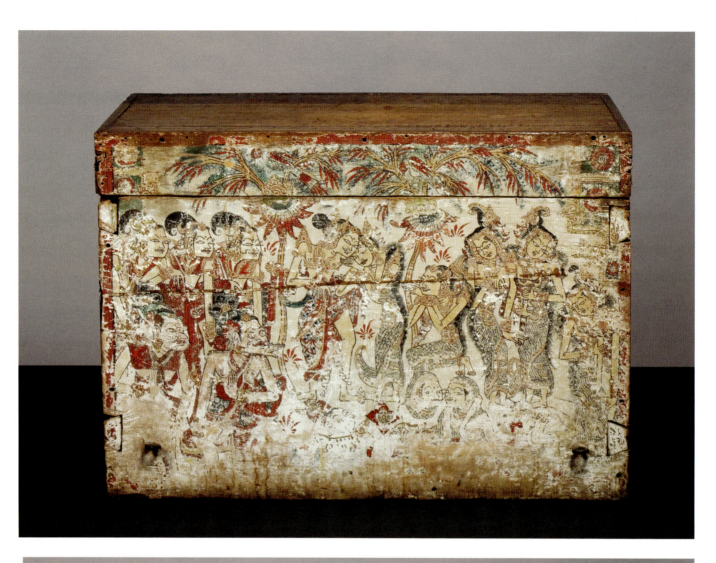

This finely painted box was collected in Bali by W. O. J. Nieuwenkamp, one of the first European artists in Bali and a famous collector and champion of the arts of the island.[1] Nieuwenkamp visited Bali both before and immediately after the Dutch gained colonial control in a series of military campaigns in the early 1900s. The Balinese had been resistant to relinquishing sovereignty and were renowned as fierce defenders of their territory. When the Dutch forces advanced on the kingdoms of southern Bali in 1906 and in 1908, the Balinese rulers knew their days were numbered. They marched into the gunfire of the Dutch troops in a dramatic mass action called a *puputan*, or "ending." Those not killed by the soldiers killed themselves or each other.

Nieuwenkamp was appalled by the events, and did his best to save works of art from the looting and burning of the palaces that followed the fall of the courts. Photos of much of his collection, including this box, were published in a 1924 German catalogue.

This box is a remnant of court life in southern Bali. It was probably used to carry sacred textiles or other valuables. The paintings, made with traditional stone-ground pigments, illustrate themes from the Malat, a very important story in pre-conquest Bali that was illustrated in paintings and performed in the dance dramas *gambuh* and *arja*.[2] The stories in the Malat are also called Panji tales, after the legendary East Javanese prince who features in many of the stories. Originating in East Java in perhaps the twelfth or thirteenth century, versions of these stories spread through much of Southeast Asia.

In one episode of the story, a princess, Rangkesari, is kidnapped to be a wife of the king of Lasem, but she threatens suicide to avoid consummating the coercive union. Lasem and his allies eventually enter into battle with Prince Panji and Rangkesari's brother, the king of Melayu, but they are defeated.

On one side of the box, the panel is starkly divided, with aristocratic men and their attendants on the left side and a group of noblewomen and their servants on the right. In the center of the panel, framed by two stylized trees, one man stands with his arm around a woman's shoulders, his head bowed down toward her. Her hands are clasped in a gesture of respect, and her head leans in toward him. The man — Rangkesari's brother, the king of Malayu — has picked his sister out of a group of the wives of Lasem and his allies. The women are on their way to ritually kill themselves after the deaths of their husbands, but Rangkesari is given a reprieve.

On the other side, we see the victorious kings seated under parasols at the left. Below them lie the stiff corpses of the defeated Lasem and his allies. The widows kneel around their husbands' bodies and dramatically plunge daggers into their own chests.[3] Blood spurts from

70 Royal storage box, approx. 1850–1900

Klungkung
Wood and pigments
H: 20½ in; W: 18½ in; L: 30⅜ in
Asian Art Museum, Acquisition made possible by Richard Beleson, 2007.4.a–.b

1 Bruce W. Carpenter, *W.O.J. Nieuwenkamp: First European Artist in Bali* (Singapore: Periplus Editions, 1997).

2 Adrian Vickers, *Journeys of Desire: A Study of the Balinese Text Malat* (Leiden: KITLV, 2005).

3 The suicide of widows was a practice that continued in Bali into the early twentieth century. Early European visitors to the island were horrified by the custom, especially when widows jumped into the funeral pyres of their husbands. Catherine Weinberger-Thomas, Jeffrey Mehlman, and David Gordon White, *Ashes of Immortality* (University of Chicago Press, 2000), 1–13.

their wounds. One of the women has pierced her mouth before stabbing her chest; her blood drips from her lips down onto the wounds of the dead king. Perched in the trees above them two crows, harbingers of bad luck, stare intently.

One end of the box shows three officials of the court, recognizable by their hair (or lack thereof) and headdresses: a noblemann (*arya*), a commander in chief (*tumengggung*), and a bald chamberlain (*demang*).⁴ The other end is badly damaged but seems to show a man of high rank (Panji?).⁵

NR

4 Vickers, *Journeys of Desire*, 30.

5 Thanks to Thomas Cooper and Adrian Vickers for help in identifying these scenes.

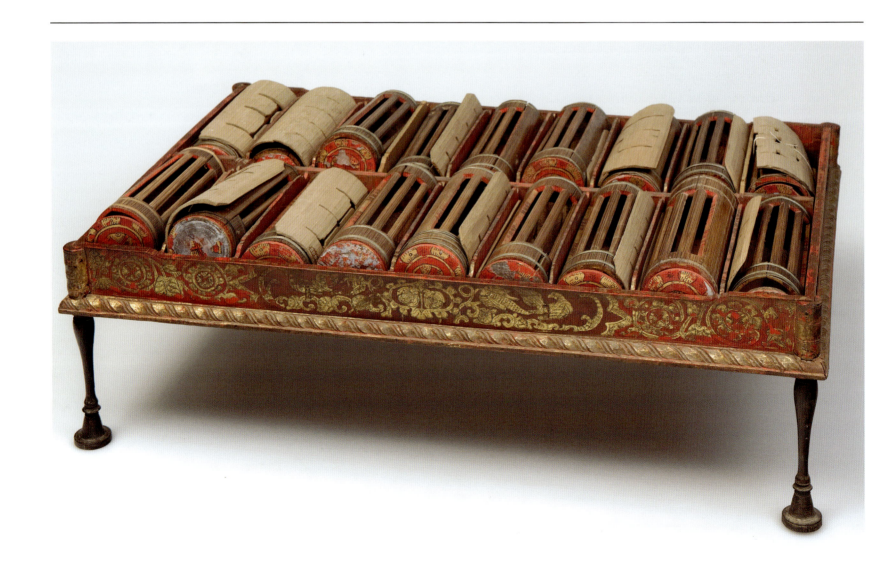

An important item of furniture is associated with cricket fighting: a footed tray to hold the bamboo tubes in which the crickets are kept. Such trays are often greatly prized by their owners. This finely crafted tray (*penarangan*), with spaces for eighteen little bamboo tubes, is painted red and decorated with black and gold figures.[1] Appearing among these fanciful freehand drawings are bird, animal, and plantlike forms, including what could be a scorpion or a gecko. Such creatures, especially if caught in the act of fighting, are added to the cricket's diet. The cricket tubes (*bungbung jangkrik*) are stoppered at either end and have carved slats that let in light and air. The tubes are of a plain bamboo, and the stoppers painted with simple decoration. Often, however, cricket tubes are made from a decorative species of bamboo (such as the spotted *tiing tutul*).

Cricket fighting is known all over Bali, although the number of aficionados is very small compared to the legions of cockfighting enthusiasts. Like cockfighting, cricket fighting is a man's pastime, and is sometimes organized into special clubs (*seka jangkrik*) that hold the fights, complete with gambling, as also occurs with cockfighting. A particular species of cricket, the *jangkrik kalung*, is sought for fighting. Where it is found is important; it is said that a cricket found in a temple is uncommonly lucky, but should be fought only once. The crickets are trained, exercised, and fed special diets. Players have their own, often secret, recipes (*sadek*) comprising a variety of different substances, intended to strengthen their fighting instincts.

The fight takes place in an open space at whose center is the fighting arena. In its simplest form this consists of a long piece of bamboo split lengthwise, but it may instead be a specially carved stand (*panuruan, patulangan*), another piece of cricket furniture that can be finely crafted. The crickets available for fighting on a given day are examined by the players, and suitable opponents are chosen by goading them into action using "quills," called *kekilit*, made of a particular variety of grass. When all is ready, the tubes containing the crickets are placed in the fighting arena, separated by a divider. The divider is removed, the crickets are provoked into action, and the fight begins. Crickets are rarely killed in these combats, although injury can occur. A cricket with just one leg, in fact, has a special name, *jangkrik kipa*. The winner is the cricket that forces its opponent to retreat.

Cricket fighting is also known in Java and in other parts of Southeast Asia. It is possible that the pastime was introduced from China, which has a long history of keeping crickets, especially for their song.

DSF

71 Table and bamboo tubes for cricket fighting, approx. 1900–1930

Painted wood, bamboo

Table: H: 7¼ in; W: 20⅞ in; D: 14¼ in

Bamboo tubes: L: 5⅞ in; D: 2 in

Collection, Tropenmuseum, Amsterdam (the Netherlands), 1936-10a–s

[1] Purchased from Mrs. E. W. Sayers-Stern, 1949.

Holding the cricket tube in his hand, a cricket aficionado exercises his cricket using a special quill. Next to him are the cricket trays. Budakeling (Karangasem). *Photo David Stuart-Fox.*

It is difficult to determine the original purpose of this small slit drum. Made from a hollowed-out piece of wood, slit drums are one of the oldest types of percussion instruments. In Bali they are called *kulkul* and are commonly found in villages. Balinese temples have an open-air tower from which one or more *kulkul* are vertically hung. These drums are often hollowed-out logs the size of a human being. Occasionally the top end of the drum is carved with a human or animal face. If two *kulkul* are hung as a pair, they often produce different tones, one low and one high. They are beaten to gather the community for ceremonial occasions and are also used in emergencies, such as military attacks or natural disasters. The rhythm and pitch of the drumming indicate the reason the drums are sounded. Hildred Geertz describes the sounds of the *kulkul* at the Pura Desa in Batuan as being an essential part of "the confrontation with the gods themselves, when [the drums] are beaten continuously, forming a ladder of sound that stretches between the upper worlds and the human world."[1] As with many Balinese objects that help mediate between the two worlds, the drums at Pura Desa Batuan are treated with special care, clothed in a sacred *poleng* cloth, and given daily offerings.

Kulkul can be found in other parts of the Balinese landscape. Most neighborhood organizations (*banjar*) have one, and they are also sometimes found hanging from sacred trees outside temples. (See the far right of the painting in cat. no. 41.) Local organizations may have small *kulkul*, also used to gather members or crowds.[2] *Kulkul* made out of bamboo, called *tektekan,* are used in gamelan, especially in Tabanan.

This small drum is carved in the likeness of a fish. Like almost all depictions of animals in Bali, the fish has a slightly frightening countenance, with bared pointed teeth. There is minimal wear on the sides of the drum, indicating little use. It was possibly an object carved for a tourist, by an artist experimenting with traditional forms in unconventional ways. Slit drums of this type and size, though, were also found in East Java, and it is possible that this one is related to that tradition.[3]

NR

72 Slit drum, approx. 1950

Wood

L: 20⅞ in.; W: 5⅛ in; D: 4½ in

National Museum of Ethnology, Leiden, the Netherlands, 5480-13

1 Hildred Geertz, *The Life of a Balinese Temple: Artistry, Imagination, and History in a Peasant Village* (Honolulu: University of Hawaii Press, 2004), 124.

2 Ida Bagus Gde Judha Triguna et al., *Peralatan hiburan dan kesenian tradisional daerah Bali* (Departemen Pendidikan dan Kebudayaan, Direktorat Jenderal Kebudayaan, Direktorat Sejarah dan Nilai Tradisional, Bagian Proyek Penelitian, Pengkajian dan Pembinaan Nilai Budaya Bali, 1993), 101.

3 Bruce Carpenter, *Javanese Antique Furniture and Folk Art: The David B. Smith and James Tirtoprodjo Collections* (Singapore: Editions Didier Millet, 2009), fig. ii40.

Gamelan Semar Pagulingan

Musical ensembles composed primarily of metallophones, xylophones, drums, and gongs, and occasionally supplemented by flutes, stringed instruments, and vocalists, are known in Indonesia as gamelan.[1] Unlike what is found in Western orchestras, the majority of instruments in most gamelan are percussive; the word *gamelan* is derived from the Javanese root *gamel-*, meaning to hammer or strike. All instruments in an ensemble are tuned to, and intended to be played with, that ensemble alone. The complex and multilayered music produced by the Balinese gamelan is marked by interlocking patterns of paired instruments that are tuned slightly apart to produce a shimmering, pulsating resonance.

There are over thirty types of gamelan in Bali today, ranging from large sets with dozens of instruments to simple pairs of metallophones.[2] Temples, palaces, and villages, as well as many other groups and individuals, may own one or more gamelan ensembles. Royal courts were known to have several separate sets for different occasions and moods. The instruments displayed here (beginning on p. 280) come from a type of gamelan called Semar Pagulingan. The word *Semar* refers to Semara, the god of love, and *pagulingan* means sleeping chambers. This type of ensemble was once found exclusively in a court setting, played outside the pavilions where the king slept and entertained his consorts. This type of primarily seven-toned gamelan is famed for producing sweet, sensuous music. Its repertoire is based on an older type of gamelan called the gamelan *gambuh*, which was performed primarily on large bamboo flutes to accompany courtly dance dramas.

With the decline of the Balinese courts in the early twentieth century and the rise of a new style of village-based gamelan called *kebyar*, the courtly gamelan Semar Pagulingan lost favor, and few ensembles of this type remain today.[3] The Canadian composer Colin McPhee (1900–1946) noted that by 1931 this type of gamelan "had all but vanished."[4]

In his memoir of his six years in Bali, McPhee describes visiting blacksmiths to commission some additional instruments to supplement a rare gamelan Semar Pegulingan that had been loaned to him.

> There was something dark and secret about their ancient craft, for they had to do with metal, cold mysterious product of the underworld, charged with magic power. For centuries they manufactured from the same substance the instruments of both music and death, the resonant gongs, the spears and thin-edged krises. In their craft the elements of life and death were strangely united. For a gong when struck can (or once could) dispel the demons, bring rain, wind; or give, when bathed in, health and strength. And music, which is the most ecstatic voice of life, rang from the bronze keys even as they were hammered out in forges, over fire that had burned from time immemorial.[5]

---

1 For more general information on gamelan in Bali, see Lisa Gold, *Music in Bali: Experiencing Music, Expressing Culture* (New York: Oxford University Press, 2005); Michael Tenzer, *Balinese Music* (Berkeley and Seattle: Periplus Editions, 1991); I Wayan Dibia and Rucina Ballinger, *Balinese Dance, Drama and Music: A Guide to the Performing Arts of Bali*, illustrated edition (Singapore: Periplus Editions, 2004); Colin McPhee, *Music in Bali: A Study in Form and Instrumental Organization in Balinese Orchestral Music* (New York: Da Capo Press, 1976).

2 Dibia and Ballinger, *Balinese Dance, Drama and Music*, 22.

3 In the last few decades there has been a revival of music using this type of gamelan, with attempts to recreate older styles or create new ones.

4 Colin McPhee, *Music in Bali* (New Haven, CT: Yale University Press, 1966), 140.

5 Colin McPhee, *A House in Bali* (New York: John Day, 1946), 189–190.

Although much has changed since McPhee's sojourn in Bali in the 1930s, the instruments of a gamelan are still considered to be imbued with special powers. Most rehearsals and performances begin with a small offering to the instruments themselves, and every thirty weeks gamelan are ritually purified on a special day called Tumpek Wayang. Legends say the first gamelan was first created by the god of love, Semara, and his spouse, Ratih, and then copied by other gods, and eventually by the kings of earth as well.[6] Music is believed to have the power to move between the seen and unseen worlds. It serves as an offering and is an important component of most ritual ceremonies. The sound of the gamelan calls the gods down to this world, entertains them while they visit, and escorts them back to the heavens.

Archives of the Tropenmuseum indicate that this gamelan was purchased from the ruler of the eastern Balinese kingdom of Karangasem, Anak Agung Gedé Agung, in 1938 or 1939.[7] The son of the ruler recalls that his father once had three complete gamelan Semar Pagulingan ensembles in his court. According to him, one was given as a gift to the queen of the Netherlands, one melted down to make a new gamelan *kebyar*, and a third retained at the palace.[8]

Gamelan are made up of a variety of instruments. The Semar Pegulingan in the Tropenmuseum collection comprises thirty-five instruments: two drums, two upright gongs, a single horizontal gong, a *trompong* (a series of small gongs set into a frame), twenty-eight metallophones, and one *rincik* (small cymbals set on a base). Presumably the set would have originally included a flute (*suling*) and two lyres (*rebab*), as are found in other sets. It is likely that the bases of the instruments are made of jackfruit wood, which is commonly used for this purpose, but some may be made from teak.[9] The resonators are cut tubes of bamboo, and the keys are made from bronze. The different style of decoration on a few of the instruments, and the differing shapes of keys on others, has led some scholars to hypothesize that they were not original to the ensemble. There are many irregularities in the Tropenmuseum's Semar Pagulingan ensemble. In her dissertation, Ireen van der Endt questions whether the set is a seven-toned gamelan or if it actually contains instruments that were combined from two five- and six-toned gamelan ensembles (perhaps from the other two sets owned by the ruler of Karangasem).[10]

NR

6 Adrian Vickers, "The Realm of the Senses: Images of the Court Music of Pre-Colonial Bali," *Imago Musicae* 2 (1985): 146–147.

7 The archives are probably referring to Anak Agung Agung Anglurah Ketut Karangasem, who ruled in Karangasem, 1908–1950.

8 Ireen van der Endt, "Van Koninklijke Slaapkamer naar Rommelzolder: een Beschrijving van de Semar Pagulingan in het Tropenmusem" (Universiteit van Amsterdam, 1996), 31–33. This third gamelan Semar Pagulingan was later sold to the Gunarsa Museum in Klungkung. Letters in the archives of the Tropenmuseum discuss the details of the payment for the gamelan.

9 Van der Endt, "Van Koninklijke Slaapkamer naar Rommelzolder: een Beschrijving van de Semar Pagulingan in het Tropenmusem," 82–83.

10 Van der Endt, "Van Koninklijke Slaapkamer naar Rommelzolder: een Beschrijving van de Semar Pagulingan in het Tropenmusem." Among the puzzling questions is why the gamelan is described as having a seven-tone scale system, when the ornamentation instruments have six keys.

This vertically hanging gong (*kemong*) is the smaller of the two standing gongs in the Tropenmuseum's gamelan Semar Pegulingan. Gongs are one of the most important instruments in an orchestra, and may be given honorific names. Most large hanging gongs in Balinese gamelan are imported from Java.[1] A primary function of suspended gongs in gamelan music is to punctuate the rhythmic units of a musical composition. The large gongs are used to define the end of a metric cycle, while a smaller gong like this would be used to mark subphrases. In Bali kettle gongs, like this one, have deep rims and surfaces that slant toward a raised boss in the center. When a padded mallet hits the raised knob, it produces a high-pitched sound that was described by Colin McPhee as "a prolonged and penetrating tone of remarkable beauty and purity."[2]

The decoration on the framework of the suspended gongs in this Semar Pagulingan set is particularly beautiful. As with the other instruments in the ensemble, the main colors used are black, red, and gold. The decoration on the frame can be divided into three sections. At the very bottom, a line of black separates the instrument from the ground. A similar border of black defines the inner framework surrounding the gong itself. The base has two large pedestals connected by a raised arch of wood beneath the bronze gong. This part of the frame is painted red and not decorated except for a depiction of an open many-petaled flower that is carved directly below the center of the gong. The gong's block-shaped feet show a deeply carved depiction of a coral reef. Small fish, sea snakes, long-clawed shrimp, and a crab emerge from or dart into holes in the coral. Some scholars have hypothesized that this watery world, with its poisonous snakes and clawed crustaceans, depicts the *tatamanan*, a water park representing the underworld of demons and the middle world of men.[3] Gongs are sometimes associated with water. The word *ombak*, or wave, refers both to waves in the water and the sound waves produced by the gong. Some scholars suggest that the gong is seen as a tree rooted in water, from which all life comes and is returned.[4]

The sides rise up in intricately carved tendrils of leaves and flowers to form an inverted U around the gong. Crowning this frame, a larger flower is depicted in profile. Tendrils also rise from the frame's shoulders. The shape of the frame mimics the shape of a gateway to a temple, with the flower placed where one would find a *kala*/Boma monster face on a temple, and the flared wings mimicking the pattern of the *makara* (a mythical aquatic creature whose head with raised nose is often depicted in architecture).[5]

NR

73 *Kemong*, approx. 1900–1930

Karangasem, East Bali

Wood, bronze, string, pigments

H: 23⅝ in; W: 21¾ in; D: 7¼ in

Collection, Tropenmuseum, Amsterdam (the Netherlands), 1340-13

1 Michael Tenzer, *Gamelan Gong Kebyar* (University of Chicago Press, 2000), 47.

2 Colin McPhee, *Music in Bali: A Study in Form and Instrumental Organization in Balinese Orchestral Music* (New York: Da Capo Press, 1976), 29.

3 Sue Carole DeVale and I Wayan Dibia, "Sekar Anjar: An Exploration of Meaning in Balinese Gamelan," *The World of Music* 33, no. 1: 16–17.

4 Sue Carole DeVale and I Wayan Dibia, "Sekar Anjar: An Exploration of Meaning in Balinese Gamelan," 33–35.

5 A similar shape is also seen in *mimbars* (mosque pulpets) in Bali; see the *mimbar* of Gelgel in pl. 21 of Moh. Ali Fadillah, "L'art ancien des mimbar dans les mosquées de Bali," *Archipel* 44, no. 1 (1992): 111. Presumably the same woodcarvers worked for a variety of patrons using a similar vocabulary of motifs.

This instrument, called a *gender rambat*, is a metallophone with thirteen bronze bars that hang over bamboo resonators set in the wooden base. The instrument stands upon a richly carved trapezoidal foot. The keys are suspended over the base on cords that run through holes on either side of each key. Traditionally, the musician would strike the keys with two mallets with disks at the tip. After striking each key the musician would damp it with his hand, to keep the sound crisp. This particular type of instrument is not common today in gamelan ensembles.

Like many of the other instruments in the gamelan ensemble, the *gender rambat* is painted a deep red with gold highlights. As with all the instruments in the group, colors seem to have been applied from dark to light, with black first, then red and finally gold. The foot of the instrument is carved with a scrolling pattern of flowers and leaves. The ends have a pentagon containing a carving of a partially opened large flower. A long panel rises above, with twining tendrils and leaves. At the level of the keys is a large flower in full bloom. Two rounded flaps curve slightly outward. Their outer surfaces are carved with a pattern that looks like the spreading tail feathers of a bird, possibly Garuda, mount of the god Wisnu. Garuda is a symbol of the celestial world. Three stylized flowers grow from a twisting leafy stalk carved on the inside of these flaps.

NR

74 *Gender rambat gede, approx. 1900–1930*

Karangasem, East Bali

Wood, bronze, bamboo, string, pigments

H: 27.4 in; W: 45.3 in; D: 11.8 in

Collection, Tropenmuseum, Amsterdam (the Netherlands), 1340-10

There are two pairs of large and small instruments called *gangsa jongkok* in the Tropenmuseum gamelan. These instruments have six bronze keys, increasing in size from left to right. Today most metallophones, especially in South Bali, have bronze bars that are strung by cords above resonators contained in a wooden frame. But in the past Balinese gamelan had more instruments in which the keys rested directly on the wooden base, cushioned only by a small rubber, felt, or straw pad to dampen the vibration.

The instrument is played with a hammer-shaped mallet with a head of wood or horn. The word *jongkok* means to squat, and indicates that the keys rest on the base, rather than hanging over it as they do on the *gender rambat* (cat. no. 74). Another term for the instrument is *gangsa pacek*. *Pacek,* nail, refers to the wooden pins that rise from the base. The keys, which are perforated at either end, are held in place when positioned on these pins.

The base is block shaped, but flares out like a cresting wave on the sides. Unlike the other instruments in the gamelan ensemble, the four instruments of this type are painted in several colors. Besides black, red, and gold, one also sees white, blue, and shades of pink. This difference in decoration may indicate that the instruments were originally part of a different ensemble.

The *gangsa jongkok* is painted front and back with an image of a single animal in a niche surrounded by filler motifs. These motifs look like horizontal teardrops or flaming ovals and are said to symbolize the wind and clouds. They are commonly found in paintings produced in the village of Kamasan. On the side of the instrument facing the audience is a pale rose tiger with gold stripes outlined in black and red. His head is raised and his teeth and tongue can be seen. On the side facing the player is a golden animal with fur or bristles depicted by fine black lines. The head and legs appear to be those of a dog, but the tail resembles that of a goat. The animal can be identified as a goat because it resembles depictions of goats drawn and identified on palm leaf manuscripts.[1]

The three other *gangsa jongkok* also have paintings of animals on their sides, which have been identified as apes, goats, and tigers. These animals are characters in an animal fable (Tantri tale) in which a mother goat outwits a tiger and ape.[2] Tantri tales are derived from Indian animal fables like the Panchatantra, or from Javanese and Balinese collections of the same type. Reliefs on temples in Central and East Java indicate the popularity of these morality tales between the ninth and fifteenth centuries.[3] In temple reliefs, a single animal might sometimes be portrayed in a tendril-filled niche. It seems these stories were familiar enough that the characters alone could suggest the stories to a viewer.

NR

75 *Gangsa jongkok cenik,* approx. 1900–1930

Karangasem, East Bali
Wood, bronze, pigments
H: 7½ in; W: 13¾ in; D: 7⅛ in
Collection, Tropenmuseum, Amsterdam (the Netherlands), 1340-34

[1] Ireen van der Endt, "Van Koninklijke Slaapkamer naar Rommelzolder: een Beschrijving van de Semar Pagulingan in het Tropenmusem" (Universiteit van Amsterdam, 1996), 103, 139.

[2] C. Hooykaas, *Tantri Kamandaka : een Oudjavaansche Pantjatantra-Bewerking* (Bandoeng: Nix und Co., 1931), 161–167.

[3] For an in-depth discussion of early depictions of Tantri tales, see Marijke Klokke, *The Tantri Reliefs on Ancient Javanese Candi* (Leiden: KITLV Press, 1993). Pages 103–104 discuss the fable of the goat that outwits the tiger.

76 *Gangsa jongkok gede,* approx. 1900–1930

Karangasem, East Bali
Wood, bronze, pigments
H: 9⅝ in; W: 15⅞ in; D: 8⅞ in
Collection, Tropenmuseum, Amsterdam (the Netherlands), 1340-33

This instrument, like cat no. 75, is a metallophone in which the keys lie directly on the base rather than being suspended above it. Instruments of this sort are still used in northern and northeastern Bali, but rarely found in the south.

Like the smaller *gangsa jongkok* (cat. no. 75), this instrument has animals painted on both sides. On the audience side a tiger crouches with its head raised, showing its sharp teeth and protruding tongue. The animal's body is painted red with stripes outlined in black and filled in with pink. On the player's side, an ape sits with his left hand grasping his genitals and his right raised as though in conversation. The ape is painted a pale blue with darker blue spots outlined with gold. As with the other instruments of this type in the ensemble, these animals probably refer to an animal fable about a goat that outwits a tiger and an ape.

NR

A *curing* is a metallophone whose keys rest atop an hourglass-shaped base. The fifteen keys in this instrument are slightly angled so that they are lower at the musician's side and higher facing the audience. They are perforated only on one side, and held onto the base by small pegs. Instruments of this type are seen in Balinese paintings, but rarely encountered in ensembles on the island today.[1] The hourglass shape is reminiscent of instruments in the Javanese gamelan. The presence of this type of instrument in the Semar Pagulingan gamelan is thought to indicate the ensemble's roots in Javanese Hindu traditions brought to Bali in earlier centuries. There are two pairs of *curing* in the Tropenmuseum's Semar Pagulingan gamelan.

The base is painted red and is decorated at the corners of the foot, the waist, and directly below the keys. Two flaps rise from the ends of the instrument, angling outward at a forty-five-degree angle. They are decorated with large opposed S shapes carved in openwork. The rest of these side flaps are full of floral and plant motifs. Since decorative motifs are usually quite similar among instruments in an ensemble, it is possible that the *curing* as well as the *gangsa jongkok* might be from a different ensemble than are the other instruments in this group.

NR

77 *Curing*, approx. 1900–1930

Karangasem, East Bali

Wood, bronze, pigments

H: 16⅞ in; W: 36⅝ in; D: 9⅛ in

Collection, Tropenmuseum, Amsterdam (the Netherlands), 1340-29

1 Adrian Vickers, "The Realm of the Senses: Images of the Court Music of Pre-Colonial Bali," *Imago Musicae* 2 (1985): 164.

Legong dancers of Bali

Perhaps the most famous of all Balinese dances is *legong*, a dance traditionally performed only by young girls who have not yet reached puberty.[1] European visitors, transfixed by the dance, recorded the dancers in drawings, paintings, photographs, and film. In 1931 fifty Balinese musicians and *legong* dancers represented the Dutch colonies at the Paris Colonial Exposition, where they were seen by thousands of Europeans (in six months there were thirty-three million registered visitors to the exposition).[2]

Images of young dancers were often used to promote Bali in travel pamphlets and posters. In 1935 the film *Legong: Dance of the Virgins* was released in New York to great popular success. It had been filmed entirely in Bali two years earlier. The melodramatic film exploited images of bare-breasted young women and promoted the notion of the "exotic" other. Nevertheless, the film did provide a look at life in Bali in the early 1930s and recorded performances and ceremonies beyond the *legong*.

In their 1938 book, *Dance and Drama in Bali,* Beryl de Zoete and Walter Spies described the *legong* dancers:

> In front of the gamelan kneel three small dancers, resplendent in gold and jewels and bright-coloured stuffs overlaid with gold leaf; literally encased and buckled in with gold. Huge golden flowers strewn over purple or crimson skirts, gold lozenges on close-fitting emerald sleeves, gold stoles magenta-lined, gold Garudas at their waist and on their winged head-dresses, crowned with flowers; their small bodies tightly wound in the same glittering stuffs, so that it seems as if no movement would be possible … All have the same glittering precision in their infinitely supple gestures.[3]

There are over a dozen dances in the *legong* repertoire, most deriving from the Hindu epics or the Malat (stories of the East Javanese prince Panji). The most commonly performed today is called *Lasem,* and derives from a Malat story of a princess, Rangkesari, who is kidnapped by the King of Lasem.[4] (See cat. nos. 21 and 70 for images of this princess.) The narrative is enacted through highly stylized movements, marked by synchronization both among the dancers and with the gamelan. Without changing costume, the dancers take on different roles in the story, with a narrator describing the scene.

There are many theories about the origins of the *legong* tradition.[5] Some legends describe its creation by the gods. One commonly repeated narrative attributes its inspiration to celestial nymphs who danced in a dream of the eighteenth-century king I Dewa Agung

---

[1] Beryl de Zoete and Walter Spies wrote in 1938 that boys occasionally danced in *legong*, but to my knowledge that practice no longer exists. Beryl de Zoete and Walter Spies, *Dance and Drama in Bali* (London: Faber and Faber, 1938), 218.

[2] Marieke Bloembergen, *Colonial Spectacles* (Singapore: NUS Press, 2006), 269–316; Nicola Savarese and Richard Fowler, "1931: Antonin Artaud Sees Balinese Theatre at the Paris Colonial Exposition," *The Drama Review (1988–)* 45, no. 3 (Autumn 2001), 51–77.

[3] De Zoete and Spies, *Dance and Drama in Bali*, 220–221.

[4] I Wayan Dibia and Rucina Ballinger, *Balinese Dance, Drama and Music: A Guide to the Performing Arts of Bali*, illustrated edition (Singapore: Periplus Editions, 2004), 78–79.

[5] For a summary, see Stephen Davies, "The Origins of Balinese Legong," *Bijdragen tot de Taal-, Land- en Volkenkunde* 164, no. 2/3 (2008); Adrian Vickers, "When Did Legong Start? A Reply to Stephen Davies," *Bijdragen tot de Taal-, Land- en Volkenkunde* 165, no. 1 (2009).

Made Karna. From his visions, the king choreographed a masked dance for young girls. This profoundly sacred trance dance, known as Sanghyang Topeng, is believed by some to be the source of *legong*. Recent scholarship has questioned this conventional story of the origins of the dance form, suggesting that older forms of trance dance may have taken on characteristics of *legong* in the 1930s. Other scholars have suggested looking more closely at a form of dance drama called *gambuh*, which was very popular in the nineteenth century, and from which much of the repertoire of *legong* derives.[6]

In the past *legong* was known as courtly entertainment, but today it is widely performed in many settings. It is referred to as a secular dance because it is not performed in the sacred innermost courtyard of a temple, but like all dance it is considered to be an offering by its performers to the gods.[7]

NR

[6] Stephen Davies, "The Origins of Balinese Legong," 197–198; Adrian Vickers, "When Did Legong Start? A Reply to Stephen Davies," 5–6.

[7] In the early 1970s, in response to mass tourism, a seminar was held to discuss the sacredness of different genres of Balinese dance. A tripartite system was devised in which some dances were considered open to the public, some could be performed in conjunction with a ritual, and the most sacred were reserved (generally) for the innermost compound of a temple. This imposed division does not precisely correspond to the actual complexity of Balinese ceremonial life. Dibia and Ballinger, *Balinese Dance, Drama and Music*, 10–11.

78 Crown of a *legong* dancer's costume (*gelungan*), before 1939

Rawhide, pigments, rattan, glass, metal

H: 11 in; W: 17⅛ in; D: 9⅜ in

Collection, Tropenmuseum, Amsterdam (the Netherlands), 1403-7a

Perhaps the most distinctive feature of a Balinese dancer's costume is the headdress. The crown of a *legong* dancer's costume is made of gilt rawhide, often ornamented with glass or mica. The intricately cut leather rises to a point in the back, while the front of the headdress is often decorated with wire branches (*bancangan*) holding glittering leaves of metal that wave as the dancer moves. Fresh frangipani flowers, which quiver and release their sweet scent, are used as well at the front of the headdress. At the base in the rear is a stylized depiction of the head of Garuda, the mythical bird of Hinduism beloved in Indonesia.

Although today the *legong* dance is often seen in abbreviated form in performances for tourists, it is also performed in its full length for ceremonial occasions. Certain headdresses, such as the ones at Pura Desa in Sumerta, Denpasar, are considered sacred and are stored in shrines in the village temple. These headdresses are thought to induce trance among the dancers, who wear them while performing on the tenth full moon of the lunar calendar.[1]

NR

1 I Wayan Dibia and Rucina Ballinger, *Balinese Dance, Drama and Music: A Guide to the Performing Arts of Bali*, illustrated edition (Singapore: Periplus Editions, 2004), 78.

A *legong* dancer's costume consists of several elements. The legs are wrapped with a cloth often decorated with designs of gold (*kain prada*). The dancer typically wears a shirt whose long sleeves are also decorated in gold. The girl's torso is bound by a long strips of cloth wrapped from the hips to the chest. Sashes and belts further bind the waist and ornament the rear of the dancer. The dancer wears a shoulder cover (as seen below at left), often made of intricately perforated hide that has been gilded. She wears a long apron of gilt cloth or rawhide that ties below her armpits and hangs below her waist. Finally a necklace, armbands, ear plugs, and a fan complete the glittering costume.

The apron seen here is cut through with delicate geometric and floral designs. The name for the garment, *lamak*, is a term commonly used for long banner-like offerings that hang from altars during ceremonies, especially during the New Year's festivities of Galungan. (See "Palm leaf and Silkscreen: Balinese Lamak in Transition" on p. 61 for a detailed discussion of *lamak*.)

NR

79 Shoulder cover for a *legong* dancer's costume (*sesimping*)

Rawhide, gold pigments
H: 13⅝ in.; W: 15¼ in.
Collection, Tropenmuseum, Amsterdam (the Netherlands), 1403-7c

80 Apron for a *legong* dancer's costume (*lamak*), before 1939

Rawhide, gold pigments, wood, mirrored glass
H: 23¾ in.; W. 24¾ in.
Collection, Tropenmuseum, Amsterdam (the Netherlands), 1403-7d

81 Shoulder cover for a *legong* dancer's costume (*sesimping*), 1800–1900

Klungkung, Bali

Cloth, gold

H: 6½ in; W: 15 in

National Museum of Ethnology, Leiden, the Netherlands, 1684-30

Like the shoulder cover seen in cat. no. 79, this component of a *legong* dancer's costume would have been worn over a tight-fitting blouse. Made with gold sheet repoussé that has been attached to a velvet cloth, this delicately crafted object was likely part of a costume for a dancer at the Klungkung court. The gold sheet has been formed into leaves, tendrils, and flowers, and cut out to expose the cloth underneath. From an examination of the cloth on the back of the shoulder cover we can tell that the velvet was once green, but most traces of color have faded from the front. Because of the fragility of the material, the shoulder cover is hinged in the front, so that the dancer could put it on and remove it more easily.

NR

These two photographs depict young Balinese dancers. The photographers, dates, and locations of the photographs are unknown, as are the identities of the dancers. The floor and hung backdrop suggest that the photographs were taken indoors, perhaps in a studio in the early 1900s. The three dancers stare directly at the photographer, looking slightly wary. An indication that the photographs were not taken in conjunction with actual dance performances is that the costumes are somewhat incomplete. The dancers wear elements of a *legong* costume — rounded necklaces, long aprons, and elaborate headdresses — but they are not wearing the lower garments, torso cloths, and shoulder covers that are commonly worn for performances.

Young dancers were a favorite subject of early European photographers. Whether staged in studios or furtively snapped at a village bathing site, photographs of "exotic" girls and women of the Indies were published in postcards, travel brochures, and books, and served to promote an image of Bali as an Edenic isle.

NR

82 Three young dancers from Bali, approx. 1900–1930

Unknown photographer
Photograph from glass negative
H: 7⅛ in; W: 5⅛ in (original plate)
Collection, Tropenmuseum, Amsterdam (the Netherlands), 10004866

83 Young dancer from Bali, approx. 1900–1930

Unknown photographer
Photograph from glass negative
H: 7⅛ in; W: 5⅛ in (original plate)
Collection, Tropenmuseum, Amsterdam (the Netherlands), 10004871

From the size and shape of this superb gold leaf–patterned textile (*kain prada*), it is not certain whether it was to be worn or to be used as decoration.[1]

As clothing, it would have been a man's chest cloth (*saput* or *kampuh*) that was tied under the armpits and fell to the knees, worn by a man of princely descent or by a dancer.[2] A narrow band, sometimes attached to the textile, sometimes separate from it, fastened it around the chest, so that the precious material and the total pattern remained visible.

Other items of clothing, such as men's head cloths and women's breast cloths, which have different sizes and structures, are also sometimes decorated with the *prada* (gold leaf) technique. Because gold leaf is such a precious and fragile material, *kain prada* are worn only on special occasions, such as tooth-filing ceremonies or weddings.

Since there is no attached belt, it is most likely, however, that this *kain prada* was used as a backdrop, *tabing*, to decorate the back panel of a shrine or pavilion. But whether this *kain prada* was used as an item of expensive festive clothing or as decoration for a building, the context was probably one of the wealthy courts of Bali, probably in the late nineteenth or early twentieth century.

Traditionally, *kain prada* was made exclusively by men, usually the same artisans (*sangging*) who made paintings and drawings to order for palace use. Creating *prada* patterns involved the same artistic skills as these activities, because the ornaments were created freehand. Drawing the motif outlines was called *orten* or *macawi*. Thin gold leaf of mainly Chinese origin was applied to the cloth by means of fish glue, *ancur*.[3]

The black background of this precious silk is adorned throughout with a bold and fluent pattern of flowers, winding tendrils, and leaves. The borders are decorated with a triangular *tumpal* design, mainly consisting of entwined plant elements, and intertwined swastikas or *banji* associated with ancient solar symbols (see cat. no. 69). In the center of the textile, a stylized lotus flower (*padma*) bears a swastika or *banji* motif at its heart. In the four corners of the center field are flower motifs seen from the side. The central *padma*, represented

84 Cloth patterned with gold leaf (*kain prada*), approx. 1875–1925

Silk, gold leaf

H: 36⅝ in; W: 45⅛ in

Collection, Tropenmuseum, Amsterdam (the Netherlands), 2359-1

1 On all four sides of this *kain prada* are small holes, suggesting the use of pins to hang the cloth on a wall. But since the cloth as given to the museum was fastened in a wooden frame, we do not know whether the *kain prada* was also used as a decoration in Bali. The textile was a gift from J. Caland Marsman.

2 For an example worn by a dancer, see W. O. J. Nieuwenkamp, *Zwerftochten op Bali* (Amsterdam: Elsevier, 1910), 3.

3 Tjokorde Gdé Rake Soekawati, "Nijverheid en kunstnijverheid op Bali," *Mededeelingen van de Kirtya Liefrinck-van der Tuuk 15* (1941), 12–13; Urs Ramseyer, *The Art and Culture of Bali* (Oxford: Oxford University Press, 1977), 70, 89, 108; J. E. Jasper and Mas Pirngadie, *De inlandsche kunstnijverheid in Nederlandsch Indië, III. De batikkunst* ('s-Gravenhage: Mouton, 1916), 79–80.

4 M. L. Nabholz-Kartaschoff, "Perada: Gilded Garments for Humans, Gods and Temples," in Brigitta Hauser-Schäublin, Marie-Louise Nabholz-Kartaschoff, and Urs Ramseyer, *Textiles in Bali* (Berkeley: Periplus, 1991), 52–57.

Ink drawing made in Boeboenan (Bubunan, Buleleng) by W. O. J. Nieuwenkamp, depicting a dancer wearing a *kain prada*. *Photo Stichting Museum Nieuwenkamp.*

with eight leaves around the center, is in Balinese cosmology a symbol of the center of the universe. In the *nawa sanga* system of cosmological ordering, the multicolored *padma* (lotus) is the attribute of the all-encompassing deity Siwa. This divinity is situated in the center of the world, in the middle of the wind rose. The number eight, referring to the directions of the compass, is Siwa's sacred number. The composition of the center field as a whole, with four flowers around a central flower, also refers to the cardinal directions.

The overall structure of the cloth, while full of elegant details, is beautifully symmetrical and avoids an impression of being overly crowded. The balanced effect is enhanced by the contrast between the black background and the shining gold of the *prada* ornamentation.

Today *kain prada* are still widely produced and used in Bali by people of all castes. The cloths are used as festive clothing and garments for dancers, and also as temple decorations. But due to its high cost, real gold is almost never used, and most *prada* patterns are silkscreened on the cloth with bronze pigments or applied with plastic gold foil.[4]

FB

These masks of Barong and Rangda are part of a complete set of masks and costumes for the characters of the Calonarang drama.[1] The masks almost certainly originate from either Badung or Gianyar, where the Calonarang drama is most often performed. However, it is not known whether the set was specially put together for this purchase, or whether it was obtained as a set from an existing Calonarang dance group. The set also includes five *jauk* and five *telek* masks, the former representing male characters, the latter refined female ones.

THE CALONARANG STORY AND DANCE-DRAMA

As a narrative, the Calonarang has a long history. The colophon of one manuscript gives the date 1462, and the text may be even older. The story is still popular in Bali, as literature, as dance-drama, and, occasionally, as shadow puppet performance. The narrative is set in East Java in the eleventh century, during the time of King Airlangga. The widow Calonarang has a beautiful daughter, Ratna Manggali, but because her mother is feared for her magic powers, no one will marry Ratna Manggali. In anger, Calonarang — in her wrathful form as Rangda — brings pestilence to the land, aided by her pupils, known as *leyak*, the term still used in Bali for practitioners of black magic. It is finally only though the power of the priest Mpu Bharadah that she is defeated and the land restored to well-being. The story is believed to have a basis in historical events.[2]

According to one view, the dance-drama Calonarang, at least as it is now known, originated about 1890 in the Batubulan area (Gianyar), using elements from various dance and drama genres, such as *gambuh*.[3] At least one element, the dance of the *leyak* pupils, may descend from old Tantric rites. The history of Rangda herself can also be traced back to Tantric antecedents, for she is associated with Durga, the wrathful form of Siwa's consort, goddess of the "death temple" (*pura dalem*) and of the graveyard. The role of the Barong in this drama is to help extricate Rangda from her black magic activities. The Barong's followers attack Rangda, but her powers force them to turn their *kris* against themselves. Finally, holy water from the Barong's beard helps bring Rangda back to her senses.

Barong and Rangda are perhaps Bali's most iconic images, and the relationship between them is complex.[4] Most visitors to Bali see them in performance as part of the Barong and Rangda dance-drama (also called the "Barong and *kris*" dance). As plot, this dance performance uses the story of Dewi Kunti, mother of the five Pandawa brothers, and their roles in this dance have to a large extent determined how visitors and Balinese alike view them. The common view portrays this dance as a struggle between good, represented by the Barong, and evil,

85 Rangda mask, before 1929

Possibly by I Gusti Made Gde
Denpasar, Badung
Wood, pigments, parchment, rawhide, hair
H: 31½ in; W: 14¼ in; D: 6¾ in
Tropenmuseum, Amsterdam, 1116-14a

86 Barong mask, before 1929

Possibly by I Gusti Made Gde
Denpasar, Badung
Wood, pigments, rawhide, antlers, hair
H: 10¼ in; W: 19¼ in; D: 15¾ in
Tropenmuseum, Amsterdam, 1116-1a

1 They were purchased in 1937 through the good offices of H. J. Jansen, assistant resident of South Bali.

2 In this interpretation, Rangda represents Mahendradatta, wife of the Balinese king Udayana, mother of Airlangga.

TWO MASKS 297

represented by Rangda. This dance, however, is an artistic creation of the twentieth century, and its concept of a struggle between good and evil does not accurately reflect the nature of these two supernatural beings.⁵ The dance was, in fact, developed from a traditional ritual without plot or story, as is indicated by the oral tradition and early written sources. Both figures also make appearances in temple festivals, where they have their own shrines, and in religious processions, often one without the other. The Barong plays a special protective role during the period of Galungan. Yet neither can be understood without the other.

BARONG: ORIGINS, SYMBOLISM, PRODUCTION, HISTORY

The term *barong* refers to a variety of masks, and also to the figures attached to the masks, associated with supernatural beings. The different kinds of masks and figures have their own qualifying names based on the animal or character presented.⁶ Most kinds of *barong* are operated by two performers, one carrying the head and working the mask, the other acting as hind legs, in the manner of the Chinese lion dance. Only the giant *barong landung* (cat. no. 93) and the "primitive" *barong brutuk* of Trunyan are carried by a single performer.⁷ All *barong* carried by two performers represent animals, the most common and most prestigious by far being the *barong ket* (*keket*, *ketket*). This mythological beast is known as Banaspati Raja, "Lord of the Forest," a name with important religious connotations. He is never addressed as *barong,* but rather by such high honorific titles as Batara Gede (Great God) or Ratu Gede (Great Lord).

The mask is the most sacred part of the *barong*, its locus of supernatural power. It is not worn, but instead is carried in front of the face, its moveable lower jaw operated by the hands. The hard repeated clap of the jaws is its characteristic sound; a *barong* does not talk. Creating a *barong* intended for ritual (rather than for tourist performances) requires special ceremonies at key points in the process, beginning with the cutting of the wood from the "pregnant" swelling of a sacred tree, usually the *pule* (*Alstonia scholaris*). Specialist artisans carve and paint the mask, which includes wild or demonic characteristics such as fangs and bulbous eyes. Antlerlike protuberances on top of the mask are likened to the prongs of the thunderbolt or *vajra*. Of special significance is the beard, believed to have potent curative powers, which is made of hair from a prepubescent girl.

The body of the *barong* consists of a bamboo or rattan framework covered with the *barong*'s "hair." This is usually created from *praksok* (or *piraksok*), specially prepared fibers of the pandanus plant, though occasionally more exotic substances are used, such as peacock or crow feathers. The figure's high, sweeping tail is made of sugar palm fiber, with little bells

3 I Made Bandem and Fredrik Eugene deBoer, *Balinese Dance in Transition: Kaja and Kelod* (Kuala Lumpur: Oxford University Press, 1995), 113–125. Another source suggests a date of about 1825, also in Gianyar (I. G. B. N. Pandji et al., *Ensiklopedi musik dan tari Daerah Bali* [Jakarta: Departemen Pendidikan dan Kebudayaan, Proyek penerbitan buku bacaan dan sastra Indonesia dan daerah, 1979], 83). On Calonarang, see also Beryl de Zoete and Walter Spies, *Dance and Drama in Bali* (London: Faber and Faber, 1938), 116–133.

4 One cannot be certain that the two figures have always been associated. Perhaps they have independent origins, and only later did myth and ritual bring them together.

5 Philip Frick McKean, *A Preliminary Analysis of the Inter-action between Balinese and Tourists: The "Little," "Great," and "Modern" Traditions of a Culture* (Denpasar: Museum Bali, Direktorat Museum, Ditdjen, Kebudajaan, Dep. P. & K. 1971), 9–10, says that Cokorda Oka of Singapadu first developed this dance, with its story of Dewi Kunti, for the Balinese dance group performing at the 1931 International Exposition in Paris, using specially made nonsacred masks.

6 There is an extensive literature concerning the *barong*; important works include Beryl de Zoete and Walter Spies, *Dance and Drama in Bali* (London: Faber and Faber, 1938); Jane Belo, *Bali: Rangda and Barong* (Locust Valley, NY: Augustin, 1949); I Made Bandem and Fredrik Eugene deBoer, *Balinese Dance in Transition: Kaja and Kelod* (Kuala Lumpur: Oxford University Press, 1995); Angela Hobart, *Healing Performances of Bali: Between Darkness and Light* (New York: Berghahn Books, 2003); Michele Stephen, "Barong and Rangda in the context of Balinese religion," *Review of Indonesian and Malaysian Affairs* 35, 1 (2001); Michele Stephen, *Desire, Divine and Demonic: Balinese Mysticism in the Paintings of I Ketut Budiana and I Gusti Nyoman Mirdiana* (Honolulu: University of Hawai'i Press, 2005).

attached. The crown, broad collar, and other ornaments are made of cut-out leather, painted and gilded, flashing with little mirrors. Altogether, he is a magnificent creature.

After completion, the *barong* undergoes rituals of empowerment conducted by a high priest, which prepares it for the presence of unseen spiritual forces from the *niskala* world. The *pasupati* ritual occurs in the temple, followed later by *ngerehang*, a magically charged ritual that takes place at night in the graveyard. Sacred letters inscribed on the inside of the mask during these rituals are sometimes visible on examples in museums.

The history of the *barong* in Bali is a matter of considerable debate.[8] The numerous *barong ket* observable throughout Bali are similar and easily recognizable, and their number probably increased during the twentieth century.[9] It is said that they all descend from a prototype created toward the end of the nineteenth century by Cokorda Gede Api of Singapadu (Gianyar).[10] Lacking definite sources, the nature of earlier forms of *barong* is unclear, but presumably they were influenced by animal figures such as the *singa*. The similarity of the Balinese *barong* to the *singa barong* dance figures on Java, to Boma masks on temples in Bali and ancient Java, and to Batak *singa* house ornaments, all areas of Indic influence, raises the possibility of wider relationships.

Whatever its relationship (if any) with one-person masks or figures, the development of the four-legged *barong* is often associated with influence from the Chinese lion dance, a form that dates back to the Tang dynasty (618–906).[11] This dance is generally associated with Buddhism. Whether its introduction into Indonesia dates back to such an early period is a matter of conjecture; later, certainly, the dance was present among local Chinese communities, presumably in Bali as well as elsewhere in the archipelago. Rather similar *barong*-like lion figures are sometimes depicted as mounts of deities in Tantric art from Tibet and China, which is usually Buddhist in nature. Despite certain demonic aspects, the *barong* is regarded as a protective deity, similar to the Tantric Buddhist protective deities who appear in ferocious form.

Banaspati Raja (Lord of the Forest), an alternative name for the *barong ket*, is also the name of one of the four "spirit siblings" (*kanda empat*) that accompany a human being from conception through life and beyond. In Bali's spiritual worldview, to which the concept of *buana alit* (microcosm) and *buana agung* (macrocosm) is fundamental, the *barong ket* is considered the macrocosmic, one might say community-level, equivalent of the spirit sibling Banaspati Raja, who is associated with placenta, and with Iswara, god of the east.[12] Protective if properly honored, with power against black magic, these spiritual beings can also cause harm if neglected. Further discussion of the meaning of *barong* revolves around its relationship with Rangda.

7 The *barong kedingding* masks of Mandangan (Gianyar) are also carried by one performer, but these are derived from Ramayana *wayang wong* masks representing monkeys (I Made Bandem and Fredrik Eugene deBoer, *Balinese Dance in Transition: Kaja and Kelod* [Kuala Lumpur: Oxford University Press, 1995], 56–58). *Barong brutuk* masks are humanlike rather than animal-like.

8 The word *barong* itself is believed to derive from the word for bear, *barwang*. But what, if any, role that animal played in the development of the *barong* is unknown; it has never been present on Bali.

9 A survey from 1988–1989, in *Data sarana kebudayaan Daerah Bali* (Denpasar: Dinas Kebudayaan Propinsi Daerah Tingkat I Bali, 1988/1989) gives a count of 524 *barong*s of all sorts in Bali, well over half being in the regions of Badung (127) and Gianyar (168). The numbers from Buleleng (2), Jembrana (8), and Karangasem (21) indicate the unevenness of *barong* distribution.

10 I Made Bandem and Fredrik Eugene deBoer, *Balinese Dance in Transition: Kaja and Kelod* (Kuala Lumpur: Oxford University Press, 1995), 105–106.

11 Michele Stephen, "Barong and Rangda in the context of Balinese religion," *Review of Indonesian and Malaysian Affairs* 35, 1 (2001), 168, suggests that the form of the *barong* is described in the textual tradition of the creation of the world, and that the Chinese lion-dog was not the source of its form but rather provided a visual model for what a lion looked like.

12 Michele Stephen, "Barong and Rangda in the Context of Balinese Religion," *Review of Indonesian and Malaysian Affairs* 35, 1 (2001), 162–165. Angela Hobart, *Healing Performances of Bali: Between Darknessa nd Light* (New York: Berghahn Books, 2003), 208–212.

RANGDA: A FIGURE WITH COMPLEX SYMBOLISM AND ASSOCIATIONS

Rangda the "witch" (as she is often referred to in Western publications), Rangda the angry "widow" (the literal meaning of the word), Rangda as an aspect of the fierce Hindu goddess Durga—this female figure with horrific and terrifying aspects is all of these.[13] "Witch" she may be in certain contexts, but her highly ambiguous nature is far more complex, and her powers encompass protection as well as destruction. This mask has Rangda's typical iconography: fearsome fangs in a cavernous mouth emanating fire, an enormous lolling tongue with bursts of flame, flaring nostrils, and bulging eyes. Her costume adds to her ferocity: wild disheveled hair, huge pendulous breasts, enormously long outstretched fingernails. And she always carries a white cloth behind which she hides her hideous face, or which she waves with threatening intent. In ritual contexts this cloth is inscribed with sacred syllables of power. She is almost always danced by a specialist male dancer, for strength is needed for this physically exacting role; the dancer must also be spiritually strong.

Unlike the Barong, which is rarely represented in temple sculpture, figures of Rangda are quite common. They are almost always found in the *pura dalem*, the so-called "death temple" close to the graveyard and cremation ground. Here the resident deity, generally referred to as Ratu Batari Dalem, is identified as Durga, the wrathful transformation of Siwa's spouse Uma. The iconography of Rangda is directly related to that of Durga, a goddess of major importance in ancient Bali and Java. She was originally depicted as Durga Mahisasuramardini, slayer of the buffalo demon, but gradually her character changed. She took on demonic aspects and became associated with the graveyard, all indications of Tantric beliefs and practices, especially "left-handed" sects and their related "left-handed" (black) magic. The goddess's demonic appearance is said to be the form that Uma took when cursed by Siwa to live on earth as punishment for her marital infidelity, where as Durga she caused the destruction of the created world. The myth continues with Siwa, desirous of his wife, also descending to earth in his demonic form of Kala. Their reunion negates Durga's destructive powers, and the two deities return to their benevolent aspects. This myth is the source of an important Balinese tradition linking the *barong* with Siwa/Kala and Rangda with Uma/Durga.[14] The enacted combat between Barong and Rangda represents the act by which Siwa/Kala brings Uma/Durga under control and restores the welfare of the created world.

---

13 Rangda is mentioned in almost every book about Bali, usually in association with Barong. See titles cited in note 5; also Claire Fossey, *Rangda, Bali's Queen of the Witches* (Bangkok: White Lotus, 2008). In Balinese society, there is a certain negative connotation about the status of a widow. Widows are not infrequently suspected of involvement in black magic.

14 This is analyzed at length in Michele Stephen, "Barong and Rangda in the Context of Balinese Religion," *Review of Indonesian and Malaysian Affairs* 35, 1 (2001), but is also mentioned by earlier writers such as Hans Neuhaus, "Barong," *Djawa* 17 (1937), and Katharane Edson Mershon, *Seven Plus Seven: Mysterious Life-Rituals in Bali* (New York: Vantage Press, 1971), 43–44.

15 Museum records identify the barong mask as "*barong ket*," the kind of mask normally used in a Calonarang performance. But the addition of the deer antlers is certainly unusual, and would seem sufficient to identify the mask as a "deer barong" (*barong manjangan*); its ears also seem rather deerlike. Since there is no information as to how the set was brought together, it is uncertain whether such a deer barong was sometimes used in Calonarang performances.

16 P. A. J. Moojen, B*ali: Verslag en voorstellen aan de Regeering van Nederlandsch-Indië* (Batavia: Bond van N.I. Kunstkringen en N.I. Heemschut, 1920), 6. After the great earthquake of 1917, I Gusti Made Gde was appointed to oversee rebuilding of Pura Besakih, Bali's most important temple.

ANALYSIS OF MASKS AND THEIR INSCRIPTIONS

The features of the barong mask are typically those of a *barong ket*, yet it contains many features that are anomalous for such a mask.[15] Were those features just the whim of a craftsman making a mask for a foreign buyer? Was it included in the Calonarang set simply because it was available? There are no sure answers, but the inscriptions inside the masks suggest a curious history.

On the inside of both masks are inscriptions in Balinese script; each inscription mentions the same two dates, 1937 and 1929. It would seem that the inscriptions on both masks were written at different times. The older part begins with a name and a place: "I Gusti Madé Gdé, Pamcutwan, Grencéng," referring (in modern spelling) to the Banjar Gerenceng, in Pemecutan, Denpasar. Then follows a short text which I am unable to read entirely, but it mentions the "*gupinur jendral*" (governor-general), and ends with the date "15-10-[19]29." The later part of the inscription consists, in the case of the *barong* mask, of just the date "6-1-1937," and in the case of the Rangda mask the same 1937 date, repeating the name and place. The most likely interpretation is that the masks date from at least 1929, and that I Gusti Made Gde added the 1937 date when he received the request from Mr. Jansen, the assistant resident.

I have been unable to determine whether any special event took place on the dates mentioned. Perhaps relevant is the fact that 1929 was the year when the Governor-General "restored" the former Balinese rulers to their positions. The mention of the Governor-General, and the fact that all dates follow the Western rather than the Balinese calendar, suggest that these masks were originally made for a secular purpose. No sacred syllables are visible, such as are often found on sacred masks.

A further question is whether I Gusti Made Gde was the carver of the masks or just the owner. This question cannot be answered with certainty; the Balinese did and do write their names on objects that they own. However, I Gusti Made Gde may not be just another otherwise unknown Balinese. He is quite probably the same "artistic (*kunstnijvere*) Gusti Madé Gdé of Badung (Denpasar)" who "amongst the Balinese had a very good reputation as master-builder,"[16] and who after the great earthquake of 1917 was appointed to oversee rebuilding of Pura Besakih. It is that possible he is the carver of the mask.

DSF

Below top: A *barong ket* (sometimes also identified as a tiger *barong*) dances during a ceremony in Kerambitan (Tabanan). *Photo Francine Brinkgreve.*

Below bottom: A *barong ket* and two Rangda are placed in a pavilion and honored with offerings during a temple festival at Pura Pusering Jagat, Pejeng (Gianyar). *Photo Francine Brinkgreve.*

87 Rangda, 1929

By K. T. Satake

Photograph from glass negative

H: 4¾ in; W: 3⅝ in (original plate)

Tropenmuseum, Amsterdam, 10004670

This photograph portrays Rangda dancing during a performance.[1] Members of a gamelan orchestra are visible behind the dancer, by the wall of a palace or temple. It is not known where the photograph was taken. Neither can it be said, from this single Rangda figure, which specific type of dance performance is taking place.

The photograph was published in a large-format volume of K. T. Satake's photographs, bearing the title *Camera-beelden van Sumatra, Java & Bali/Camera pictures of Sumatra, Java & Bali,* published by Satake himself in 1935 and printed in England.[2] A number of early color photographs are included in the publication. Satake was a Japanese photographer who had a photography studio, the Tosari Studio, in Surabaya in the 1920s and 1930s. Japanese photographers were active in many parts of the Netherlands East Indies during the later Dutch colonial period.

DSF

1 Another copy of the same photograph exists in the Tropenmuseum collection, numbered 60042916. The museum website provides links to the photographer "S. Satake" and the Tosari Studio, without stating that he made the photograph. A search by name of photographer does produce this photograph among many others in the Tropenmuseum collection. Apparently S. Satake is an error for K. T. Satake. The photograph was a gift of J. C. van Eerde.

2 The photograph appears on page 272.

For such a small island, Bali has a remarkably diverse array of textiles. Some are simply woven, while others demonstrate intricate craftsmanship. Natural dyes create subdued colors, while aniline dyes generate candy-colored hues. Textiles commissioned by the upper classes were traditionally ornamented by gold and silver supplementary threads, but a simple handspun cotton cloth can have much greater ritual significance. Many Balinese cloths have specific roles in the ritual lives of the community.

This textile is a *cepuk*, a cloth made by a complicated process in which the weft threads are dyed with a pattern before the textile itself is woven. This method of patterning cloth (known as ikat) involves tying bundles of threads tightly so that they resist absorbing dye when the threads are dipped into a dye vat. *Cepuk* are most often made of cotton, like this handspun example, but are also occasionally woven from silk. They are distinguished by a deep red background, a framework of thin stripes in white, and other colors that divide the textile into a center field and borders. Many different patterns are possible in the main field of this type of textile, and certain patterns have higher ritual significance.[1] Always present are rows of small white triangles running down the longitudinal borders. This motif is known as *gigin barong*, or teeth of the Barong, a well-known Balinese mythical protective creature (see cat. nos. 85 and 89).

Many scholars have observed similarities between *cepuk* and the imported Indian double-ikat textiles from Gujarat (*patola*). *Patola* were highly valued throughout the archipelago and treasured as heirlooms. The Balinese textile specialist Marie-Louise Nabholz-Kartaschoff suggests that the ritual hierarchy of *cepuk* patterns may depend on their similarity to *patola* cloths.[2] The pattern on this *cepuk* is known as *cendana kawi*, and is considered the highest class of this type of textile. The word *cepuk* means "being brought face to face with someone" and may indicate being brought into contact with the divine. *Cendana* is a type of fragrant sandalwood, and *kawi* means creation.[3]

Textiles of this type could be used in a number of ways: as the waist cloth (*kamben*) or shoulder cloth for the sorceress Rangda in the Calonarong dance-drama; as garb for deities and people in trance; and as shrouds for members of the highest caste.[4]

NR

88 Ceremonial cloth (*kamben cepuk*), approx. 1900–1930

Southern Bali

Cotton

H: 30 in; W: 102 in

Asian Art Museum, gift of Betty N. Alberts, F2006.31

[1] Marie-Louise Nabholz-Kartaschoff, "A Sacred Cloth of Rangda: Kamben Cepuk of Bali and Nusa Penida," in *To Speak with Cloth*, ed. Mattiebelle Gittinger (Los Angeles: UCLA Fowler Museum of Cultural History, 1989), 181–197.

[2] Marie-Louise Nabholz-Kartaschoff, "A Sacred Cloth," 197.

[3] Marie-Louise Nabholz-Kartaschoff, "A Preliminary Approach to Cepuk Cloths from South Bali and Nusa Penisda," in *Indonesian Textiles: Symposium 1985* (Cologne: Ethnologica, 1991), 124.

[4] For an explanation of the many ritual uses of *cepuk*, see Marie-Louise Nabholz-Kartaschoff, "Cepuk: Sacred Textiles from Bali and Nusa Penida," in *Textiles in Bali* (Berkeley; Singapore: Periplus Editions, 1991), 94–114.

This photograph shows a daytime performance of a *barong ket* accompanied by three *jauk* dancers. The performance is being held in an open space whose location is not known. An eager crowd is present to enjoy the dance, the children in front within touching distance of the *barong*. In origin, *jauk* and their female equivalents, called *telek,* are thought to be characters in a folk play involving the *barong*, of the kind observed by the Dutch visitor Julius Jacobs in 1881.[1] This photograph may depict such a dance.

The photograph is in an album donated to the Tropenmuseum by Augusta de Wit (1864–1939), who visited Bali from October to late December 1911. The photograph was probably made either by de Wit herself or by Carl Gründler, and probably dates from 1910 or 1911.[2]

DSF

89 *Barong ket* with *jauk* dancers, approx. 1910–1911

By an unknown photographer, probably Augusta de Wit (1864–1939) or Curt Gründler
Photograph from glass negative
H: 4⅜ in; W: 6¼ in (original plate)
Tropenmuseum, Amsterdam, 60049079

1 I Made Bandem and Fredrik Eugene deBoer, *Balinese Dance in Transition: Kaja and Kelod* (Kuala Lumpur: Oxford University Press, 1995), 106–107.

2 For further details, see cat. no. 95.

Barong Masks

90 Lion *barong* (*barong singa*), approx. 1900–1925 (page 310)

Wood, pigments, rawhide, horsehair

H: 11¾ in; W: 21¼ in; D: 27¼ in

Tropenmuseum, Amsterdam, 740-43

91 Boar *barong* (*barong bangkal*), approx. 1900–1925 (bottom)

Wood, pigments, palm leaf ribs, boar teeth, boar bristles

H: 11¾ in; W: 5⅞ in; D: 16½ in

Tropenmuseum, Amsterdam, 1772-608

92 Tiger *barong* (*barong macan*), approx. 1900–1930 (top)

Mas, Gianyar

Wood, pigments

H: 10¼ in; W: 21¾ in; D: 11⅞ in

National Museum of Ethnology, Leiden, the Netherlands, 2407-51

Most varieties of *barong* known in Bali represent four-legged creatures danced by a pair of dancers, one for the forelegs and mask, the other for the hind legs (cat. no. 85). Along with the *barong ket,* a mythological leonine beast, *barong* masks occasionally portray a number of other animals: the lion (*singa*), tiger (*macan*), boar (*bangkal*), deer (*manjangan*), cow (*lembu*), dog (*asu*), and elephant (*gajah*).[1] Among these, the tiger and boar are probably the most common. The bodies of such *barong* are covered in an appropriate "hair," but not with the whitish leaves typically found on the *barong ket*. It is not entirely clear why these animals were chosen as *barong*. With the exception of the lion and elephant, all these animals were once or are still found in Bali, either wild or domesticated. Formerly tiger, deer, and pigs were wild animals of Bali; so too, perhaps, the *banteng,* from which the Bali cow is domesticated. The Bali tiger (*Panthera tigris balica*) became extinct probably by the mid-twentieth century. Yet the tiger, a much-feared animal, is still the focus of ritual, often shamanic in nature, in Java and especially Sumatra, where tigers still roam. Although these various animals make their appearances within Hindu and Buddhist mythology and art (for example, the boar as avatar of Vishnu), it is not known whether this animal lore played a role in the development of animal *barongs* in Bali. Local cults and trance directives are possible sources of inspiration.

90 LION *BARONG* (*BARONG SINGA*)

In museum records this *barong* is given the name *barong singa*.[2] It is distinct in form from the *barong ket,* which perhaps was partly inspired by it. The *singabarong* is well known in Java, where it appears in folk performances.

91 BOAR *BARONG* (*BARONG BANGKAL*)

This *barong* mask portrays a mature boar with full-grown tusks, the literal meaning of the word *bangkal*, which is one of several words for "pig" in Balinese.

The mask was from the collection of Georg Tillmann (1882–1941), a major collector of Indonesian art. Originally on loan, the collection was donated to the Tropenmuseum by his son. It was bought in Klungkung by Carel Groenevelt (1899–1973), an art dealer based in Yogyakarta who collected in Bali in the 1930s.[3]

92 TIGER *BARONG* (*BARONG MACAN*)

This *barong macan* mask originated from Mas (Gianyar), a leading center of woodcarving, and especially mask carving, to the present day. Traces of paint are found inside the mask.

1 For illustrations, see Gregor Krause, *Bali* (Hagen: Folkwang, 1926), 169 (cow), claimed by Volker Gottowik (*Der Erfindung des Barong: Mythos, Ritual und Alterität auf Bali* [Berlin: Reimer, 2005], 68–69) to be the oldest known photograph of a *barong*; Beryl de Zoete and Walter Spies, *Dance and Drama in Bali* (London: Faber and Faber, 1938), pl. 32 (tiger, boar, cow, elephant); Judy Slattum, *Masks of Bali: Spirits of an Ancient Drama* (San Francisco: Chronicle Books, 1992), 107–111 (boar, lion, tiger, cow, deer). According to Slattum, there are also *barong* masks, documented but not photographed, representing the buffalo (*kebo*), dragon (*naga*), horse (*jaran*), goat (*kambing*), and quail (*puuh*). This list is perhaps partly derived from Beryl de Zoete and Walter Spies, *Dance and Drama in Bali* (London: Faber and Faber, 1938), 113, and J. Kats, "Barong op Bali," *Djawa* 4 (1924), 140. The Museum Bali possesses *barong* masks of the tiger, lion, cow, deer, boar, and elephant (*Saraswati* 18 [1981], 15); this list may be incomplete.

2 This mask was a gift of F. James, 1932.

3 On Tillmann, see Koos van Brakel, et al., *A Passion for Indonesian Art: The George Tillman (1882–1941) Collection at the Tropenmuseum Amsterdam* (Amsterdam: Royal Tropical Institute, 1996); on Groenevelt, see Hanneke Hollander, *Een man met een speurdersneus: Carel Groenevelt (1899–1973), beroepsverzamelaar voor Tropenmuseum en Wereldmuseum in Nieuw-Guinea* (Amsterdam: Royal Tropical Institute, 2007).

The Bali tiger once existed in jungled mountain areas. It seems likely that in Bali as in other parts of Indonesia, the tiger was a focus of ritual.

It is unknown whether the mask was made for sale or was a deconsecrated mask. It is uncertain whether Kleiweg de Zwaan purchased the mask in the late 1930s, when artworks for tourists were already commonplace, or during an earlier visit. Johannes Pieter Kleiweg de Zwaan (1875–1971), a well-known medical and physical anthropologist, was also interested in ethnography.

DSF

Left: A tiger *barong* (*barong macan*) makes an appearance at a temple festival at Bunut Bolong (Tabanan). *Photo David Stuart-Fox.*

Right: A pig *barong* (*barong bangkal*) on the beach at Sanur (Denpasar) during a purificatory *melis* ceremony. *Photo Brent Hesselyn.*

Opposite page: Jero Gede and Jero Luh, the giant male and female *barong landung* figures, perform for villagers during the period before Kuningan. Abiansemal (Badung). *Photo Brent Hesselyn.*

Barong landung are giant figures or puppets, each carried on the shoulders of a single male performer.[1] With their bearers, they reach a height of some three meters, towering over performance spectators. Sometimes *barong landung* consist of a couple, considered husband and wife; a complete set consists of a family of four or five, the puppets of the children being somewhat smaller in size. As with other *barong*, the masks are the seat of the figures' power. The main male figure, Jero Gede (Honorable Sir),[2] has dark features and prominent teeth. In contrast, his wife, Jero Luh (Honorable Lady), has white features, a prominent forehead, a sweet smile, and slanted eyes that are generally thought of as characteristically Chinese.

The "stranger" characteristics of the female figure are explained through a legend in which a Balinese king, often identified as Jayapangus, who is said to have been dark and ugly, took a Chinese lady as his wife. In one version locating the story in the Batur region, where the old capital was situated, the king's new attachment provoked the wrath of his first wife, Dewi Danu, who used her power to burn the couple to ashes.[3] The dark features of the male figure are also said to represent a Dravidian from South India. Other stories associate Jero Gede with Jero Gede Macaling, a demonic figure from the neighboring island of Nusa Penida, who is believed to visit Bali in the sixth month of the lunar year, bringing disease, especially cholera. The female figure is thought to reflect Chinese cultural influence, which is considerable in Bali. Although the origin of these figures remains uncertain, Chinese influence is indeed likely.[4]

The distribution of *barong landung* in Bali is very uneven, but they are especially popular in the southern Bali regions of Badung and Gianyar. They are regarded as village protective figures. Although making an appearance at festivals of certain village temples, *barong landung* are particularly associated with the festive Galungan and Kuningan period. During these ten days, they are taken on walkabout in and beyond the village, where in the presence of appreciative crowds they perform dances and songs of a humorous and often bawdy nature, accompanied by music.[5] These pantomimic performances are believed to repel misfortune and illness. Once a lunar year, just prior to Nyepi, they are taken in procession to the seaside for a ceremony of purification, where they make a particularly striking impression.

The two masks here are part of a set of four, the other two representing a son and daughter. They were acquired by the museum in 1937 from J. A. Houbolt, a Dutch journalist and later art dealer with a special interest in Bali dating to the early 1930s. The masks are said to have come from Dangin Puri, Denpasar, but it is not known whether they were "decommissioned" masks, or made for sale.

DSF

93 *Barong landung* mask: Jero Gede (male), before 1937

Wood and pigments, animal fur
H: 10¼ in; W: 13⅜ in; D: 6½ in
Tropenmuseum, Amsterdam,
1156-40

94 *Barong landung* mask: Jero Luh (female), before 1937

Wood and pigments
H: 6¼ in; W: 9⅛ in; D: 5½ in
Tropenmuseum, Amsterdam,
1156-41

1 *Barong* here is used in the broad sense of a puppet or figure carried by human performers; *landung* means tall, with reference to a body. *Barong landung* are mentioned in many books on Bali, for example, Beryl de Zoete and Walter Spies, *Dance and Drama in Bali* (London: Faber and Faber, 1938), 113–115; see especially Angela Hobart, *Healing Performances of Bali: Between Darkness and Light* (New York: Berghahn Books, 2003) and Volker Gottowik, *Der Erfindung des Barong: Mythos, Ritual und Alterität auf Bali* (Berlin: Reimer, 2005).

2 *Gede* means large or big, but is also used as a term of address for an eldest son.

3 Hobart, *Healing Performances of Bali: Between Darkness and Light*, 128–129.

4 In Taiwan, and perhaps elsewhere, rather similar large-scale figures are carried in procession during festivities honoring the goddess of the sea, Mazu (Matsu), including male figures wearing dark-faced masks, comparable to that of Jero Gede. Mazu is also honored by those of Chinese heritage throughout Southeast Asia. For a discussion of Chinese cultural influence in Bali, see Made Sulistyawati, ed., *Integrasi budaya Tionghoa ke dalam budaya Bali: sebuah bunga rampai* (Denpasar: Penerbit Universitas Udayana, 2008).

5 Hobart, *Healing Performances of Bali: Between Darkness and Light*, 186–192.

This photograph shows a gathering of *barong landung* in what seems to be a temporary shelter roofed with plaited coconut fronds. There are seven figures in all, three female and four male. Since at least two *barong landung* groups are present, the gathering perhaps took place during a temple festival or a Galungan visit. The audience is predominantly children, some carrying banners and processional paraphernalia.[1] Perhaps a drama is taking place, although the children seem to be more interested in the photographer. It is not known where the photograph was taken.

The donor, Augusta de Wit (1864–1939), is an important colonial Dutch Indies author of both fiction and travel writing, especially concerning Java. She visited Bali from October to late December 1911, writing about it in a series of letters in the *Nieuwe Rotterdamsche Courant*, later worked into her book *Natuur en menschen in Indië* (*Nature and People in [Netherlands] India*), published in 1914. During her travels in Bali and elsewhere she made an extensive collection of photographs, taken by herself and by other photographers, including a German architect called Curt Gründler, who lived in Bali around 1910.[2] Photographs by Gründler are published in de Wit's book. The photograph of the *barong landung* was probably made either by de Wit herself or by Gründler, and probably dates from 1910 or 1911.

DSF

95 *Barong landung* figures, approx. 1910

By unknown photographer, probably Augusta de Wit (1864–1939) or Curt Gründler
Photograph from glass negative
H: 5⅛ in; W: 7⅛ in (original plate)
Tropenmuseum, Amsterdam,
10004870

1 For other early photographs of *barong landung*, see KITLV collection nos. 9828 and 9829, dating from about 1920.

2 Website of KIT collections, http://collectie.tropenmuseum.nl/nbasicsearch.asp?lang=en&showtype=single+objects&field1=ccIdentifier&operator1=all&searchfor1=T34&sort=crelevance. Biographical data on Gründler are scarce. Apparently he lived on Bali for some time (years?). His arrival there was connected with the Frankfurt Sunda-Expedition of 1909–1910, led by Johannes Elbert, to whom he was an assistant (C. Lekkerkerker, *Bali en Lombok: overzicht der litteratuur omtrent deze eilanden tot einde 1919* [Rijswijk: Blankwaardt & Schoonhoven, 1920], 348–349). While on Bali, Gründler was requested by the assistant resident of South Bali, W. F. J. Kroon, to participate in plans to build a museum, together with Balinese architects (information from the website of the KIT collection). Gründler was involved in early construction of what eventually became the Museum Bali. He also was involved in collecting and art dealing; the museum in Frankfurt purchased objects from him (Achim Sibeth, ed., *Being Object, Being Art* [Frankfurt am Main: Museum für Völkerkunde, 2009], 178–179). He was murdered in Arabia around 1914 (Lekkerkerker, *Bali en Lombok: overzicht der litteratuur omtrent deze eilanden tot einde 1919*, 349).

Five Balinese Masks

Masks are used in various dance-dramas and ritual performances in Bali. The earliest mention of masked performers may be in a copper plate inscription from 896 CE, in which a masked dancer is listed among the other performers at court.[1] Perhaps the most famous masks are those of Barong and Rangda (see cat. nos. 85 and 86), but masks play a part in many other traditions as well.

Forms of dramatic performance in Bali have undergone remarkable changes in the last century, with the decline of some genres like *gambuh* and the rise of many innovative styles. Many forms of masked performance mentioned by ethnologists in the 1930s are rarely or no longer encountered today. Because of these changes, it is difficult to determine the original uses of many masks dating from the early twentieth century.

These five masks could all have been used in a type of performance called *wayang wong*. The word *wayang* means shadow and *wong* means person; thus the term refers to human enactments of stories commonly told in shadow puppet performances. The Indian Ramayana is a major source of material for *wayang wong* performances. This great story revolves around Rama, an incarnation of the Hindu god Wisnu, and his battle with the demon king, Rawana. Especially popular are recountings of the episodes in which Rama leads his monkey army to rescue his wife, Sita, who has been kidnapped by Rawana.

In *wayang wong* performances, the monkey army includes a number of hybrid part-simian creatures, as well as monkeys. According to I Made Bandem and F. E. deBoer,

> These "monkeys" are no mere simians — many of them are hybrid creatures resulting from intermarriage of a monkey with a tiger, for example, or a bird, or a cow. The monkeys in Wayang Wong are mythical beings; in them ancient Balinese protectors in the form of benevolent mythical animals survive in thin disguise.[2]

Masks used in performances of this story are considered sacred and for most of the year are stored in village temples. They may be taken out of their shrines to receive offerings, but performances with the masks are uncommon today.[3] Sacred masks are more than just objects that are treated with care and reverence; they are powerful sites of connection between the human and divine worlds. As Hildred Geertz writes, "Masks are seen as aids not only in visualizing the divine powers but also in providing them momentary material manifestations."[4]

The process of making sacred masks involves far more than just artistic ability. Numerous rituals and offerings are involved in their production, culminating in their being ritually brought to life by a priest. The masks are stored in the village temple, given offerings on the appropriate days, and cremated when no longer functional. When a new mask is commissioned, the wood is chosen from a specific type of tree, often a *pule* (*Alstonia scholaris*) tree, which grows near the village cremation grounds. A swelling in the bark of the tree indicates that it is ready or "pregnant" (*beling*) and can be harvested.

Old masks, and some masks still made today, are painted with pigments made locally, such as white from ground pig bone, black from soot, and yellow from ochre clay, as well as with imported colors such as red and gold leaf from China. After the pigment is mixed with a binder, a hundred or more layers of paint may be applied to achieve the proper hue. These masks would all once have had perforated and gilt leather side ornaments (*sekar-taji*) that framed the masks and attached to the headdresses.

The carving and painting of all these masks (except the monkey mask) suggest that they were made by the same artist. Although masks were traditionally not signed, artists and other experts can identify the work of master carvers.

NR

1 Leon Rubin and I. Nyoman Sedana, *Performance in Bali* (Routledge, 2007), 104.

2 I Madé Bandem and Fredrik Eugene deBoer, *Kaja and Kelod* (Oxford University Press, 1981), 67.

3 Perfomances still take place in Batuan, Mas, and Tejakula. I Wayan Dibia and Rucina Ballinger, *Balinese Dance, Drama and Music: A Guide to the Performing Arts of Bali*, illustrated edition (Singapore: Periplus Editions, 2004), 62.

4 Judy Slattum, *Balinese Masks: Spirits of An Ancient Drama* (Hong Kong: Periplus Editions, 2003), 6.

96 Elephant mask, perhaps 1900–1940

Wood, leather, rattan, and pigments
H: 8⅛ in; W 11¼ in; D: 7⅞ in
Collection of W. E. Bouwman

Elephant masks can be seen in several contexts of Balinese performance. A form of protective deity (*barong*) is the *barong gajah*, or elephant *barong*. Masks for *barong*, though, are generally larger than this one; they usually have a hinged jaw, and are held in front of the dancer's face by protruding poles.

Another dance-drama in which an elephant plays a role is the *Amad Mohamad* story in the *gambuh* repertoire. *Gambuh* is believed to be the oldest Balinese dance-drama form in Bali today, and the source of many other musical and dramatic genres.[1] Tales of the prince Panji form the basis of many *gambuh* performances, but other Javanese stories like the Muslim *Amad Mohamad* and the historical romance *Rangga Lawe* also are significant sources. The *Amad Mohamad* story includes a white elephant belonging to the king of Egypt. Although most *gambuh* performances today do not feature masked dancers, Walter Spies and Beryl de Zoete describe a dancer in a blue mask appearing in such a performance witnessed in the 1930s. The elephant mask worn by the dancer in an accompanying photograph resembles this mask.[2]

Elephant masks are also seen in *wayang wong* performances of episodes derived from the Ramayana. Among the animals fighting with Rama's monkey army, one can sometimes find a variety of other animals, including elephants.[3]

This mask has the open mouth and bulging eyes characteristic of demonic animal masks. The artist has captured the texture of the elephant's trunk and the wrinkled skin of its ears. The tusks are placed forward so as not to interfere with the fangs at the back of the mouth. On the interior of the mask, a sacred syllable, *ongkara*, is roughly painted.

NR

1 Marianne Ariyanto, "Gambuh: The Source of Balinese Dance," *Asian Theatre Journal* 2, no. 2 (Autumn 1985): 221–230; Adrian Vickers, *Journeys of Desire: A Study of the Balinese Text Malat* (Leiden: KITLV, 2005).

2 Beryl de Zoete and Walter Spies, *Dance and Drama in Bali* (London: Faber and Faber, 1938), 142, 291–292, pl. 65.

3 De Zoete and Spies, *Dance and Drama in Bali,* 142, 291–292, pl. 65.

This mask combines aspects of close observation of a bird in nature with elements of fantasy. The shape of the bird's beak and the placement the nostrils at its base are naturalistically depicted, but the rows of small teeth are an embellishment. There is a tendency in Balinese art from this period to depict all animals and fierce characters with open mouths and bared teeth. An unusual feature of this mask is its lack of protruding canine fangs, which are commonly seen on other masks of animals.

Bird masks are used to perform a number of characters from the Hindu epics. One of the most common bird characters is Jatayu, who valiantly tries to rescue Sita as she is being abducted by the demon Rawana. Another important bird character is Garuda, the mount of the god Wisnu, who plays a role in rescuing Rama in another episode of the Ramayana, as well as appearing in other stories. The same mask could be used for either character. Two other bird characters in *wayang wong* are Goaksa and Winata, avian members of the monkey army.[1] In an illustration of Goaksa made in the late nineteenth century, the bird (with a monkey's body) does not have prominent fangs.[2] A video of a 2009 performance at the Pura Desa Batuan shows two bird-headed dancers, one whose mask is fangless like this one, and one whose mask does have fangs.[3]

This mask has a sacred syllable, *ongkara*, very roughly painted on the interior.

NR

97 Bird mask, perhaps 1900–1940

Wood, leather, rattan, and pigments
H: 8¼ in; W: 10¼ in; D: 9⅛ in
Collection of W. E. Bouwman

1 De Zoete and Spies, *Dance and Drama in Bali*, 154.

2 H. I. R Hinzler, *Catalogue of Balinese Manuscripts in the Library of the University of Leiden and Other Collections in the Netherlands* (Leiden: E. J. Brill, 1986), fig. 3390-62.

3 *Bali: "Celebration in Pura Desa Batuan" Wayang Wong #1*, 2009, http://www.youtube.com/watch?v=Q3wQ-frKDIc&feature=youtube_gdata.

98 Bird mask, perhaps 1900–1940

Wood, leather, and pigments
H: 8⅛ in; W: 9½ in; D: 7½ in
Collection of W. E. Bouwman

While similar to the bird mask in cat. no. 97, this mask more closely resembles masks of Garuda and Jatayu made in recent times.[1] Like many images of animals in Balinese art, the bird is given protruding eyes and large fangs, features that emphasize his animal nature. The mask has three small pointed horns at the top of the forehead and a single small one at each temple. Judy Slattum calls these *padang astra*, symbols of magical power.[2]

Although Jatayu is a relatively minor character in the Ramayana, the bird does play a dramatic role in his attempts to rescue the kidnapped Sita. Wounded by Rawana, Jatayu manages with his dying breath to tell Rama of Sita's fate. Describing the graceful and evocative choreography of the character in dance performances, Beryl de Zoete and Walter Spies observed in the 1930s that the role of Jatayu was generally danced by an older and highly experienced dancer.

As noted in the entry for cat. no. 97, the bird-headed creatures Goaksa and Winata are members of Rama's monkey army and dance together. This mask could also represent one of those characters.

NR

1 Judy Slattum, *Balinese Masks: Spirits of An Ancient Drama* (Hong Kong: Periplus Editions, 2003), 81.

2 Slattum, *Balinese Masks*, 61.

With its long snout and flaming split tongue, this mask probably represents a mythical serpent or *naga*. It is similar to a mask in the collection of the Rijksmuseum voor Volkenkunde, Leiden (inv. no.2407-54), which is described as a mask used in the *barong* play. Although the *barong naga* is a known type of *barong* or protective deity, the shape of this mask is quite different from the larger *barong* mask with hinged jaws and poles for handling.[1]

Numerous *naga* play important roles in Hindu mythology, including the serpents Anantaboga and Basuki. If this mask were used in an episode of the Ramayana in a *wayang wong* performance, it could represent Drua, a snake member of Rama's monkey army.[2] The tooling of the leather of the flames on the snake's tongue is particularly delicate, as are the designs on the mask's leaf-shaped earrings (*rumbing*). For an example of a *rumbing*, see cat no. 66.

NR

99 Serpent (*naga*) mask, perhaps 1900–1940

Wood, leather, rattan, and pigments
H: 8 in; W: 10¼ in; D: 6¼ in
Collection of W. E. Bouwman

[1] Margaret Coldiron, *Trance and Transformation of the Actor in Japanese Noh and Balinese Masked Dance-Drama* (E. Mellen Press, 2004), 212.

[2] Beryl de Zoete and Walter Spies, *Dance and Drama in Bali* (London: Faber and Faber, 1938), 154.

100 Monkey mask, perhaps 1900–1940

Wood, leather, rattan, and pigments
H: 7⅛ in; W: 8¾ in; D: 5⅛ in
Collection of W. E. Bouwman

This monkey mask was most likely made for a performance of an episode of the Ramayana, a popular subject for the genre of dance-drama called *wayang wong*. There are several important monkey characters in the Ramayana, including the rival king brothers, Subali and Sugriwa, who are often depicted with red faces. The heroic and loyal aide to Rama, Hanoman, the white monkey, plays a starring role in the story; he is accompanied by a host of other monkey troupes.

Another masked performance in which monkey masks are encountered is an exorcistic dance called Barong Kedingkling. This dance involves many dancers with costumes of the major monkey characters from the Ramayana. The dancers move from the courtyard of the temple throughout the village and then back to the temple.

This mask is subtly different from the other four masks in this group (cat. nos. 96–99). The artist used fine lines to indicate the fur of the monkey. Thin, black curving lines are painted on the exposed lips of the animal's open mouth. The fangs are also emphasized with black outlines. This mask has only two small horns at the apex of the forehead, while the others in this group have three.

NR

Bali and the World Expositions

In the pavilions of the world fairs of the late 1880s to early 1930s, European countries sought to promote their empires through representations of their colonial territories.[1] It was in the world fairs in Paris (1889, 1900, 1931), Amsterdam (1883), and Brussels (1910) that the Netherlands, one of the world's largest colonial powers at the time, presented everything from transplanted "Javanese" villages to Buddhist and Hindu statuary to dancing troupes from Bali.

Hundreds of thousands of Europeans attended these fairs, including such luminaries in the arts as Claude Debussy, Emile Zola, Paul Gauguin, and Antoine Artaud. The presentation of Indonesian dance and music had a major impact on visiting Europeans. Some were genuinely interested in the structure and content of the performances; others came to ogle the very young and "exotic" dancers.[2] As documented by Marieke Bloembergen, the Dutch nation's presentation of the "Indies" reflected its own changing colonial strategies. While remarkable works of art were collected and commissioned for these fairs, the selection of objects often represented Dutch colonial concerns and preconceptions. Early fairs focused on agricultural goods and products, while later expositions emphasized the Hindu and Buddhist antiquities of Central Java, and the artists and performers of the islands.[3]

NR

Poster of Balinese dancers for the International Colonial Exposition, Paris, 1931. *P. A. J. Moojen Tropenmuseum, Amsterdam 3204-382.*

1 Marieke Bloembergen, *Colonial Spectacles: The Netherlands and the Dutch East Indies at the World Exhibitions, 1880–1931* (Singapore: Singapore University Press, 2006).

2 Bloembergen, *Colonial Spectacles*, 132–149.

3 For an analysis of the Dutch pavilion of the 1931 International Colonial Exposition in Paris, see Frances Gouda, *Dutch Culture Overseas: Colonial Practice in the Netherlands Indies, 1900–1942* (Singapore: Equinox Publishing [Asia], 2008), 194–236.

101–106 Statues of Batara Guru, Uma, Yama, Bregu, Kalika, and Krisna, 1899

Painted wood

Buleleng, North Bali

Tropenmuseum, Amsterdam, Commissioned by C. M. Pleyte,
15-158, 15-157, 15-182a, 15-172, 15-174, 15-175

These six statues (*togog*) are part of a large pantheon of more than thirty polychromatic wooden statues, made to order in Buleleng, North Bali, in 1899. The entire pantheon of statues was collected in connection with plans for the Dutch colonial pavilion at the Paris World Exhibition of 1900. There they were exhibited as Group no. 89: *Collection de statues en bois polychrome représentant des divinités de l'île de Bali; A. Divinités Hindoues*.[1] After the Paris World Exhibition, they were also exhibited in the Stedelijk Museum in Amsterdam in 1901 and again in 1915.[2]

COLONIAL PROJECTS, COLLECTORS, AND AMBITIONS

According to the collector of the statues, C. M. Pleyte, the Dutch government decided to exhibit remnants of famous Javanese Hindu architecture and sculpture, together with recent Hindu-Balinese objects, for a very specific purpose. The intention was to present in Europe the then unfamiliar and little studied Hindu-Balinese iconography. This aim was explicitly mentioned in the official report of the exhibition.[3] With this kind of display — "for the first time shown in Europe," as was stressed in the guidebook — the Dutch sought to show the importance and uniqueness of their colony's culture.[4] The director of the Rijks Ethnographisch Museum in Leiden (now the National Museum of Ethnology), J. D. E. Schmeltz, regarded the colorful group of statues as one of the most interesting parts of the exhibited ethnographic materials from the archipelago.[5]

To study and collect material for the upcoming world exhibition, Cornelis Marinus Pleyte visited the Netherlands Indies from 1898 until 1899. Born in 1863, the son of the director of the National Museum of Antiquities in Leiden, for most of his working life Pleyte was involved with museums and collections. Beginning in 1882 he worked in the Ethnographic Museum in Leiden (the present-day National Museum of Ethnology), and in 1887 he became curator of the Ethnographic Museum of the Royal Zoological Society, "Natura Artis Magistra," in Amsterdam. In 1897 he became a member of one of the committees for the organization of the Dutch contribution to the Paris exhibition. After his collection journey, he worked on the exhibition in Paris, and on the "Indische" exhibition in the Stedelijk Museum in 1901. Pleyte enjoyed the colonies so much that he returned in 1902 to work in Batavia, where he became curator of the museum of the renowned Batavia Society, a post he retained until his death in 1917. During his last years as curator, he was assisted by the retired government official H. J. E. F. Schwartz, the same person who accompanied and advised Pleyte during his collection journey in Bali in 1898–1899.[6]

---

1 *Exposition universelle internationale de 1900 à Paris: Guide à travers la section des Indes Néerlandaises, groupe XVII (colonisation)* (La Haye: Nijhoff, 1900), 225–226.

2 *Gids voor den bezoeker van de Indische tentoonstelling in het Stedelijk Museum te Amsterdam* (Amsterdam: Stedelijk Museum, 1901), 65–69; J. C. van Eerde, *Gids voor de tentoonstelling betreffende Oud-Javaansch en hedendaagsch Balisch Hindoeïsme* (Amsterdam: Koloniaal Instituut, 1915), 71–90; see also photograph 60040500 KIT in album ALB-0068. The statues are also described in B. M. Goslings, *Gids in het Volkenkundig Museum, II. Bali en Lombok* (Amsterdam: Koninklijke Vereeniging Koloniaal Instituut, 1927), 84–88.

3 C. M. Pleyte, "Herinneringen uit Oost-Indië: Bali," *Tijdschrift van het Koninklijk Nederlandsch Aardrijkskundig Genootschap*, 2nd series, 18 (1901), 35–37; *Verslag der Centrale Commissie tot inrichting van de afdeelingen van Nederland en zijne koloniën en tot behartiging van de belangen der inzenders in die afdeelingen op de Wereldtentoonstelling te Parijs in 1900* ('s-Gravenhage, 1901), 209.

Herman Johannes Elias Frans Schwartz, born in Indonesia in 1863, was educated to become a civil servant in Batavia. He worked for twelve years in Bali, spoke the language fluently, and was widely praised by the government for his knowledge of the culture of Bali and his sensitivity in dealing with the Balinese. Besides his political work, Schwartz, with his wide knowledge of Balinese culture and language, was also very helpful to visitors to Bali with cultural interests, such as Pleyte and W. O. J. Nieuwenkamp.[7]

WOODCARVING AND STATUARY

In Balinese art, large-scale statues and woodcarvings were commonly found as parts of architectural pillars and supports. Large, freestanding wooden statues of deities are not traditional in Balinese culture. The six in this group are in some cases copies, of stone sculptures in temples. There are several functions for stone sculptures and reliefs in temple architecture, including protecting the entrance of the temple against evil, illustrating important episodes from Hindu epic literature, and amusing and entertaining (Balinese: *ameng-ameng*) the deities when they visit their temple.[8] With the exception of some ancient statues, stone sculptures are not intended to be worshiped as are the small god figures, *arca, pratima,* and *pralingga.* These small images serve as receptacles into which the gods are requested to descend. Such sculptures are visible only during temple festivals, or when the gods are carried in procession (*makihis, melihis*) to visit other temples or as part of purification rituals.[9]

Pleyte and Schwartz identified the stone sculptures from which these six wooden statues were copied in different temples in North Bali. For instance, the original versions of Batara Guru and Uma stood in front of the main shrine in the house temple of Ida Nyoman Karang in the village of Sawan. This same artist was also involved in the making of a beautiful palanquin (cat. no. 25).[10] Other woodcarvers lived in Pengastulan and Banjar.[11] The source for Bregu was a temple image in Sukasada,[12] and Krisna was copied from one of the temples in Kubutambahan.[13] The source locations for Yama and Kalika are not mentioned in the reports, but as terrifying figures, examples in stone were probably found as guardian figures in many temples. We do not know whether the wooden statues were exact copies of the stone sculptures, or whether the artists also found inspiration in dancers and actors who performed the adventures of deities, kings, and princes. The postures of some of the statues, especially their feet with upturned toes, are reminiscent of actors or dancers. The figures of the more important gods have anthropomorphic characteristics and are dressed in classical attire; their sumptuous clothing and jewelry resemble those of royalty and high nobility.

4 Marieke Bloembergen, *De Koloniale Vertoning: Nederland en Indië op de wereldtentoonstellingen (1880–1931)* (Amsterdam: Wereldbibliotheek, 2002), 206–210.

5 J. D. E. Schmeltz, "Verslag over een bezoek aan de Wereldtentoonstelling te Parijs in october en november 1900," *Jaarverslag van het Rijksmuseum voor Volkenkunde* (1901), 49.

6 N. J. Krom, "Levensbericht van C.M. Pleyte Wzn.," *Jaarboek van de Maatschappij der Nederlandsche Letterkunde* (1919), 5–25.

7 Francine Brinkgreve and David Stuart-Fox, "Collecting after Colonial Conflict: Badung and Tabanan 1906–2006," in ed. Pieter ter Keurs, *Colonial Collections Revisited* (Leiden: CNWS Publications, 2007).

8 J. C. van Eerde, "Hindu-Javaansche en Balische eeredienst," *Bijdragen tot de Taal-, Land- en Volkenkunde* 65 (1911), 21.

9 F. A. Liefrinck, "Balische godenbeelden," *Feestbundel van taal-, letter-, geschied- en aardrijkskundige bijdragen ter gelegenheid van zijn tachtigsten geboortedag aan Dr. P.J. Veth, door eenige vrienden en oud-leerlingen aangeboden* (Leiden: Brill, 1894), 205.

10 Pleyte, "Herinneringen uit Oost-Indië: Bali," 44.

11 Pleyte, "Herinneringen uit Oost-Indië: Bali," 924.

12 Pleyte, "Herinneringen uit Oost-Indië: Bali," 234.

13 Pleyte, *Indonesian Art: Selected Specimens of Ancient and Modern Art and Handwork from the Dutch Indian Archipelago* (The Hague: Nijhoff, 1901), 39.

14 *Guide à travers la section des Indes Néerlandaises; groupe XVII...*, 225–226. The other *dieux de premier rang* were: Brahma, Saraswati, Wisnu, Dewi Sri, Mahadewa, Parvati or Dewi Danu, Kala, Durga, Ganesa, Kama, Rati, Baruna, Indra or Surya, and Rahu; *dieux de second rang*: Brahma *murti*, Raksasa, Buta, Widadara, Widadari, Basuki.

15 *Verslag der Centrale Commissie tot inrichting van de afdeelingen van Nederland en zijne Koloniën en tot behartiging van de belangen der inzenders in die afdeelingen op de Wereldtentoonstelling te Parijs in 1900*, 220, plate between 224 and 225.

16 J. C. van Eerde, *Gids voor de tentoonstelling betreffende Oud-Javaansch en hedendaagsch Balisch Hindoeisme*, 25, 70–71.

Notably, the deities in these wooden examples are often represented without the typical iconographical attributes found in classical Hindu-Javanese sculpture.

The exposition catalogue divides the statues into two groups: "Deities of first rank," which includes Uma, Batara Guru, and Yama, and "Deities of second rank," including Bregu, Kalika, and Krisna.[14] It is not clear who invented this classification of deities into two ranks; it is not a traditional Balinese concept. In Bali, Krisna and Kalika are usually not regarded as deities, whereas Bregu, as son of Brahma, is. This particular hierarchy was also not represented in the World Exposition display of the "Balinese pantheon," as the group of statues was called. They were exhibited in the center of one of the pavilions, on a round pyramid in the shape of a lotus flower, on four levels. An illustration of the installation shows that Bregu was placed on a higher level than Yama.[15]

The statues are painted in bright colors and with different skin colors. Batara Guru, Uma, and Yama have white skin, whereas Bregu, Kalika, and Krisna, have more naturalistic light brown skin. It is not clear whether these colors are significant, since they do not entirely correspond to traditional Balinese color classifications. Only white for Batara Guru as a manifestation of Siwa, and for Uma as his spouse, relate to the usual color scheme of the Trimurti, in which Siwa is represented as white, Brahma red, and Wisnu black.

The anthropomorphic statues of the deities (Batara Guru, Uma, Yama, and Bregu) wear crowns, *gelung kurung* or *gelung candi,* often with a *garuda mungkur* (the mythical bird Garuda looking backward) at the rear as a protective talisman, or gilded flowers in their hair. Decorative bands are wound around their breasts or waists, and caste cords are draped from shoulder to sides. Their hip cloths in some cases are painted with the actual patterns used in gold-patterned *kain prada* (see cat. no. 84). Jewelry includes a band around the forehead with precious stones (*patitis*), ear ornaments (*sekar taji*), and collar-shaped shoulder covers (*bapang*), while bands and rings adorn arms and legs and fingers. Long fingernails are a hallmark of high status. Uma and Bregu, especially in the refined features of their faces, are represented as a handsome young princess and prince.

The figures of a terrifying nature (Yama, Kalika, and Krisna) have frightening features including bulging eyes, fangs, protruding tongues, loose curly hair, substantial body hair, and claws like animals".[16]

FB

Siwa is the highest-ranking deity in Balinese Hinduism. As Batara Guru he possesses the highest wisdom and spiritual teachings of humankind. In Javanese Hindu iconography, Batara Guru is represented as an old, pot-bellied man with a beard and just two arms, carrying a water pot and rosary. But in this statue he is depicted as an attractive young man with four arms, two of them holding a container with holy water, a third one carrying flowers, and one that forms a *mudra*.

101 Batara Guru

H: 44⅛ in; W: 11 in; D: 11⅜ in

Collection, Tropenmuseum, Amsterdam (the Netherlands), 15-158

102 Uma

H: 36⅝ in; W: 10⅝ in; D: 9⅛ in

Collection, Tropenmuseum, Amsterdam (the Netherlands), 15-157

Uma is Siwa's faithful spouse, the creative force in marital unity. She is often manifested as goddess of the lake (Dewi Danu) or mountain (Giriputri). Here she is represented as a princess, and she carries no specific attributes.

Yama, the much-feared god of the underworld, determines whether the souls of the dead will be allowed to go to heaven or must go to hell. His terrifying nature is usually indicated by a red skin color, rather than white, as in this example. In this case, body hair, and especially bulging eyes and impressive fangs, convey his fearsome characteristics. In his right hand he carries a thunderbolt (*vajra*) as weapon.

103 Yama

H: 49¼ in; W: 12⅝ in; D: 11¾ in

Collection, Tropenmuseum, Amsterdam (the Netherlands), 15-182a

104 Bregu

H: 55⅛ in; W: 13¾ in; D: 11¾ in

Collection, Tropenmuseum, Amsterdam (the Netherlands),
15-172

Bregu is one of the seven sons of Brahma. The Balinese worship him as god of cockfighting. In his right hand the figure carries a container made of coconut shell (*cacupu*).

Kalika is one of the followers of Durga, the terrifying goddess of death and destruction. In her right hand this frightening figure carries the head of a slain enemy, and human hair hangs from her neck ornament.

105 Kalika

H: 41¼ in; W: 14¼ in; D: 13 in
Collection, Tropenmuseum, Amsterdam (the Netherlands),
15-174

106 Krisna

H: 45¼ in; W: 14¼ in; D: 12⅝ in

Collection, Tropenmuseum, Amsterdam (the Netherlands), 15-175

17 For a discussion of *pamurtian* figures, including that of Krisna, see C. Hooykaas, "Pamurtian in Balinese Art," *Indonesia* 12 *(1971),* 1–20.

18 C. M. Pleyte, *Indonesian Art: Selected Specimens of Ancient and Modern Art and Handwork from the Dutch Indian Archipelago* (The Hague: Nijhoff, 1901), 39.

The collector C. M. Pleyte chose this statue of the so-called *pamurtian,* or terrifying form of Krisna, for inclusion in his album of Indonesian art.[17] He described it there as follows:

Polychromatic, wooden statuette with seven elaborately carved heads, one above the other, three in front and two on each side, the uppermost crowned with a magnificent glung chandi [*gelung candi*]. The statuette represents Krishna in full war dress, having four arms of which the two hindermost are armed with a sword and a club, the latter surmounted by a vajra — thunderbolt. The left forehand holds a bunch of flames, the right one presses down the waistcloth. The figure is an excellent specimen of Balinese woodcarving, and is carefully painted and gilt…. Krishna is the eighth avatara — descent — of Vishnu to destroy Kansa, the representative of the principle of the evil, at the end of the Dvapara or third age of the world. For that purpose the god was born as eighth son of Devaki, Vasudeva's spouse, on the eighth day of the dark half of the month Badra. He had a black skin…. Only in his later years he succeeded in slaying Kansa. Though this was the chief task of Krishna, yet he accomplished others. For instance, he killed his own son Bhoma, born from his female counterpart Prithivi, the goddess of earth. Bhoma, from his terrestrial origin, was a Danava or Titan, a much dreaded demon. After doing much mischief he even attacked Indra and subdued him. Then it was that his father descended as Krishna incarnate, and as his mother (the earth) constantly provided him with fresh vigour slew the demon by lifting him from the ground. To this battle the statuette refers. It was copied from the stone Krishna figure, which with that of Bhoma, is found before the entrance of the temple at Kubutambahan, a village on the north coast of the island.[18]

FB (101–106)

Miguel Covarrubias and *Island of Bali*

The Mexican artist Miguel Covarrubias (1904–1957) was already an established artist when he and his wife, Rose, first traveled to Bali in 1930. He had moved to New York at the age of nineteen and gained fame primarily as a caricaturist, designing covers and illustrations for *Vanity Fair* and the *New Yorker,* among other publications.

Covarrubias first became aware of Bali through the photographs of Gregor Krause, whose exotic images drew many other visitors to the island. Upon their arrival, the Covarrubiases quickly befriended members of the expatriate community, including the influential German artist Walter Spies. Covarrubias was fascinated by Balinese life, and particularly by rituals, offerings, and festivals. His friend Gusti Alit Oka recalled that, with his dark skin and Balinese dress, Covarrubias blended in with the villagers.[1] His efforts to learn the language, and his enthusiasm for new and novel experiences, also made him popular. Rose, a dancer and photographer, shared her husband's love for exploring Balinese culture. As Covarrubias documented his experiences in paintings and sketches, his wife recorded their surroundings through an extensive body of photographs. The Covarrubiases spent nine months in Bali, then returned in 1933 for another extended visit.

In 1937 Covarrubias published *Island of Bali*, a detailed account of the many aspects of Balinese life that he had observed. The book contains numerous illustrations by Miguel and photographs by Rose. While the book shares the romanticism of many other works published about the island, it is a remarkable source of information about the art, ritual life, and customs of parts of Bali in the 1930s.

NR

1 Adriana Williams, *Covarrubias and Bali*, 1st printing (Singapore: Didier Millet, 2005), 25.

In this painting, entitled *Tanah Bali,* or Land of Bali, Miguel Covarrubias succinctly illustrates the defining geographical features of the island. A trail of volcanoes bisects the land with the two largest, Gunung Batur and Gunung Agung, dominating the east. Smoke rises from the still-active crater of Batur, while the sacred lake, Danau Batur, fills the caldera. Terraced rice fields descend the fertile slopes to the southern shores. The most sacred temple, Pura Besakih, is on the southern slope of the most sacred mountain, Gunung Agung. Other famous temples dot the island. The west of the island, where in Covarrubias's day the last Bali tiger was nearing extinction, is dry and wild. The animals depicted in this area are all ones that Covarrubias observed when he went camping in this remote region.[1] Fishermen in traditional double outriggers sail in the southern waters, while in the north a large tourist ship approaches the northern town of Singaraja. The boat, the S.S. *Ophir,* was one of the vessels of the Royal Packet Navigation Company (KPM) that sailed between the islands in the archipelago.

Covarrubias draws from Balinese iconography in his depiction of a crowned sea serpent (*naga*) in the upper right of the painting. The figure of a mermaid (*minarupa luh*) with large earplugs is also taken from Balinese imagery. A two-headed sea serpent sucks water from the ocean and sprays it out as rain. In Bali the double-headed serpent was believed to represent the rainbow and a path between earth and the heavens.[2] It appears that portions of this painting are incomplete. A compass in the lower right corner is unpainted, as is the northern region near Buleleng.

NR

107 *Tanah Bali,* approx. 1930–1937

By Miguel Covarrubias
(Mexican, 1904–1957)
Gouache on paper
H: 14 in; W: 21 in
Prints and Photographs Division, Library of Congress, Washington, D.C., 98509203

1 Adriana Williams, *Covarrubias and Bali*, 1st printing (Singapore: Didier Millet, 2005), 22–23.

2 Miguel Covarrubias, *The Eagle, the Jaguar, and the Serpent: Indian Art of the Americas*, 1st edition (New York: Knopf, 1954), 45.

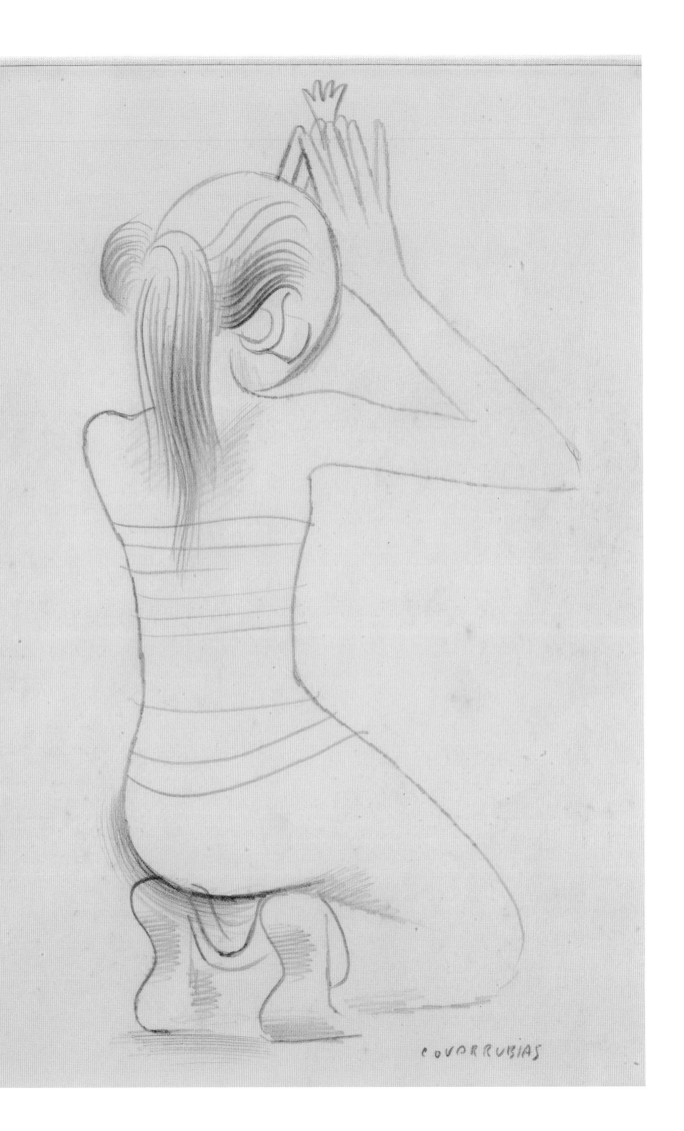

Miguel Covarrubias could have encountered this sight of a young woman praying on any number of occasions. Women bear the bulk of the responsibility for daily offerings and prayer around the house compound and in front of places of commerce. On ceremonial occasions women carry offerings to temples, where they pray and are blessed by priests.

Although locations and types of ceremony vary, most worship involves incense, flowers, and water. Women kneel and men sit cross-legged in front of a coconut leaf offering tray (*canang*) filled with flowers, fruit, and the ingredients for preparing a betel quid. The first prayer may be performed with open hands; then one flower (often a white frangipani) is held up between the fingertips of the raised hands, with the thumbs touching the forehead. Next, a selection of colored flowers is held between the fingers. Other flowers are held up a third time, then the hands are held empty in front of the chest again. If the prayer takes place at a temple, a priest or one of his attendants sprinkles holy water on the worshiper, and into the devotee's cupped hands to drink and to wet the face and head. Grains of rice are then pressed on the temples and throat; a few grains may be eaten as well.

Covarrubias was a famous caricaturist before he came to Bali, and here he captures the female form with a few quick lines. Despite the simplicity of the sketch, we can recognize the worshiper's posture, costume, hairstyle, and earplugs as uniquely Balinese.

NR

108 Sketch of a praying woman, approx. 1930–1937

By Miguel Covarrubias
(Mexican, 1904–1957)
Graphite on paper
H: 9½ in; W: 7 in
Collection of Lily Edith Belcher, San Francisco

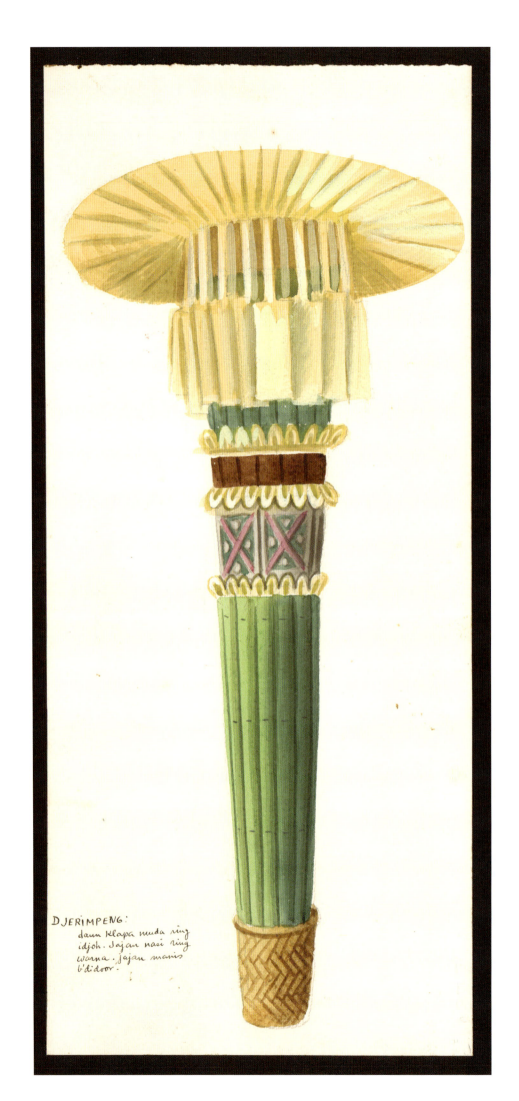

DJERIMPENG:
daun klapa muda ring
idjoh. Jajan nasi ring
warna. jajan manis
b'didoor.

Many visitors to Bali have been fascinated by the extensive variety of offerings made by women (mostly) to present to the gods at temples. The sight of rows of women walking down the roads of villages bearing offerings on their heads was common in the 1930s, when the Mexican artist Miguel Covarrubias visited Bali, and remains common today. Covarrubias's interest extended beyond snapshots and sketches. He recorded a variety of offerings in paintings, but he also upon occasion took note of the materials with which the offerings were made or the places where he saw them.

Balinese families make offerings every day the year, and many are not as picturesque as the ones that have been observed by visiting travelers. The names of offerings vary, and many may be specific to certain villages or communities. Covarrubias entitles this painting *Djerimpeng,* which in modern-day spelling is *jerimpen.* Tall cylindrical offerings like this one are built within a basket base supporting a bamboo frame. Multicolored rice cakes encircle the cylinder. It is topped by a *sampian*, or crown made from coconut fronds.

The words on the bottom left of the painting list the components of the offering: "Coconut fronds of green color : Colored rice cakes : Sweet cakes : b'didoor [?]"

NR

109 *Djerimpeng* (offering), approx. 1930–1937

By Miguel Covarrubias
(Mexican, 1904–1957)
Gouache on paper
H: 12¼ in; W: 5½ in
Prints and Photographs Division, Library of Congress, Washington D.C., 98509139

A Balinese woman carrying a large offering. *Photo Gregor Krause, before 1912.*

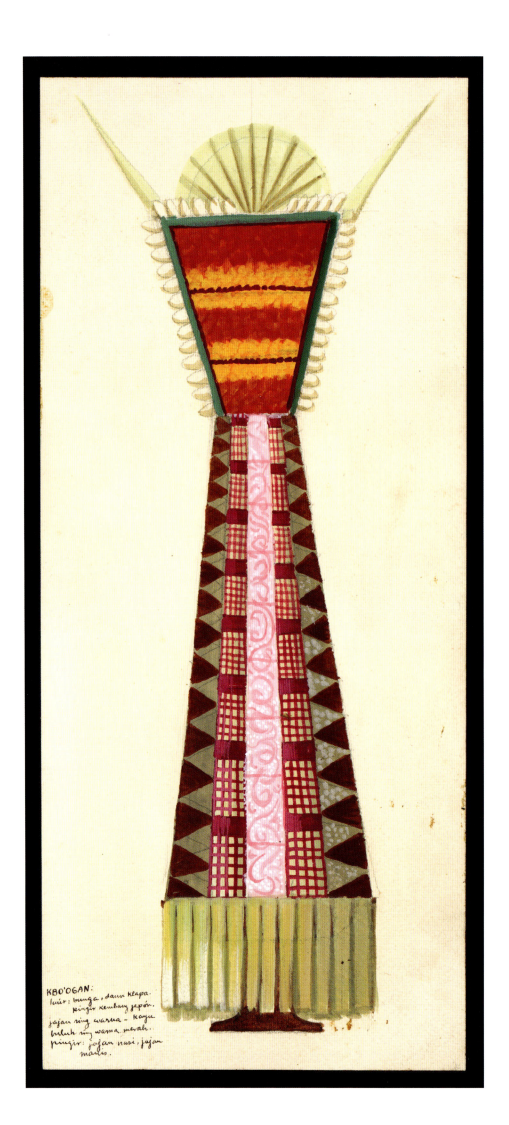

KBO'OGAN:
luir: bunga, daun klapa.
pingir kembang jepun.
jajan sing warna - kayu
buluh sing warna merah.
pingir: jajan nasi, jajan
manis.

A common sight in Bali is that of women carrying large conical offerings on their heads as they make their way to village temples. Women prepare this type of offering on temple anniversaries and other ceremonial occasions throughout the year. After a priest at the temple blesses the offering and its essence is given to the gods, the family can take it home and consume it.

Kbo'ogan (or *gebogan,* as it is more commonly spelled) is a general term for this category of offering, which varies regionally. These offerings often consist of fruit, flowers, rice cakes, and coconut fronds. They differ in size but can reach as high as eight feet tall. The offerings are built on a footed wooden tray (*dulang*) (cat. no. 37), a metal bowl (*bokor*) (cat. no. 36), or an enamel bowl. The styles of arranging the components vary by region, but arrangements often begin with layers of fruit attached by wood or bamboo spikes to the porous trunk of a banana tree. Upper layers may have rice cakes and decorations made from coconut leaves and flowers. Covarrubias lists the components of this offering on the lower left of the painting: flowers, coconut fronds, frangipani flowers, colored rice cakes, red bamboo, and sweet rice cakes.

Elements of offerings have changed in recent times. Wooden platforms have been replaced by painted metal bases. Some women use Styrofoam instead of banana trunks as the offering's core, and imported fruits are used as decoration. Coconut palm frond decorations were once formed by attaching leaves with small slivers of bamboo, but now one can also see metal staples being used.

NR

110 *Kbo'ogan* (offering), approx. 1930–1937

By Miguel Covarrubias
(Mexican, 1904–1957)
Gouache on paper
H: 12¼ in; W: 5½ in
Prints and Photographs Division, Library of Congress, Washington, D. C., 98509142

BEBITÉRA

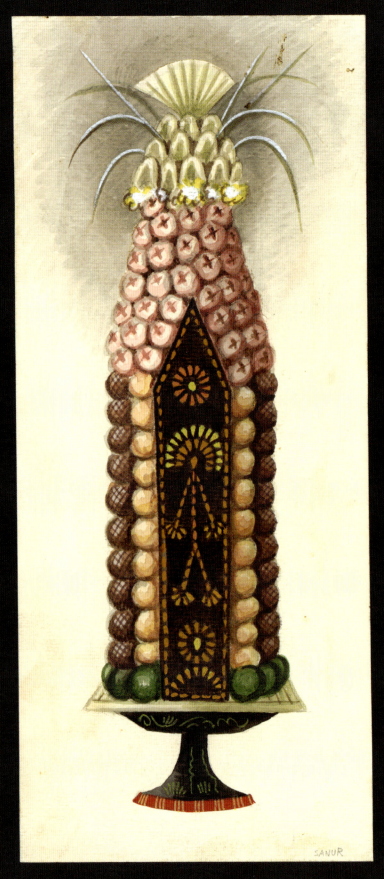

SANUR

In Bali, offerings play an essential part in the ritual life of the community, and one can find hundreds of different types of these carefully made gifts to the deities, demons, and ancestors. Names, shapes, and components vary from region to region and according to the type of ritual or ceremony attended. These three images depict offerings that the artist Covarrubias must have observed during his time in Bali in the 1930s. The titles of these paintings presumably indicate the village where each offering was made.

These three paintings provide a modest glimpse of the diversity of materials used in Balinese offerings. Some components can be found in almost all offerings: incense, flowers, and rice. Offerings for the lower-ranking spirits often contain meat. Other gifts to the gods contain tempting foods and treats: fruits, crispy rice crackers, rice cakes, and the ingredients for making a betel quid. Covarrubias captures some of the colors, shapes, and textures of these towering forms.

The Bebitera offering image depicts an entire roasted and splayed chicken, as well as cones of rice, rice cakes, soursop (*sirsak*), and green bananas. The Sanur offering has a variety of fruit, including the distinctive crosshatched skin of the snakefruit (*salak*). A banner (*lamak*) with a human form (*cili*), an auspicious symbol, decorates the front. Finally, the Tegal Sibang offering has a skirt of cut palm fronds concealing the wooden base. A tall cylinder of rice cakes and fruit rises to a crown of red-orange and white flowers.

NR

111–113 Three paintings of offerings

111 *Bebitera* (offering from the village of Bebitera), approx. 1930–1937

By Miguel Covarrubias
(Mexican, 1904–1957)
Watercolor and pencil on paper
H: 9¾ in; W: 4¼ in
Prints and Photographs Division, Library of Congress, Washington, D.C., 98509136

112 *Sanur* (Offering from the village of Sanur), approx. 1930–1937

By Miguel Covarrubias
(Mexican, 1904–1957)
Watercolor and pencil on paper
H: 9.¾ in; W: 4¼ in
Prints and Photographs Division, Library of Congress, Washington, D.C., 98509103

113 *Tegal Sibang* (offering from the village of Tegal Sibang), approx. 1930–1937

By Miguel Covarrubias (Mexican, 1904–1957)
Watercolor and pencil on paper
H: 9¾ in; W: 4⅝ in
Prints and Photographs Division, Library of Congress, Washington, D.C., 98509107

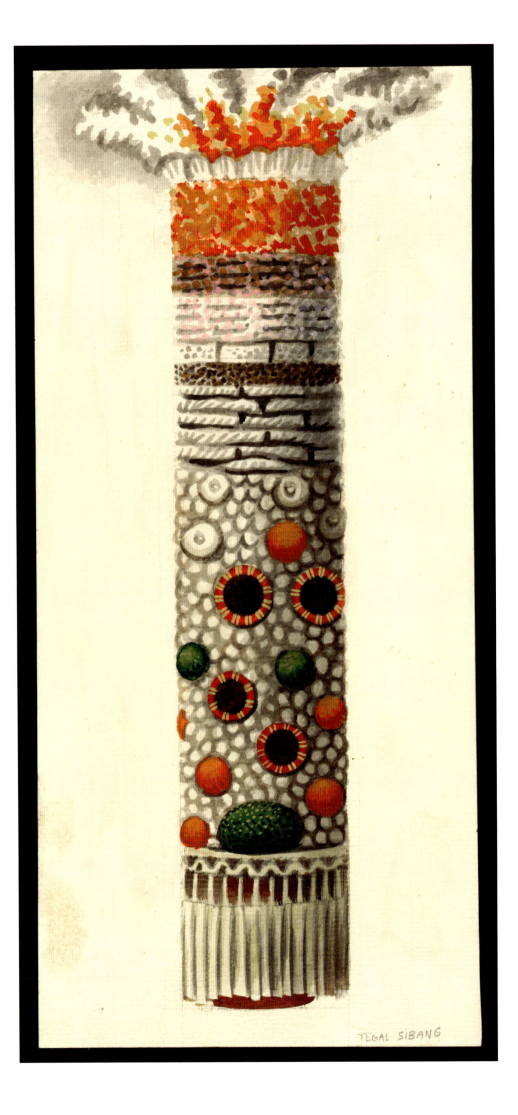

The striking figures depicted in this watercolor are giant puppets. The pair is jointly referred to as *barong landung*. (See cat. no. 95 for a photograph depicting such figures circa 1910, and cat. nos. 93 and 94 for masks of these characters.) The black male on the right is known as Jero Gede, and the white female is Jero Luh. These protective effigies are often seen during the important ten-day Galungan holiday that occurs every 210 days. During this period, they are carried on men's shoulders and may be walked within and between villages, particularly in the south of Bali.

The couple in Covarrubias's painting bears close resemblances to the figures in the early photograph. Jero Gede's white eyebrows accentuate his round black cheeks and mirror the striking whiteness of his large, protruding teeth. He wears a black-and-white checked cloth (*poleng*), a type of textile reserved for sacred and powerful figures. His wife, Jero Luh, has white skin, a protruding forehead, and eyes that are commonly described as indicating her Chinese origin. In both the photograph and this painting, Jero Luh wears a simple unpatterned skirt and a patterned shoulder cloth. This type of cloth is recognizable as a silk batik known as *lok can*, which was historically produced on the north coast of Java, in the villages of Juana and Rembang, and exported to Bali. These textiles were made by and for the Peranakan (mixed Chinese and Indonesian) community and for export. This textile is another signifier of Jero Luh's Chinese ethnicity.

In *Island of Bali*, Covarrubias describes seeing four *barong landung* puppets during a festival at Pura Sakenan, on the island of Serangan off the southern coast of Bali.[1] He was particularly struck by how these sacred figures engaged in bawdy language and "made my polite Balinese friends blush." On another occasion, while Covarrubias was living in the village of Belaluan in the home of young prince Gusti Alit Oka, a special performance of *barong landung* was arranged for his birthday.[2]

NR

114 *Barong landung* figures, approx. 1930–1937

By Miguel Covarrubias
(Mexican, 1904–1957)
Watercolor on paper
H: 15⅜ in; W: 10½ in
Prints and Photographs Division, Library of Congress, Washington, D.C., 98509197

[1] Miguel Covarrubias, *Island of Bali* (New York: Alfred A. Knopf, 1937), 287.

[2] Adriana Williams, *Covarrubias and Bali*, 1st printing (Singapore: Didier Millet, 2005), 24.

Balinese funerary ceremonies have long been fascinating to outsiders. In this watercolor Covarrubias depicts two bull-shaped sarcophagi (*patulangan lembu*) into which corpses would be placed for cremation. Sarcophagi come in a variety of other animal or composite animal forms, but the bull is generally reserved for nobility and those of the highest caste.[1] The framework of the sarcophagus is made from wood and bamboo. The top of the bull's torso is constructed so that it can be removed for the placement of the body. After the animal's form is complete, it is covered with paper and then cloth, often velvet. Finally it is decorated with textiles, yarn, mirrors, colored paper, or other bright ornaments. According to Fred Eiseman, a black bull sarcophagus was for a man, and yellow for a woman.[2] But in *Island of Bali*, Covarrubias notes that bull sarcophagi were used for men and cow sarcophagi for women, and clearly the yellow animal here is not female.[3] In general, these bovine effigies could be quite anatomically accurate, with carved hoofs and even moving genitalia.[4]

On the day of the cremation, the sarcophagus is carried on a bamboo framework through the village to the cremation grounds. A huge tower carrying the corpse winds its way down the same path. The corpse is transferred from the tower into the sarcophagus, and after rituals performed by a priest, both structures are burned. The cremation is just one small (but spectacular) step in the long and complex ceremonies surrounding the death of an individual.

NR

115 Burial bulls (*patulangan lembu*), approx. 1930–1937

By Miguel Covarrubias
(Mexican, 1904–1957)
Watercolor on paper
H: 9 in; W: 11½ in
*Prints and Photographs Division,
Library of Congress*, Washington,
D. C., 98509149

1 Eiseman notes that there are occasional exceptions to this rule. Fred Eiseman, *Bali: Sekala and Niskala* (Berkeley: Periplus Ed., 1990), 118.

2 Eiseman, *Bali*, 118; Hinzler describes how differently shaped sarcaphagi were used by the different castes, "In former days the bull was used for a male brahman and the cow for a female brahman, the lion for a ksatriya, the deer for a *wesya* and the gajah mina, fish-elephant, and cecekakan [fish-tailed], for a jaba." H. I. R Hinzler, *Catalogue of Balinese Manuscripts: In the Library of the University of Leiden and Other Collections in the Netherlands* (Leiden: E. J. Brill, 1986), 398.

3 Miguel Covarrubias, *Island of Bali* (New York: Alfred A. Knopf, 1937), 373.

4 Eiseman, *Bali*, 119.

The Novelist Vicki Baum in Bali

A popular Austrian novelist named Vicki Baum was among the many Westerners who made their way to Bali in the 1930s. Baum wrote that she first became aware of the island through photographs taken by a doctor who had lived there. She is surely referring to the photographs of Gregor Krause (1883–1959), a German physician who took approximately four thousand photographs while working in Bali between 1912 and 1914. A selection of his photographs was exhibited in several European cities and appeared in numerous publications, including a two-volume set published in 1920.[1]

Baum was the author of many novels, the most famous of which had been made into the Hollywood film *Grand Hotel,* starring Greta Garbo, Joan Crawford, and Lionel Barrymore. In 1935 Baum traveled to Bali, where, like many other famous tourists, she spent time with the German expatriate Walter Spies. She drew upon his deep knowledge of the island in her novel *Tale of Bali*, published in 1937.[2] The story recounts the 1906 ritual end (*puputan*) of the court of Badung in the face of the Dutch troops.[3]

At the time of Baum's visit to Bali, several Western artists were involved in actively encouraging new styles, genres, and techniques of practice among Balinese artists. Walter Spies (1880–1942), a multitalented German artist, first came to the island in 1927. He settled in Bali and became deeply immersed in its culture, acting as a guide and advisor to many of the Western visitors who followed, including Vicki Baum. In 1929 the Dutch painter Rudolf Bonnet (1895–1978) also came to Bali. In 1936 he and Walter Spies, Gusti Nyoman Lempad, and Cokorda Gede Agung Sukawati, among others, founded the Pita Maha Arts Movement, which encouraged young artists working in new styles. A later visitor to the island, the Mexican artist and caricaturist Miguel Covarrubias, closely observed Balinese culture and made many dozens of sketches of aspects of daily life. His stylized sketches often featured the sinuous elongation of forms, a feature also found in much of the early woodcarving in the modern style.

Many of the works collected by Baum are examples of this new style of carving for the tourist market.

NR

---

1 The two-volume set was published in German as *Bali: Geist, Kunst und Leben Asiens, erster Teil:Land und Volk, zweiter Teil: Tänze, Tempel, Feste* (Bali: Spirit, Art and Life of Asia. Part one: Land and People; part two: Dance, Temple, Ceremony). In 1922 a one-volume book of photographs was published.

2 The novel refers to a Dutch source for her knowledge of Balinese life; this source was in fact Walter Spies.

3 As noted by Adrian Vickers, Baum's story suggests that the tragic event was inevitable and the result of the pride of the Balinese aristocracy. She also praises the Dutch colonizers after the event, writing, "since then the Dutch have carried out an achievement in colonization that reflects the highest credit on them." Vicki Baum, *A Tale from Bali* (New York: The Literary Guild, 1938), 10.

116 Mask of a refined woman, approx. 1935

Wood

H: 7½ in; W: 6¾ in

Asian Art Museum, Vicki Baum Bali Collection; Gift of Wolfgang Lert and Ruth Clark Lert, 1992.37

This mask reflects the new artistic styles that were developing in Bali during the early decades of the twentieth century. The colonization of the island led to the decline of the Balinese courts, previously the major patrons of the arts. With the increase of visitors from the West in the 1920s and 1930s, Balinese artisans began producing artworks solely for the tourist market. A tourist mask could be made without the ritual requirements of a sacred mask. For instance, the carver would not have to carefully monitor the type of wood chosen, the day the carving began, and the purification and consecration of the completed object. Perhaps the clearest physical difference between masks like this one created for the tourist market and masks used in performance is the unpainted surface.

This mask bears some resemblance to masks of refined female characters (Raja Putri) used in dance performances. The slight smile, downcast glance, and large earplugs are all attributes of the ideal noblewoman.

NR

Like the mask also collected by Vicki Baum (cat. no. 116), this statue was made for the tourist market. A signature on the bottom of the statue reads Ida Bagus Putu Hemas, which probably indicates a known woodcarver from the southern village of Mas. In an article describing woodcarving in south Bali, Ida Bagus Putu is mentioned as the brother of I Gelodog. Ida Bagus Putu is described as the less fantastic and experimental of the two.[1]

This statue depicts a scene from the *Arjunawiwaha*, an East Javanese poem describing the exploits of Arjuna, one of the heroes of the Mahabharata epic.[2] This text was very popular in Bali, as evidenced by the abundant palm leaf manuscripts and painted images of the poem.[3] In this statue Arjuna flirts with Supraba, a heavenly nymph who will become his wife. The figures' raised shoulders and angular poses are reminiscent of Balinese dancers.

NR

117 Arjuna and Supraba, approx. 1935

Mas, South Bali
Perhaps by Ida Bagus Putu
H: 14 in; W: 8 in
Wood
Asian Art Museum, Vicki Baum Bali Collection; Gift of Wolfgang Lert and Ruth Clark Lert, 1992.43

NOTES FROM OPPOSITE PAGE

1 Rudolf Bonnet, "Beeldende Kunst in Gianjar," *Djawa* 16 (1936), 62.

2 Mpu Kanwa, *Arjunawiwāha: The Marriage of Arjuna of Mpu Kanwa*, trans. S. O. Robson (Leiden: KITLV Press, 2008).

3 For an illustration of Arjuna and Supraba that is very similar to this sculpture, see the Ubud artist Ida Bagus Anom's drawing of the subject in the Rijksmuseum voor Volkenkunde, B135-41.

In the background of this painting, a smoldering volcano spews out the words "Goodbye" and "Good Luck," while curlicues of smoke emerging from the volcano in the foreground spell "Welcome." In the middle of the painting, on a small outrigger canoe, Margaret Mead and Gregory Bateson make their way between islands. The painting was commissioned by Made Kaler, Mead and Bateson's research assistant, when the couple was about to depart Bali to conduct research in New Guinea. In the painting, the sorrow of the Balinese is evident as they stand on the shore in postures of grief with the distinctive architecture of the island behind them. In contrast, New Guinean villagers rush with excitement toward the approaching anthropologists, arms raised in greeting.

In the early 1930s young artists of Batuan, encouraged by the European artists Spies and Bonnet, began producing new styles of painting. These small black-and-white works on paper were very different from the colorful stylized paintings on cloth that had been produced traditionally. Instead of portraying scenes from the Hindu epics or legends, they primarily depict aspects of contemporary village life and visions of local demons and spirits.[1] Rather than being intended for use in the temple or court, they were created to be sold to tourists.

While in Bali, Mead and Bateson had collected more than twelve hundred paintings and sketches, most of which came from the village of Batuan.[2] They also interviewed artists, intending to study what the images could tell them about the psychology of the Balinese.

According to the anthropologist Hildred Geertz, who studied Mead and Bateson's collection:

> The pictures Mead and Bateson collected are best understood as bicultural products, bound up in the meaning systems and aesthetic ideas of several cultures at once. Made within Western pictorial conventions, they draw almost entirely from Balinese culture for their images. This dual ancestry had uneven effects on the pictures, since their makers did not understand the Western tradition of pictorial art very deeply. They saw the few examples of European drawing and painting that had made their way to Bali, but through eyes that had been complexly trained within their own culture. Yet for the paintings of the village of Batuan at least, adoption of certain Western conventions seems to have given them a new way to look at themselves and their lives.[3]

The artist who made this painting, I Ketut Ngendon, was encouraged to paint by his

118 *Goodbye and Good Luck to Margaret Mead and Gregory Bateson,* 1938

By I Ketut Ngendon (1903–1948)
Batuan, Bali
Ink on paper
Collection of Mary Catherine Bateson

---

1 Hildred Geertz, *Images of Power* (University of Hawai'i Press, 1994).
2 Geertz, *Images of Power,* 97.
3 Geertz, *Images of Power,* 19.

cousin, who had met Spies and Bonnet. Ngendon incorporated perspective, shading, and active figures in a variety of poses into his work, and seems to have had more exposure to, and interest in, Western painting styles than did other artists of Batuan. During the Japanese occupation of 1942–1945, Ngendon went to Java, where he became involved in nationalist politics. Upon his return to Bali he was involved with the movement for independence, but was caught and executed by the Dutch in 1948. Geertz writes:

> While Ngendon used pictures and dance performances to make money, this was not his primary motive. It was Western modernity and Western forms of power that fascinated him. All the evidence we have indicates that Ngendon felt an increasing resentment at being prevented from sharing the advantages of Western life and at the colonial patterns of domination and appropriation of Balinese talents for outsiders' pleasures.[4]

NR

4 Hildred Geertz, *Images of Power* (University of Hawai'i Press, 1994), 19.

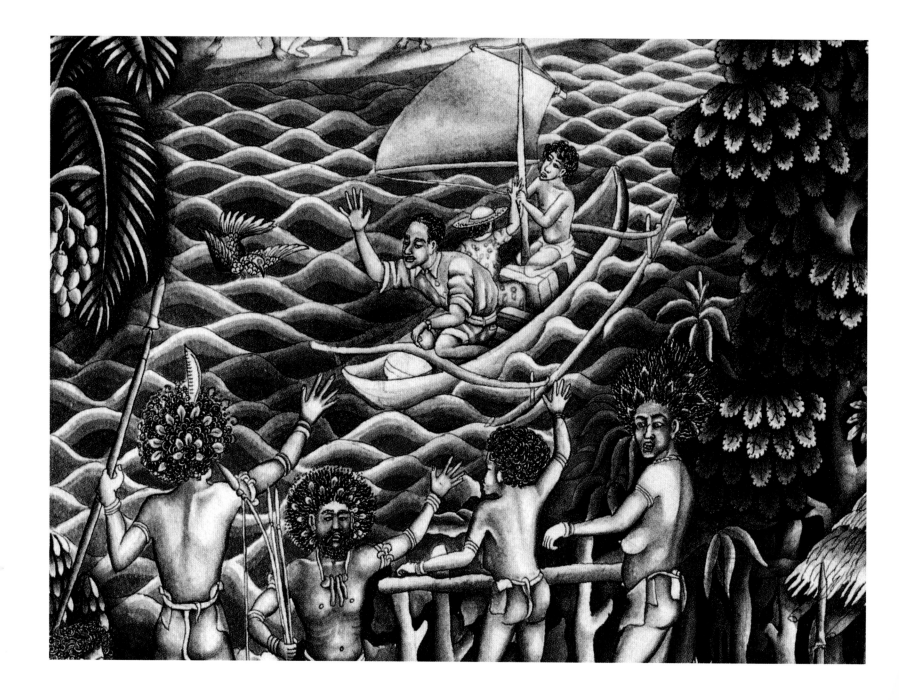

Balinese shadow puppets from the Margaret Mead Collection

These shadow puppets (*wayang kulit*) were collected by the eminent anthropologist Margaret Mead between late 1936 and early 1938, when Mead and her husband, Gregory Bateson, were conducting research in Bali. After her return to the United States, Mead donated more than three hundred puppets to the American Museum of Natural History. Pioneers of visual anthropology, Mead and Bateson documented their stay in Bali with approximately 35,000 photographs and 33,000 feet of motion picture film, including photographs and films of the process of making puppets.

Unlike many early collectors, Mead and her research assistant, Made Kaler, took careful notes about the puppets, their artists, and the artistic process. She commissioned a number of puppets and bought others from *dalang* (puppet masters). She lists the collection sources as three *dalang* from Sebatu and Negara, in Gianyar province, South Bali; one *dalang* in Penglipuran, Bangli province, South Bali; a *dalang* in Buleleng, North Bali; and a few miscellaneous sources in Bangli and Batuan.

Thirty-four of the puppets were commissioned from an artist named I Wara of Negara.[1] Mead became aware of I Wara through the composer Colin McPhee, who gave Mead one of I Wara's puppets and told her it was a fine example from one the best *wayang* makers in Bali.[2] She visited the artist in the fall of 1937 and ordered "55 guilders worth of wayngs [sic]."[3] The artist's grandfather had been a *dalang*, but upon his death I Wara's father had to sell his full collection of *wayang* to pay for the cremation ceremonies. I Wara slowly built up his own collection with models, mostly from from Klungkung, with the hope of one day becoming a *dalang* himself. When Mead met him, he was a professional *wayang* maker who sold his work in Badung.

Many of the puppets in the collectioin are characters derived from the Mahabharata.[4] In Balinese shadow puppet theater, this repertoire (*wayang parwa*) is more popular than stories from the other major Indian epic, the Ramayana.[5] Other sources for *wayang* repertoire include indigenous stories and legends from East Java, but these are infrequently performed. The Mahabharata revolves around the conflicts between the five Pandawa brothers and their cousins, the one hundred Korawa brothers. Their rivalry results in a great and terrible war that tests the character of all involved. Only portions of these long and complicated stories are told during the all-night-long performances, or in the shorter ritual daytime performances.

At the center of the performance is the *dalang*, who alone manipulates the puppets, provides the voices, and directs the gamelan. The *dalang* relates the narrative from memory, chants in Old Javanese, speaks in a variety of formal levels appropriate to the status of different characters, and improvises comic dialogue that engages the audience.

NR

---

1 I Wara is described as coming from Negara. Today the town of Negara is known as the capital of the Jembrana province in West Bali. It is likely that I Wara came from a different Negara, a village and former kingdom that was incorporated into the village of Batuan, where Mead and Bateson conducted research.

2 Mead writes that McPhee's puppet actually "is so thin it could never be used and is a fragile style which has been developed for sale." Amusingly, Mead notes that later McPhee told her that he thought I Wara's puppets were cold and lifeless.

3 Mead writes that I Wara was "slight, eager, fey, intelligent and adaptive. He asks his wife's opinion on all practical points, how long he will take to do his [*wayangs*], how much advance he needs, etc."

4 For an overview of *wayang kulit* in Bali, see Angela Hobart, *Dancing Shadows of Bali: Theatre and Myth* (London; New York: KPI, distributed by Methuen Inc. Routledge and Kegan Paul, 1987).

5 Fredrik E. deBoer, I Made Bandem, and I Ketut Madra, "'The Death of Kumbakarna' of I Ketut Madra: A Balinese Wayang Ramayana Play," *Asian Theatre Journal* 9, no. 2 (Autumn 1992), 147.

119 Dwijakangka, approx. 1930–1938[1]

Hide, wood, pigment, spring, plant fiber, metal (modern)
L (with rod): 24½ in; L: 14¾ in; W: 6¾ in
American Museum of Natural History, 70.0/8201

1 This puppet was bought from I Wara of Negara. The puppet was modeled after a puppet from Klungkung.

2 In Mead's notes the older spelling of Doewidjakangka is used. This older Dutch spelling is used in her notes for many other characters as well. Her notes also include the Balinese gender identifiers "I" and "Ni" in front of character's names, for example, I Bima and Ni Batara Doerga.

Dwijakangka (more commonly known as Yudistira) is one of the names used in Bali for the eldest of the Pandawa brothers, one of the heroes of the Mahabharata.[2] In one episode of the epic, Yudistira and his brothers are exiled. They must spend twelve years living in the forest, followed by one year living in disguise. If recognized during that final year, they must repeat the twelve years of exile. During the thirteenth year, each of the brothers conceals his identity. Yudistira impersonates a Brahman, and becomes the advisor to King Wirata, who has been friendly to the Pandawas in the past. At Wirata's court, Yudistira is given the assumed name Dwijakangka. Yudistira's brothers likewise disguise themselves to take on other positions at the king's court.

Yudistira is considered the most refined of the Pandawa brothers; he is known for his truthfulness and righteousness. His facial features, with narrow eyes, a delicate mouth, and a straight nose, are indications of his restrained and gentle nature. Here, in his disguise, he wears a long cloak over trousers, dress that is common to Brahman priests and sages. His hair is tied back in a kind of chignon also common to holy men. Although he is admired for his loyalty and his attention to duty, he is not as popular in Bali as are his brothers Bima and Arjuna.

NR

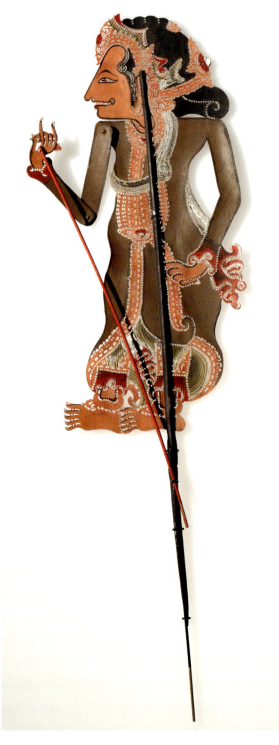

Arjuna is the third of the five Pandawa brothers, the heroes of the Mahabharata. Like Yudistira, he is a very refined character and has similar delicate features. But in contrast to his elder brother, Arjuna wears more jewelry and a patterned lower garment with sashes behind the waist. Rising distinctively in a wave above his head, his hair is arranged in a style called *supit urang* (pincers of a crab).

Arjuna is known as an unequalled warrior and an irresistible lover, and various narratives recount both his exploits on the battlefield and his romances with a number of beautiful women.[1] A popular story in Indonesia involves Arjuna's meditation and attainment of a magical weapon, the *pasopati*. (See episodes from this story with cat. no. 54).

This puppet was bought from I Wara of Negara. It is based on a model from Klungkung.

NR

120 Arjuna, approx. 1930–1938

Hide, wood, string, plant fiber, metal

L (with rod): 22⅜ in; L: 15¾ in; W: 9¾ in

American Museum of Natural History, 70.0/8199

[1] According to Angela Hobart, Balinese villagers consider Arjuna to be the son of Semara, god of love, rather than of Indra, as described in Indian versions of the epic. Angela Hobart, *Balinese Shadow Play Figures: Their Social and Ritual Significance* (London: British Museum Dept. of Ethnography, 1985), 40.

121 Bima, approx. 1930–1938

By I Wara

Hide, wood, string, plant fiber, metal

L (with rod): 28 in; L: 14⅝ in; W: 18⅛ in

American Museum of Natural History, 70.0/8194

Bima's physical features are broader and coarser than those of his brothers Yudistira and Arjuna. As with other fierce figures, his eyes are large and round, and he wears a curling mustache. His body is painted black. Bima wears a black-and-white checked cloth called *poleng* wrapped around his waist, exposing his powerful thighs. This type of textile is a sacred symbol in Bali, often associated with spirits of the netherworld. The balance of black and white is said to represent the cosmic duality of the universe. Among puppets, *poleng* cloth patterns are found only on characters that are believed to have supernatural powers, such as Bima, Hanoman, and Twalen.

The puppet's coarser features indicate the character's rough and impulsive nature. His long thumbnails, *kuku pancanaka*, are a sign of his descent from the wind god Bayu, and serve as deadly weapons. Bima's strong-willed but loyal nature is much admired in Bali, and he is the main character in several Balinese adaptations of episodes from the Mahabharata.

This puppet was bought by Margaret Mead from the artist and is based on a model from Klungkung.

NR

Many of the stories that are told in shadow puppet performances are derived from Indian epics, which are well known by the Balinese. In the Ramayana, the hero Rama must rescue his wife, who has been kidnapped by the demon king Rawana. Rama joins with troops of monkey allies to journey to Rawana's kingdom. Rawana's brother is the demon Kumbakarna, a fearsome giant. Although he disapproves of his brother's actions, Kumbakarna feels it is his duty to support him; he joins the fight against Rama and his monkey army. After a fierce battle, Kumbakarna is killed by Rama.[1]

Kumbakarna is shown here with all the attributes of a *wayang* villain: wild curling hair, bulging round eyes, a snub nose, and sharp teeth. The depiction is unusual because it lacks the headdress usually found on puppets of Kumbakarna. Despite the fact that he is a fierce character and Rama's antagonist in the story, Kumbakarna is still a somewhat sympathetic character. His loyalty to his brother is seen as an admirable attribute.

This puppet, bought from I Wara of Negara, was modeled on a puppet made by Dalang Djandjang of Batujang.

NR

122 Kumbakarna, approx. 1930–1938

Hide, wood, string, plant fiber
L (with rod): 28¾ in; L: 18⅞ in; W: 11¾ in
American Museum of Natural History, 70.0/8202

1 Fredrik E. deBoer, I Made Bandem, and I Ketut Madra, ""The Death of Kumbakarna" of I Ketut Madra: A Balinese Wayang Ramayana Play," *Asian Theatre Journal* 9, no. 2 (Autumn 1992): 141–200.

123 Bala *raksasa*, demon warrior, approx. 1930–1938

Hide, wood, pigment, plant fiber

L (with rod): 18¾ in; L: 13⅛ in; W: 8 in

American Museum of Natural History, 70.0/8217

Raksasa are powerful demons and skillful warriors. They are described in the Ramayana as members of the army of the villainous Rawana (himself a ten-headed *raksasa*), and in the Mahabharata as frightening dwellers of the forest. Bloodthirsty and terrifying, they have the ability to shift shapes and to assume human form for nefarious purposes. Balinese religion is full of malevolent spirits, and shadow puppet artists were adept at portraying a wide variety of evil beings.

The demon's wild hair, round eyes, and bared teeth instantly identify it as a coarse creature. Although these demonic figures were feared, images of them are often found in temple architecture, where they serve as spiritual protectors. Mead's collection contains many examples of this type of character. Her notes indicate that artists had freer range to innovate when creating demons and clowns. This puppet was bought from I Wara of the village of Negara. It is modeled on a puppet made by Gusti K. Roengsia of Negari.

NR

Although lions never existed in Indonesia, they must have been familiar from Indian sources from an early date: they are depicted in some of the earliest stone monuments of the islands. Lions play important roles in Hindu and Buddhist mythology and also in Tantri tales, the animal fables that were very popular in Java and Bali.

This lion's body is painted red with white spots and has flames spiking from the tail and head. Wings encircle the animal's shoulders. The creature's mouth is open, exposing sharp teeth, and his eyes are round and bulging. Lions with these same characteristics were also carved from wood (cat. no.27) and used as vehicles for the gods in religious rituals. This type of depiction may also have a connection to the *barong*, a mythical creature encountered in Balinese dance-dramas and revered on the island.[1]

Unlike the other puppets in this catalogue created by the artist I Wara, this puppet was not produced to Margaret Mead's commission. Rather, Mead purchased it in the village of Bangli in South Bali.

NR

124 Lion (*singa*), approx. 1930–1938

By I Wara

Hide, wood, pigment, string

L (with rod): 17¼ in; L: 14¾ in; W: 12 in

American Museum of Natural History, 70.0/8191

[1] The *barong* in its most common form is thought by some to be related to the lion dance traditions of China. For more on *barong*, see cat. nos. 85 and 86.

125 Batara Anantaboga, god of the snakes, approx. 1930–1938

By Dalang Sebeng

Hide, wood, pigment, plant fiber, metal

L (with rod): 29½ in; L: 16⅞ in; W: 10⅛ in

American Museum of Natural History, 70.0/8098

[1] Mead calls the puppet Betara Anteboga, father of Taksasa. There are several variations on the name of the character, but it is most commonly known as Anantaboga.

Naga (mythical snakelike creatures) play a large role in Hindu mythology, and several snake deities are important in Balinese mythology. According to Margaret Mead's notes, this puppet represents the ruler of the underworld, a serpent called Anantaboga or Antaboga.[1] In one legend, as a youth Anantaboga had the form of a *naga*, but due to his devotion to the gods and his helpfulness to them, he was given divine status and allowed to assume other forms. He is shown here with a dragon's head, a human body, and a snake's tail. As lord of the *naga*, Anantaboga wears a rounded crown and elaborate jewelry. Other versions of this puppet have a torso covered with green scales, but the body of this one looks more like that of a monkey.

A Balinese folktale also associates Anantaboga with the production of rice. It relates that once the king of the gods, Batara Guru, was holding a celebration. Anantaboga was upset because, since he lacked hands, he could not bring anything. His tears fell and turned into three eggs, which he put into his mouth to take to the god. En route he stopped to speak, and two of the eggs fell out and hatched into a boar and a rat. The third egg he presented to Batara Guru, and when it hatched, the goddess Dewi Sri emerged. The other goddesses were jealous and killed Dewi Sri. From the spot where she was buried, the first rice grew.

This puppet was purchased from the artist Dalang Sebang and modeled after a puppet from the village of Sebatu. Mead noted that Sebeng "was illiterate, exceedingly ingenious in construction of odd characters, and specially good at handling comics. His attributions of classical characters are somewhat doubtful."

NR

The goddess Durga is well known in Bali. Of the three temples found in most Balinese villages, the *pura dalem* is dedicated to Durga and her consort, Siwa. This temple is generally located near the cemetery and cremation grounds and is called the temple of death. Durga is strongly associated with both black magic and healing.[1] She shares characteristics with the wrathful Indian deity Kali; both are connected to darkness and annihilation. Durga is seen not only as a destructive force but also as a creative one, who is linked in myths to the creation of all life.[2]

The Durga puppet is used in a number of shadow puppet plays that are performed to protect an individual or community from harmful forces. She is seen in *wayang Sudamala*, a play performed for purification purposes, and she is linked to Rangda in performances of the Calonarang, an exorcistic tale that also forms the basis of a famous dance-drama. Performances of this play are rare, because *dalang* (puppet masters) are uneasy with dramatizing stories that test "their capacity to combat and contain malevolent forces and energies."[3] This puppet was bought from the artist. It is based on a model from Sebatu.

NR

126 Batara Durga, goddess of death, approx. 1930–1938

By Dalang Sebeng
Hide, wood, string, plant fiber, metal
L (with rod): 28⅞ in; L: 16⅞ in; W: 9⅜ in
American Museum of Natural History, 70.0/8150

1 Angela Hobart, *Healing Performances of Bali: Between Darkness and Light*, 1st edition (New York: Berghahn Books, 2005), 108–112.

2 Hobart, *Healing Performances,* 110.

3 Hobart, *Healing Performances,* 112.

127 *Pamurtian, supernatural form of Krisna*, approx. 1930–1938

By Dalang Sebeng

Hide, wood, string, plant fiber, metal

L (with rod): 31¼ in; L: 24⅜ in; W: 14¾ in

American Museum of Natural History, 70.0/8009

1 C. Hooykaas, "Pamurtian in Balinese Art," *Indonesia* 12 (October 1971): 1–20.

2 Hooykaas, "Pamurtian in Balinese Art," 1–20.

3 Hooykaas, "Pamurtian in Balinese Art," 11.

In *wayang kulit* performances, a character can be depicted by more than one shadow puppet, depending on the episode of a story or the mood of the character. Krisna (Sanskrit: Krishna) is an avatar of the Hindu god Wisnu, who descends to earth in times of crisis. He is generally depicted as a refined nobleman, but upon occasion he takes a much fiercer form. This type of wrathful depiction of a deity is called a *pamurtian*.[1] The root of *pamurtian* is *murti*, meaning "form"; thus the word signifies a manifestation of the god's terrible powers through corporeal transformation. A number of gods have wrathful forms, but Siwa and avatars of Wisnu are most commonly depicted as giant multiheaded demons.[2] The Balinese narrative poem Smaradahana includes a terrifying description of Siwa in his *pamurtian* form:

> Rose up then Siwa, the Supreme God, enraged; huge became his form.
> Forthwith, of His own will, He took the frightful Three Strides shape.
> Terrible and dreadful, He placed Himself in the middle of the sky.
> The demons of demons and hideous beings gazed on Him terrified, horror-struck.
>
> His form was that of Rudra, with five heads, immense,
> Horrible His hair unkempt, thick and glowing,
> Curling, red, like clouds at the doom of the Universe,
> His thousand arms, inspiring fear, He stretched in all directions.
>
> His eyes, like suns and moons, formed half a circle;
> His nostrils, flared and deep, resembled caverns;
> His mouth, tusks razor keen, was like [the entrance to the Realm of] Death;
> His teeth, grinding, begat unceasing storms and thunderclaps.
>
> He was a mountain flanked with arms and legs;
> The long hairs on His body, drooping, made it seem like twilight;
> Each placing of a foot on earth an earthquake caused;
> Earth rocked beneath his steps, as though it would be cloven."[3]

Mead's notes describe this puppet as "Pemurtian, the supernatural form into which someone is transformed, usually Kresna, *boeta sia,* nine heads." This puppet has nine heads and ten arms, each holding various weapons. Supernatural forms of wrathful deities were also often depicted in Balinese paintings, and in wood and stone. (See cat. no. 106.)

NR

This striking puppet shows the hero Abimanyu (Sanskrit: Abhimanyu) from the Mahabharata shortly before his death. The Mahabharata relates the battle between the Pandawa brothers and their cousins, the Korawas. Abimanyu was the son of Arjuna, one of the five Pandawa brothers, the heroes of the epic. His mother was Subadra, half-sister to the god Krisna.

Abimanyu's tragic role in the battle began while he was still *in utero* and overheard Krisna explaining to Subadra techniques of entering and escaping from certain military formations. Abimanyu grew up to be a famed archer who went into battle with the Pandawas against their enemies the Korawas. One day when Krisna and Arjuna were attending to battle on another front, Abimanyu was called upon to break into a circular battle formation of the enemy. Because of the knowledge he had learned in the womb, he was able to do so; but he had not learned the secret of breaking out of the formation. He fought valiantly, but he was attacked by all the Korawas simultaneously and in some accounts eventually stabbed in the back. These violations of the warrior code mark the breakdown of the rules of war and foreshadow the terrible slaughter to follow. The puppet depicts Abimanyu, already fallen from his chariot, his bow crushed, now battling singlehandedly with a sword. His body is pierced on all sides by the enemy's arrows.

The puppet was purchased from Dalang Lana of Sebatu. It was modeled from a puppet produced by I Salimoer of Djoengdjoengan (Jungjungan). In her anthropological documentation, Margaret Mead distinguished between literate puppet masters from towns in the south, and those *dalang* such as Dalang Lana, whose work, she said, was typical of illiterate mountain puppetry.

NR

128 Abimanyu, approx. 1930–1938

Hide, wood, pigment, plant fiber
L (with rod): 24¼ in; L: 15⅞ in; W: 9⅜ in; D: ¾ in
American Museum of Natural History, 70.0/7954

129 A multicolored chicken, approx. 1930–1938

By I Made Oka
Buleleng, North Bali
Hide, wood, pigment, string
L (with rod): 12¼ in; L: 8¼ in; W: 11¾ in
American Museum of Natural History, 70.0/8231

According to Margaret Mead's notes, the artist and *dalang* I Made Oka was quite specific in his designation of this puppet, describing it as a type of multicolored chicken that "can be used in the middle of a *metjaroe* offering."[1] *Metjaroe* or *mecaru* ceremonies are types of purification ritual that involve offerings to the unseen and sometimes malevolent denizens of the world, the *buta*. Offerings are given to the *buta* to honor and appease them. Many levels of *macaru* offerings exist. The simplest can involve tokens of worship composed of rice, flowers, plants, and a single chicken. The second-level offering requires the sacrifice of several chickens, whose blood must be spilled on the ground. Mead may have mistakenly written that the chicken is used in the middle of a *macaru* offering, when the informant probably meant it could be used for the middle level of such a type of ceremony. The highest level of *macaru* can involve the sacrifice of hundreds of animals, from chickens to water buffaloes.

This puppet was made in the north of Bali by an artist named I Made Oka, a cousin of Mead's research assistant, Made Kaler. Mead writes that Made Oka's puppets "are typical of N. Bali, showing far more variety and greater freedom of phantasy, combined with more ingeneous manipulative devices."[2]

NR

[1] The Balinese term *siap berumbun* is used. "Manuscript Catalog," http://anthro.amnh.org/anthropology/databases/common/catno_page.cfm?catno=70%2E0%2F%208231&curr_page=&from_anthro=yes&show_portfolio=yes.

[2] Margaret Mead, "Notes of Field Catalogue of Balinese Shadow Play Puppets" (Library of Congress, Manuscript Reading Room, Margaret Mead Papers, 1937–1938), http://www.loc.gov/exhibits/mead/images/fieldnotes/0044_gif.html.

This puppet, like the chicken puppet (cat. no. 129), was purchased in Buleleng, North Bali. Margaret Mead wrote that she encountered some of the most imaginative puppets in the north. Many of the puppets that she collected from this region depict subjects that do not derive from the Hindu epics. They include characters from local folk tales and depictions of villagers, animals, and performers. This puppet depicts two *legong* dancers who wear the characteristic headdresses and carry fans like those often used in performance. Their costumes vary in some ways from *legong* dance costumes found in South Bali; this distinction could represent either a regional variation or the whim of the artist. The bodies of the puppets are articulated in three sections, so that when the strings are pulled, the dancers move their torsos.

NR

130 Two dancing girls, *legong* dancers, approx. 1930–1938

Buleleng, North Bali

Hide, wood, string, plant fiber, metal, gilt

L (with rod): 17¼ in; L: 15 in; W: 12⅜ in

American Museum of Natural History, 70.0/800

GLOSSARY

ABIMANYU (SANSKRIT: ABHIMANYU), son of Arjuna in the Mahabharata

ADIPARWA (SANSKRIT: ADI PARVA), first book of the Mahabharata

AGAMA, religion

AGAMA TIRTA, religion of holy water, a name for the Balinese religion

AIRLANGGA, king of east Java in the eleventh century, son of a Balinese father and Javanese mother

AMAD MOHAMAD OR AHMAD MUHAMMAD, an Islamic tale enacted in Balinese dance-drama

AMERTA (SANSKRIT: AMRITA), elixir of life, nectar of the gods that grants immortality

ANANTABOGA (SANSKRIT: ANANTABHOGA), sacred cosmic naga (mythical serpent)

ANGGAPAN, small knife used to harvest rice

ARCA, statue

ARCA LINGGA, statue that is a receptacle for a deity

ARJA, a genre of sung dance drama

ARJUNA, the third of the Pandawa (Sanskrit: Pandava) brothers in the Mahabharata

ARJUNAWIWAHA, "Arjuna's Wedding," an 11th-century Javanese poem

BABAD DALEM, a chronicle of Balinese kings of Gelgel

BADE, cremation tower (see also WADAH)

BADUNG, a former kingdom, now a regency in Southern Bali

BAJRA (SANSKRIT: VAJRA), ritual object, with prongs at either end of a short stick

BALE, elevated pavilion

BALE GUMI, cremation pavilion

BALI AGA, inhabitants of the highland villages of central Bali, considered the original inhabitants of Bali

BALIAN, healer

BALIAN USADA, healer whose knowledge is based on sacred lontar books

BANASPATI RAJA, "Lord of the Forest" another name for barong ket

BANJAR, neighborhood association

BANJI, basket weave or repeated swastika pattern

BANTEN, offering

BANTEN CANANG, offering consisting of a small palm leaf container with flowers and betel quid ingredients

BARONG, a class of mostly animal-like protective spirits; also a mask with attached costume often animated by two dancers

BARONG BANGKAL, boar barong

BARONG GAJAH, elephant barong

BARONG KET, a lionlike barong

BARONG LANDUNG, protective effigies in the shape of giant male and female figures

BARONG MACAN, tiger barong

BARONG SINGA, lion barong

BARUNA (SANSKRIT: VARUNA), Balinese god of the ocean

BASUKI (SANSKRIT: VASUKI), king of the naga (mythical serpents)

BATARA (SANSKRIT: BHATTARA), god, also spelled Bhatara

BATARA GURU, an epithet for Siwa (Sanskrit: Shiva) as Supreme Teacher

BATARA SEDANA, god of wealth, consort of Dewi Sri

BATARI (SANSKRIT: BHATTARI), a goddess, also spelled Bhatari

BAYU, (SANSKRIT: VAYU), god of the wind

BEBALI, a genre of mostly handspun textiles with a ritual function

BEGAWAN BREGU, see BREGU

BETEL, the leaf of the *Piper* betle plant; a mild stimulant made from the betel leaf, *areca* nut, and the mineral slaked lime (calcium hydroxide)

BHUJANGGA, see RSI BHUJANGGA

BIJAKSARA, sacred syllables

BIMA (SANSKRIT: BHIMA), a Pandawa (Sanskrit: Pandava) brother in the Mahabharata

BOKOR, a round bowl with a low flaring rim often used to hold offerings

BOMA (SANSKRIT: BHAUMA), son of the earth goddess and Wisnu (Sanskrit: Vishnu); his face is often used to ornament temple gateways

BRAHMAN OR BRAHMANA, the highest ranked of the four castes; associated with priests

BREGU (SANSKRIT: BHRIGU), the Balinese god of cockfighting, one of the seven great sages created by Brahma

BUANA AGUNG, the "great world," the macrocosmic world of the outer environment

BUANA ALIT, the "little world," the microcosmic world of the individual

BULELENG, former kingdom, now a regency in northern Bali

BUTA, also spelled bhuta, demonic spirits

BUTA KALA, demonic spirits

BUTA YADNYA, rituals directed toward demonic forces

CALONARANG, an exorcistic story that is the basis for the Barong and Rangda dance drama

CANANG, betel quid, and a small offering containing betel quid

CANDI, name used for Hindu and Buddhist temples in Java

CANDI BENTAR, split gate, often in a temple wall

CARATAN, spouted water vessel

CARU, offering for netherworld deities

CENIGA, a coconut leaf decoration serving as a base for offerings

CEPUK, sacred cloth made with the ikat technique

CILI, human-shaped fertility figures, sometimes representing the rice goddess

CINTIA, also Acintia, the inconceivable supreme deity, sometimes represented by a stylized figure of a man with one foot raised and hands clasped in front of the chest

DADIA, clan

DALANG, master puppeteer

DANAU, lake

DENPASAR, capital of Bali, former capital of the kingdom of Badung

DESA, place, village

DEWA (SANSKRIT: DEVA), god

DEWA YADNYA, rituals directed toward the gods

DEWI (SANSKRIT: DEVI), goddess

DEWI KUNTI, mother of the three eldest Pandawa (Sanskrit: Pandava) brothers in the Mahabharata

DEWI MELANTING, goddess of seeds

DEWI PERTIWI (SANSKRIT: PRITHIVI), goddess of the earth

DEWI SRI (SANSKRIT: SHRIDEVI), goddess of rice and fertility

DHYANAMUDRA, a gesture of meditation with hands in the lap, palms turned upward

DRUA, a snake member of Rama's army in Balinese versions of the Ramayana

DWIJAKANGKA (SANSKRIT: KANKA), the name taken by Yudistira (Sanskrit: Yudhishthira) during exile

DULANG, footed wooden tray

DURGA, consort of Siwa (Sanskrit: Shiva), associated with the temple of death

ENDEK, Balinese textile made with the weft ikat technique

GALUNGAN, a ten-day-long Balinese holiday, occurring every 210 days, in which the deified ancestors return to visit

GAMBUH, a type of dance drama; the oldest surviving theatrical genre in Bali

GAMELAN, musical ensembles primarily composed of metallophones and percussive instruments

GAMELAN SEMAR PAGULINGAN, a type of gamelan once reserved for the nobility, associated with the sleeping chambers of the king

GARUDA, mythical bird and the mount of Wisnu (Sanskrit: Vishnu)

GARUDA MUNGKUR, decorative ornament shaped like a Garuda head, often found on the rear of a headdress

GARUDEYA, a story derived from the Mahabharata telling of the feats of Garuda

GEBOGAN, a type of offering

GELGEL, a former Balinese kingdom, particularly powerful in the sixteenth century

GELUNGAN, headdress

GERINGSING, a type of double-ikat textile in which the threads of both the warp and weft have been dyed with a pattern before the cloth is woven

GIGIN BARONG, "teeth of a barong," a decorative motif of triangles

GOAKSA, a crow-headed character in Balinese versions of the Ramayana

GUNUNG, mountain

GUNUNG AGUNG, the most sacred mountain in Bali

HANOMAN (SANSKRIT: HANUMAN), the monkey hero of the Ramayana

IBU PERTIWI, see Dewi Pertiwi

IKAT, a method of textile ornamentation in which the pattern is dyed into the threads before weaving

INDRA, Hindu god and king of the heavens

ISWARA (SANSKRIT: ISHVARA), a manifestation of the Hindu god Siwa (Sanskrit: Shiva)

JABA, outside; also another name for sudra, or the caste of the majority of Balinese

JATAYU (SANSKRIT: JATAYUS), the heroic vulture of the Ramayana

JAUK, a male genre of masked dance, presenting demonic characters

JAYAPANGUS, Balinese king reigning in the late twelfth century

JEJAITAN, palm leaf constructions made for ritual purposes

JEMBRANA, former kingdom, now a regency in western Bali

JEMPANA, palanquin

JERIMPEN, tall cylindrical offerings

JERO GEDE, the main male character of the barong landung

JERO LUH, the main female character of the barong landung

KAIN, cloth, lower garment

KAIN PRADA, cloth decorated with gold

KAJA, upridge, toward the mountains

KAJANG, ritual cloth used in death rituals

KALA, time

KALA, demonic spirits

KALA, god of time and death; see also BUTA KALA

KALA RAHU (SANSKRIT: RAHU), demon who plays a part in myths about the eclipse

KALIKA, a follower of Durga

KAMA (SANSKRIT: KAMADEVA), also known as Semara, god of love

KAMASAN, village in the Klungkung regency known for its community of painters

KAMBEN, waist cloth

KANDA EMPAT, the four "spirit siblings," unseen spiritual companions that are thought to accompany an individual from the womb throughout life; they are linked to the amniotic fluid, blood, *vernix caseosa,* and afterbirth

KARANG, motif or arrangement; a rock or reef motif

KARANG BINTULU, one-eyed monster motif

KARANG TAPEL, mask motif

KARANG GOAK, crow motif

KARANGASEM, former kingdom, now a regency in eastern Bali

KARTIKEYA, son of Siwa (Sanskrit: Shiva) and Parwati (Sanskrit: Parvati)

KAWI, the Old Javanese language and idioms derived from it

KAWITAN, kin group or origin group

KEBYAR, energetic style of village-based gamelan developed in the early twentieth century

KEKAWIN, also spelled kakawin, Old Javanese metrical poem

KELOD, downridge, toward the sea

KEPENG, Chinese coins with hole in the center used in Balinese offerings

KETIPAT, rice cooked inside a packet of plaited coconut leaves

KORAWA (SANSKRIT: KAURAVA), the antagonists of the Mahabharata

KORI AGUNG, large gateway

KRISNA OR KRESNA (SANKRIT: KRISHNA), an avatar of the Hindu god Wisnu (Sanskrit: Vishnu)

KRIS, dagger

KSATRIA (SANSKRIT: KSHATRIYA), caste associated with rulers and warriors

KULKUL, split drum

KUMBAKARNA (SANSKRIT: KUMBHAKARNA), the demon brother of Rawana (Sanskrit: Ravana) in the Ramayana

KUMARA, god of infants in Bali, probably in some way related to the Sanskrit Kumara/Kartikeya

KUNINGAN, the last day of Guningan, when the deified ancestors depart

KUWERA (SANSKRIT: KUBERA), god of wealth and a directional deity

LAMAK, a rectangular hanging used as a base for offerings and as decoration for altars or shrines; also used to describe an apron-like component of dance costumes
LAMAK SABLON, permanent silkscreened lamak
LAKSMANA (SANSKRIT: LAKSHMANA), brother of Rama in the Ramayana
LASEM, town along the north coast of Central Java, an important early port
LEGONG, a dance performed by young girls
LEMBU, bull, or a sarcophagus shaped in the form of a bull
LENGKA (SANSKRIT: LANKA), kingdom of Rawana (Sanskrit: Ravana)
LEYAK, demonic spirits associated with sorcery
LONTAR, a type of palm, leaves are used in offerings and for manuscripts
LUDRA (SANSKRIT: RUDRA), a fierce aspect of Siwa (Sanskrit: Shiva)

MACARU, see CARU
MADURA, island off the northeastern coast of Java
MAHABHARATA, a Sanskrit epic poem, popular throughout Southeast Asia, revolving around the conflict between the Pandawas (Sanskrit: Pandavas) and their cousins the Korawas (Sanskrit: Kauravas)
MAHADEWA (SANSKRIT: MAHADEVA), deity associated with the mountains, especially Gunung Agung; can be considered a manifestation of Siwa (Sanskrit: Shiva)
MAJAPAHIT, an East Javanese dynasty founded in 1293 and falling in the early sixteenth century
MAKARA, mythical aquatic creature whose head with upturned nose is often found on architectural ornaments
MALAT, tales of courtly romance revolving around Prince Panji, and other members of the East Javanese royal courts
MALUKU, also known as the Moluccas, islands in the eastern Indonesian archipelago, source of valuable spices
MANTRA, ritual incantation
MANUSA YADNYA, life cycle rituals
MAWINTEN, a consecration ritual of a pemangku priest
MELASTI, ritual cleansing in the sea or a body of holy water
MELAYU, kingdom in southwestern Sumatra, mentioned in inscriptions between the 7th and 13th centuries
MERU, sacred mountain of Indic mythology
MERU, a shrine with an odd number of tiered roofs
MUDRA, symbolic gesture often of the hands

NAGA, mythical serpent
NAGA BANDA, large bamboo and wood dragonlike serpent used in royal cremation ceremonies
NAGARAJA, serpent king
NAGARAKRTAGAMA, a court chronicle of the east Javanese Majapahit dynasty
NAWA SANGA, the concept of the cosmic space and its division into nine, the eight directions of the compass plus the center
NGABEN, cremation ritual
NILARUDRAKA (SANSKRIT: TARAKASUR), a powerful demon
NINI, bundle of rice stems used as a temporary residence for the rice goddess
NISKALA, the world of unseen spiritual forces
NYEPI, Balinese lunar new year's day

ODALAN, temple anniversary festival
ONGKARA (SANSKRIT: AUM OR OM), a sacred syllable

PACANANGAN, a box with compartments for the ingredients of a betel quid
PADI, rice on the stalk
PADMA, lotus
PADMASANA, lotus throne, a raised stone shrine with empty seat for deities; also a crosslegged position
PALINGGIH, seat for the visit of the gods
PAMURTIAN, wrathful form of a deity
PANDAWA (SANSKRIT: PANDAVA), the five heroic brothers of the Mahabharata epic
PANDE, metalworker
PANDE, the name of the clan or descent group associated with blacksmiths
PANDE MAS, goldsmith
PANJI, hero prince of the Malat
PARARATON, Javanese text describing the history of the Singasari and Majapahit dynasties
PARBA, painted wooden panel sometimes used as the back of a pavilion
PARISADA HINDU DHARMA INDONESIA, official organization for Hindu affairs

PASEK, the largest Balinese clan or descent group
PASOPATI (SANSKRIT: PASHUPATA), magic weapon given to Arjuna in the Mahabharata
PATOLA, Indian textiles with double ikat designs, imported cloths were considered heirlooms in Indonesia
PATRA, situation
PATRA, plant motifs
PATRA CINA, foliate motif, thought to derive from Chinese designs
PATA SARI, a meandering floral motif
PATRA SAMBLUNG, vegetal scroll pattern
PATULANGAN, sarcophagus in the shape of an animal
PATULANGAN LEMBU, sarcophagus in the shape of a bull
PEDANDA, high priest of the Brahman caste
PEDANDA BUDA, a high priest of the Brahman caste whose rituals include Buddhist as well as Saivite elements
PEDANDA ISTRI, female high priest of the Brahman caste
PEDANDA SIWA, high priest of the Brahman caste
PENASAR, jester or clown-servant
PENJOR, arching bamboo poles decorated with palm leaf ornaments
PEMANGKU, a priest with lower level of consecration than a high priest (pedanda)
PERTIWI (SANSKRIT: PRITHIVI), earth goddess
PIS BOLONG, Chinese coins with hole in the center used in Balinese offerings
PITA MAHA, an art association founded in 1936 in Ubud by Walter Spies, Rudolf Bonnet, Cokorda Agung Gede Sukawati, and a number of Balinese artists
PITRA YADNYA, rituals directed toward the ancestors
POLENG, a black and white checked textile with spiritual significance
POROSAN, a betel quid
PRALINGGA, statue that is a receptacle for a deity
PRASASTI, inscription
PRATIMA, statue that is a receptacle for a deity
PUPUTAN, finishing or ending; the name given to the mass actions in which Balinese rulers and their courts marched into enemy fire or took their own lives rather than surrender
PURA, Balinese temple
PURA BESAKIH, the most important state temple of Bali, located on the slopes of Mount Agung
PURA DALEM, death temple
PURA DESA, village temple
PURA PUSEH, navel temple, for the worship of village founders
PURI, palace
PUSAKA, sacred heirloom

RAKSASA (SANSKRIT: RAKSHASA), powerful demon
RAMAYANA, a Sanskrit epic poem, popular throughout Southeast Asia, revolving around Rama and the abduction of his wife, Sita, by the demon king Rawana (Sanskrit: Ravana)
RAMBUT SEDANA, deity of wealth, also known as Batara Sedana
RANGDA, literally widow, but also refers to a wrathful female deity
RANGGA LAWE, a historical romance relating episodes from the history of the Majapahit dynasty
RANGKESARI, Prince Panji's beloved princess in the Malat
RATIH (SANSKRIT: RATI), goddess of love, consort of Semara
RAWANA (SANSKRIT: RAVANA), demon king who kidnaps Sita, the wife of Rama in the Ramayana
RERAJAHAN, magic drawings
RSI, title for some priests of non-Brahman castes
RSI BHUJANGGA, a priest from the bhujangga waisnawa clan, of the sudra caste
RSI YADNYA, ritual for priests
RUMBING, leaf-shaped earrings worn by men
RWA BHINEDA, a doctrine of duality and the balance of opposing forces

SAMBU (SANSKRIT: SHAMBU), a manifestation of Siwa (Sanskrit: Shiva)
SAMPIAN, a decorative palm leaf construction made of coconut leaf fronds
SANGGING, artist
SANGKU, a holy water vessel with straight sides
SANTI, an implement of a Buddhist priest
SANGKARA (SANSKRIT: SHANGKARA), Balinese deity of vegetation, a manifestation of Siwa (Sanskrit: Shiva)
SAPTA RSI (SANSKRIT: SAPTA RISHI), seven great sages created by Brahma
SAPUT, a secondary waistcloth worn over a kamben on formal occasions
SARASWATI (SANSKRIT: SARASVATI), goddess of learning
SARPAMUKA, a monkey with a snake-face in Indonesian versions of the Ramayana
SEKALA, the seen world

SEMARA, also known as Kama, god of love
SENDI, base or socle for an architectural pillar
SENGGUHU, a type of priest who often conducts rites for demonic forces, of the sudra caste
SESIMPING, shoulder cover for a dancer's costume
SINGA (SANSKRIT: SINGHA), lion
SINGASARI, an East Javanese dynasty (1222–1292)
SIRIH, the Indonesian name for the betel (*Piper betle*) plant; also used to describe the betel quid and its components as a whole
SIWA (SANSKRIT: SHIVA), a Hindu deity, highest god of the Balinese Hindu pantheon
SMARADAHANA, an Old Javanese poem describing the god of love's destruction by Siwa (Sanskrit: Shiva)
SONGKET, a textile with supplementary metallic threads woven into the weft
SRI SEDANA, Dewi Sri and Batara Sedana as a pair
STUPA, a Buddhist dome shaped monument or reliquary
SUBALI (SANSKRIT: VALI), one of the rival monkey king brothers in the Ramayana
SUBENG, plug-like jewelry for the lobes of the ear
SUDAMALA, a story derived from the Mahabharata, often linked to purification rituals
SUDRA (SANSKRIT: SHUDRA), caste associated with commoners
SUGRIWA (SANSKRIT: SUGRIVA), one of the rival monkey king brothers in the Ramayana
SULINGGIH, priests who have undergone the highest level of consecration
SUPIT URANG, style of hair resembling the pincers of a crab that is seen on wayang-style depictions of characters from the Hindu epics
SUPRABA (SANSKRIT: SUPRABHA), a heavenly nymph; Arjuna's wife in the Arjunawiwaha
SWAMBA, a rounded holy water pot

TABANAN, former kingdom, now a regency in south central Bali
TANTRI, animal fables derived from the Indian Panchatantra or similar Javanese or Balinese compilations
TELEK, a form of masked dance; telek dancers may accompany Rangda in performances
TENGET, sacred or spiritually charged
TIRTA, holy water
TRIAKSARA, three sacred syllables, ang, ung, mang, used in Balinese ritual
TRIWANGSA, the three upper castes
TRIMURTI, the deities Siwa (Sanskrit: Shiva), Wisnu (Sanskrit: Vishnu) and Brahma
TUKANG, artisan
TUKANG BANTEN, specialist in offering making
TUMPAL, a pattern of interlocking triangular designs often found on textiles
TUMPEK WAYANG, sacred day for musical instruments, dance equipment, puppets and puppeteers
TWALEN, a god in the guise of a jester-like servant and advisor to the protagonists in depictions of the Hindu epics

UMA, consort of Siwa (Sanskrit: Shiva)

WADAH, funerary tower
WAHANA (SANSKRIT: VAHANA), mount or vehicle for a deity
WANGSA (SANSKRIT: VANGSA), caste
WARNA (SANSKRIT: VARNA), caste
WAYANG KULIT, painted and perforated shadow puppets
WAYANG PARWA, shadow puppet repertoire based on the Mahabharata
WAYANG WONG, a form of dance drama often enacting episodes of the Ramayana
WEDUNG, ceremonial knife
WESIA (SANSKRIT: VAISHYA), caste associated with merchants and minor officials
WIBHISANA (SANSKRIT: VIBHISHANA), brother of Rawana (Sanskrit: Ravana) in the Ramayana
WILMANA, the mount of the demon Rawana (Sanskrit: Ravana)
WINATA (SANSKRIT: VINATA), mother of Garuda
WIRATA (SANSKRIT: VIRATA), the king with whom the Pandawa (Sanskrit: Pandava) brothers spent a year in exile
WISNU (SANSKRIT: VISHNU), the Hindu deity, also known in the form of his avatars, Rama and Krisna (Sanskrit: Krishna)

YADNYA, rituals
YAMA, Hindu god of the underworld
YUDISTIRA (SANSKRIT: YUDHISHTHIRA), the eldest of the Pandawa (Sanskrit: Pandava) brothers in the Mahabharata

BIBLIOGRAPHY

Acri, Andrea. "Shaivism in Ancient Indonesia: The Sanskrit-Old Javanese 'Tutur' Literature from Bali." *The Drama Review* 45, no. 3 (Autumn 2001), 51–77.

Adini, Ni Made Mawi. "Siapa suka lamak sablon?" *Sarad: Majalah gumi Bali* 1, no. 1 (January 2000): 7–8.

———. "Siapa suka lamak sablon?" *Sarad: Majalah gumi Bali* 1, no. 4 (April 2000): 10–11.

Agung Rai Gallery of Fine Art. *Selected Paintings from the Collection of the Agung Rai Fine Art Gallery*. Edited by Abby Ruddick. Peliatan: Agung Rai Fine Art Gallery, 1992.

Angelino, P. de Kat. "Barong op Djawa." *Djawa* 4 (1924): 140–141.

———. "Over de smeden eneenige andere ambachtslieden op Bali." *Tijdschrift voor indische taal-, land- en volkenkunde* 60; 61 (1921): 140–141, 370–424.

Angelino, P. de Kat, and Tyra de Kleen. *Mudra's op Bali: Handhoudingen der priesters*. 's Gravenhage: Adi-Poestaka, 1922.

Angst, Walter. *Wayang Indonesia: die phantastische Welt des indonesischen Figurentheaters*. 1st ed. Konstanz: Stadler, 2007.

Aravamuthan, T.G. *Portrait Sculpture in South India*. London: India Society, 1931.

Ardika, I Wayan. "Archaeological Traces of the Early Harbour Town." In *Burials, Texts and Rituals*, edited by Brigitta Hauser-Schäublin and I Wayan Ardika, 1:149–157. Göttinger Beiträge zur Ethnologie. Göttingen: Universitätsverlag Göttingen, 2008.

———. "Blanjong: An Ancient Port Site in Southern Bali, Indonesia." In *Form, Macht, Differenz: Motive und Felder ethnologischen Forschens*, edited by Elfriede Hermann, Karin Klenke, and Michael Dickhadt, 251–258. Göttingen: Universitätsverlag Göttingen, 2009.

Ardika, I Wayan, and Peter Bellwood. "Sembiran: The Beginnings of Indian Contact with Bali." *Antiquity* 65, no. 247 (1991): 221–232.

Ariyanto, Marianne. "Gambuh: The Source of Balinese Dance." *Asian Theatre Journal* 2, no. 2 (Autumn 1985): 221–230.

Bali: Further Studies in Life, Thought, and Ritual. The Hague: W. van Hoeve, 1969.

Bali: Kringloop van het leven: Tentoonstelling, 17 December 1965–31 Mei 1966, Ethnografisch Museum-Delft. Delft: Ethnografisch Museum Delft, 1965.

Bali: Studies in Life, Thought, and Ritual. The Hague: W. van Hoeve, 1960.

BALI: "Celebration in Pura Desa Batuan," Wayang Wong #1, 2009. http://www.youtube.com/watch?v=Q3wQ-frKDIc&feature=youtube_gdata.

Balische kunst uit eigen bezit. Amsterdam: Tropenmuseum, Amsterdam, 1952.

Ball, Katherine. *Animal Motifs in Asian Art: An Illustrated Guide to Their Meanings and Aesthetics*. Mineola, NY: Dover Publications, 2004.

Bandem, I Made. "Topeng in Contemporary Bali." In *Mask, The Other Face of Humanity*, 1–18. Quezon City, Philippines: Rex Bookstore, Inc., 2002.

Bandem, I Madé, and Fredrik Eugene DeBoer. *Balinese Dance in Transition: Kaja and Kelod*. 2nd ed. Kuala Lampur; NY: Oxford University Press, 1995.

Barth, Fredrik. *Balinese Worlds*. Chicago: University of Chicago Press, 1993.

Bataviaasch Genootschap van Kunsten en Wetenschappen. *Verhandelingen van het Bataviaasch Genootschap der Kunsten en Wetenschappen*. Vol. 21. Batavia: Egbert Heemen, 1847.

Bateson, Gregory. "An Old Temple and a New Myth." *Djawa* 17 (1937): 291–307.

Baum, Vicki. *A Tale from Bali*. New York: The Literary Guild, 1938.

Bellwood, Peter. "The Origins and Dispersals of Agricultural Communities in Southeast Asia." In *Southeast Asia: From Prehistory to History*, 21–40. London; NY: Routledge-Curzon, 2004.

Belo, Jane. *Rangda and Barong*. Vol. 16. Monographs of the American Ethnological Society. Locust Valley, NY: Augustin, 1949.

Bernet Kempers, A. J. *Bali Purbakala*. Djakarta: Penerbitan dan Balai Buku Indonesia, 1956.

———. *Monumental Bali: Introduction to Balinese Archaeology & Guide to the Monuments*. Berkeley; Singapore: Periplus Editions, 1991.

———. *The Kettledrums of Southeast Asia: A Bronze Age World and Its Aftermath*. Vol. 10. Modern quaternary research in Southeast Asia. Rotterdam: Balkema, 1988.

Bintarti, D. D. "Analisis Fungsional Nekara Perunggu dari Lamongan, Jawi Timur." In *Pertemuan ilmiah arkeologi III (PIA III), Ciloto, 22–23 Mei 1983*, 81–91. Jakarta: Proyek Penelitian Purbakala, Jakarta, Departemen Pendidikan dan Kebudayaan, 1985.

———. "Hasil penelitian benda-benda perunggu dan besi di Indonesia." In *Rapat evaluasi hasil penelitian arkeologi I, Cisarua, 8–13 Maret 1982*, 79–98. Jakarta: Pusat Penelitian Arkeologi Nasional, 1983.

Bloembergen, Marieke. *Colonial Spectacles: the Netherlands and the Dutch East Indies at the World Exhibitions, 1880–1931*. Singapore: Singapore University Press, 2006.

———. *De koloniale vertoning: Nederland en Indië op de wereldtentoonstellingen (1880–1931)*. Amsterdam: Wereldbibliotheek, 2002.

Bodrogi, Tibor. *Kunst van Indonesië*. Den Haag: Gaade, 1971.

Bonnet, Rudolf. "Beeldende Kunst in Gianjar." *Djawa* 16 (1936): 60–73.

Boon, James A. "Review: Bali: An Entree via the Mosque." *Current Anthropology* 36, no. 5 (December 1995): 884–886.

Bosch, F. D. K. "De inscriptie op het Aksobhya-beeld van Gondang Lor." *Tijdschrift voor Indische Taal-, Land- en Volkenkunde* 59 (1920): 498–528.

Brakel, J., David Van Duuren, and I. C. van Hout. *A Passion for Indonesian Art: The Georg Tillmann (1882–1941) Collection at the Tropenmuseum, Amsterdam*. Amsterdam: Royal Tropical Institute, 1996.

Brakel, Koos van. *Charles Sayers, 1901–1943: Pioneer Painter in the Dutch East Indies*. Amsterdam: KIT Publishers, 2004.

Brandes, J. "Een Buddhistisch monniksbeeld, en naar aanleiding daarvan het een en ander over eenige der voornaamste mudrás." *Tijdschrift voor indische taal-, land- en volkenkunde* 48 (1906): 37–56.

Brinkgreve, Francine. "Balinese Rulers and Colonial Rule: The Creation of Collections, and Politics." In *Indonesia: The Discovery of the Past*, edited by Endang Sri Hardiati and Pieter ter Keurs, 122–145. Amsterdam: KIT Publishers, 2006.

———. *De lamak als loper van bergtop naar mensenwereld: betekenis van regionale verschillen in materialen, kleuren en motieven van rituele decoraties op Bali*. Leiden: Oosters Genootschap in Nederland, 1996.

———. "Offerings to Durga and Pretiwi in Bali." *Asian Folklore Studies* 56, no. 2 (1997): 227–251.

———. "The Woven Balinese Lamak Reconsidered." In *Weaving Patterns of Life: Indonesian Textile Symposium 1991: [held from August 26th to August 30th 1991 in Basel]*, edited by Marie-Louise Nabholz-Kartaschoff, Ruth Barnes, and David J Stuart-Fox, 135–153. Basel: Museum of Ethnography, 1993.

———. "W. O. J. Nieuwenkamp en zijn vorstelijke leeuwendoosje." *Aziatische Kunst* 36, no. 3 (September 2006): 2–15.

Brinkgreve, Francine, and Itie van Hout. "Java: Gifts, Scholarship and Colonial Rule." In *Indonesia: The Discovery of the Past*, edited by Endang Sri Hardiati and Pieter ter Keurs, 100–121. Amsterdam: KIT Publishers, 2006.

Brinkgreve, Francine, and David Stuart-Fox. "Collecting after Colonial Conflict: Badung and Tabanan 1906–2006." In *Colonial Collections Revisited*, edited by Pieter ter Keurs, 145–185. CNWS Publications, 2007.

———. *Offerings: The Ritual Art of Bali*. Sanur, Bali: Image Network Indonesia, 1992.

Brownrigg, Henry. *Betel Cutters from the Samuel Eilenberg Collection*. New York: Thames and Hudson, 1992.

Budaya Indonesia: kunst en cultuur in Indonesië/Arts and Crafts in Indonesia. Amsterdam: Tropenmuseum/Royal Tropical Institute, 1987.

Budiarti, Hari, and Francine Brinkgreve. "Court Arts of the Sumatran Sultanates." In *Sumatra: Crossroads of Cultures*, edited by Francine Brinkgreve and Retno Sulistianingsih, 121–151. Leiden: KITLV Press, 2009.

Callenfels, P. V. van Stein. "Epigraphica Balica: I." *Verhandelingen van het Bataviaasch Genootschap van Kunsten en Wetenschappen* 66, no. 3 (1926).

Calò, Ambra. *The Distribution of Bronze Drums in Early Southeast Asia: Trade Routes and Cultural Spheres*. BAR International Series 1913. Oxford: Archaeopress, 2009.

Carpenter, Bruce W. *Javanese Antique Furniture and Folk Art: The David B. Smith and James Tirtoprodjo Collections*. Singapore: Editions Didier Millet, 2009.

———. *W. O. J. Nieuwenkamp: First European Artist in Bali*. Singapore: Periplus Editions, 1997.

Christie, Jan Wisseman. "Texts and Textiles in 'Medieval' Java." *Bulletin de l'Ecole française d'Extrême-Orient* 80, no. 1 (1993): 181–211.

Clune, Frank. *To the Isles of Spice with Frank Clune: A Vagabond Voyage by Air from Botany Bay to Darwin, Bathurst Island, Timor, Java, Celebes and French Indo-China*. Sydney: Angus and Robertson, 1940.

Coast, John. *Dancing Out of Bali*. Singapore: Periplus Editions, 2004.

Coldiron, Margaret. *Trance and Transformation of the Actor in Japanese Noh and Balinese Masked Dance-drama*. Lewiston, NY: E. Mellen Press, 2004.

Cool, Wouter. *De Lombok expeditie*. Batavia: G. Kolff, 1896.

Cooper, Thomas L. *Sacred Painting in Bali: Tradition in Transition*. Bangkok: Orchid Press, 2006.

Covarrubias, Miguel. *Island of Bali*. New York: Alfred A. Knopf, 1937.

———. *The Eagle, the Jaguar, and the Serpent: Indian Art of the Americas*. 1st ed. New York: Knopf, 1954.

Creese, Helen. "Balinese Babad as Historical Sources; A Reinterpretation of the Fall of Gelgel." *Bijdragen tot de Taal-, Land- en Volkenkunde* 147, no. 2 (1991): 236–260.

———. *In Search of Majapahit: The Transformation of Balinese Identities*. Clayton, Vic.: Monash University, Monash Asia Institute, 1997.

———. "Ultimate Loyalties: The Self-Immolation of Women in Java and Bali." *Bijdragen tot de taal-, land- en volkenkunde van Nederlandsch-Indië* 157, no. 1 (2001): 131–166.

———. *Women of the Kakawin World*. Armonk, NY: M. E. Sharpe, 2004.

Creese, Helen, Darma Putra, and Henk Schulte Nordholt, eds. *Seabad Puputan Badung: Perspektif Belanda dan Bali*. 1st ed. Jakarta: Pustaka Larasan, 2006.

Crucq, K. C. *Bijdrage tot de kennis van het Balisch doodenritueel*. Santpoort: C.A. Mees, 1928.

Danandjaja, James. *Kebudayaan petani Desa Trunyan di Bali*. Jakarta: Pustaka Jaya, 1980.

Dapperen, J.W. van. "Het padimesje." *Nederlandsch-Indië Oud & Nieuw* 15, no. 9 (January 1931): 257–289.

Data sarana kebudayaan daerah Bali. Denpasar, Bali: Dinas Kebudayaan Propinsi Daerah Tingkat I Bali, 1988.

Davies, Stephen. "Balinese Legong: Revival or Decline?" *Asian Theatre Journal* 23, no. 2 (Fall 2006): 314–341.

———. *Musical Works and Performances*. Oxford: Oxford University Press, 2001.

———. "The Origins of Balinese Legong." *Bijdragen tot de Taal-, Land- en Volkenkunde* 164, no. 2 (2008): 194–211.

De kunst van Bali: verleden en heden. Den Haag: Haags Gemeentemuseum, 1961.

DeBoer, Fredrik E., I Made Bandem, and I Ketut Madra. "'The Death of Kumbakarna' of I Ketut Madra: A Balinese Wayang Ramayana Play." *Asian Theatre Journal* 9, no. 2 (Autumn 1992): 141–200.

DeVale, Sue Carole, and I Wayan Dibia. "Sekar Anjar: An Exploration of Meaning in Balinese Gamelan." *The World of Music* 33, no. 1 (1991): 5–55.

Dibia, I Wayan, and Rucina Ballinger. *Balinese Dance, Drama and Music: A Guide to the Performing Arts of Bali*. Illustrated edition. Singapore: Periplus Editions, 2004.

Dongen, Paul L. F. van, Matthi Forrer, and William R. van Gulik, eds. *Topstukken uit het Rijkmuseum voor Volkenkunde/Masterpieces from the National Museum of Ethnology*. Leiden: Rijksmuseum voor Volkenkunde, 1987.

Dunningham, Margaret M. *The Barongs of Bali: Rangda and Other Temple Rituals, Observations of the Balinese Folk Religion*. Point Wells, New Zealand: Dunningham, 1974, 196.

Duuren, David van. *Krisses: A Critical Bibliography*. Ext. and impr. ed. Wijk en Aalburg, The Netherlands: Pictures Publishers, 2002.

———. *The Kris: An Earthly Approach to a Cosmic Symbol*. Wijk en Aalburg, The Netherlands: Pictures Publishers, 1998.

Eerde, J.C. van. *Gids voor de tentoonstelling betreffende Oud-Javaansch en hedendaagsch Balisch Hindoeïsme*. Amsterdam: Kolonial Instituut, 1915.

———. "Hindu-Javaansche en Balische eeredienst." *Bijdragen tot de taal-, land- en volkenkunde*, 65 (1911): 1–39.

Eggebrecht, Eva. *Versunkene Königreiche Indonesiens*. Edited by Arne Eggebrecht. Mainz: P. von Zabern, 1995.

Eiseman, Fred B., Jr. *Bali, Sekala and Niskala, Vol. 1: Essays on Religion, Ritual, and Art*. 4th ed. Berkeley: Periplus Editions, 1996.

———. *Bali, Sekala and Niskala, Vol. 2: Essays on Society, Tradition, and Craft*. Revised. Berkeley: Periplus Editions, 1996.

———. *Woodcarvings of Bali*. Berkeley: Periplus Editions, 1988.

Ekawana, I Gusti Putu. "Sawa Widhana dalam Prasasti Bali." In *Proceedings Analisis Hasil Penelitian Arkeologi I*, 178–193. Jakarta: Departemen Pendidikan dan Kebudayaan, 1990.

Encyclopaedie van Nederlandsch-Indie. 's-Gravenhage: Nijhoff, 1917.

Endt, Ireen van der. "Van Koninklijke Slaapkamer naar Rommelzolder: een Beschrijving van de Semar Pagulingan in het Tropenmusem." Amsterdam: Universiteit van Amsterdam, 1996.

Ethnographische Kostbarkeiten: Aus den Sammlungen von Alfred Buhler im Basler Museum für Völkerkunde. Basel: Museum für Völkerkunde, 1970.

Exposition universelle internationale de 1900 à Paris: Guide à travers la section des Indes Néerlandaises, groupe XVII (colonisation). La Haye: Nijhoff, 1900.

Fadillah, Moh. Ali. "L'art ancien des mimbar dans les mosquées de Bali." *Archipel* 44, no. 1 (1992): 95–114.

Ferdinandus, Pieter. *The Role of Musicians During the Old Javanese and Balinese Period*. Jakarta: Pusat Penelitian Arkeologi Nasional Proyek Penelitian Arkeologi Jakarta, 2000.

Fischer, Joseph. "Balinese Embroideries." *Jurnal seni* VIII, no. 4: 333–348.

———. *Story Cloths of Bali*. Berkeley: Ten Speed Press, 2004.

Fischer, Joseph, and Thomas L. Cooper. *The Folk Art of Bali: The Narrative Tradition*. Kuala Lumpur; New York: Oxford University Press, 1998.

Fontein, Jan. *The Sculpture of Indonesia*. Washington, DC; New York: National Gallery of Art; H. N. Abrams, 1990.

Forge, Anthony, and Australian Museum. *Balinese Traditional Paintings: A Selection from the Forge Collection of the Australian Museum, Sydney*. Sydney: Australian Museum, 1978.

Fossey, Claire. *Rangda, Bali's Queen of the Witches*. Bangkok: White Lotus, 2008.

Fraser, J. J. "De Weefkunst in de afdeeling Boeleleng (Bali)." *Tijdschrift voor het Binnenlandsch Bestuur* 35 (1908): 324–333.

Gamelan Semar Pegulingan; Naxos Digital Services. *INDONESIA Gamelan Semar Pegulingan Music from Bali*. Hong Kong: Naxos Digital Services Ltd., 2008.

Geertz, Hildred. *Images of Power: Balinese Paintings Made for Gregory Bateson and Margaret Mead*. Honolulu: University of Hawai'i Press, 1994.

———. *Kinship in Bali*. Chicago: University of Chicago Press, 1975.

———. *Tales from a Charmed Life: A Balinese Painter Reminisces*. Honolulu: University of Hawai'i Press, 2005.

———. *The Life of a Balinese Temple: Artistry, Imagination, and History in a Peasant Village*. Honolulu: University of Hawai'i Press, 2004.

Gids voor den bezoeker van de Indische tentoonstelling in het Stedelijk Museum te Amsterdam. Amsterdam: Stedelijk Museum, 1901.

Gittinger, Mattiebelle. *To Speak with Cloth: Studies in Indonesian Textiles*. Los Angeles: Museum of Cultural History, University of California, 1989.

Glover, Ian, and Peter Bellwood, eds. *Southeast Asia from Prehistory to History*. London; New York: RoutledgeCurzon, 2004.

Gold, Lisa. *Music in Bali: Experiencing Music, Expressing Culture*. New York: Oxford University Press, 2005.

Gomperts, Amrit, Arnoud Haag, and Peter Carey. "Rediscovering the Royal Capital of Majapahit." *IIAS Newsletter* 53 (Spring 2010): 12–13.

Gonda, J. *Sanskrit in Indonesia*. 2nd ed. New Delhi: International Academy of Indian Culture, 1973.

Goris, R. *Bali: Atlas Kebudajaan; Cults and Customs; Cultuurgeschiedenis in beeld*. 's-Gravenhage: W. van Hoeve, 1955.

———. *Bijdrage tot de kennis der oud-javaansche en balineesche theologie*. Leiden: A. Vros, 1926.

———. *Prasasti Bali*. 2 vols. Bandung: N. V. Masa Baru, 1954.

———. *Sekte-sekte di Bali*. Jakarta: Bhratara, 1974.

———. "The Position of the Blacksmiths." In *Bali: Studies in Life, Thought, and Ritual*. The Hague: W. van Hoeve, 1960, 289–299.

Goslings, B. M. *Gids in het Volkenkundig Museum, II. Bali en Lombok*. Amsterdam: Koninklijke Vereeninging Koloniaal Instituut, 1927.

Gottowik, Volker. *Die Erfindung des Barong: Mythos, Ritual und Alterität auf Bali*. Berlin: Reimer, 2005.

Gouda, Frances. *Dutch Culture Overseas: Colonial Practice in the Netherlands Indies, 1900–1942*. Singapore: Equinox Publishing (Asia), 2008.

Goudriaan, Teun, and Christiaan Hooykaas. *Stuti and Stava (Bauddha, Śaiva and Vaisnava) of Balinese Brahman Priests*. Verhandelingen der Koninklijke Nederlandse Akademie van Wetenschappen, Afd. Letterkunde, nieuwe reeks 76. Amsterdam: North-Holland Pub. Co., 1971.

Groeneveldt, W. P. "Hindoe-Javaansche portretbeelden." *Tijdschrift voor Indische Taal-, Land- en Volkenkunde* 50 (1907): 140–146.

Groneman, I. *In den Kedaton te Jogjakarta: oepatjara, ampilan en toneeldansen*. Leiden: E. J. Brill, 1888.

———. *The Javanese kris*. Leiden: C. Zwartenkot Art Books and KITLV Press, 2009.

Hagerdal, Hans. "Bali in the Sixteenth and Seventeenth Centuries; Suggestions for a Chronology of the Gelgel Period." *Bijdragen tot de Taal-, Land- en Volkenkunde* 151, no. 1 (1995): 101–124.

Hamilton, Roy. www.lunacommons.org, February 25, 2010. http://www.lunacommons.org/luna/servlet/detail/MOAC~100~1~122652~17268:Textile,-chair-covering-Indonesia?qvq=q:bali+fowler;lc:AMICO~1~1,BardBar~1~1,ChineseArt-ENG~1~1,CORNELL~3~1,CORNELL~9~1,ESTATE~2~1,FBC~100~1,HOOVER~1~1,JCB~1~1,LTUHSS~20~20,MOAC~100~1,PRATTPRT~12~12,PRATTPRT~13~13,PRATTPRT~21~21,PRATTPRT~9~9,RUMSEY~8~1,RUMSEY~9~1,Stanford~6~1&mi=39&trs=83.

———. *The Art of Rice: Spirit and Sustenance in Asia*. Los Angeles: UCLA Fowler Museum of Cultural History, 2003.

Hamzuri. *Petunjuk Singkat tentang Keris*. 2nd ed. Jakarta: Proyek Pengembangan Museum Nasional Departemen Pendidikan & Kebudayaan, 1983.

Hardiati, Endang Sri, and Pieter ter Keurs, eds. *Indonesia: The Discovery of the Past*. Amsterdam: KIT Publishers, 2006.

Hauser-Schäublin, Brigitta. "'Bali Aga' and Islam: Ethnicity, Ritual Practice, and 'Old-Balinese' as an Anthropological Construct." *Indonesia* 77 (April 2004): 27–55.

———. "Sembiran and Julah Sketches of History." In *Burials, Texts and Rituals*, edited by Brigitta Hauser-Schäublin and I Wayan Ardika, 1:9–68. Göttinger Beiträge zur Ethnologie. Göttingen: Universitätsverlag Göttingen, 2008.

Hauser-Schäublin, Brigitta, and I Wayan Ardika, eds. *Burials, Texts and Rituals*. Vol. 1. Göttinger Beiträge zur Ethnologie. Göttingen: Universitätsverlag Göttingen, 2008.

Hauser-Schäublin, Brigitta, Marie-Louise Nabholz-Kartaschoff, and Urs Ramseyer. *Textiles in Bali*. Berkeley; Singapore: Periplus Editions, 1991.

Hegemann, Hans-Werner. *Schnitzkunst und Plastik aus Indonesien aus dem Reichsmuseum für Völkerkunde Leiden, Holland*. Erbach: Deutschen Elfenbeinmuseum, 1977.

Heringa, Rens. "Tilling the Cloth and Weaving the Land: Textiles, Land and Regeneration in an East Javanese Area." In *Weaving Patterns of Life: Indonesian Textile Symposium 1991: [held from August 26th to August 30th 1991 in Basel]*, edited by Marie-Louise Nabholz-Kartaschoff, Ruth Barnes, and David J. Stuart-Fox, 155–176. Basel: Museum of Ethnography, 1993.

Hinzler, H. I. R. *Catalogue of Balinese Manuscripts: In the Library of the University of Leiden and Other Collections in the Netherlands*. 2 vols. Leiden: E. J. Brill, 1986.

Hirsch, Philip, and Carol Warren. *The Politics of Environment in Southeast Asia*. London: Routledge, 1998.

Hobart, Angela. *Aesthetics in Performance: Formations of Symbolic Construction and Experience*. New York: Berghahn Books, 2005.

———. *Balinese Shadow Play Figures: Their Social and Ritual Significance*. London: British Museum Dept. of Ethnography, 1985.

———. *Dancing Shadows of Bali*. London; New York: KPI; Distributed by Methuen Inc. Routledge & Kegan Paul, 1987.

———. *Healing Performances of Bali: Between Darkness and Light*. New York: Berghahn Books, 2003.

———. *The Peoples of Bali*. Oxford: Blackwell Publishers, 1996.

Hobart, Mark. "Rethinking Balinese Dance." *Indonesia and the Malay World* 35, no. 101 (2007): 107–128.

Hoevell, G. W. W. C. van "Kleine Notizen und Correspondenz." *Internationales Archiv für Ethnographie* 17 (1905): 221.

Hollander, Hanneke. *Een man met een speurdersneus: Carel Groenevelt (1899–1973), beroepsverzamelaar voor Tropenmuseum en Wereldmuseum in Nieuw-Guinea*. Amsterdam: KIT Publishers, 2007.

Hoop, A. N. J. Th. à Th. van der. *Indonesische Siermotieven/Ragam-ragam perhiasan Indonesia/Indonesian ornamental design*. Jakarta: Koninklijk Bataviaasch Genootschap van Kunsten en Wetenschappen, 1949.

———. "De ethnografische verzamling." *Jaarboek Koninklijk Bataviaasch Genootschap von Kunsten en Wetenschappen* 8 (1941).

Hooykaas, Christiaan. *A Balinese Temple Festival*. Bibliotheca Indonesica 15. The Hague: Martinus Nijhoff, 1977.

———. *Agama Tirtha: Five Studies in Hindu-Balinese Religion*. Amsterdam: N. V. Noord-Hollandsche uitgevers maatschappij, 1964.

———. *Balinese Bauddha Brahmans*. Vol. 80. Verhandelingen der Koninklijke Nederlandse Akademie van Wetenschappen, Afd. Letterkunde, nieuwe reeks. Amsterdam: North-Holland Pub. Co., 1973.

———. *Drawings of Balinese Sorcery*. Leiden: E. J. Brill, 1980.
———. "Pamurtian in Balinese Art." *Indonesia* 12 (October 1971): 1–20.
———. "Patola and Gringsing: An Additional Note." *Bijdragen tot de Taal-, Land- en Volkenkunde* 134, no. 2 (1978): 356–359.
———. "Santi: A Ritualistic Object from Bali." *Asia Major* 11, no. 1 (1964): 78–83.
———. *Surya-Sevana: The Way to God of a Balinese Siva Priest*. Verhandelingen Koninklijke Nederlandse Akademie van Wetenschappen, Afd. Letterkunde, nieuwe reeks, dl. 72, no. 3. Amsterdam: Noord-Hollandsche U. M., 1966.
———. *Tantri Kāmandaka: een Oudjavaansche Pañtjatantra-Bewerking*. Bandoeng: Nix und Co., 1931.
———. *Tovenarij op Bali: magische tekeningen uit twee Leise collecties*. Amsterdam: Meulenhoff, 1980.
Hooykaas, Jacoba. "The Balinese Realm of Death." *Bijdragen tot de Taal-, Land- en Volkenkunde* 112 (1956): 74–87.
Howe, L. E. A. "An Introduction to the Cultural Study of Traditional Balinese Architecture." *Archipel* 25, no. 1 (1983): 137–158.
Howe, Leo. *Hinduism & Hierarchy in Bali*. Oxford: James Currey, 2001.
———. *The Changing World of Bali: Religion, Society and Tourism*. London: Routledge, 2005.
I Ketut Budiana: Illusory View from the Balinese Spiritual Cosmos. Tokyo: Tokyo Station Gallery, 2003.
Jacknis, Ira. "Margaret Mead and Gregory Bateson in Bali: Their Use of Photography and Film." *Cultural Anthropology* 3, no. 2 (1988): 160.
Jasper, J. E., and Mas Pirngadie. *De inlandsche kunstnijverheid in Nederlandsch Indië IV, De goud- en zilversmeedkunst*. 's-Gravenhage: Mouton, 1927.
———. *De inlandsche kunstnijverheid in Nederlandsch Indië V, De bewerking van niet-edele metalen koperbewerking en pamorsmeedkunst*. 's-Gravenhage: Mouton, 1930.
Jenkins, Ron, and I Nyoman Catra. "Taming the Tourists: Balinese Temple Clowns Preserve Their Village Traditions." *On Tourism* 2, no. 2 (January 16, 1998): 23–27.
Jessup, Helen Ibbitson. *Court Arts of Indonesia*. New York: Asia Society Galleries in association with H. N. Abrams, 1990.
Juynboll, H. H. *Catalogus van 's Rijks Ethnographisch Museum 7, Bali en Lombok*. Leiden: E. J. Brill, 1912.
———. "De geschiedenis van Garuda." In *Koninklijk Instituut voor Taal- Land- en Volkenkunde van Nederlandsch-Indië: Gedenkschrift uitgegeven ter gelegenheid van het 75-jarig bestaan op 4 Juni 1926*. 's-Gravenhage: Nijhoff, 1926.
———. *Gids voor de tentoonstelling van ethnographische voorwerpen van Bali*. Vol. 16. Publicatie uit 's Rijks Ethnographisch Museum 2. Leiden: Van Doesburgh, 1907.
Kal, Pienke. *Yogya Silver: Renewal of a Javanese Handicraft*. Amsterdam: KIT Publishers, 2005.
Kaler, I Gusti Ketut. *Ngaben: mengapa mayat dibakar?* 1st ed. Denpasar: Yayasan Dharma Naradha, 1993.
Kam, Garrett. *Perceptions of Paradise: Images of Bali in the Arts*. Ubud: Yayasan Dharma Seni Museum Neka, 1993.
Kanwa, Mpu. *Arjunawiwaha: The Marriage of Arjuna*. Translated by S. O. Robson. Leiden: KITLV Press, 2008.
Karitiwa, Suwati, ed. *Treasures of the National Museum, Jakarta*. Jakarta: Buku Antar Bangsa, 1997.
Kaset-siri, Charnvit. "The Statement of Chinkak on Bali." *Indonesia* 7 (1969): 83.
Kern, H. "De Sanskrit-inscriptie van 't Mahaksobhya-beeld te Simpang." *Tijdschrift voor Indische Taal-, Land- en Volkenkunde* 52 (1910): 99–108.
———. "Naschrift." *Internationales Archiv für Ethnographie* 10 (1897): 160.
Kern, Hendrik. "De Nagarakrtagama." In *Verspreide geschriften: onder zijn toezicht verzameld*, VIII:1–32. 's-Gravenhage: Nijhoff, 1918.
Keurs, Pieter ter, ed. *Colonial Collections Revisited*. Leiden: CNWS Publications, 2007.

Khan Majlis, Brigitte. *Indonesische textilien: wege zu Göttern und Ahnen*. Stadt Köln: Rautenstrauch-Joest-Museum für Völkerkunde, 1984.
Klokke, Marijke. *The Tantri reliefs on Ancient Javanese Candi*. Leiden: KITLV Press, 1993.
Kraan, Alfons. *Bali at War: A History of the Dutch-Balinese Conflict of 1846–49*. Clayton, Vic.: Centre of Southeast Asian Studies, Monash University, 1995.
Kraan, Alfons van der. "Bali: Slavery and Slave Trade." In *Slavery, Bondage, and Dependency in Southeast Asia*, edited by Anthony Reid, 315–340. New York: St. Martin's Press, 1983.
———. "Human Sacrifice in Bali: Sources, Notes, and Commentary." *Indonesia* 40 (October 1985): 89–121.
Krause, Gregor. *Bali: Geist, Kunst und Leben Asiens, erster Teil: Land und Volk, zweiter Teil: Tänze, Tempel, Feste*. Hagen: Folkwang-Verlag G.m.b.H, 1920.
Krom, N. J. "Levensbericht van C.M. Pleyte Wzn." *Jaarboek van de Maatschappij der Nederlandsche Letterkunde te Leiden* (1919): 5–25.
Kruyt, Alb. C. "De rijstmoeder inder Indischen Archipel." *Verslagen en Mededeelingen der Koninklijke Akademie van Wetenschappen. Afdeeling Letterkunde*. 4e, no. 5 (1903): 361–411.
Kunst, Jaap. *Hindu-Javanese Musical Instruments*. 2nd ed. Koninklijk Instituut voor Taal-, Land- en Volkenkunde translation series 12. The Hague: Martinus Nijhoff, 1968.
Kusumawati, Ayu. "Catatan tentang tempat pengerjaan logam di Budaga dan hubungannya dengan upacara agama di Bali." In *Pertemuan ilmiah arkeologi III (PIA II), 25–29 Pebruari 1980 di Jakarta*, 749–755. Jakarta: Proyek Penelitian Purbakala, Jakarta, Departemen Pendidikan dan Kebudayaan, 1982.
de Laat, Sonya. "Multipicilty of Balinese Characters." *Nexus* 16, no. 1 (2003): 1–17.
Langewis, Laurens. "A Woven Balinese Lamak." In *Lamak and Malat in Bali and A Sumba Loom*, 31–47. Amsterdam: Royal Tropical Institute, 1956.
Lansing, J. S., A. J. Redd, T. M. Karafet, J. Watkins, and I. W. Ardika. "Reply [to: 'Indian traders in Ancient Bali: A Reconsideration of the Evidence']." *Antiquity* 80, no. 307 (March 2006). http://antiquity.ac.uk/projgall/lansing/index.html#response.
Lansing, John Stephen. *Evil in the Morning of the World: Phenomenological Approaches to a Balinese Community*. Ann Arbor: Center for South and Southeast Asian Studies, University of Michigan, 1974.
———. "Foucault and the Water Temples." *Critique of Anthropology* 20, no. 3 (2000): 309–318.
———. *Priests and Programmers: Technologies of Power in the Engineered Landscape of Bali*. Princeton: Princeton University Press, 1991.
———. *The Three Worlds of Bali*. New York: Praeger, 1983.
Lefèvre, Vincent. *Lumières de soie: soieries tissées d'or de la collection Riboud: exposition, Paris, Musée national des Arts asiatiques-Guimet, 27 oct. 2004–24 janv. 2005*. Paris: Réunion des Musées Nationaux, 2004.
Leidelmeijer, Frans. *Art deco beelden van Bali (1930–1970): van souvenir tot kunstobject*. Zwolle: Waanders, 2006.
Lekkerkerker, Cornelis. *Bali en Lombok: overzicht der litteratuur omtrent de eilanden tot einde 1919*. Rijswijk: Blankwaardt en Shoonhoven, 1920.
Liefrinck, F. A. "Balische Godenbeelden." In *Feestbundel van taal-, letter-, geschied- en aardrijkskundige bijdragen ter gelegenheid van zijn tachtigsten geboortedag aan Dr. P. J. Veth, door eenige vrienden en oud-leerlingen aangeboden*, 205–208. Leiden: E. J. Brill, 1894.
Limburg Stirum, O. J. H. Graaf van. "Reisindrukken van Bali, meer in het bijzonder van Boeleleng en Bangli." *Tijdschrift van het Nederlansch Aardrijkskundig Genootschap*, 2e 4 (1887): 3–33.
Loebèr, J. A. Jr. *Been-, hoorn- en schildpadbewerking en het vlechtwerk in Nederlandsch-Indië*. Geillustreerde beschrijving van Indische kunstnijverheid 7. Amsterdam: Koloniall Instituut, 1916.

Lohuizen-de Leeuw, J. E. van. "The Dikpalakas in Ancient Java." *Bijdragen tot de Taal-, Land- en Volkenkunde* 111 (1955): 356–384.
Lovric, Barbara. "Bali: Myth, Magic, and Morbidity." In *Death and Disease in Southeast Asia: Explorations in Social, Medical and Demographic History*, edited by Norman G. Owen, 117–141. Melbourne: Asian Studies Association of Australia, 1987.
Lueras, Leonard. *Fire: A Balinese Journey of the Soul*. Gianyar, Indonesia: Yayasan Sekar Manggis, 1994.
Lunsingh Scheurleer, Pauline, ed. *Asiatic Art in the Rijksmuseum*. Amsterdam: Meulenhoff/Landshoff, 1985.
Lunsingh Scheurleer, Pauline. "Skulls, Fangs, and Serpents: A New Development in East Javanese Iconography." In *Southeast Asian archaeology 1998: Proceedings of the 7th International Conference of the European Association of Southeast Asian Archaeologists, Berlin, 31 August–4th September 1998*, edited by Wibke Lobo and Stefanie Reimann, 189–204. Hull Centre for South-East Asian Studies University of Hull; Berlin: Ethnologisches Museum, Staatliche Museen zu Berlin Stiftung Preussischer Kulturbesitz, 2000.
———. "The Javanese Statue of Garuda Carrying Wisnu and Candi Kidal." *Artibus Asiae* 69, no. 1 (2009): 189–218.
Lunsingh Scheurleer, Pauline, and Marijke J. Klokke. *Ancient Indonesian Bronzes: A Catalogue of the Exhibition in the Rijksmuseum Amsterdam with a General Introduction*. Leiden; New York: E. J. Brill, 1988.
MacRae, Graeme. "The Value of Land in Bali: Land Tenure, Landreform [sic], and Commodification." In *Inequality, Crisis and Social Change in Indonesia: The Muted Worlds of Bali*, edited by Thomas Reuter, 143–165. London; New York: RoutledgeCurzon, 2003.
Majlis, Brigitte Khan. *The Art of Indonesian Textiles*. New Haven, CT: Yale University Press, 2007.
Mann, Richard I. *Treasures of Bali: A Guide to Museums in Bali*. Jakarta: Gateway Books International, published in collaboration with the Museums Association of Bali (HIMUSBA), 2006.
"Manuscript Catalog," n.d. http://anthro.amnh.org/anthropology/databases/common/catno_page.cfm?catno=70%2E0%2F%208231&curr_page=&from_anthro=yes&show_portfolio=yes.
Martin, Petra. "Was die Natur und der Mensch des merkwurdigen Tropenlandes erzeuren ...: Wolf Curt von Schierbrand und seine Sammlungen." *Kleine Beiträge aus dem Staatlichen Museum für Völkerkunde Dresden* 17 (1999).
Masquelier, Adeline. *Dirt, Undress, and Difference: Critical Perspectives on the Body's Surface*. Bloomington: Indiana University Press, 2005.
Maxwell, Robyn. *Sari to Sarong: Five Hundred Years of Indian and Indonesian Textile Exchange*. Canberra: National Gallery of Australia, 2003.
———. *Textiles of Southeast Asia: Tradition, Trade and Transformation*. Revised. Hong Kong: Periplus, 2003.
McPhee, Colin. *A House in Bali*. New York: John Day, 1946.
———. *A House in Bali*. Kuala Lumpur: Oxford University Press, 1979.
———. *Music in Bali; a Study in Form and Instrumental Organization in Balinese Orchestral Music*. New Haven: Yale University Press, 1966.
Mead, Margaret. "Notes of Field Catalogue of Balinese Shadow Play Puppets." Library of Congress, Manuscript Reading Room, Margaret Mead Papers, 1937. http://www.loc.gov/exhibits/mead/images/fieldnotes/0044_gif.html.
Mershon, Katharane Edson. *Seven Plus Seven: Mysterious Life Rituals in Bali*. New York: Vantage Press, 1971.
Michiels van Verduynen, L. *Verslag der Centrale Commissie tot inrichting van de afdeelingen van Nederland en zijne koloniën en tot behartiging van de belangen der inzenders in die afdeelingen op de wereldtentoonstelling te Parijs in 1900*. 's-Gravenhage, 1902.
Miksic, John. *Icons of Art*. 1st ed. [Menteng, Jakarta]: BAB Pub. Indonesia, 2006.

Moens, J. L. "Een Boddhapratista." *Tijdschrift voor Indische Taal-, Land- en Volkenkunde* 60 (1921): 78–85.

———. "Het Berlijnsche Ardhanari-beeld en de bijzettings beelden van Krtanagara." *Tijdschrift voor Indische Taal-, Land- en Volkenkunde* 73 (1933): 123–150.

———. "Hindu-Javaansche portretbeelden: Çaiwapratista en Boddhapratista." *Tijdschrift voor Indische Taal-, Land- en Volkenkunde* 58 (1919): 493–527.

Moojen, Pieter Adriaan Jacobus. *Kunst op Bali, Inleidende Studie tot de Bouwkunst*. Den Haag: Adi Poestaka, 1926.

Mookerjee, Ajit, and Madha Khanna. *The Tantric Way: Art, Science, Ritual*. Boston: New York Graphic Society, 1977.

Nabholz-Kartaschoff, Marie-Louise. "A Preliminary Approach to Cepuk Cloths from South Bali and Nusa Penisda." In *Indonesian Textiles: Symposium 1985*, 123–131. Cologne: Ethnologica, 1991.

———. "A Sacred Cloth of Rangda: Kamben Cepuk of Bali and Nusa Penida." In *To Speak with Cloth*, edited by Mattiebelle Gittinger, 181–197. Los Angeles: UCLA Fowler Museum of Cultural History, 1989.

———. "Cepuk: Sacred Textiles from Bali and Nusa Penida." In *Textiles in Bali*, 94–114. Berkeley; Singapore: Periplus, 1991.

———. "The Textiles of Sembiran." In *Burials, Texts and Rituals*, edited by Brigitta Hauser-Schäublin and I Wayan Ardika, 69–117. Göttingen: Universitätsverlag Göttingen, 2008.

Naerssen, F. H. van. "Oudjavaansche oorkonden in Duitsche en Deensche verzemelingen." Leiden: Universiteit Leiden, 1941.

Nala, Ngurah. *Aksara Bali dalam Usada*. 1st ed. Surabaya: Pāramita, 2006.

Neka, Suteja. *The Development of Painting in Bali: Selections from the Neka Art Museum*. 2nd ed. Ubud, Bali, Indonesia: Yayasan Dharma Seni Museum Neka, 1998.

Nerina de Silva. "The analysis and conservation of a newly-found drum from Lumajang, Java." In *Southeast Asian Archaeology 1990: Proceedings of the Third Conference of the European Association of Southeast Asian Archaeologists*, edited by Ian Glover, 227–232. Hull: Centre for South-East Asian Studies, 1992.

Neuhaus, Hans. "Barong." *Djawa* 17 (1937): 230–241.

Nieuwenkamp, W. O. J. *Bali en Lombok: uitvoerige geillustreerde reisherinneringen en studies omtrent land en volk, kunst en kunstnijverheid*. Edam: De Zwerver, 1906.

———. *Beeldhouwkunst van Bali*. 's-Gravenhage: H. P. Leopold, 1928.

———. *Bouwkunst en beeldhouwkunst van Bali*. 34. pl. 48. 48. 's-Gravenhage, 1947.

———. *Bouwkunst van Bali*. Inlandse kunst van Nederlandsch Oost-Indië 1. 's-Gravenhage: Leopold, 1926.

———. *Een Florentijnsche villa: "Riposo dei Vescovi" S. Domenico di Fiesole bij Florence*. 's-Gravenhage: Leopold, 1938.

———. *Inlandsche Kunst Van Nederlandsch Oost-Indië*. 's-Gravenhage: H. P. Leopold, 1926.

———. *Zwerftochten op Bali*. Amsterdam: Elsevier, 1910.

Noszlopy, Laura. Untitled review in *Journal of the Royal Asiatic Society* 14, no. 3. Third series (November 2004): 287–289.

Oja, Carol. *Colin McPhee: Composer in Two Worlds*. Washington: Smithsonian Institution Press, 1990.

Ottino, Arlette. *The Universe Within: A Balinese Village through Its Ritual Practices*. Paris: Karthala, 2000.

Pameran patung singa koleksi Museum Bali. Denpasar: Museum Bali, 1978.

Panji, I G. B. N., and I Made Bandem. *Ensiklopedi Musik dan Tari daerah Bali*. Jakarta: Departemen Pendidikan dan Kebudayaan Proyek Penerbitan Buku Bacaan dan Sastra Indonesia dan Daerah, 1979.

Parkin, Harry. *Batak Fruit of Hindu Thought*. Madras: Christian Literature Society, 1978.

Patera, I Wayan. "Sanggah Dawin in the Life of Pacung Community." In *Burials, Texts and Rituals*, edited by Brigitta Hauser-Schäublin and I Wayan Ardika, 1:119–128. Göttinger Beiträge zur Ethnologie. Göttingen: Universitätsverlag Göttingen, 2008.

Pelras, Ch. "Lamak et tissus sacres de Bali." *Objets et Mondes* 8, no. 4 (1967): 255–278.

Picard, Michel. *Bali: Cultural Tourism and Touristic Culture*. Singapore: Archipelago, 1996.

———. "The Discourse of Kebalian." In *Staying Local in the Global Village*, edited by Raechelle Rubinstein and Linda Connor, 15–50. Honolulu: University of Hawaii Press, 1999.

———. "What's in a Name? Agama Hindu Bali in the Making." In *Hinduism in Modern Indonesia: A Minority Religion between Local, National, and Global Interests*, edited by Martin Ramstedt, 56–75. London; New York: RoutledgeCurzon, 2004.

Pigeaud, Th. *Java in the 14th Century: A Study in Cultural History*. 5 vols. The Hague: Martinus Nijhoff, 1960.

———. *Literature of Java: Catalogue Raisonné of Javanese Manuscripts in the Library of the University of Leiden and Other Public Collections in the Netherlands*. Leiden: Leiden University Press, 1980.

Pleyte, C. M. "Herinneringen uit Oost-Indie: Bali." *Tijdschrift van het Nederlansch Aarddrijkskundig Genootschap, 2e* 18 (1901): 34–66, 233–259, 584–627, 909–931.

Pleyte, C.M. *Indonesian art: Selected Specimens of Ancient and Modern Art and Handwork from the Dutch Indian Archipelago*. The Hague: Nijhoff, 1901.

Pollman, Tessel. "Margaret Mead's Balinese: The Fitting Symbols of the American Dream." *Indonesia* 49 (October 1989): 1–35.

Prapanca, Mpu. *Desawarnana: (Nagarakrtagama)*. Translated by S. O. Robson. Leiden: KITLV Press, 1995.

Pringle, Robert. *A Short History of Bali: Indonesia's Hindu Realm*. Crows Nest, N. S. W.: Allen & Unwin, 2004.

Putra, Ny. I Gst. Ag. Mas. *Upakara Yadnya*. Denpasar, 1974.

Ramseyer, Urs. *Clothing, Ritual and Society in Tenganan Pegeringsingan (Bali)*. Basel, Switzerland: Birkhäuser, 1984.

———. *The Art and Culture of Bali*. New ed., with pictorial emendations. Basel: Museum der Kulturen Basel, 2002.

Ramseyer, Urs, and Marie-Louise Nabholz-Kartaschoff. "Songket: Golden Threads, Caste and Privilege." In *Textiles in Bali*, 32–50. Berkeley; Singapore: Periplus Editions, 1991.

Ramseyer, Urs, and I Gusti Panji Trisna, eds. *Bali: Living in Two Worlds: a Critical Self-Portrait*. Basel: Museum der Kulturen, Basel; Schwabe, 2001.

Ramstedt, Martin, ed. *Hinduism in Modern Indonesia: A Minority Religion between Local, National, and Global Interests*. London; New York: RoutledgeCurzon, 2004.

Rao, T. A. Gopinatha. *Elements of Hindu Iconography*. 2 vols. Madras: The Law Printing House, 1904.

Ratzel, Friedrich. *Völkerkunde, Zweiter Band: Die Naturvölker Ozeaniens, Amerikas und Asiens*. Leipzig: Verlag des Bibliographischen Instituts, 1886.

"Recente tentoonstellingen van Indonesische kunst te Amsterdam, Parijs, Hagan en Munchen." *Nederlandsch-Indië Oud & Nieuw* 13 (1928): 125–128.

Reuter, Thomas Anton. *Custodians of the Sacred Mountains: Culture and Society in the Highlands of Bali*. Honolulu: University of Hawai'i Press, 2002.

———. *Custodians of the Sacred Mountains: The Ritual Domains of Highland Bali*. Canberra: The Australian National University, 1996.

———. "Indonesia in Transition: Concluding Reflections on Engaged Research and the Critique of Local Knowledge." In *Inequality, Crisis and Social Change in Indonesia: The Muted Worlds of Bali*, 203–219. London; New York: RoutledgeCurzon, 2003.

———. *The House of Our Ancestors: Precedence and Dualism in Highland Balinese Society*. Leiden: KITLV, 2002.

Reuter, Thomas Anton, ed. *Inequality, Crisis and Social Change in Indonesia: The Muted Worlds of Bali*. London; New York: RoutledgeCurzon, 2003.

Rhodius, Hans. *Walter Spies and Balinese Art*. Zutphen: Published under the auspices of the Tropical Museum, Amsterdam, by Terra, 1980.

Robinson, Geoffrey. *The Dark Side of Paradise: Political Violence in Bali*. Ithaca: Cornell University Press, 1995.

Roux, C. C. F. M. "Madoereesche Krisheften." *Cultureel Indie* 8 (1946): 161–171.

Rubin, Leon, and I Nyoman Sedana. *Performance in Bali*. London: Routledge, 2007.

Sajana, Made. "Busung Bali sulit dicari." *Sarad: Madjalah gumi Bali* 1, no. 2 (2000): 58–59.

Salmon, Claudine, and Myra Sidharta. "The Hainanese of Bali: A Little Known Community." *Archipel* 60, no. 4 (2000): 87–124.

Santikarma, Degung. "The Power of 'Balinese Culture.'" In *Bali: Living in Two Worlds: A Critical Self-Portrait*, edited by Urs Ramseyer and I Gusti Panji Trisna, 27–35. Basel: Museum der Kulturen, Basel; Schwabe, 2001.

Savarese, Nicola, and Richard Fowler. "1931: Antonin Artaud Sees Balinese Theatre at the Paris Colonial Exposition." *TDR* 45, no. 3 (Autumn 2001): 51–77.

Schmelz, J. D. E. "Indonesische Prunkwaffen: Ein Beitrag zur Kunde des Kunstgewerbes in Indonesien und der ethnologischen Bedeutung des Kris." *Internationales Archiv für Ethnographie* 3 (1890): 85–118.

———. "Verslag over een bezoek ann de Wereld-tentoonstelling te Parijs in October en November 1900." In *Jaarverslag van hetRijksmuseum voor Volkenkunde*, 46–53, 1901.

Schnitger, F. M. "Een Hindo-Javaansch portretbeeld te Leiden." *Bijdragen tot de Taal-, Land- en Volkenkunde* 89 (1932): 251–252.

———. "Het portretbeeld van Anusanatha." *Bijdragen tot de Taal-, Land- en Volkenkunde* 89 (1932): 123–128.

Scholte, J. "De Slametan Entas-entas der Tenggereezen en de Memukur-ceremonie op Bali." In *Handelingen van het eerste congres voor de Taal-, Land- en Volkenkunde van Java*, 47–85. Weltevreden: Albrecht and Co., 1921.

Schulte Nordholt, Henk. *Bali, An Open Fortress, 1995–2005: Regional Autonomy, Electoral Democracy, and Entrenched Identities*. Singapore: NUS Press, 2007.

———. *The Spell of Power: A History of Balinese Politics, 1650–1940*. Leiden: KITLV Press, 1996.

Schwartz, H. J. E. F. *Gids voor den bezoeker van de ethnographische verzameling, Zaal B, Bali en Lombok*. Batavia [Indonesia]: Ruygrok & Co., 1920.

Sedyawati, Edi. "Iconographical Data from Old Javanese Kakawins." *Majalah Arkeologi* II, no. 1 (1978): 69–84.

Sibeth, Achim, ed. *Being Object, Being Art: Meisterwerke aus den Sammlungen des Museums der Weltkulturen Frankfurt am Main*. Tübingen; Frankfurt am Main: E. Wasmuth Verlag; Museum der Weltkulturen, 2009.

Siegel, Marcia B. "Liminality in Balinese Dance." *The Drama Review* 35, no. 4 (Winter 1991): 84–91.

Slattum, Judy. *Balinese Masks: Spirits of An Ancient Drama*. Hong Kong: Periplus Editions, 2003.

Smelik, J. C., C. M. Hogenstijn, and W. J. M. Janssen. *A. J. Duymaer van Twist: Gouverneur-Generaal van Nederlands-Indië (1851–1856)*. Zutphen: Walburg Pers, Deventer: Historisch Museum Deventer, 2007.

Soekatno, Endang Sri Hardiati. "Konsepsi tentang Hidup dan Kematian pada masyarakat Jawa Kuno ditinjau dari naskah." In *Proceedings Analisis Hasil Penelitian Arkeologi I*, 64–83. Jakarta: Departemen Pendidikan dan Kebudayaan, 1990.

Soekawati, Tjokorde Gde Rake. "Legende over den oorsprong van de rijst en godsdienstige gebruiken bij den rijstbouw onder de Baliers." *Tijdschrift voor Indische Taal-, Land- en Volkenkunde* 66 (1926): 423–434.

———. "Nijverheid en kunstnijverheid op Bali." *Mededeelingen van de Kirtya Liefrinck-van der Tuuk* 15 (1941).

Soekmono, R. *Candi, Fungsi dan Pengertiannya*. Jakarta: Universitas Indonesia, 1974.

———. "Perajaan "Ngasti" di Kelusu (Pejeng, Bali)." *Tijdschrift voor Indische Taal-, Land- en Volkenkunde* 85 (1957): 479–495.

Spanjaard, Helena. *Pioneers of Balinese Painting: The Rudolf Bonnet Collection*. Amsterdam: KIT Publishers, 2007.

Staal, Frits. "The Sound of Religion." *Numen* 33, no. 2 (December 1986): 185–224.

Stephen, Michele. "Barong and Rangda in the Context of Balinese Religion." *Review of Indonesian and Malaysian affairs* 35, no. 1 (2001): 137–194.

———. *Desire Divine & Demonic: Balinese Mysticism in the Paintings of I Ketut Budiana and I Gusti Nyoman Mirdiana*. Honolulu: University of Hawai'i Press, 2005.

Stingl, Heinz. *Bali: Aus dem Museum für Völkerkunde in Leipzig*. Leipzig: Prisma-Verl, 1969.

Stuart-Fox, David J. *The Art of the Balinese Offering*. Yogyakarta: Yayasan Kanisius, 1974.

———. *Bibliography of Balinese Culture and Religion: (Indonesian publications to the year 1978)*. Jakarta: Koninklijk Instituut voor Taal-Land- en Volkenkunde, 1979.

———. *Once a Century: Pura Besakih and the Eka Dasa Rudra Festival*. 1st ed. Jakarta: Penerbit Sinar Harapan and Citra Indonesia, 1982.

———. *Pura Besakih : Temple, Religion and Society in Bali*. Leiden: KITLV, 2002.

———. "Sri and Sedana at Pura Besakih, Bali." In *The Art of Rice*, edited by Roy W. Hamilton, 276–285. Los Angeles: UCLA Fowler Museum of Cultural History, 2003.

Stutley, Margaret, and James Stutley. *A Dictionary of Hinduism: Its Mythology, Folklore and Development 1500 B.C.–A.D. 1500*. London: Routledge & Kegan Paul, 1977.

Stutterheim, Willem Frederik. "Een bijzettingsbeeld van koning Rajasa." *Tijdschrift voor Indische Taal-, Land- en Volkenkunde* 79 (1939): 85–104.

———. "Enkele oudheden van Bali." *Djawa* 16 (1936): 74–87.

———. *Indian Influences in Old-Balinese Art*. London: The India Society, 1935.

———. *Oudheden van Bali*. Singaradja, Bali: Kirtya Liefrinck-van der Tuuk, 1929.

———. "Voorlopige inventaris der oudheden van Bali." *Oudheidkundig Verslag* (1925): 150–170.

———. "Voorlopige inventaris der oudheden van Bali." *Oudheidkundig Verslag* (1927): 139–150.

Suastika, I Made. "Traces of Human Life Style from the Palaeolithic Era to the Beginnings of the First Century AD." In *Burials, Texts and Rituals*, edited by Brigitta Hauser-Schäublin and I Wayan Ardika, 1:159–173. Göttinger Beiträge zur Ethnologie. Göttingen: Universitätsverlag Göttingen, 2008.

Subadio, Haryati. *Jñānasiddhânta*. Bibliotheca Indonesica 7. The Hague: Martinus Nijhoff, 1971.

Sugriwa, I Gst. Bagus. *Hari Raya Bali Hindu*. 2nd ed. Denpasar: Pustaka Balimas, 1957.

Sullivan, Gerald. *Margaret Mead, Gregory Bateson, and Highland Bali: Fieldwork Photographs of Bayung Gedé, 1936–1939*. Chicago: University of Chicago Press, 1999.

Sumner, Christina, and Milton Osborne. *Arts of Southeast Asia: From the Powerhouse Museum Collection*. Sydney: Powerhouse Museum, 2001.

Supomo, S. "The Image of Majapahit in Later Javanese and Indonesian Writing." In *Perceptions of the Past in Southeast Asia*, edited by A. Reid and David Marr, 171–185. Singapore: Heinemann Educational Books (Asia), 1979.

Surya, Rama. "Photo Essay." In *Bali: Living in Two Worlds: A Critical Self-Portrait*, edited by Urs Ramseyer and I Gusti Raka Panji Tisna, 65–93. Basel: Museum der Kulturen, Basel; Schwabe, 2001.

Sutaba, I Made. "Discovery of Late Prehistoric Burial Systems in Bali." *SPAFA journal* 9, no. 1 (Jan.–April 1999): 15–18.

———. "Newly Discovered Sarcophagi in Bali." *Archipel* 7, no. 1 (1974): 133–138.

———. "Preliminary Notes on Ancestor Statues in Bali." *Bulletin of the Indo-Pacific Prehistory Association* 16 (1997): 229–232.

Swellengrebel, J. L. "Introduction." In *Bali: Studies in Life, Thought, and Ritual*. The Hague: W. van Hoeve, 1960.

Swieten, J. van. *Krijgsverrigtingen tegen het eiland Balie in 1848*. 's Gravenhage: Doorman, 1849.

Tammens, G. J. F. J. *De Kris: Magic Relic of Old Indonesia*. 3rd ed. Eelderwolde: G. J. F. J. Tammens, 1991.

Taylor, Alison. *Living Traditions in Balinese Painting*. Peliatan, Bali: Agung Rai Gallery of Fine Art, 1991.

"Tentoonstelling van de Vereeniging 'Oost en West' van de verzameling W.O.J. Nieuwenkamp in het Stedelijk Museum te Amsterdam." *Nederlandsch-Indië Oud & Nieuw* 11 (1926): 347–352.

Tenzer, Michael. *Balinese Music*. Berkeley; Seattle: Periplus Editions, 1991.

———. *Gamelan Gong Kebyar: The Art of Twentieth-Century Balinese Music*. Chicago: University of Chicago Press, 2000.

The Asian Civilisations Museum A–Z guide to its collections. Singapore: National Heritage Board, 2003.

Thomsen, Margrit, ed. *Java und Bali: Buddhas, Götter, Helden, Dämonen*. Mainz am Rhein: P. von Zabern, 1980.

To Change Bali: Essays in Honour of I Gusti Ngurah Bagus. Denpasar: Bali Post, in association with the Institute of Socal Change and Critical Inquiry, University of Wollongong, 2000.

Tony, Fatimah Tobing. "The photogenic cannot be tamed: Margaret Mead and Gregory Bateson's Trance and Dance in Bali." *Discourse (Detroit, MI)* 28, no. 1 (Winter 2006): 5–23.

Triguna, Ida Bagus Gde Judha, I Gusti Ketut Gde Arsana, Indonesia. Bagian Proyek Penelitian, and Pengkajian dan Pembinaan Nilai-Nilai Budaya Bali. *Peralatan hiburan dan kesenian tradisional daerah Bali*. Departemen Pendidikan dan Kebudayaan, Direktorat Jenderal Kebudayaan, Direktorat Sejarah dan Nilai Tradisional, Bagian Proyek Penelitian, Pengkajian dan Pembinaan Nilai Budaya Bali, 1993.

Tuuk, H. N. van der. *Kawi-Balineesch-Nederlandsch Woordenboek*. Batavia: Landsdrukkerij, 1897.

Verslag van den Directeur ... Ministerie van Binnenlandsche Zaken, 1900.

Vickers, Adrian. *Bali, a Paradise Created*. Berkeley: Periplus Editions, 1989.

———. "Hinduism and Islam in Indonesia: Bali and the Pasisir World." *Indonesia* 44 (1987): 31.

———. *Journeys of Desire: A Study of the Balinese Text Malat*. Leiden: KITLV, 2005.

———. "The Realm of the Senses: Images of the Courtly Music of Pre-Colonial Bali." *Imago Musicæ* 2 (1985): 143–177.

———. *Travelling to Bali: Four Hundred Years of Journeys*. Kuala Lumpur; New York: Oxford University Press, 1994.

———. "When did Legong start? A reply to Stephen Davies." *Bijdragen tot de Taal-, Land- en Volkenkunde* 165, no. 1 (2009): 1–7.

Vickers, Adrian, ed. *Being Modern in Bali: Image and Change*. New Haven: Yale University Southeast Asia Studies, 1996.

Vonck, Henrice M. "The Inseparable Two: The Source of Creation in Balinese Music." In *Rhythm, A Dance in Time*, edited by Elisabeth den Otter, 37–59. Amsterdam: Royal Tropical Institute, 2001.

Voskuil, H. J. "Bij foto's van Indonesische wapens uit de verzameling Wurfbain." *Nederlandsch-Indië Oud & Nieuw* 15 (1930/1931): 379–388.

Weede, H. M. van. *Indische Reisherinneringen*. Haarlem: H.D. Tjeenk Willink, 1908.

Weinberger-Thomas, Catherine, Jeffrey Mehlman, and David Gordon White. *Ashes of Immortality*. Chicago: University of Chicago Press, 2000.

Widia, I Wayan. *Temuan nekara perunggu Banjar Panek Desa Ban Kecamatan Kubu Kabupaten Daerah Tingkat II Karangasem Bali*. (Unpublished). Denpasar: Museum Bali, 1980.

Wiener, Margaret. "Doors of Perception: Power and Representation in Bali." *Cultural Anthropology* 10, no. 4 (1995): 472.

———. *Visible and Invisible Realms: Power, Magic, and Colonial Conquest in Bali*. Chicago: University of Chicago Press, 1995.

Wijaya, Made. *Architecture of Bali: A Source Book of Traditional and Modern Forms*. Honolulu: University of Hawai'i Press, 2002.

Williams, Adriana. *Covarrubias in Bali*. Singapore: Editions Didier Millet, 2005.

Winstedt, Richard. "The Balinese Sengguhu-priest, a Shaman but not a Sufi, a Saiva, and a Vaisnava." In *Malayan and Indonesian studies essays presented to Sir Richard Winstedt on his 85th birthday*, edited by John Bastian and R. Roolvink, 267–281. Oxford: Clarendon Press, 1964.

Wirz, Paul. "Der Reisbau und die Reisbaukulte auf Bali und Lombok." *Tijdschrift voor indische taal-, land- en volkenkunde* 67 (1927): 217–346.

———. *Der Totenkult auf Bali*. Stuttgart: Strecker und Schrodër, 1928.

Woodroffe, Sir John George. *The Great Liberation*. Ganesh, 1963.

Zainalfattah. *Sedjarah Tjaranja Pemerintahan di Daerah-daerah di Kepulauan Madura dengan Hubungannja*. Pamekasan: Minerva, 1951.

Zandvliet, Kees, ed. *The Dutch Encounter with Asia, 1600–1950*. Amsterdam: Rijksmuseum, 2004.

Zimmer, Heinrich. *Myths and Symbols in Indian Art and Civilization*. The Bollingen series VI. New York: Pantheon Books, 1946.

Zoete, Beryl de, and Walter Spies. *Dance and Drama in Bali*. London: Faber and Faber, 1938.

Zoetmulder, P. *Kalangwan: A Survey of Old Javanese Literature*. The Hague: Martinus Nijhoff, 1974.

———. *Old Javanese-English Dictionary*. 's-Gravenhage: M. Nijhoff, 1982.

Zonneveld, Albert G. van. *Traditional Weapons of the Indonesian Archipelago*. C. Zwartenkot Art Books, 2001.

INDEX

Page numbers in *italics* denote illustrations; **boldface** denotes objects in the exhibition.

administrative divisions (regencies), 25–26
agriculture, 13–15, 139–41, 143, 153
Airlangga, King, 23, 36, 171, 241, 297
altar hangings (cat. 9–10), 72, 75, 83, **145**, *146*, **147**, *148–49*
Anak Wungsu, King, 23
ancestor worship
  animal bearers and, 126
  Galungan festival and, 68, 93–94
  as one element of Balinese religion, 15, 20, 21, 89
  paired figures and, 17–18, 155, 157, 161
  temple types and, 15–16
ancestral figures (cat. 15–16), 17, *154*, **155–57**, *158*, 265
animal fables. See Tantri tales
animal sacrifice, 99, 102, 113, 364
animals as deity bearers, summarized, 123–26
animism, 21, 89
architecture
  Chinese influence on, 129–30
  Garuda sculptures in, 241
  Gunung Kawi, 23
  of Javanese temples, 129, 221, 268, 285
  lion figures in, 127, 129, *131*, 181
  palace-temple parallels, 11, 27
  See also doors and gates
Arjuna. See under Mahabharata
Arjunawiwaha, 237, 239, 349
axe, ceremonial (cat. 44), *216*

Badung *puputan*. See *puputan* of Badung
barong figures
  barong ket, defined, 299
  barong ket with jauk dancers (cat. 89), *307*
  barong landung, defined, 311
  barong landung figures (cat. 95), *313*
  Chinese influence on, 11, 129, 181, 301, 311
  in Covarrubias' painting, 343
  lion puppet and, 359
  mask of Barong (cat. 86), **297**, **299**, **300**, **301**, *303*
  masks of barong landung (cat. 93–94), **311**, *312*
  mask of boar barong (cat. 91), **308**, *309*
  mask of lion barong (cat. 90), **308**, *309*
  mask of tiger barong (cat. 92), 175, **308**, *310*
  masks of, as divinities, 29–30, *94*, 171, 299
  masks of, summarized, 299, 301, 308
  of *naga* (serpents), 319
  Rangda and Barong drama, summarized, 171, 297, 299
  Siwa/Kala and, 302
  teeth of, 70, 82, 88, 108, 147, 305
Baruna, 224, 324n14
Batara Guru (cat. 101), **322–24**, *325*
Bateson, Gregory, 31, 209, 351
batik, 69, 159, 343
Baturenggong, King, 36
Baum, Vicki, 32, 216, 347, 349

bell (cat. 32), 41, *190*, **191**
betel chewing and implements
  betel cutter (cat. 69), *270*, **271**
  at court, 28–29, 122n13, 267
  ingredients, listed, 29, 89, 122, 267
  sirih boxes (cat. 68), **267–68**, *269*
  tobacco box (cat. 67), *266*, **267–68**
  See also *canang* (betel quid/offerings)
bibliography, 368–72
Bima. See under Mahabharata
bird masks (cat. 97–98), **317–18**
Blanjong inscription, 22
Boma
  on cremation towers, 209, 251
  as doorway guardian, 140, 251, 281
  sarad offerings and, 107, 108
  as son of Wisnu, 140, 330
bombings of nightclubs (2002), 33, 112, *113*
Bonnet, Rudolf, 129, 209, 347, 351–52
bowl, ceremonial (cat. 36), *196*, **197**
box, royal storage (cat. 70), 25, *272*, **273–74**
box for lontar book (cat. 40), *206*, **207**
Brahma
  Bregu as son of, 324, 328
  colors associated with, 66, 123, 324
  as four-faced, 157n10
  goose mount of, 125
  sacred syllable for, 98, 216
  Saraswati and, 82
Bregu (cat. 104), **322–24**, *328*
bronze production, early, 12, 136, 137n6, 155, 161, 193n7
Buddhism
  cult implements and, 42
  influence on Balinese Hinduism, 36, 38, 89
  introduction of, 21–22, 35
  lion figures in, 181, 221, 301, 359
  sacred syllables in, 46, 47, 214
  Sutasoma story and, 215
  See also Tantric traditions
Budiana, I Ketut, 60
Burma, 21n41, 59

calendars, 93–94, 153
Calonarang drama, 297, 299
  See also Rangda
canang (betel quid/offerings)
  composition and meaning of, 89–90, 122–23
  globe amaranth and, 64
  presentation of, 91, 335
  secularization of, 111
  on vehicles, 88, *114*
canopy, painted (cat. 47), *222*, **223–24**
caste system
  adoption of, from India, 21n43
  Brahman origins in Java, 24, 35–36, 38
  Brahman title "Ida," explained, 214
  healing profession and, 52
  kajang symbols and, 48–49, 213
  priest titles and, 37, 39

  sarcophagi shapes and, 16, 129, 181, 183, 345
  smiths' status in, 167, 257
  songket cloth and, 235
  See also royalty
ceniga hangings, *64*, 65, 67, 80, *114*
chairs (cat. 50–51), 130, 173, *232*, **233**
chicken puppet (cat. 129), *364*
Chinese coins
  gender roles and, 74
  historical summary of, 151
  on *lamak*, 61, 66, 67, 145
  in offerings, 11, 46, *48*, *91*, 96, 103, 104, 151
  on Sri Sedana figures, 14, *150*, 151
  statues made of, 120, 183
Chinese influence
  on architecture, 129–30
  on *barong* figures, 11, 129, 181, 301, 311, 343
  in general, 15, 151, 311
  Mazu (sea goddess) and, 312n4
  on woodcarving, 219, 233
  See also Chinese coins
Christians and Christianity, 15, 21, 52
cili figures
  agricultural shrines and, 14
  in Covarrubias' painting, 341
  in *lamak* embroidery, *149*
  as *lamak* motif, summarized, 72, 81–82, 145
  on *lamak nganten* (wedding), *71*, 74, 76
  on *lamak* of palm leaf, *65*, 70
  on *lamak sablon* (mass-produced), *63*, 76, 81–82, 84
  on *lamak* with mirrors and coins, *66*
  meaning of, 72, 143
  as public offerings, 88
  regional variations in, 75
  on rice cakes, 105
Cintia, 52, 58
cockfights, 99, *100*, 113–14, 139, 187, 275, 328
coin images of deities (cat. 11–14), 14, *150*, 151, *152*, 153
colonialism. See Dutch colonialism
cosmic symbols
  lotus as, 83, 178, 295–96
  naga (serpent) as, 50, 107, 175, 215, 233
  tree as, 77n16
  turtle as, 50, 107, 125, 175, 215, 233
cosmology
  cosmic directions and correspondences, 45, 96, 98–99, 102, 107, 223–24, 296
  lamak as representations of, 70, 83–84, 85
  macro- and microcosmic correspondences, 46, 69, 73, 203, 301
  mountains as cosmic axes, 13, 71, 76, 77n16, 107
  nawa sanga system, 45, 83, 224, 296
  in paintings, 60
  tree of life (*kekayonan*), 66, 68, 84, 105, 107
  unseen forces, 20, 89, 364
courtly arts, summarized, 27–30

Covarrubias, Miguel
  art collected by, 151
  barong landung figures (cat. 114), **343**, *344*
  Bebitera (cat. 111), **340**, *341*
  burial bulls (cat. 115), **345**, *346*
  cultural preservation and, 31, 32
  Djerimpeng (cat. 109), **336**, *337*
  Kbo'ogan (cat. 110), *338*, **339**
  Sanur (cat. 112), **340**, *341*
  sketch of a praying woman (cat. 108), *334*, **335**
  Tanah Bali (cat. 107), *333*
  Tegal Sibang (cat. 113), **341**, *342*
  travels to Bali, summarized, 332
  woodcarving and, 347
cremation
  ceremonies, described, 16–17, 48, *50*
  naga (serpents) and, 175
  ritual objects for, 45, 46, 48, 77
  roofed dais for cremation ritual (cat. 42), *210*, **211**
  towers, *16*, 66, 103, 209
  widows' suicide and, 231, 273n3
  See also sarcophagi
cremation shrouds (*kajang*)
  Cintia drawing style and, 59
  preparation of, 47–48
  ritual cloth for use at a cremation (cat. 43), 54, *212*, **213–15**
  sacred syllables on, 45, 46, 47, 50–51, 213–14
  symbolism of, 49–50
cricket-fighting table and bamboo tubes (cat. 71), *274*, **275**
cult implements of a Siwa high priest (cat. 32–34), 41, *190*, **191**, *192–93*

dance, *legong*
  apron for a dancer's costume (cat. 80), *291*
  crown of a dancer's costume (cat. 78), *290*
  photos of young dancers (cat. 82–83), *293*
  puppet of legong dancers (cat. 130), *365*
  shoulder covers for dancers' costumes (cat. 79, 81), *291*, *292*
  summary of, 288–89
dance, *pendet*, 40, *91*, *92*
dance dramas
  of Barong and Rangda, 29–30, 171, 297, 299, *304*
  court patronage of, 29
  gambuh performances, 25, 273, 289, 297, 314, 316
  legong and, 288, 289
  of Malat (Panji tales), 25, 30, 273, 288, 316
  wayang wong performances, 167, 301n7, 314, 316–17, 319–20
de Wit, Augusta, 307, 313
de Zoete, Beryl, 31, 288, 316, 318
death rituals
  lamak for, 74
  naga (serpents) and, 173, 175, 209

  offerings for, 16–17, 66, 93, 103–04, *105*
  palanquins, in royal funerals, 28, *29*, 237
  See also cremation; cremation shrouds (*kajang*); sarcophagi
demons
  as deities' complements, 20, 102–03
  as doorway guardians, 140, 199, 251, 281
  mantras and, 55
  offerings to, 65, 93, 94, 99, 101–03, 204, 341
  ogoh-ogoh figures, 111–12, *113*
  raksasa, 257, 358
  rituals for, 19, 40, 42, 89, 204
  wayang- vs. Cintia-style depictions of, 57–58
  See also specific demons
Dewi Melanting, 13
Dewi Pertiwi (Prithivi)
  Boma as son of, 140, 251, 330
  lamak depictions of, 71, 146
  as major deity, 13
  sarad offerings and, 107, 108
Dewi Saraswati. See Saraswati
Dewi Sri (Sri Devi)
  Anantaboga and, 360
  cili figures and, 14, 72, 105
  on *lamak*, 147, 149
  lontar figurines of Dewi Sri (cat. 6–8), 14, 72, **142**, **143**, *144*, 265
  as major deity, 13, 14
  Rambut Sedana and, 14, 151, 153, *178*
  rice harvesting and, 139
  in rice mythology, 143
  on rice sheaf paddles, 141
  sarad offerings and, 108
Djata, I Made, 209
doors and gates
  demons as guardians of, 140, 199, 251, 281
  lintel (cat. 46), **220**, **221**
  lion figures on, 127, *128*, 129, 167, 169, 217, 221
  pair of palace doors (cat. 45), 28, 121, **217**, *218*, 219
  as portals, 27, 167
  Pura Kehan gate, *28*
  stepped gateways, 11
  temple doors (cat. 22), 167, *168*, **169**
drawings of deities in the guise of priests, with demons (cat. 30–31), 187, *188–89*
drums
  as cult implements, 42
  in funeral procession, 209
  Moon of Pejeng, 12, 135, *136*
  slit drum (cat. 72), *276*, **277**
  in temple courtyard (*bale kulkul*), 67, 68, 72, 277
  tympanum of a bronze drum (cat. 1), *134*, **135–37**
dulang (cat. 37), 41, *198*, **199**, *339*
Durga
  animal vehicle of, 129
  Kalika as follower of, 329
  puppet of Batara Durga (cat. 126), *361*
  Rangda and, 112, 171–72, 297, 302, 361
  regional variations of, 18–19

Dutch colonialism
  art patronage and, 29
  art plundering and, 10, 121, 126, 219, 265
  cultural "preservation" and, 30–31, 271, 321–22
  execution of Ngendon, 352
  furniture and, 233
  governor generals, 249, 253, 254n2, 303
  Japanese photography and, 304
  palace destruction and, 26, 28, 120, 121, 217, 219
  ritual suicide ban, 231
  royal emblems and, 221
  slave trade and, 25
  Tabanan, defeat of, 26, 225, 265
  tourist art and, 193n9
  after World War II, 32
  See also puputan of Badung; puputan of Klungkung
Dutch East India Company, 10n4

ear pendants (cat. 66), 246, *264*, 265
earplugs, pair of (cat. 65), *264*, 265
earthquakes, 113, 302n16, 303
elephant mask (cat. 96), *316*
embroidery, 74, 147, 149, 200–201
environmental problems, 80, 93, 113, 115, 308

female figure (cat. 17), 17, *159*, *160–61*, 265
fertility, 11–15, 20, 71, 76, 178
  See also cili figures; Dewi Sri (Sri Devi)
footed wooden tray (cat. 37), 41, *198*, 199
funeral procession in Bali (cat. 41), *208*, 209
funerary customs. See cremation; death rituals
furniture, use of, 233

Galungan festival
  ancestor worship and, 15
  barong figures and, 299, 311, 313, 343
  lamak and, 68, 74, 75, 78, 81, 291
  pawukon calendar and, 93–94
gamelan music
  at court, 29, 278–79
  cult implements in, 42
  kulkul (slit drums) in, 277
  in photo of 1929, *304*
  in processions, 91, 112
  sarad offerings and, 108
  in temples, 9
  See also musical instruments
Gana (Ganesha), 231
Garuda
  bird masks and, 317, 318
  on court furnishings, 28, 217, 223–24
  as crown decoration, 159, 290, 324
  as Indonesian national symbol, 110
  sarad offerings and, 107, 108
  in textile designs, 261
Wisnu on Garuda (cat. 55), *240*, *241*, 243
  as Wisnu's mount, 125, 223, 241, 243, 283, 317

Gde, I Gusti Made, 297, 303
geography, 10, 11–15, 24–25, 333
glossary, 366–67
gold
  ceremonial bowl (cat. 36), *196*, *197*, 339
  court goldsmiths, 195
  ear pendants (cat. 66), *264*, 265
  earplugs, pair of (cat. 65), *264*, 265
  in textiles, 165, 291, 292, 295–96, 324
  tobacco box (cat. 67), *266*, 267–68
  water vessel (cat. 35), *194*, 195
gongs, 281
Goodbye and Good Luck to Margaret Mead and Gregory Bateson (cat. 118), *350*, 351–52
Groenevelt, Carel, 308
Gründler, Carl, 307, 313
Gunung Agung
  in Covarrubias' painting, 333
  as lamak motif, 71, 76, 77
  mythology of, 13
Gunung Kawi, 23

healers, 20, 37, 43–44, 52–56, 60, 203
Hindu epics
  bird masks and, 317
  courtly arts and, 28, 223
  dance dramas and, 30, 288
  kingship and, 23
  lamak depictions of, 147, 148
  religious practices and, 21n38, 36
  See also Mahabharata; Ramayana
Hinduism
  Balinese, as unique, 15, 20–21, 89
  Balinese vs. Indian, 18, 21
  Buddhist influence on, 36, 38, 89
  floral symbols in, 219
  Gunung Agung and, 13
  indigenous deities, 20
  introduction of, to Bali, 15, 21–22, 35–36
  lion figures in, 181, 359
  magic, in Vedic texts, 52
  orthodoxy, integration of, 83
  peacocks in, 271
  prayer rituals, summarized, 335
  Tantric influence on, 37
  Trimurti (Hindu Trinity), 66, 324
  See also cosmology; offerings; priests; and specific deities
holy water
  in Calonarang drama, 297
  ceremonial use, illustrated, *38*, *39*
  in death rituals, 17, 103
  making of, 19, 41, 43–44, 52
  presentation of offerings and, 91
  significance of, 15
  vessels for, 41, 43–44, 191, 195
Houbolt, J. A., 311

Ibu Pertiwi. See Dewi Pertiwi (Prithivi)
India
  ancient trade network and, 12–13, 21, 35, 136, 159
  Balinese vs. Indian Hinduism, 18, 21
  caste system and, 21n43
  Cintia drawing style and, 59
  Durga in, 171
  lions and, 127, 129, *178*, 221
  religious iconography and, 82–83
  swastika symbol in, 271
  textiles from, 235, 305
  time systems and, 94
Indonesia
  barong, introduction of, 301
  Dutch colonial presence in, 10, 26, 221, 253, 255
  Dutch promotion of Indonesian art, 271, 321, 322
  early civilization of, 12, 35
  food poisoning in, 109
  gamelan music in, 278
  Garuda in, 110, 241, 290
  metalworking centers in, 137n6
  religious oversight of, 20–21, 63
  rice goddesses in, 153
  Tantric traditions in, 53, 59
  textile motifs in, 235–36
  tigers in, 181, 308, 310
  after World War II, 32–33
Indra, 42, 200, 224, 229, 231, 237, 239
Islam and Muslims, 15, 21, 24, 25, 316
Iswara, 52, 98, 301

Jacobs, Julius, 307
Japanese occupation, 32, 163, 352
Java
  Arjunawiwaha and, 237, 349
  bark cloth and, 214
  batik from, 69, 159, 343
  Brahman ancestry in, 24, 35–36, 38
  bronze artifacts from, 155–56, 193n7
  ceremonial weapons in, 249
  Cintia drawing style and, 58–59
  cricket fighting in, 275
  Dewi Sri in, 153
  Durga in, 171, 302
  Dutch colonial control of, 10n4, 26, 253, 255
  Dutch promotion of Javanese culture, 321, 322
  Garuda in, 241
  geographical location of, 11
  Gunung Agung and, 13
  Majapahit dynasty, 23–24, 25, 31, 35–36, 166, 200
  musical instruments from, 136–37, 277, 281, 287
  Ngendon in, 352
  palm-leaf imports from, 80
  Sayers in, 163
  Tantri tales in, 359
  temple architecture in, 129, 221, 268, 285
  tigers in, 308
  time systems and, 93
  Udayana's alliance with, 22–23
  See also Malat (Panji tales)
Jelantik, I Gusti Ngurah Ketut, 249

kajang. See cremation shrouds (kajang)

Kala Rahu, 187, 324n14
Kaler, Made, 351, 353, 364
Kalika (cat. 105), 322–24, *329*
Kama (Semara)
  gamelan music and, 278, 279
  ritual cloth, with painting of Kama and Ratih (cat. 29), *184*, 185–86
  sarad offerings and, 107
  in Smaradahana, 186, 229, 231
Karang, Ida Nyoman, 177, 323
Kesari, King, 22
Kleiweg de Zwaan, J. P., 123, 175, 310
Klungkung puputan. See puputan of Klungkung
kneeling woman (cat. 19), *162*, 163
knives, ceremonial. See kris (ceremonial daggers); weapons, ceremonial
knives, rice-harvesting (cat. 2–3), *138*, 139
Kopang, I Gusti Wayan, 228
Krause, Gregor, 332, 347
kris (ceremonial daggers)
  Badung puputan and, 26
  Boma, ceremonial killing of, 108
  in Calonarang drama, 297
  courtly arts and, 28, 121, 245
  kris with sheath (cat. 60), *252*, 253, *254*, 255
  kris hilt depicting a demonic figure (cat. 61), *256*, 257
  kris stand in the form of a frog (cat. 58), *247*, 248
  kris stand in the form of Rawana (cat. 57), 121, *244*, *245–46*, 265
  on Prince Panji statue, 165
  ritual bloodletting and, 99
Krisna (Krishna)
  in Mahabharata, 363
  puppet of pamurtian form of Krisna (cat. 127), *362*
  statue of Krisna (cat. 106), 322–24, *330*, *331*
  as Wisnu's avatar, 241, 362
Kumara, 173
Kuwera, 224

lamak hangings
  altar hangings (cat. 9–10), 72, 75, 83, *145*, *146*, 147, *148–49*
  in Covarrubias' painting, 341
  dance costume and, 291
  function and meaning of, 61, 67–68, 85, 145
  geographical location of, 11
  Gunung Agung and, 13
  makers of, 73–74, 78, 79
  mass-produced, use of, 61–64, 79–85
  motifs, 69–73, 75–77, 81–84, 145–47, 149
  as public offerings, 88
  types of, 61, 64–66, 85
lamp (cat. 33), 41, *191*, *192*
legong. See dance, legong
Lempad, I Gusti Nyoman, 74, 347
Library of Congress, 10
lintel (cat. 46), 181, *220*, 221
Lintgensz, Aernoudt, 24, 195
lion offering box (cat. 26), *118*, *179*
  alternative function of, 121–22
  lion symbolism and, 127–31, 181

provenance of, 117, 119–20
  similar objects, 122–26, 181
lion puppet (cat. 124), *359*
literature, 23, 29, 36, 207
  See also lontar books and manuscripts; and specific literary works
litters. See palanquins
Liyer, Mangku Ketut, 43–44, 54–55, 60
Lombok, 11, 25, 199, 207, 265
lontar books and manuscripts
  box for lontar book (cat. 40), *206*, 207
  healers' use of, 53–54, 203
  of kajang samplers, 213–14
  lion figures in, 181
  lontar book with magic drawings (cat. 39), *202*, 203–05
  priest consecration rites and, 38
  Saraswati and, 82
lontar palms, 66, 67n6, 75, 145
lotus (padma)
  as cosmic symbol, 83, 178, 295–96
  Kama and, 185
  as lamak motif, 81, *82*, 83
  as purity symbol, 219
  in rerajahan, 52

magic
  Durga and, 302, 361
  Rangda and, 112, 171, 297, 302
  vs. religion, 52–53
  white vs. black, 53, 54–56
  widows and, 203n13
magic drawings. See rerajahan
Mahabharata
  Abimanyu puppet (cat. 128), *363*
  Arjuna and Suprabha (cat. 117), 216, *349*
  Arjuna puppet (cat. 120), *355*
  Bima puppet (cat. 121), *356*
  courtly arts and, 28
  Dwijakangka puppet (cat. 119), *354*
  kingship and, 23, 241
  lamak depictions of, 149
  palanquin depictions of, 237, 239
  raksasa demons in, 257, 358
  religious practices and, 21n38, 36
  as shadow-puppet subject, 353, 354–56, 363
  textile depictions of, 223
Majapahit dynasty, 23–24, 25, 31, 35–36, 166, 200
Malat (Panji tales)
  dance dramas and, 25, 30, 273, 288, 316
  Majapahit dynasty and, 23, 25
  panel depictions of, 273–74
  Prince Panji (cat. 20), 25, *164*, 165
  Princess Rangkesari (cat. 21), 25, *166*
male and female figures on their animal mount (cat. 28), 124, 181, *182*, 183
male figure (cat. 18), 17, *159*, *160*, 161, 265
Maluku Islands (Moluccas), 12, 26
map of Bali, *12*